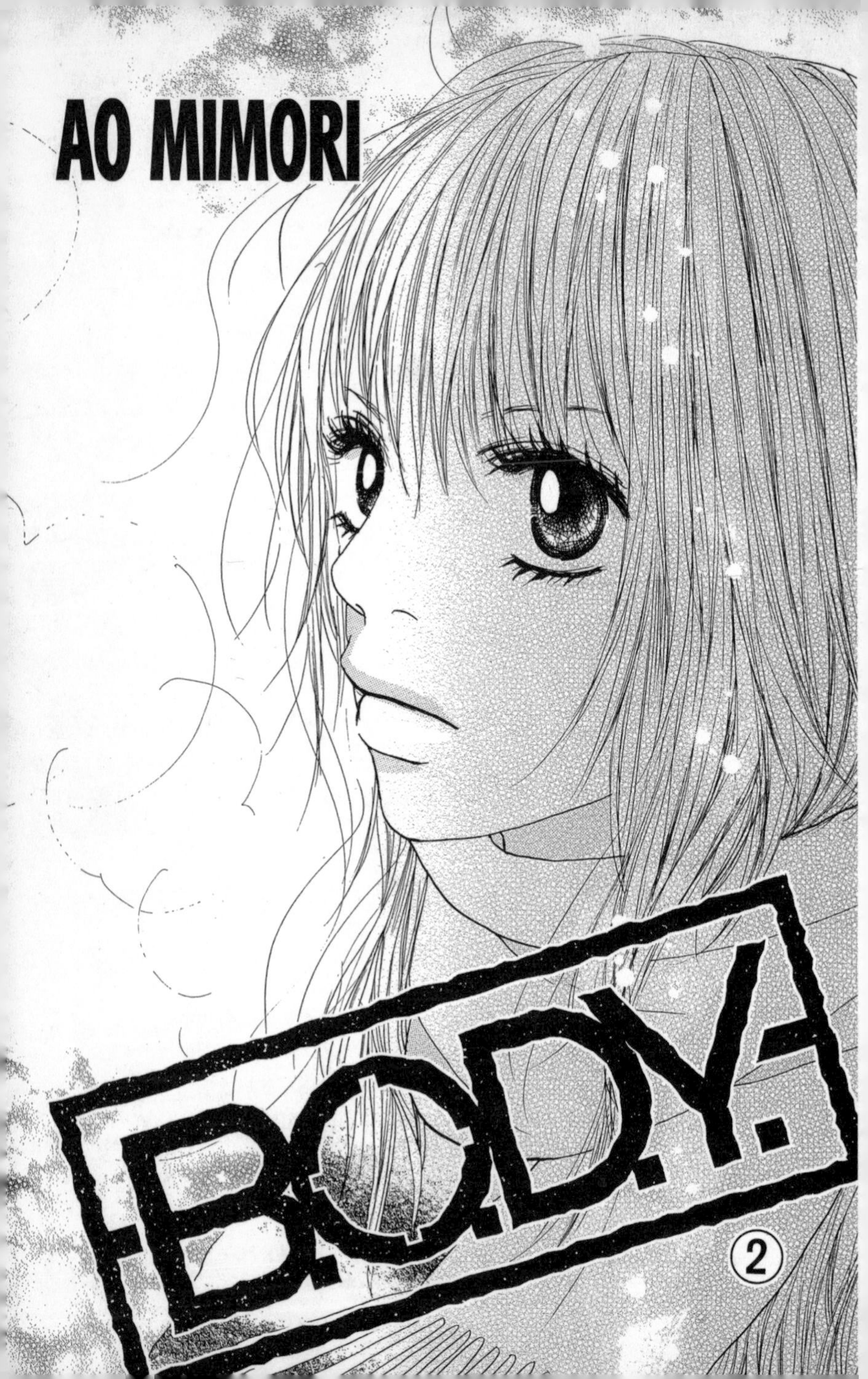
AO MIMORI
B.O.D.Y.
2

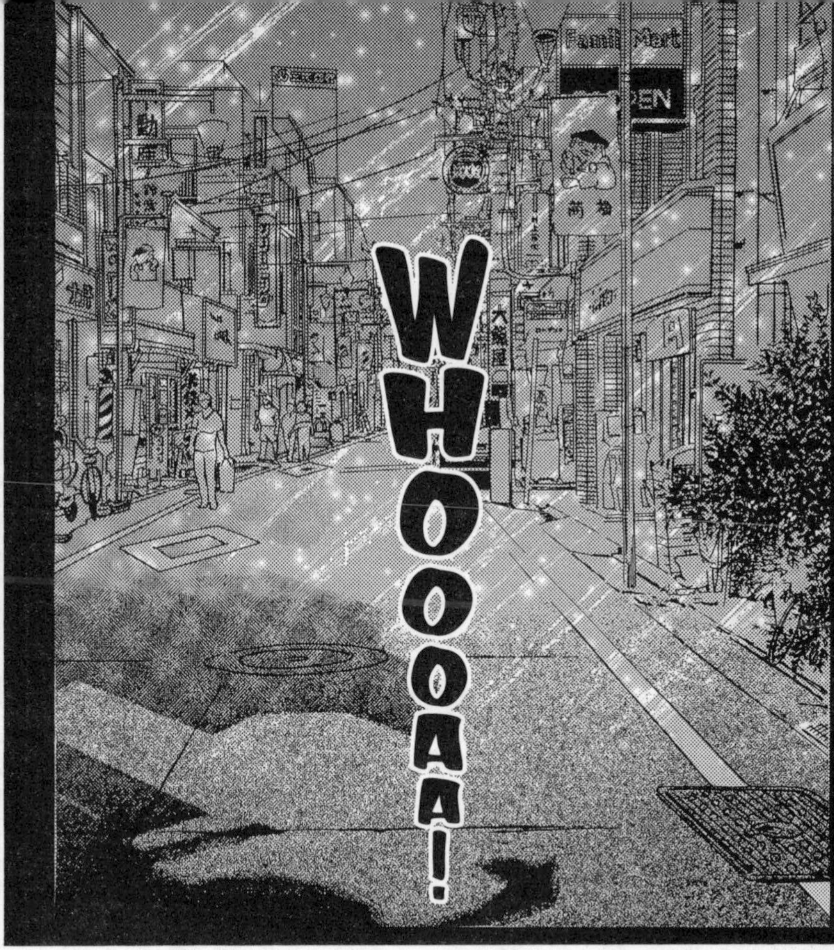
WHOOOOAA!

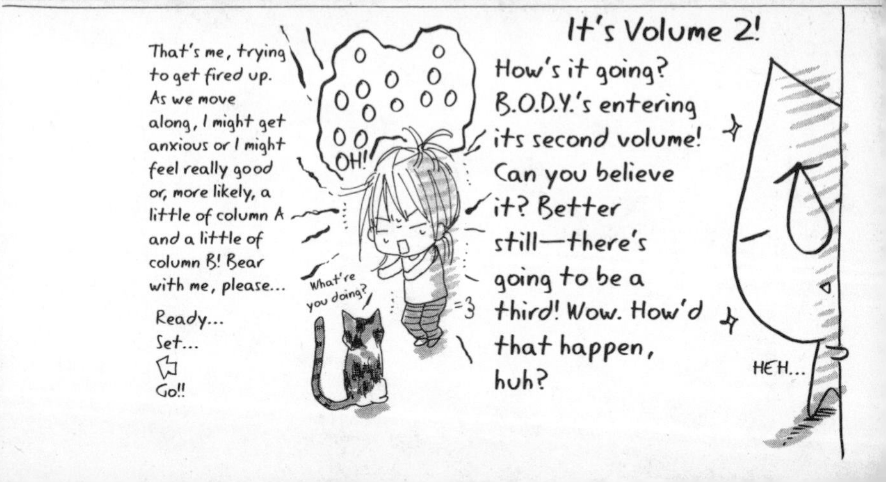
HEH...
It's Volume 2!
How's it going? B.O.D.Y.'s entering its second volume! Can you believe it? Better still—there's going to be a third! Wow. How'd that happen, huh?
OOOOOOOOOOOOOH!
What're you doing?
That's me, trying to get fired up. As we move along, I might get anxious or I might feel really good or, more likely, a little of column A and a little of column B! Bear with me, please...
Ready...
Set...
Go!!

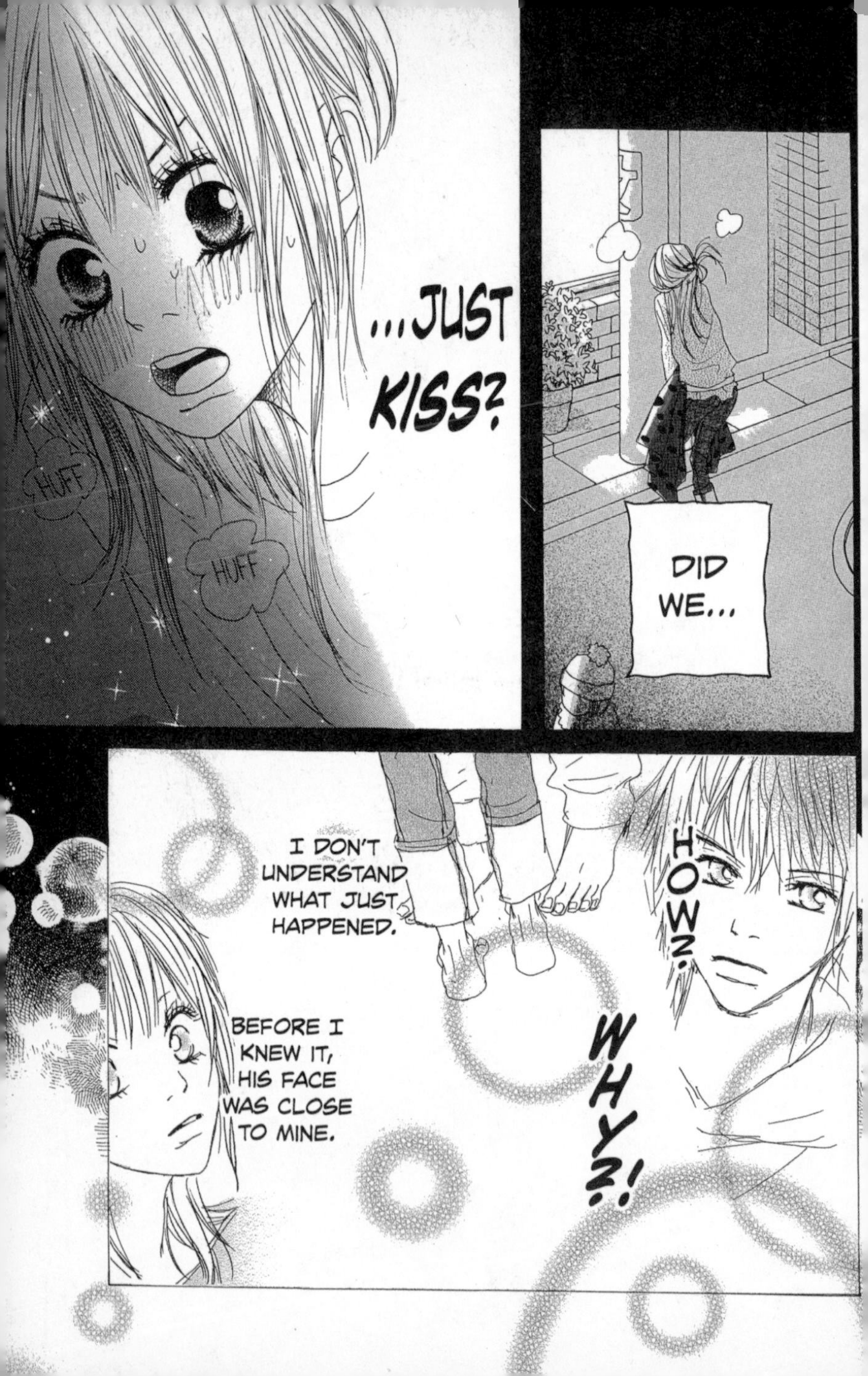
DID WE...
...JUST KISS?
HUFF
HUFF
HOW?
I DON'T UNDERSTAND WHAT JUST HAPPENED.
WHY?!
BEFORE I KNEW IT, HIS FACE WAS CLOSE TO MINE.

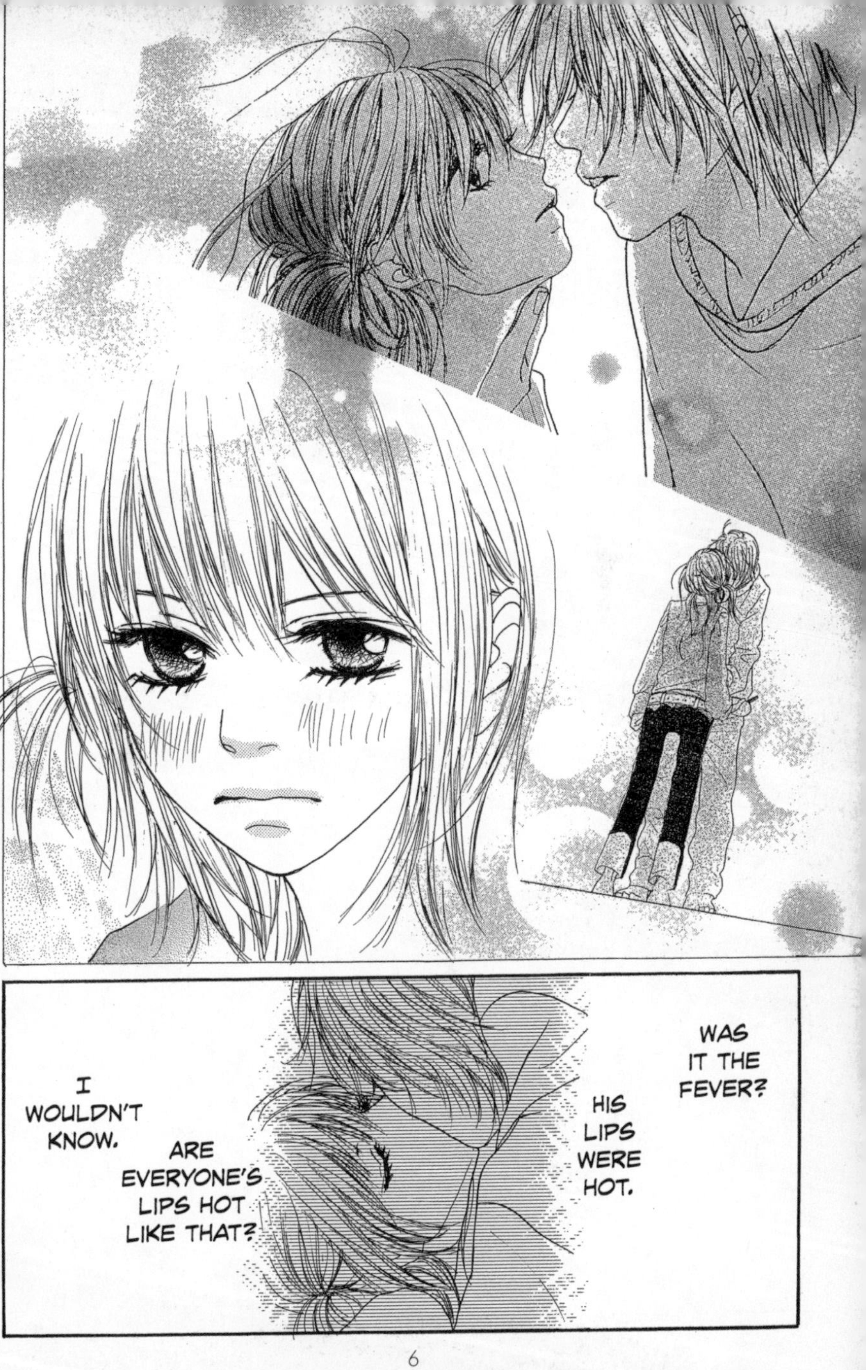
WAS IT THE FEVER?
HIS LIPS WERE HOT.
ARE EVERYONE'S LIPS HOT LIKE THAT?
I WOULDN'T KNOW.

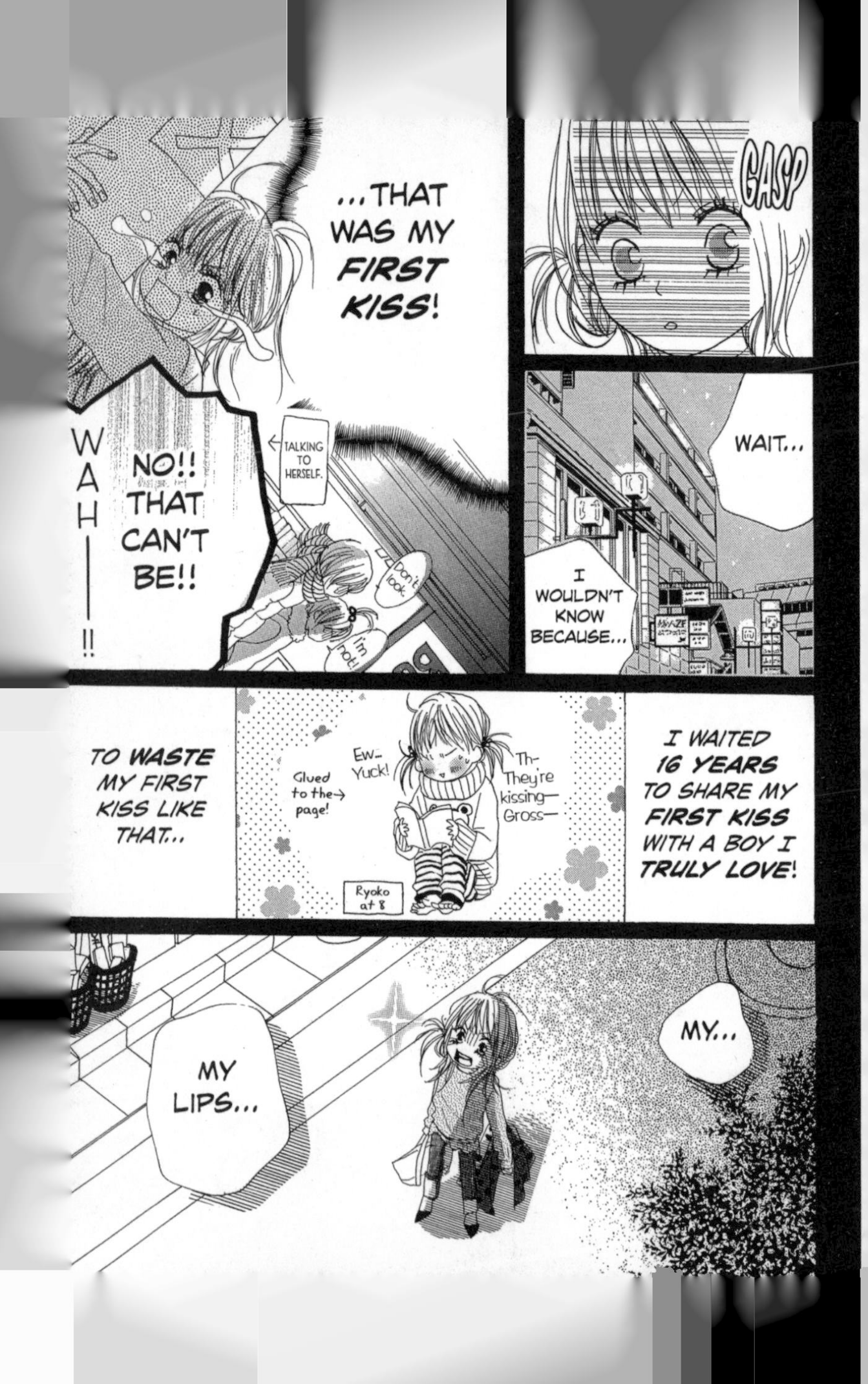
GASP
WAIT...
I WOULDN'T KNOW BECAUSE...
...THAT WAS MY FIRST KISS!
TALKING TO HERSELF.
NO!! THAT CAN'T BE!!
WAH—!!
Don't look.
I'm not!
I WAITED 16 YEARS TO SHARE MY FIRST KISS WITH A BOY I TRULY LOVE!
Th- They're kissing— Gross—
Ew.. Yuck!
Glued to the page!
Ryoko at 8
TO WASTE MY FIRST KISS LIKE THAT...
MY...
MY LIPS...

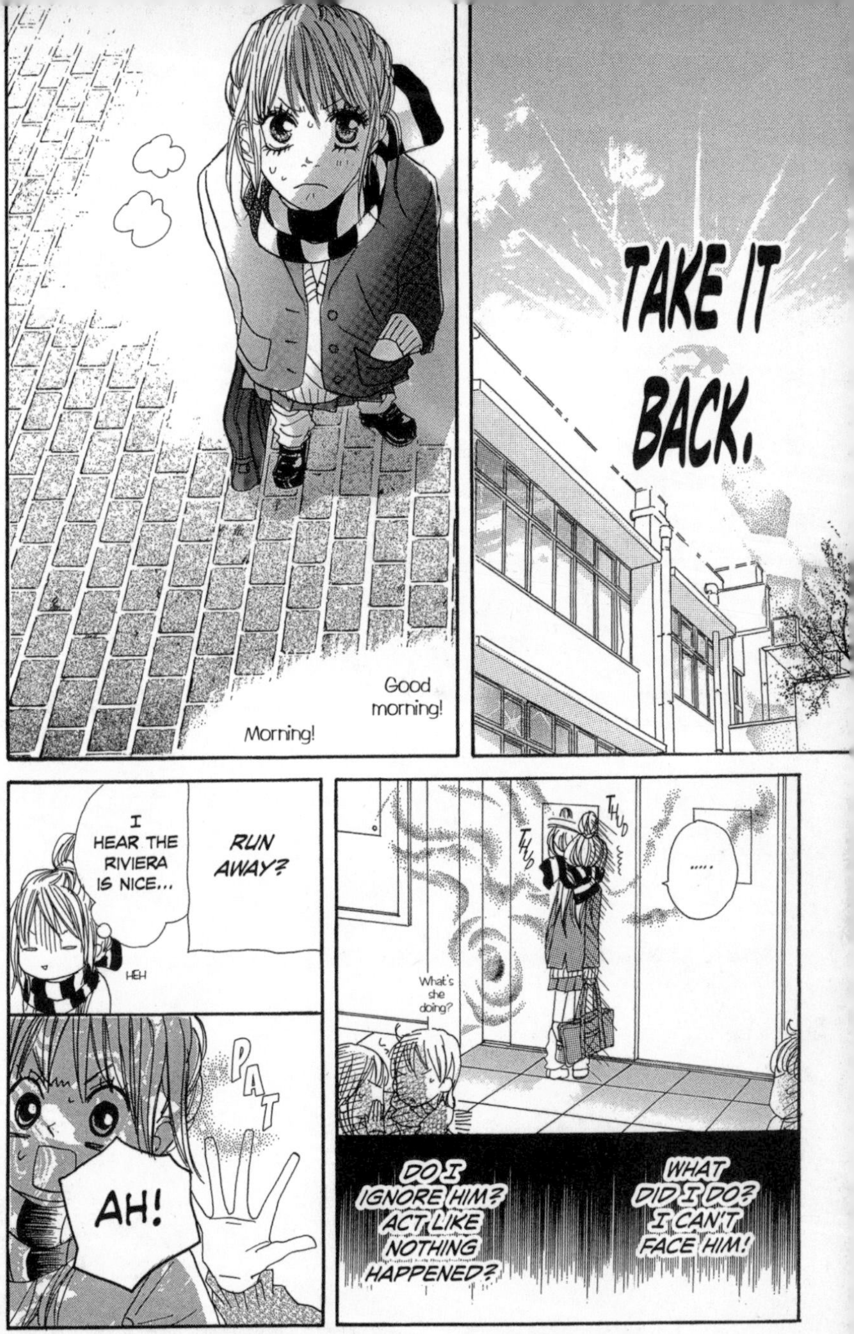
TAKE IT BACK.
Good morning!
Morning!
.....
THUD
THUD
What's she doing?
WHAT DID I DO? I CAN'T FACE HIM!
DO I IGNORE HIM? ACT LIKE NOTHING HAPPENED?
RUN AWAY?
I HEAR THE RIVIERA IS NICE...
HEH
PAT
AH!

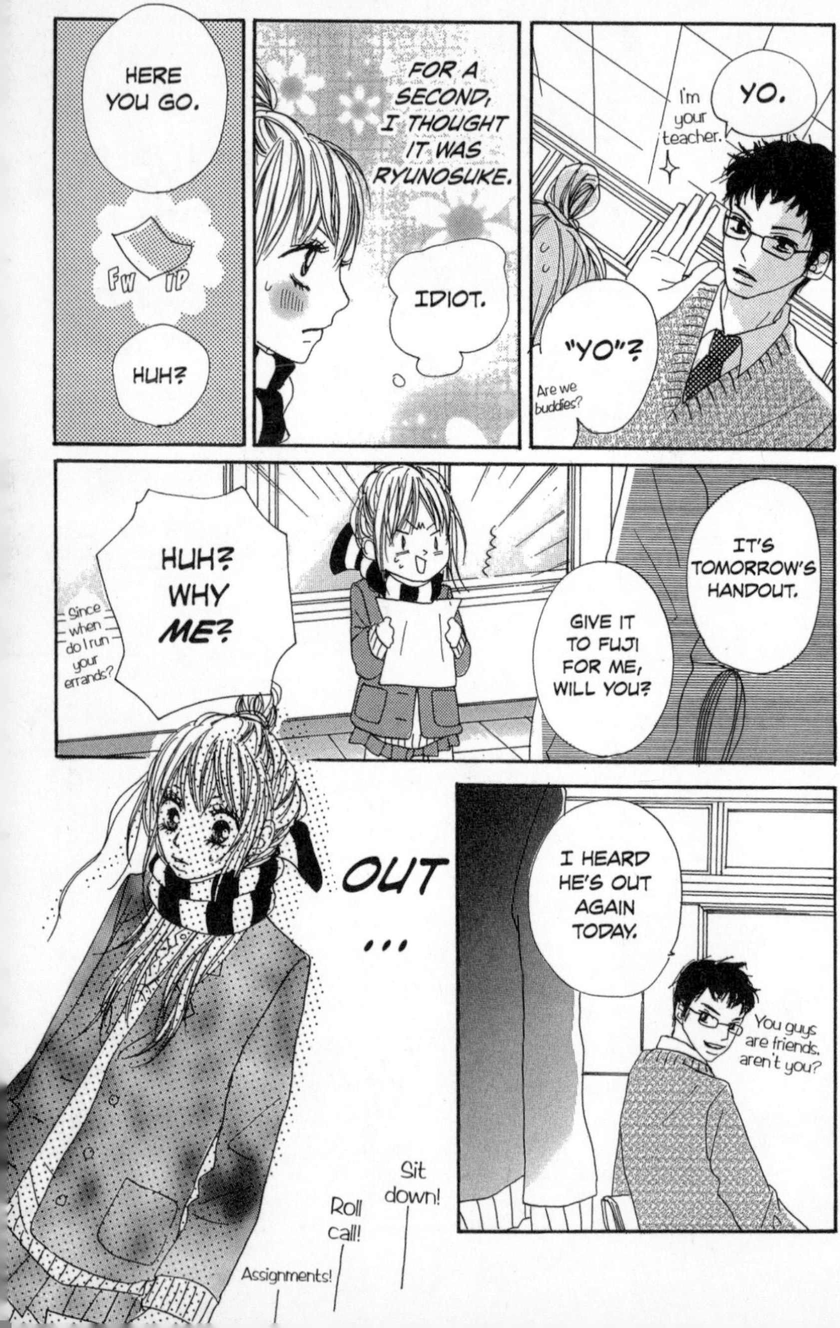
YO.
I'm your teacher.
"YO"?
Are we buddies?
FOR A SECOND, I THOUGHT IT WAS RYUNOSUKE.
IDIOT.
HERE YOU GO.
FWIP
HUH?
IT'S TOMORROW'S HANDOUT.
GIVE IT TO FUJI FOR ME, WILL YOU?
HUH? WHY ME?
Since when do I run your errands?
I HEARD HE'S OUT AGAIN TODAY.
You guys are friends, aren't you?
OUT...
Sit down!
Roll call!
Assignments!

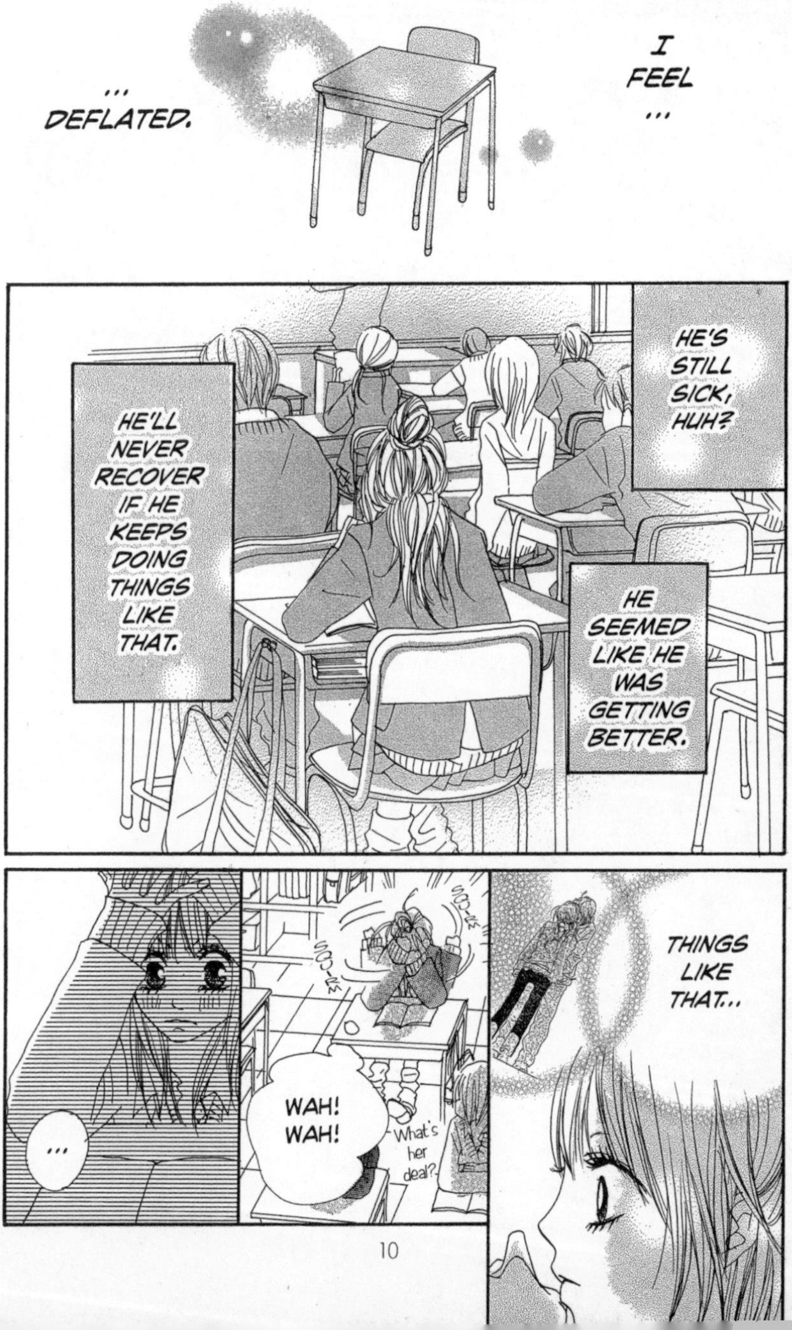
I FEEL ...
... DEFLATED.
HE'S STILL SICK, HUH?
HE SEEMED LIKE HE WAS GETTING BETTER.
HE'LL NEVER RECOVER IF HE KEEPS DOING THINGS LIKE THAT.
THINGS LIKE THAT...
WAH! WAH!
What's her deal?
...

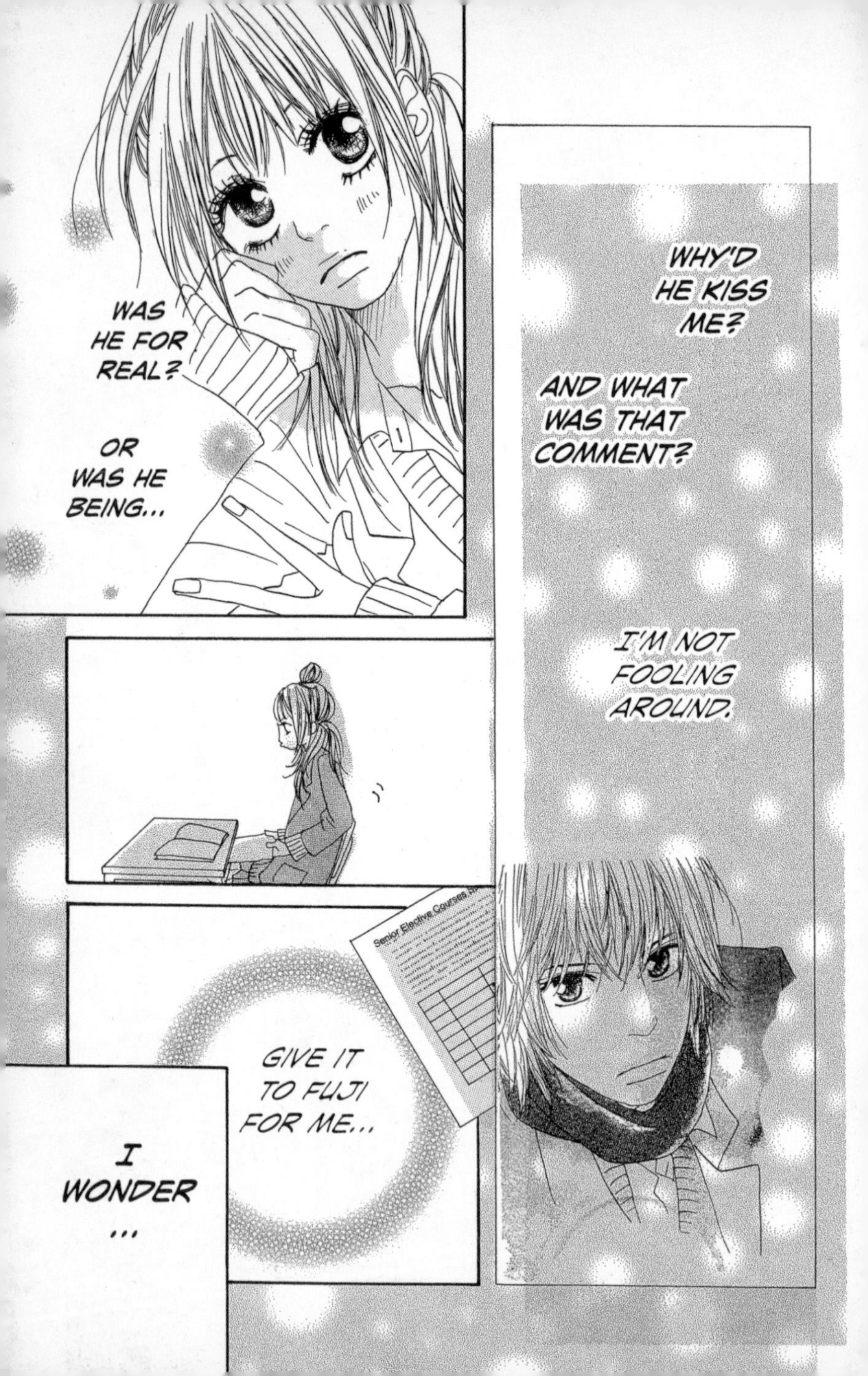
WHY'D HE KISS ME?
AND WHAT WAS THAT COMMENT?
I'M NOT FOOLING AROUND.
WAS HE FOR REAL?
OR WAS HE BEING...
Senior Elective Courses
GIVE IT TO FUJI FOR ME...
I WONDER ...

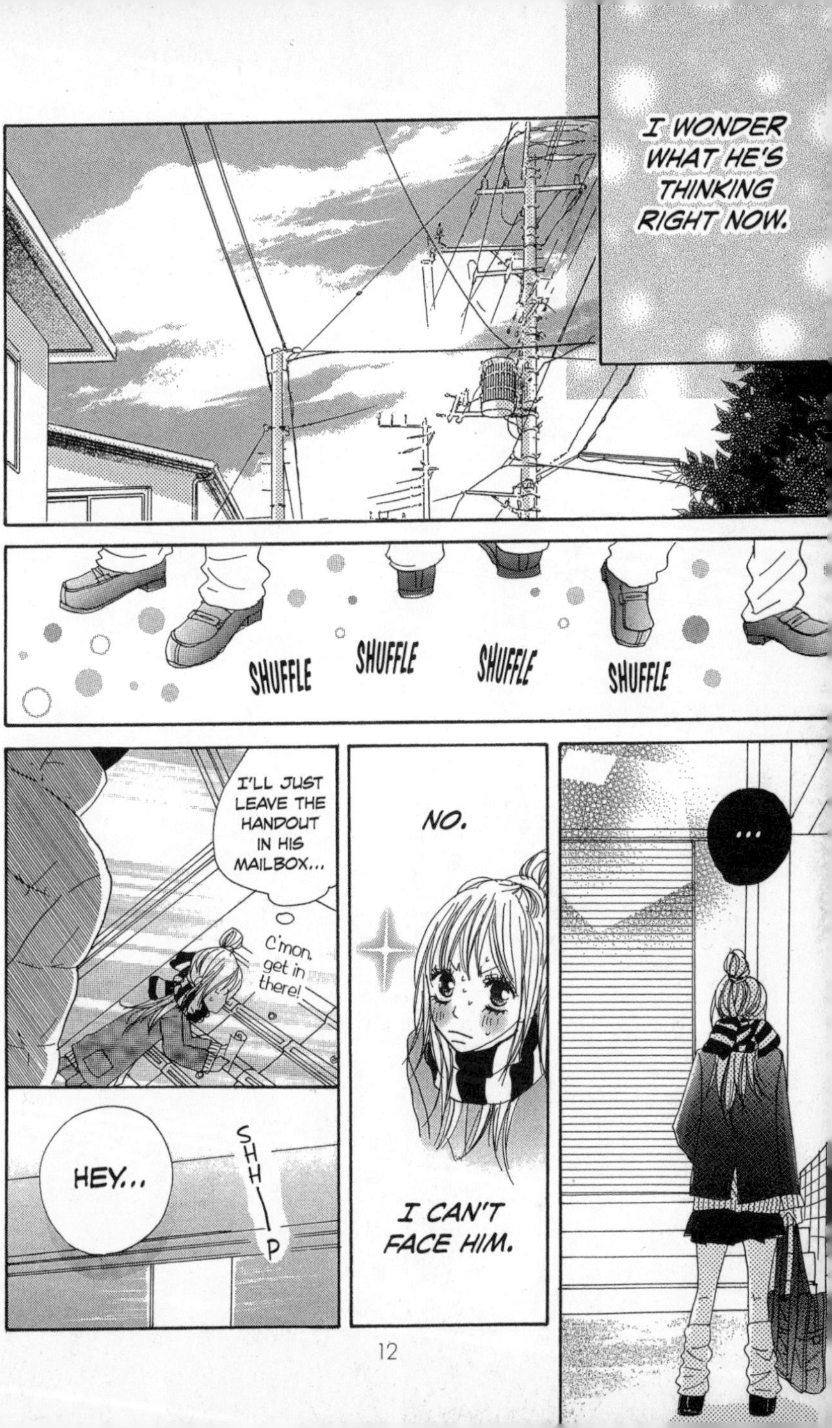
I WONDER WHAT HE'S THINKING RIGHT NOW.
SHUFFLE
SHUFFLE
SHUFFLE
SHUFFLE
...
NO.
I CAN'T FACE HIM.
I'LL JUST LEAVE THE HANDOUT IN HIS MAILBOX...
C'mon, get in there!
SHHIP
HEY...

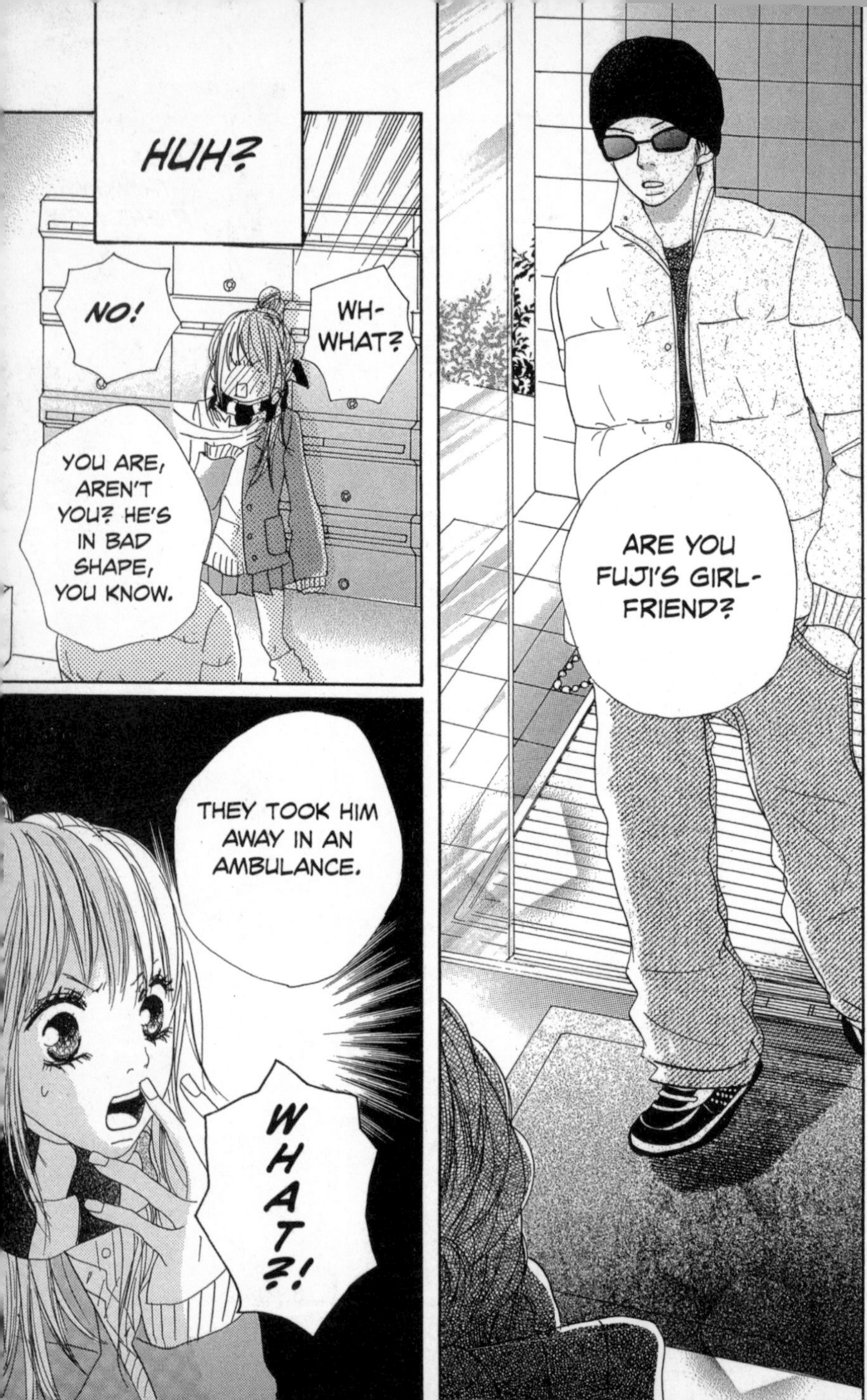
ARE YOU FUJI'S GIRL-FRIEND?
HUH?
WH-WHAT?
NO!
YOU ARE, AREN'T YOU? HE'S IN BAD SHAPE, YOU KNOW.
THEY TOOK HIM AWAY IN AN AMBULANCE.
WHAT?!

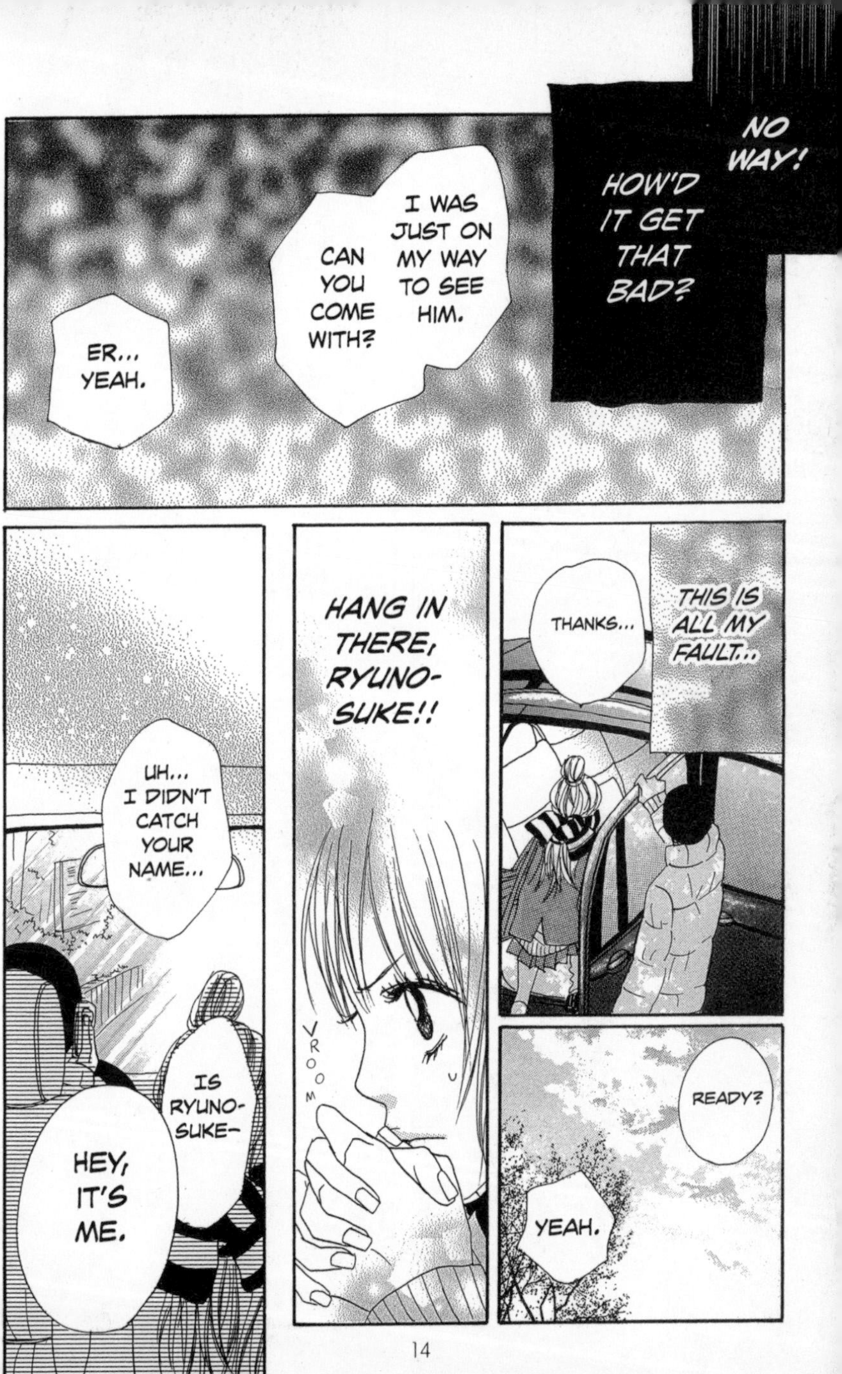
NO WAY!
HOW'D IT GET THAT BAD?
I WAS JUST ON MY WAY TO SEE HIM.
CAN YOU COME WITH?
ER... YEAH.
THIS IS ALL MY FAULT...
THANKS...
READY?
YEAH.
HANG IN THERE, RYUNO-SUKE!!
VROOM
UH... I DIDN'T CATCH YOUR NAME...
IS RYUNO-SUKE-
HEY, IT'S ME.

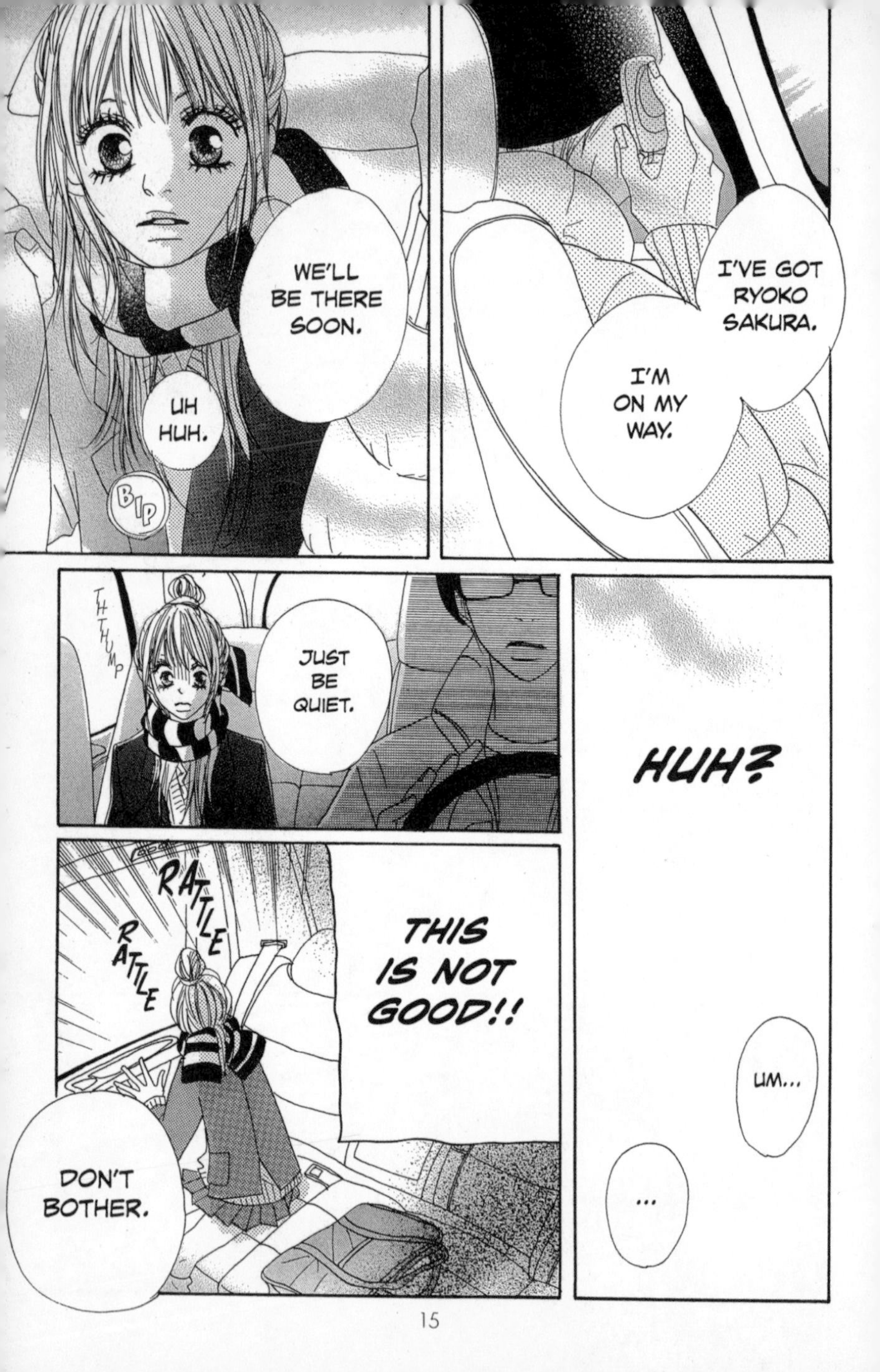
I'VE GOT RYOKO SAKURA.
I'M ON MY WAY.
WE'LL BE THERE SOON.
UH HUH.
BIP
HUH?
UM...
...
TH THUMP
JUST BE QUIET.
THIS IS NOT GOOD!!
RATTLE
RATTLE
DON'T BOTHER.

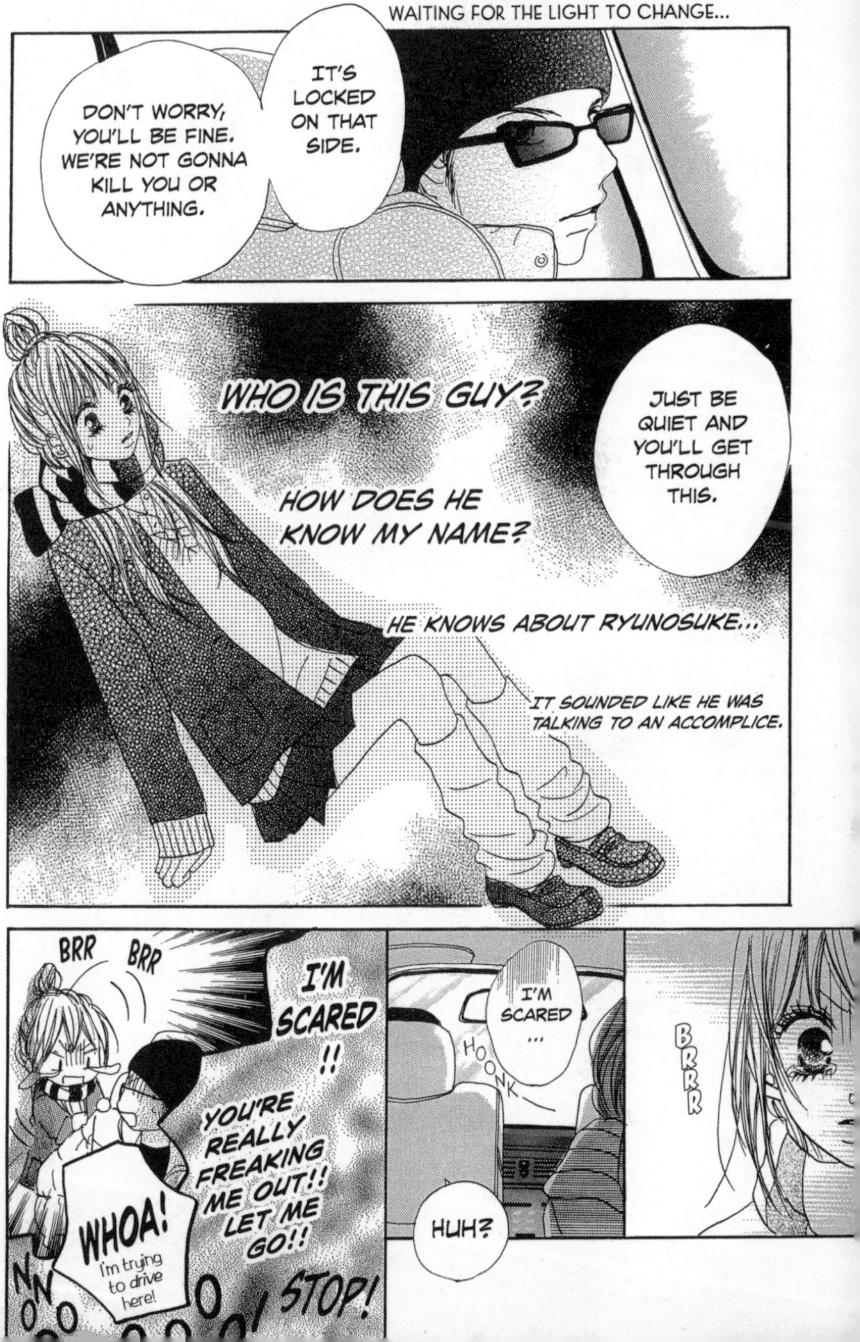
WAITING FOR THE LIGHT TO CHANGE...
IT'S LOCKED ON THAT SIDE.
DON'T WORRY, YOU'LL BE FINE. WE'RE NOT GONNA KILL YOU OR ANYTHING.
JUST BE QUIET AND YOU'LL GET THROUGH THIS.
WHO IS THIS GUY?
HOW DOES HE KNOW MY NAME?
HE KNOWS ABOUT RYUNOSUKE...
IT SOUNDED LIKE HE WAS TALKING TO AN ACCOMPLICE.
BRRR
I'M SCARED...
HOONK
HUH?
BRR BRR
I'M SCARED!!
YOU'RE REALLY FREAKING ME OUT!! LET ME GO!!
WHOA!
I'm trying to drive here!
NOOOOOOO!
STOP!

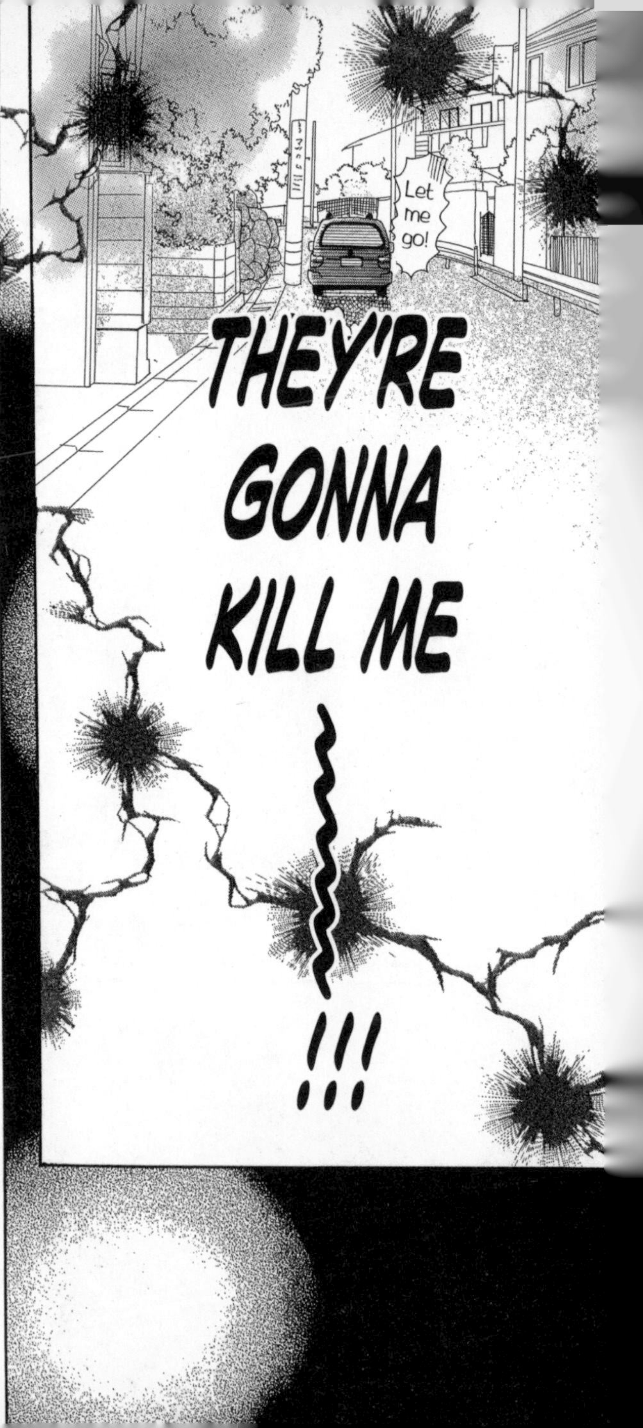
Let me go!
THEY'RE GONNA KILL ME ---!!!

Anything Goes

Mimori here! Hello again.

We plan to have five quarter-page columns in this volume, and, uh, I plan to approach them with, erm, no real *plan*.

Here's a table of contents for the bonus materials. See what I mean?

That's how it's gonna go. Those of you with time on your hands should check it out. (Don't expect miracles, though! Hee hee!)

Continued in 2—

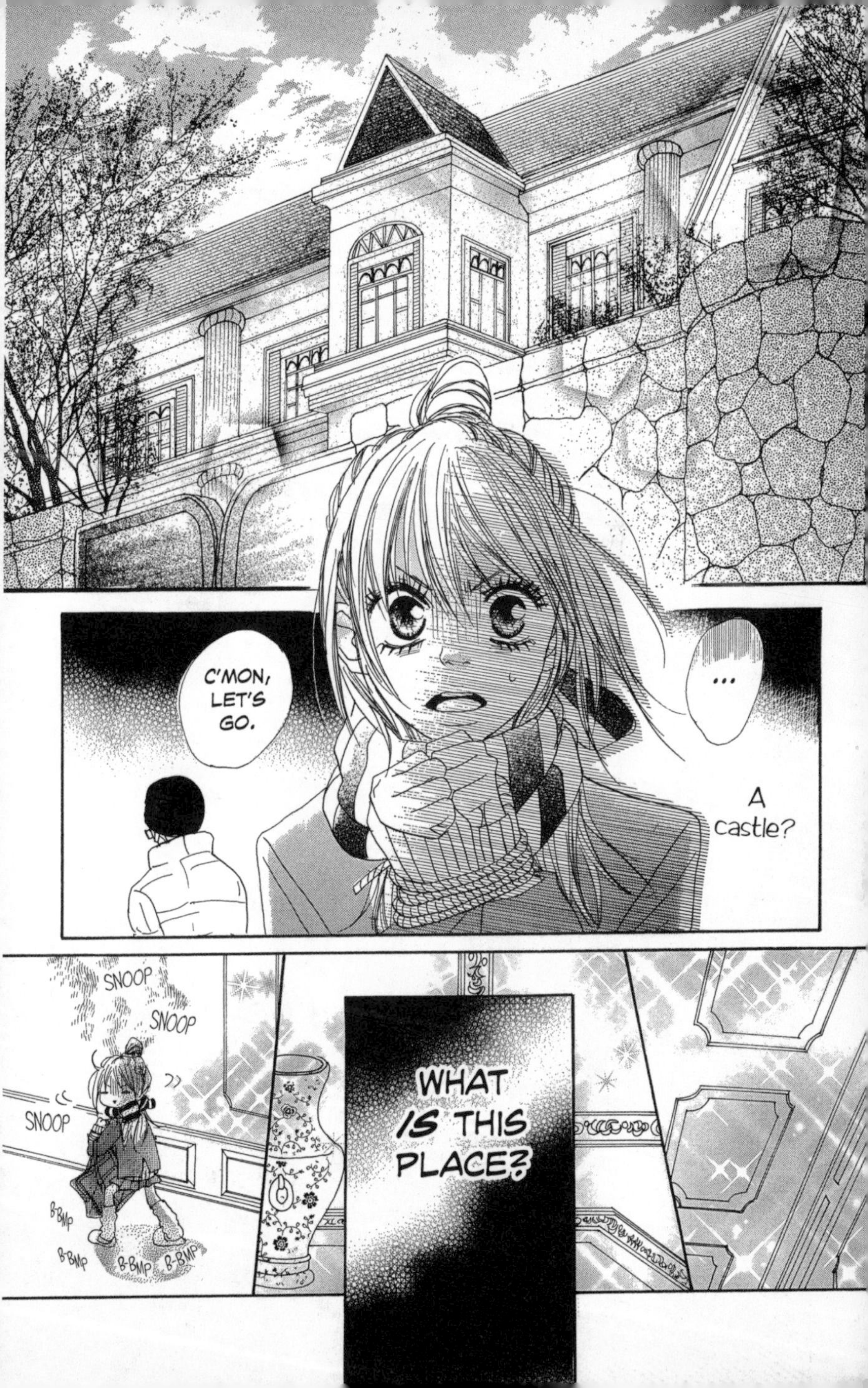
...
A castle?
C'MON, LET'S GO.
WHAT IS THIS PLACE?
SNOOP
SNOOP
SNOOP
B-BMP
B-BMP
B-BMP
B-BMP

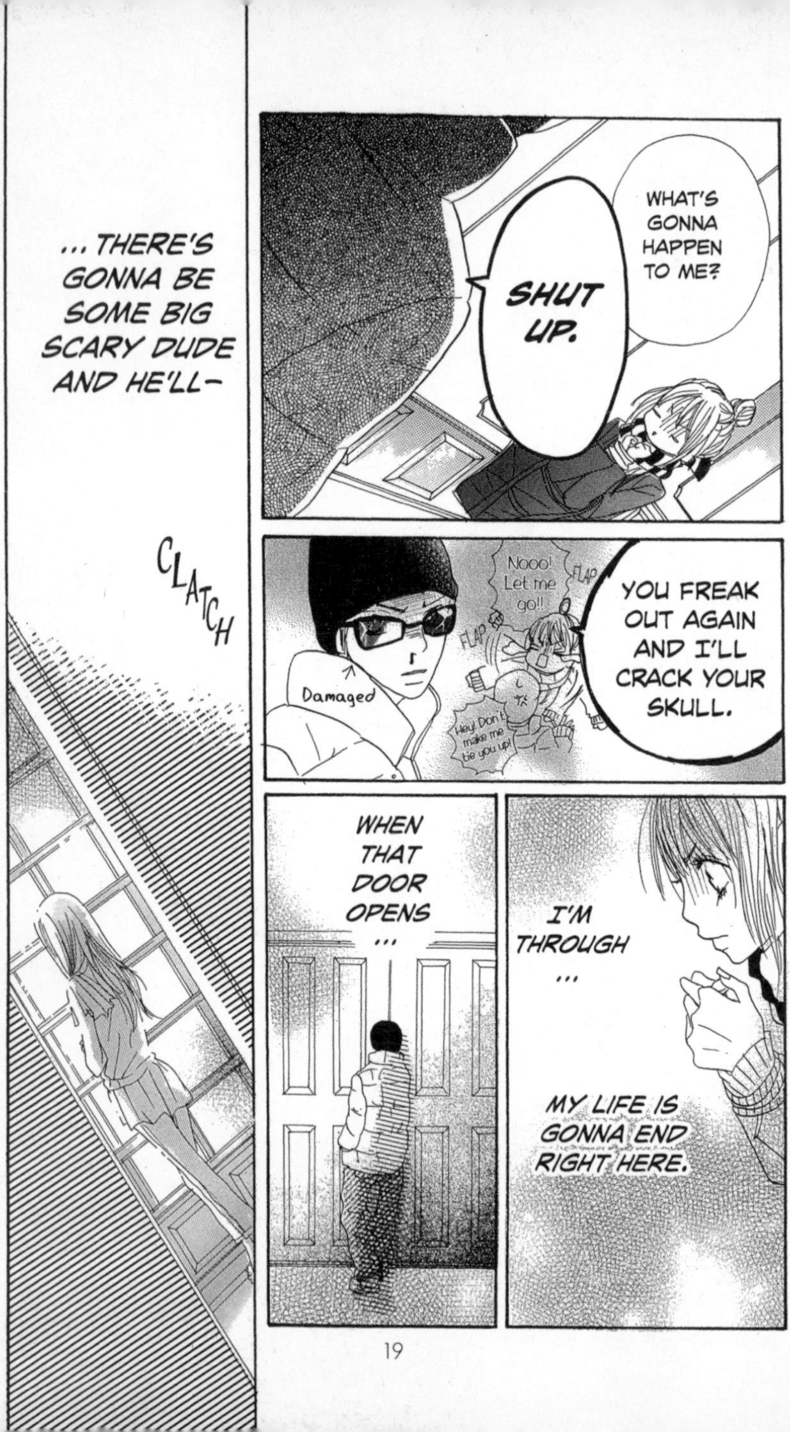
WHAT'S GONNA HAPPEN TO ME?
SHUT UP.
YOU FREAK OUT AGAIN AND I'LL CRACK YOUR SKULL.
Nooo! Let me go!!
FLAP
FLAP
Damaged
Hey! Don't make me tie you up!
I'M THROUGH ...
MY LIFE IS GONNA END RIGHT HERE.
WHEN THAT DOOR OPENS ...
...THERE'S GONNA BE SOME BIG SCARY DUDE AND HE'LL—
CLATCH

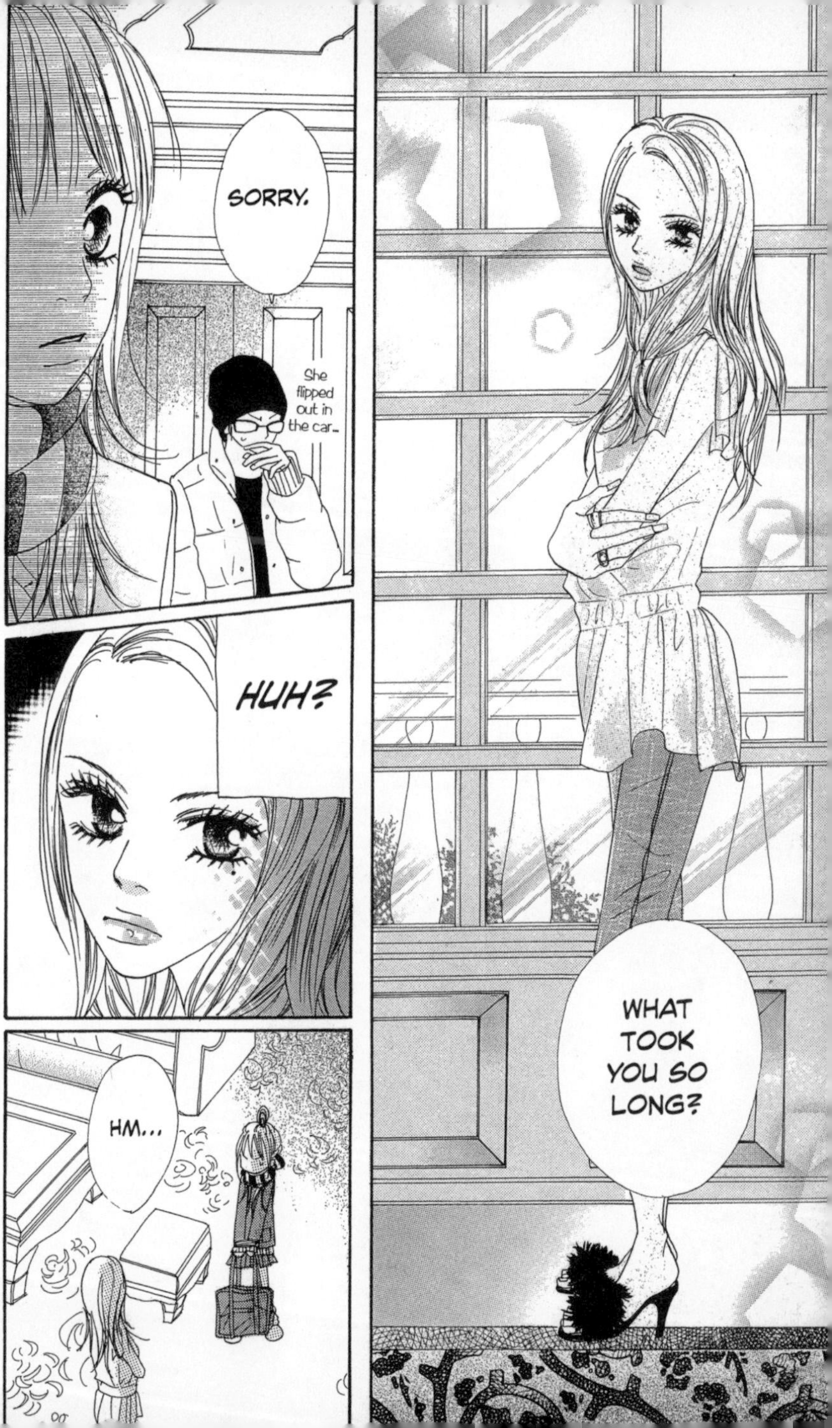
WHAT TOOK YOU SO LONG?
SORRY.
She flipped out in the car...
HUH?
HM...

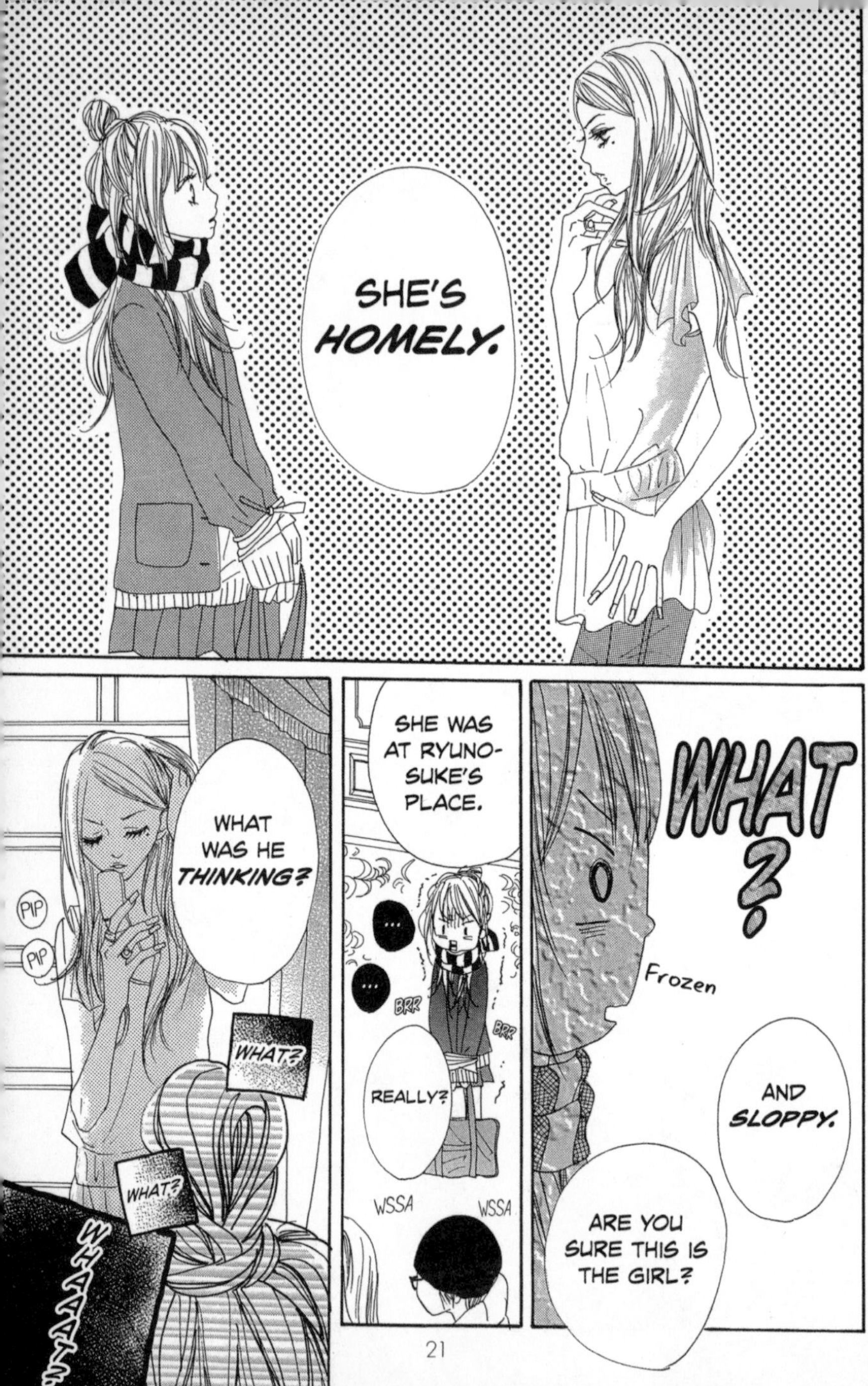
SHE'S HOMELY.
WHAT?
Frozen
AND SLOPPY.
ARE YOU SURE THIS IS THE GIRL?
SHE WAS AT RYUNO-SUKE'S PLACE.
...
...
BRR
BRR
REALLY?
WSSA
WSSA
WHAT WAS HE THINKING?
PIP
PIP
WHAT?
WHAT?

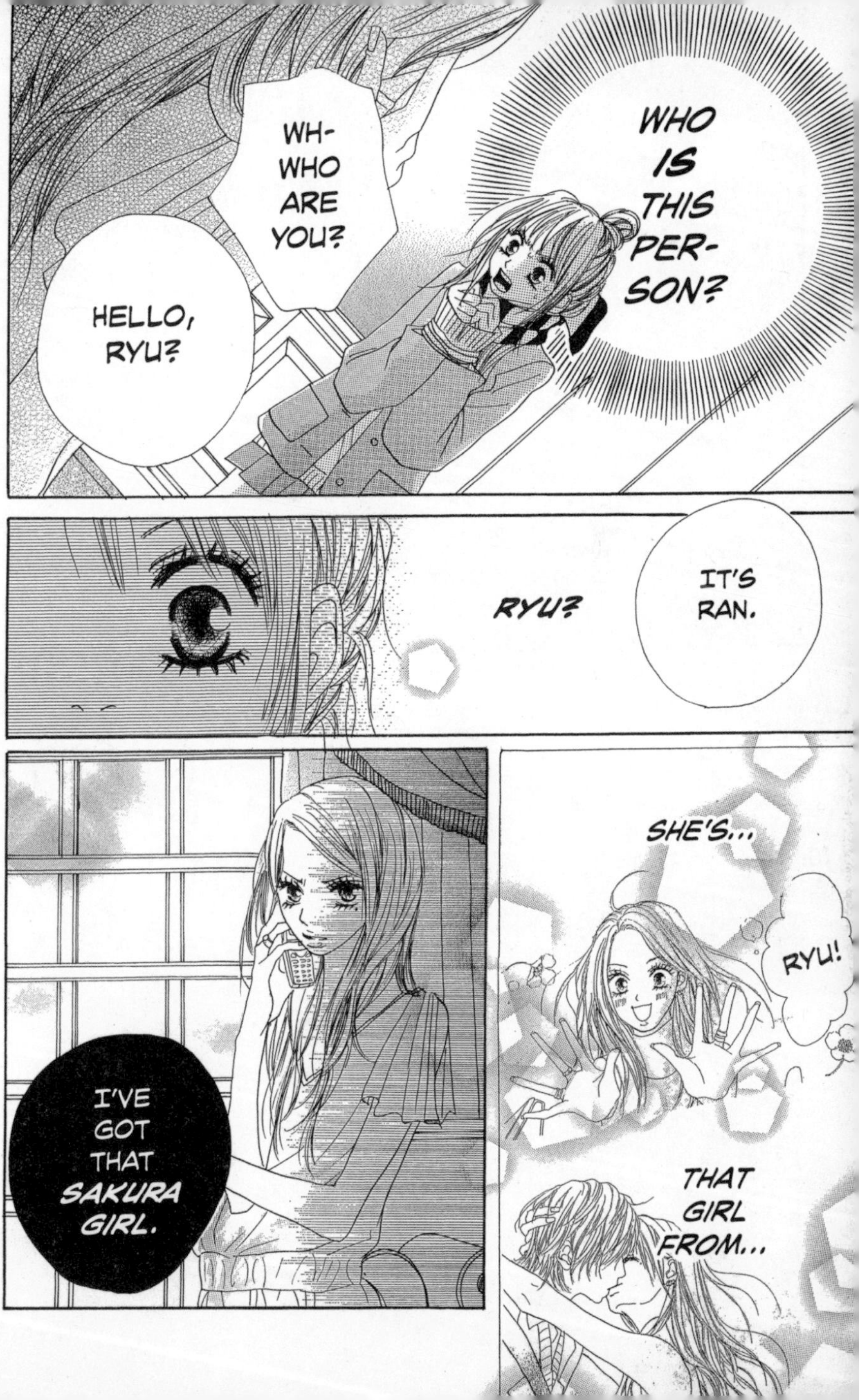
WHO IS THIS PERSON?
WH- WHO ARE YOU?
HELLO, RYU?
IT'S RAN.
RYU?
SHE'S...
RYU!
THAT GIRL FROM...
I'VE GOT THAT SAKURA GIRL.

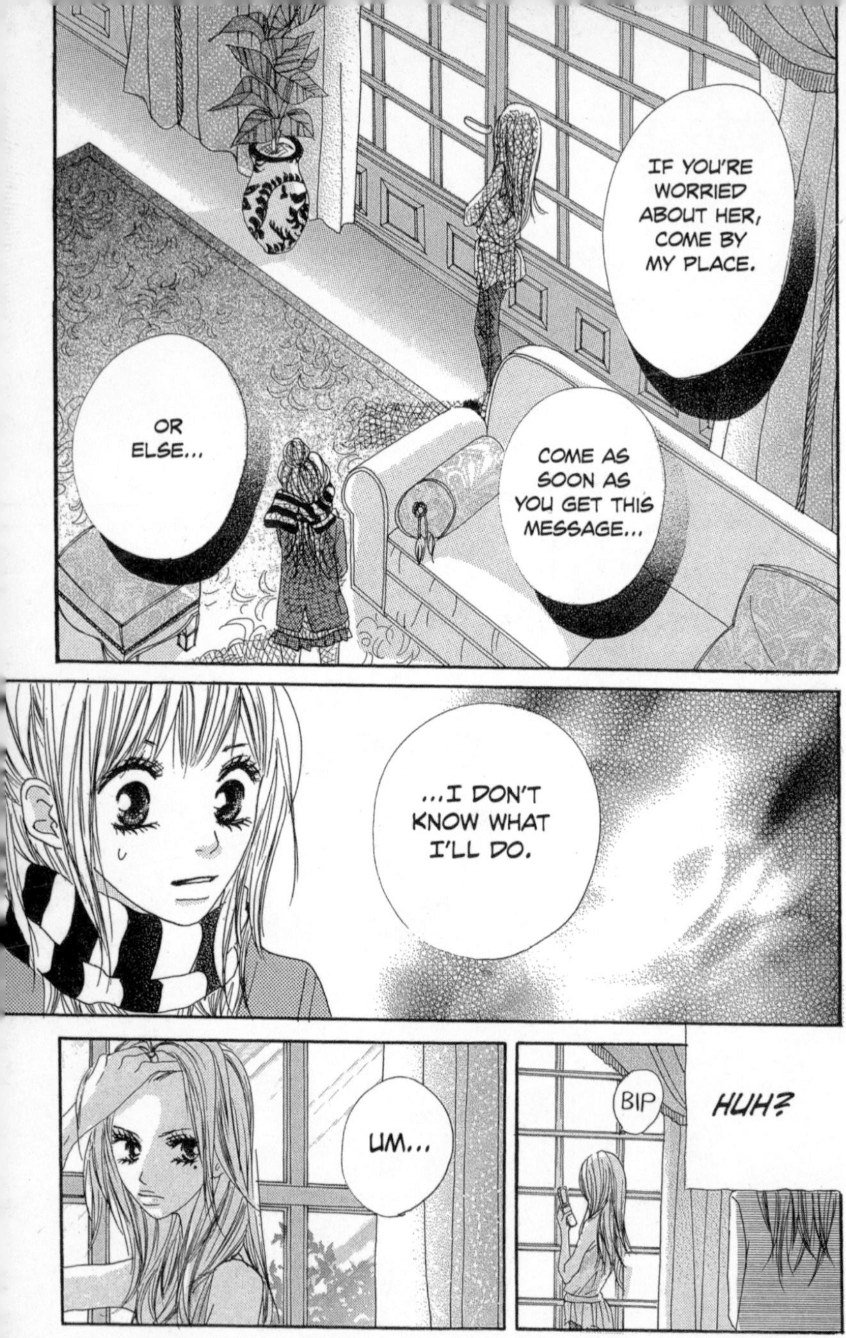
IF YOU'RE WORRIED ABOUT HER, COME BY MY PLACE.
COME AS SOON AS YOU GET THIS MESSAGE...
OR ELSE...
...I DON'T KNOW WHAT I'LL DO.
BIP
HUH?
UM...

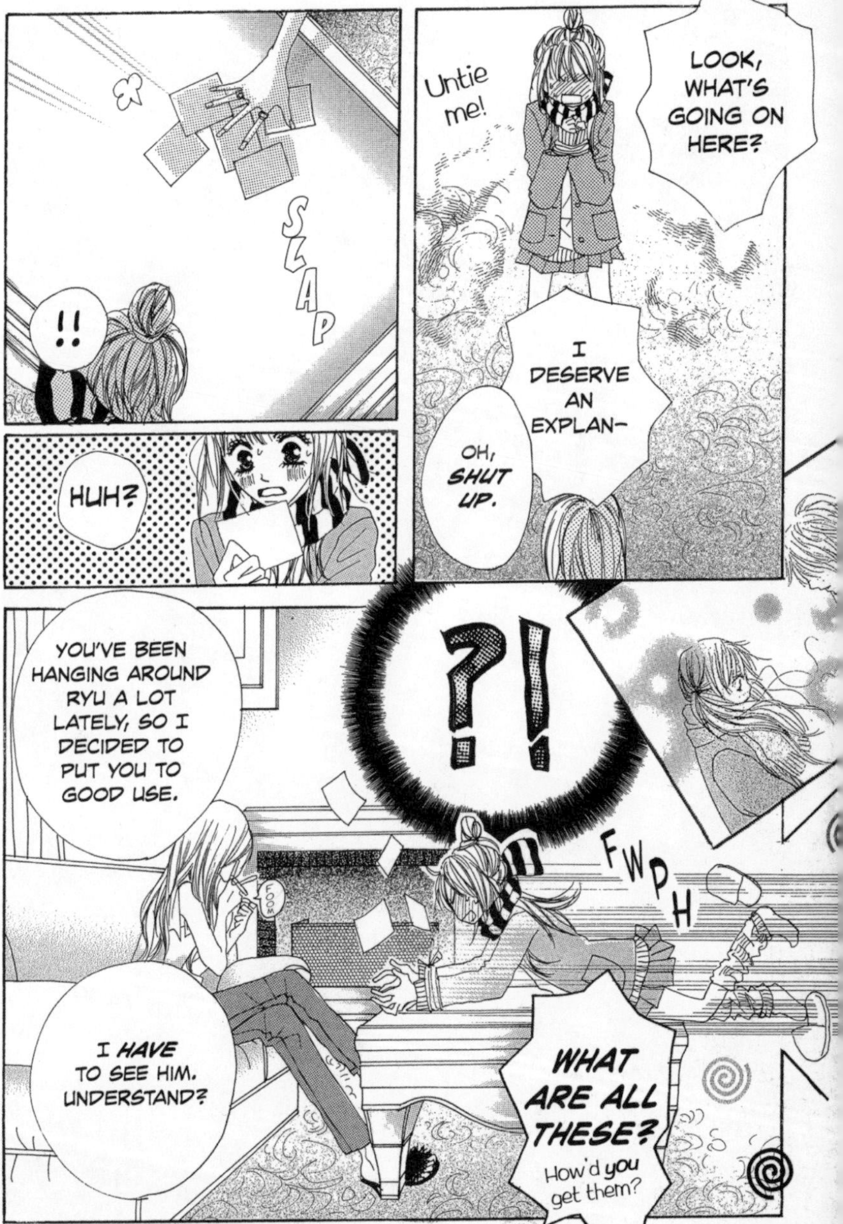
LOOK, WHAT'S GOING ON HERE?
Untie me!
I DESERVE AN EXPLAN-
OH, *SHUT UP.*
SLAP
!!
HUH?
?!
FWPH
WHAT ARE ALL THESE?
How'd *you* get them?
YOU'VE BEEN HANGING AROUND RYU A LOT LATELY, SO I DECIDED TO PUT YOU TO GOOD USE.
FOOM
I *HAVE* TO SEE HIM. UNDERSTAND?

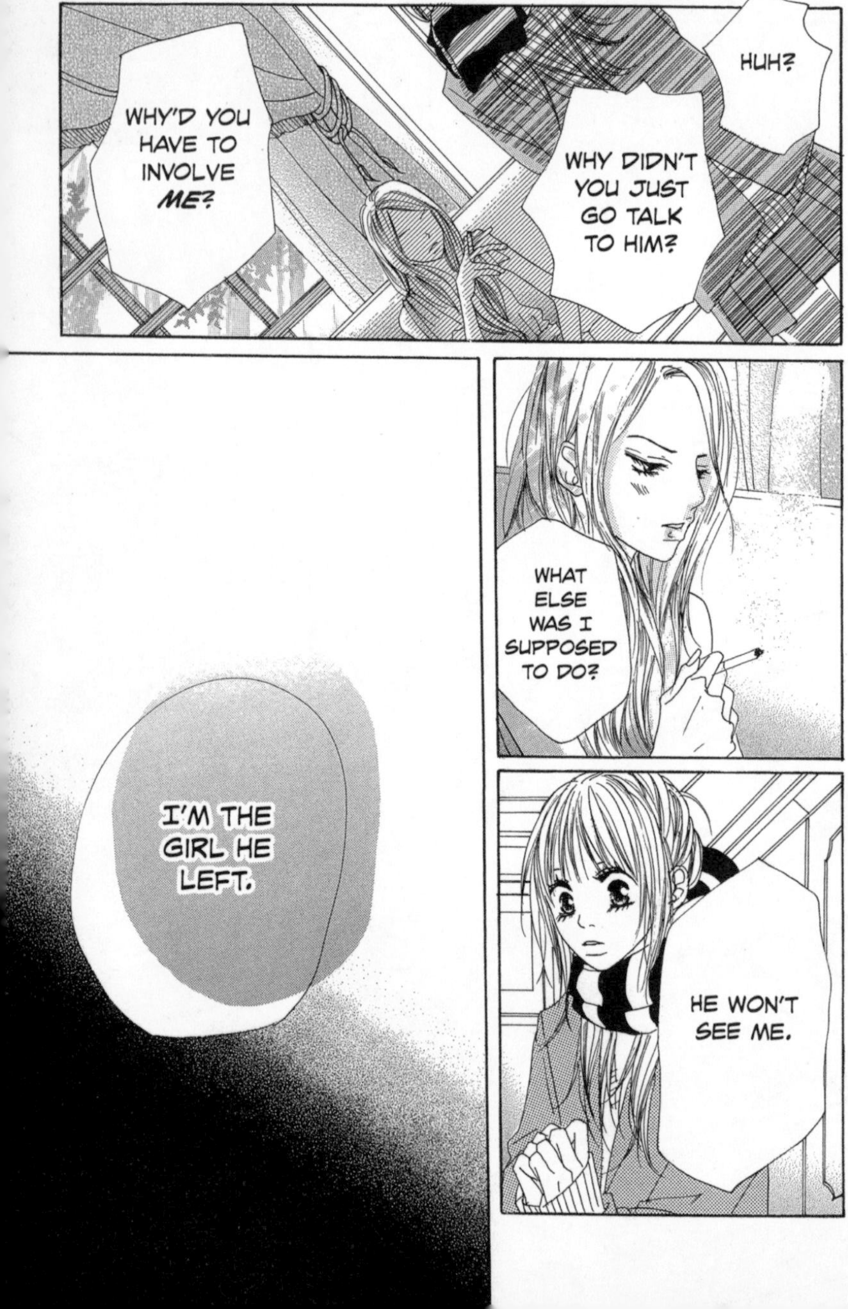
HUH?
WHY DIDN'T YOU JUST GO TALK TO HIM?
WHY'D YOU HAVE TO INVOLVE *ME*?
WHAT ELSE WAS I SUPPOSED TO DO?
HE WON'T SEE ME.
I'M THE GIRL HE LEFT.

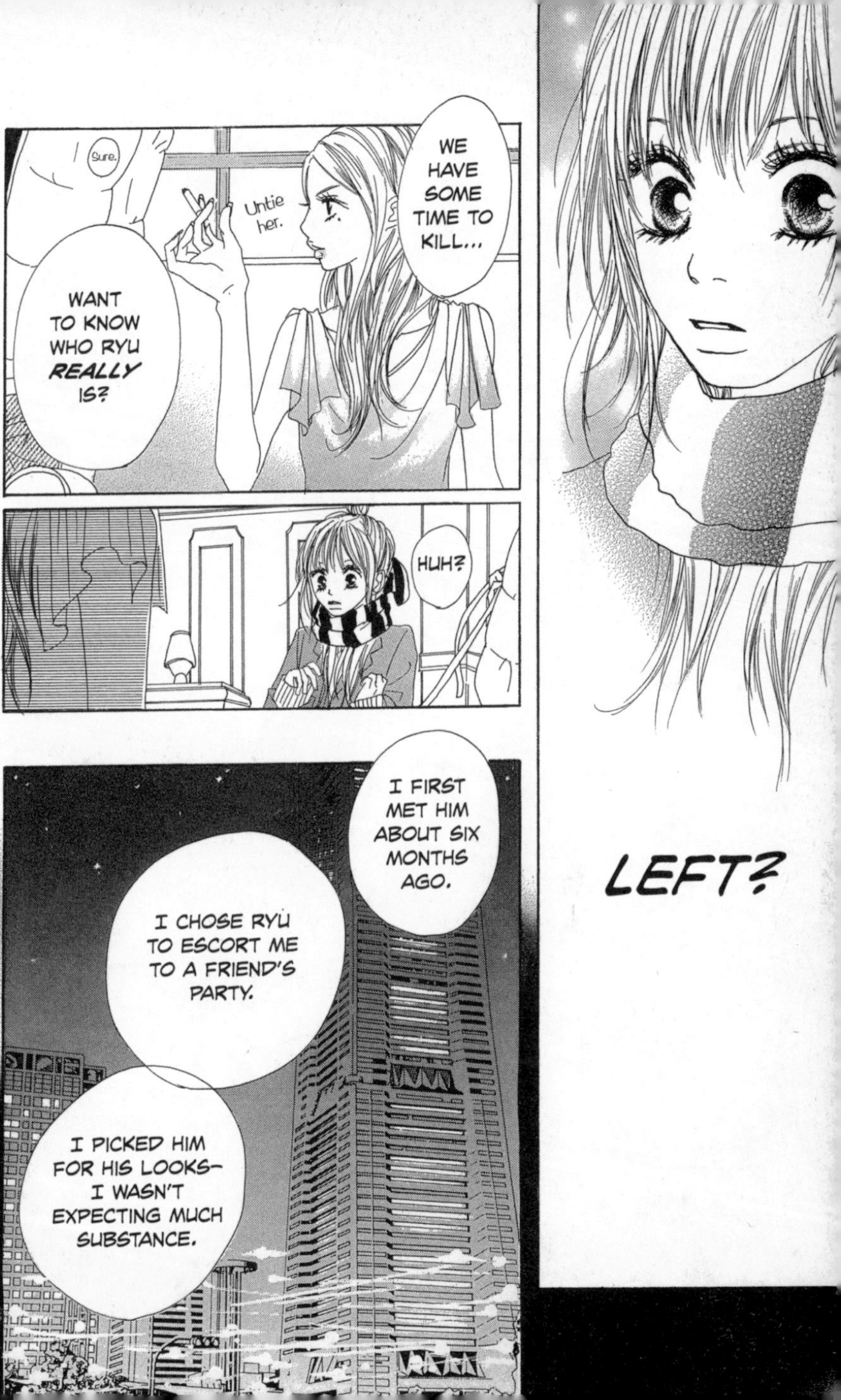
LEFT?
WE HAVE SOME TIME TO KILL...
Untie her.
Sure.
WANT TO KNOW WHO RYU *REALLY* IS?
HUH?
I FIRST MET HIM ABOUT SIX MONTHS AGO.
I CHOSE RYU TO ESCORT ME TO A FRIEND'S PARTY.
I PICKED HIM FOR HIS LOOKS— I WASN'T EXPECTING MUCH SUBSTANCE.

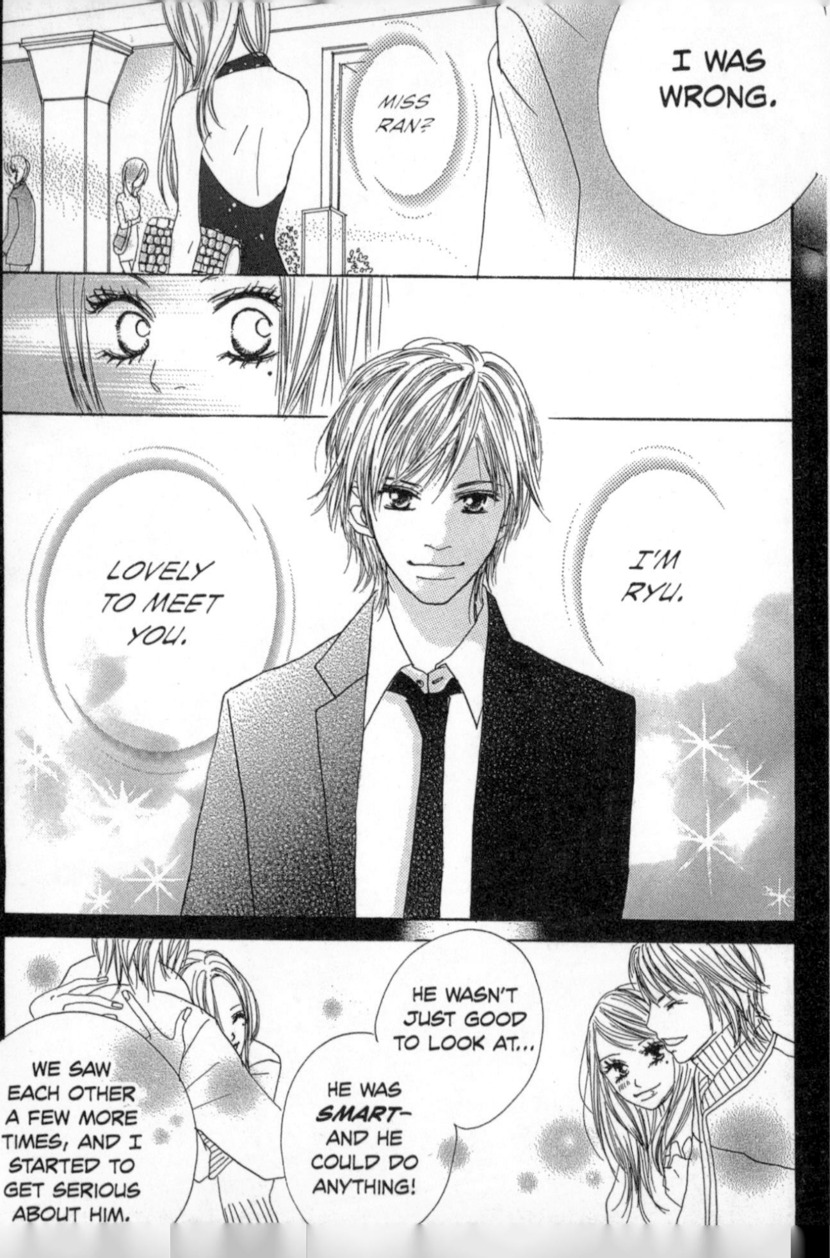
I WAS WRONG.
MISS RAN?
I'M RYU.
LOVELY TO MEET YOU.
HE WASN'T JUST GOOD TO LOOK AT...
HE WAS SMART— AND HE COULD DO ANYTHING!
WE SAW EACH OTHER A FEW MORE TIMES, AND I STARTED TO GET SERIOUS ABOUT HIM.

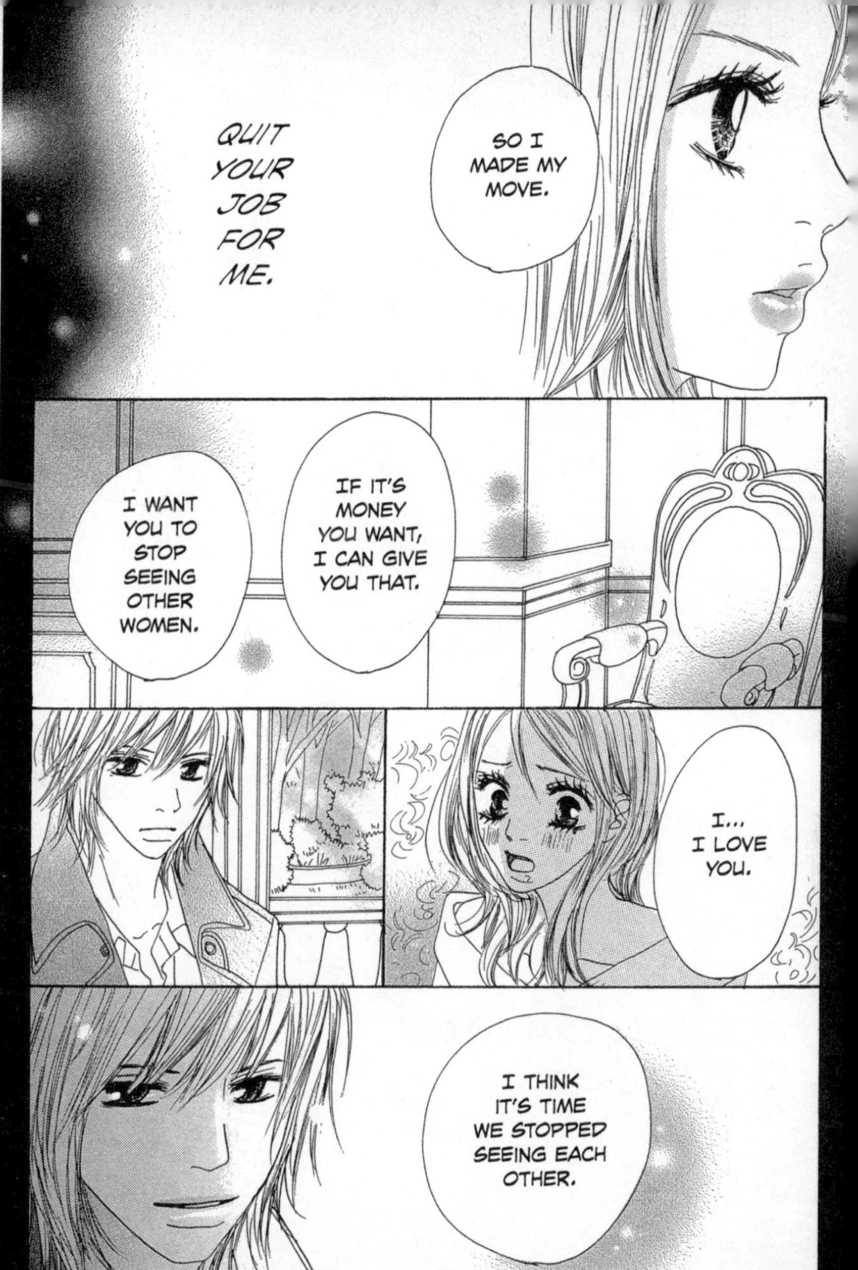
SO I MADE MY MOVE.
QUIT YOUR JOB FOR ME.
IF IT'S MONEY YOU WANT, I CAN GIVE YOU THAT.
I WANT YOU TO STOP SEEING OTHER WOMEN.
I... I LOVE YOU.
I THINK IT'S TIME WE STOPPED SEEING EACH OTHER.

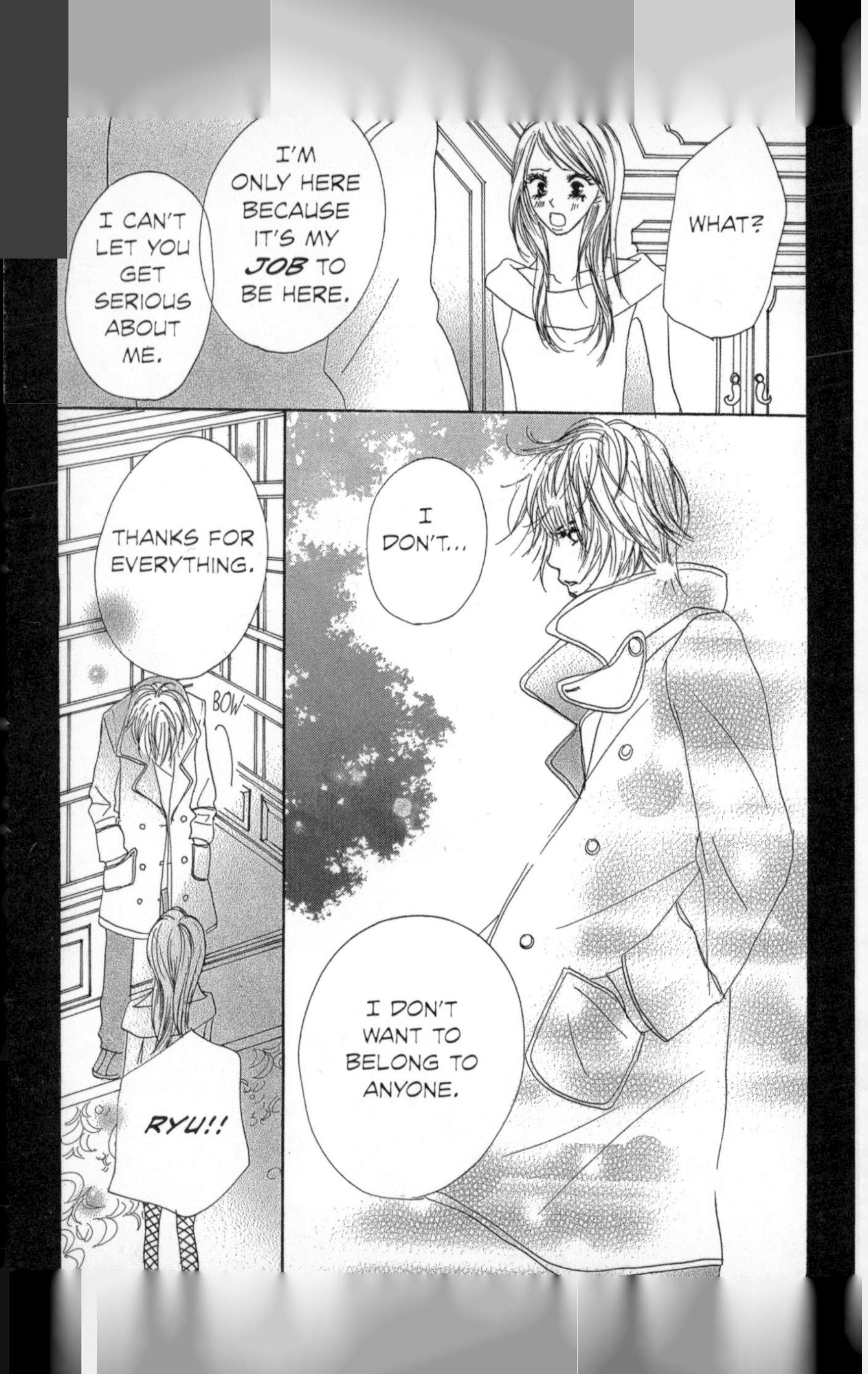
WHAT?
I'M ONLY HERE BECAUSE IT'S MY JOB TO BE HERE.
I CAN'T LET YOU GET SERIOUS ABOUT ME.
I DON'T...
I DON'T WANT TO BELONG TO ANYONE.
THANKS FOR EVERYTHING.
BOW
RYU!!

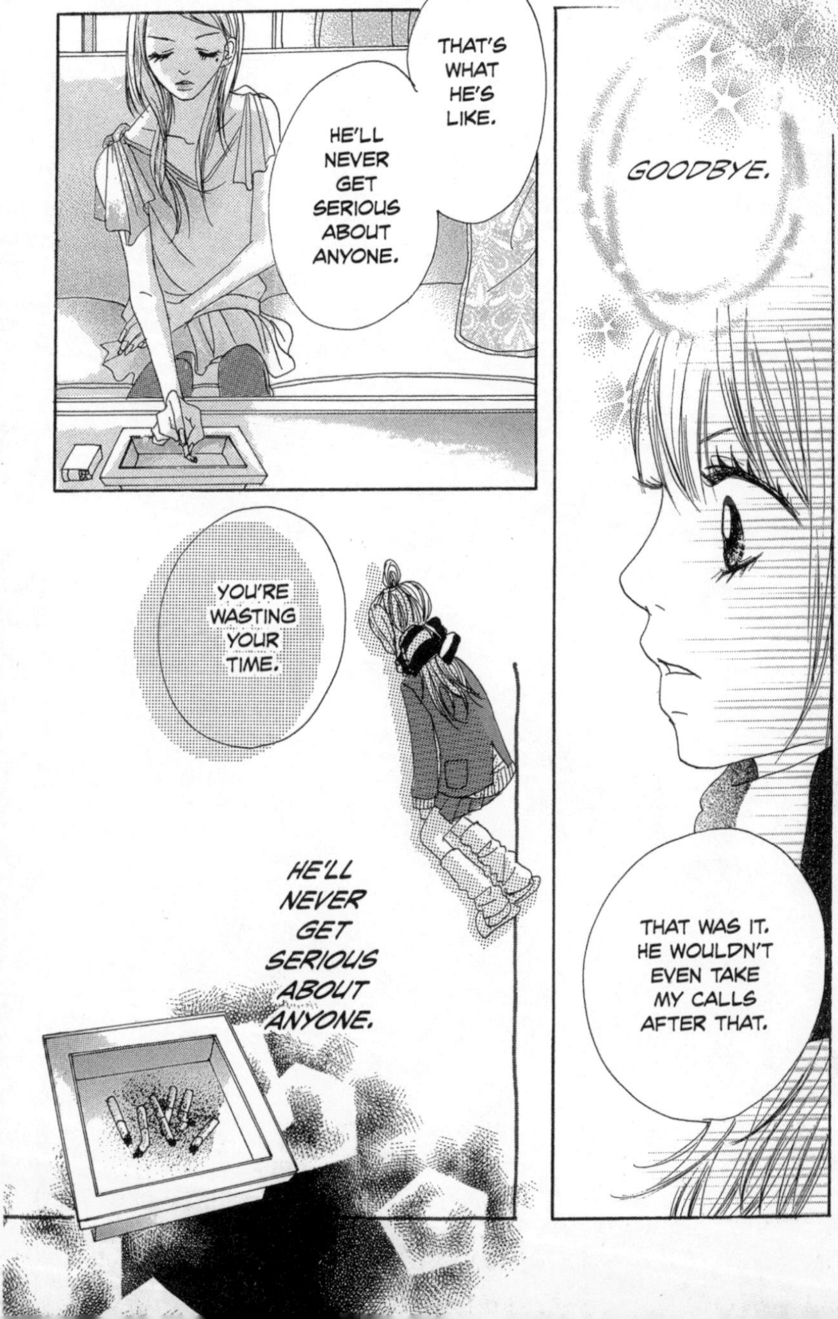
GOODBYE.
THAT WAS IT. HE WOULDN'T EVEN TAKE MY CALLS AFTER THAT.
THAT'S WHAT HE'S LIKE.
HE'LL NEVER GET SERIOUS ABOUT ANYONE.
YOU'RE WASTING YOUR TIME.
HE'LL NEVER GET SERIOUS ABOUT ANYONE.

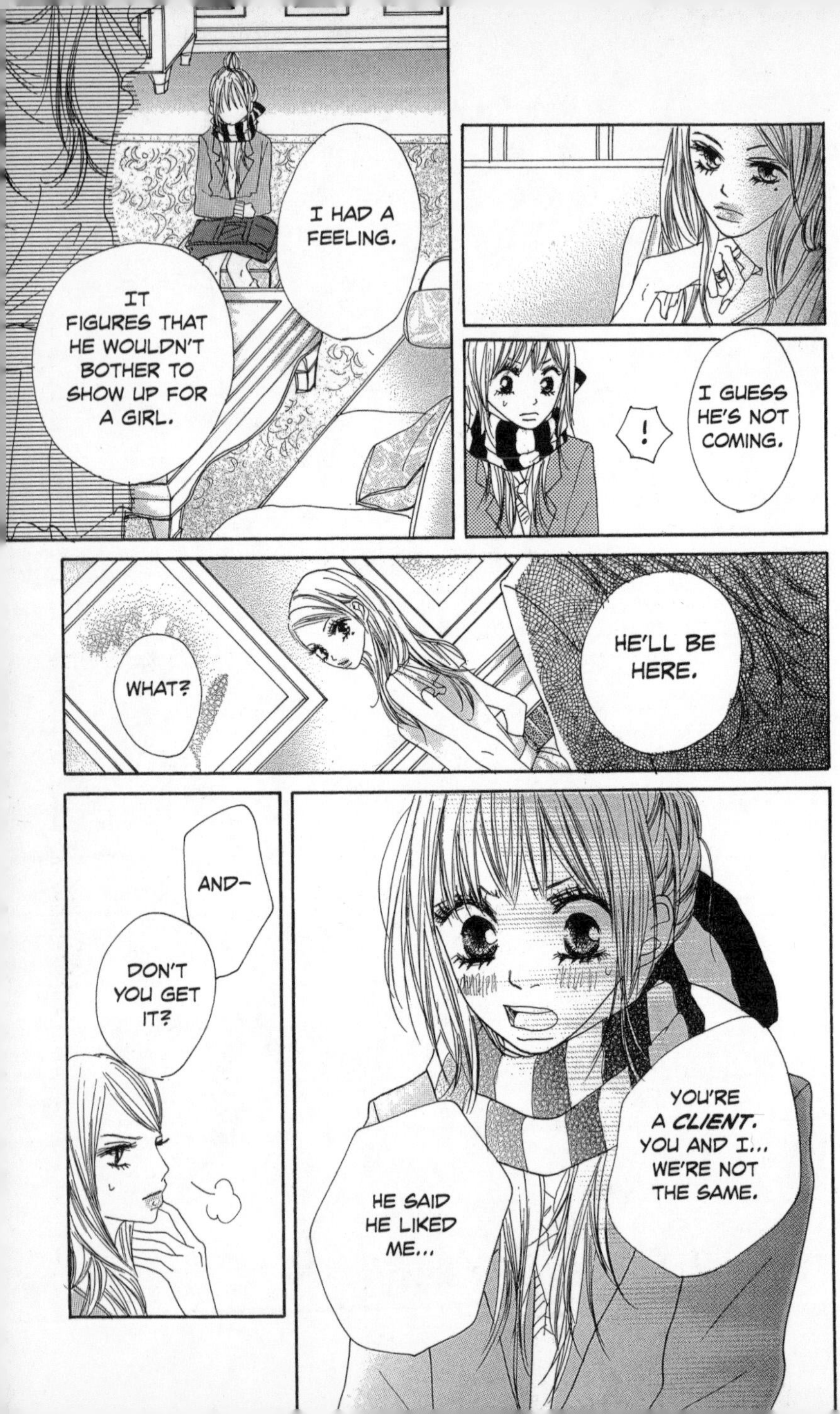

!
I GUESS HE'S NOT COMING.
I HAD A FEELING.
IT FIGURES THAT HE WOULDN'T BOTHER TO SHOW UP FOR A GIRL.
HE'LL BE HERE.
WHAT?
YOU'RE A *CLIENT.* YOU AND I... WE'RE NOT THE SAME.
HE SAID HE LIKED ME...
AND—
DON'T YOU GET IT?

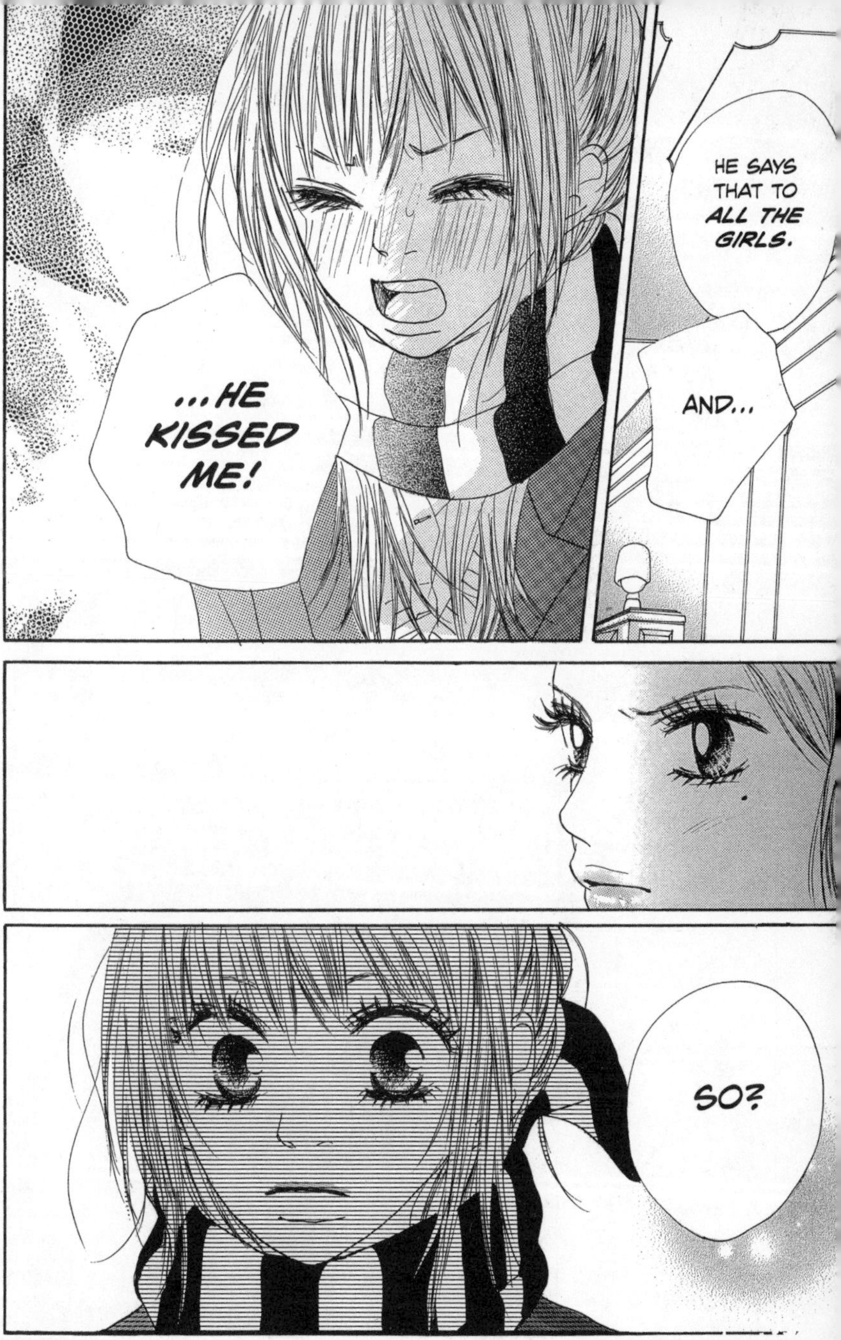
HE SAYS THAT TO ALL THE GIRLS.
AND...
...HE KISSED ME!
SO?

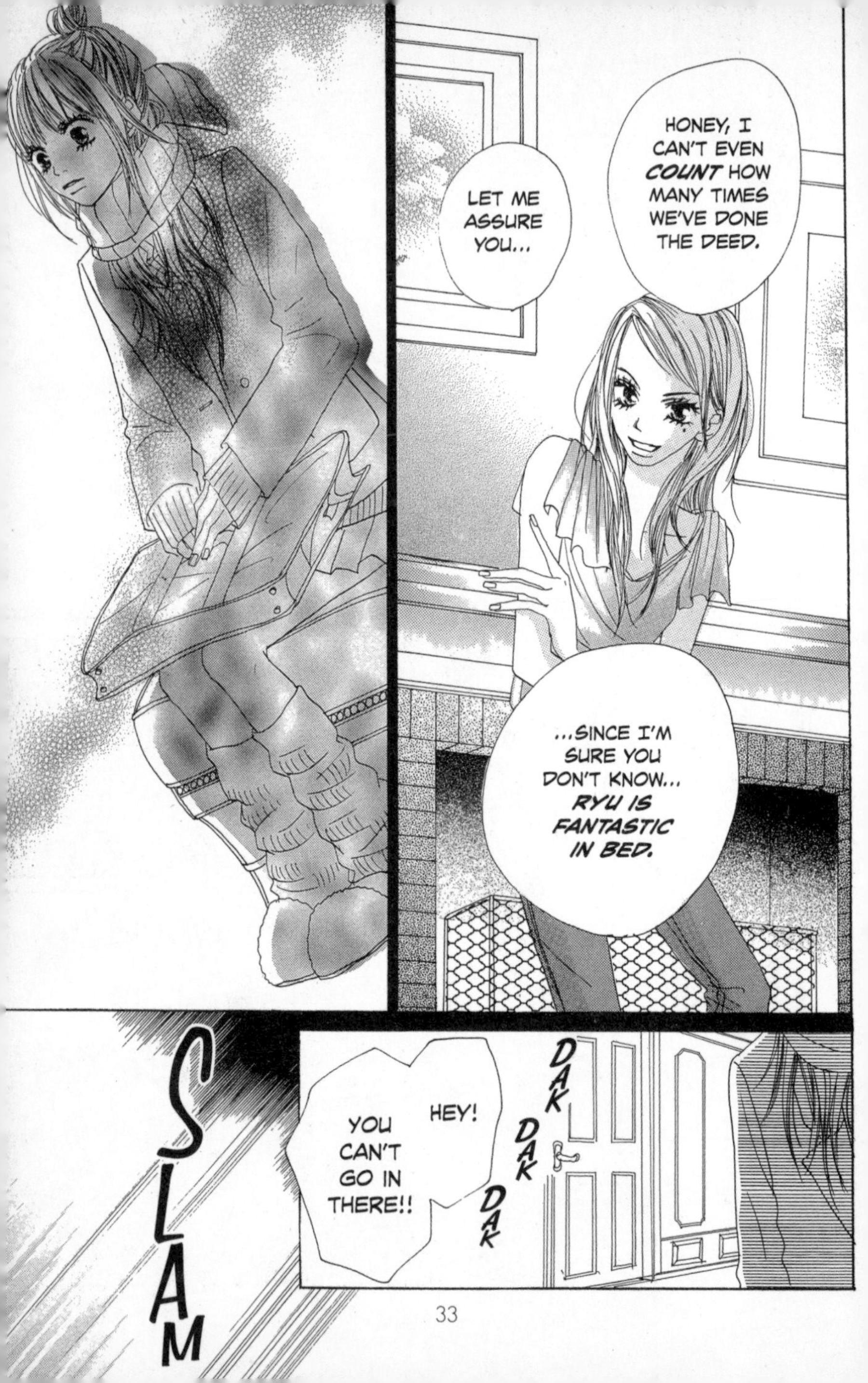
HONEY, I CAN'T EVEN COUNT HOW MANY TIMES WE'VE DONE THE DEED.
LET ME ASSURE YOU...
...SINCE I'M SURE YOU DON'T KNOW... RYU IS FANTASTIC IN BED.
DAK DAK DAK DAK
HEY!
YOU CAN'T GO IN THERE!!
SLAM

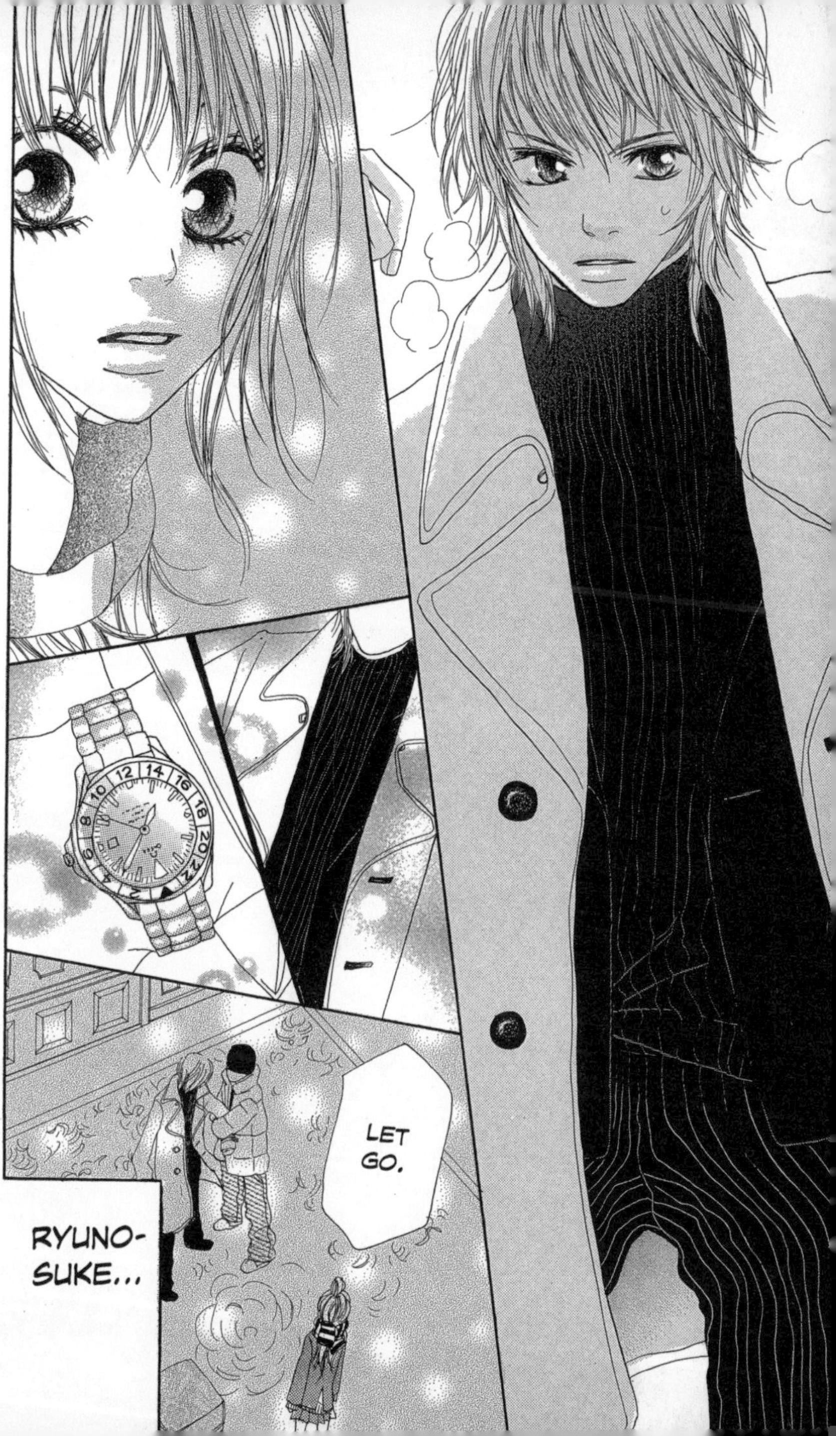
LET GO.
RYUNO-SUKE...

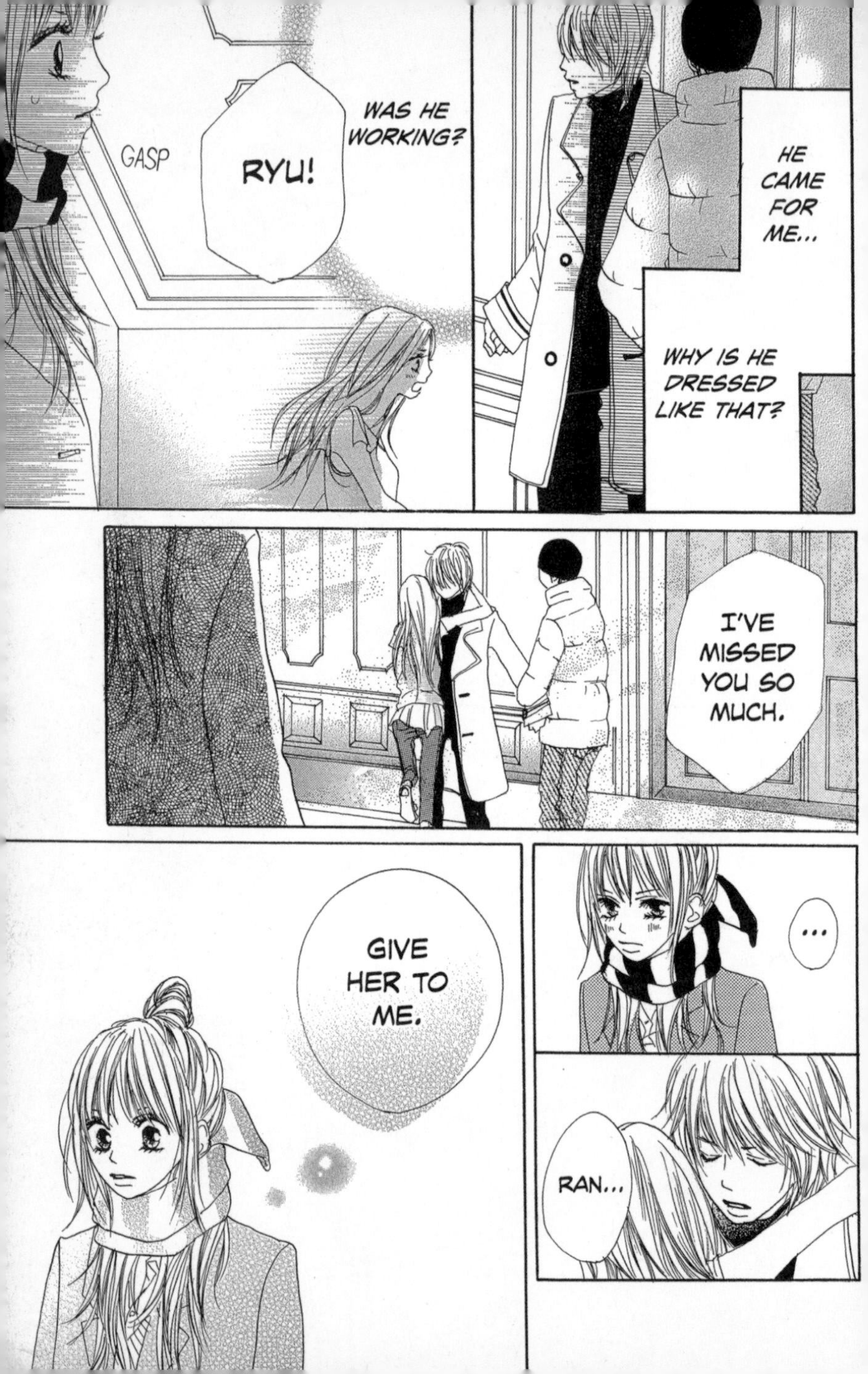
HE CAME FOR ME...
WHY IS HE DRESSED LIKE THAT?
WAS HE WORKING?
RYU!
GASP
I'VE MISSED YOU SO MUCH.
...
RAN...
GIVE HER TO ME.

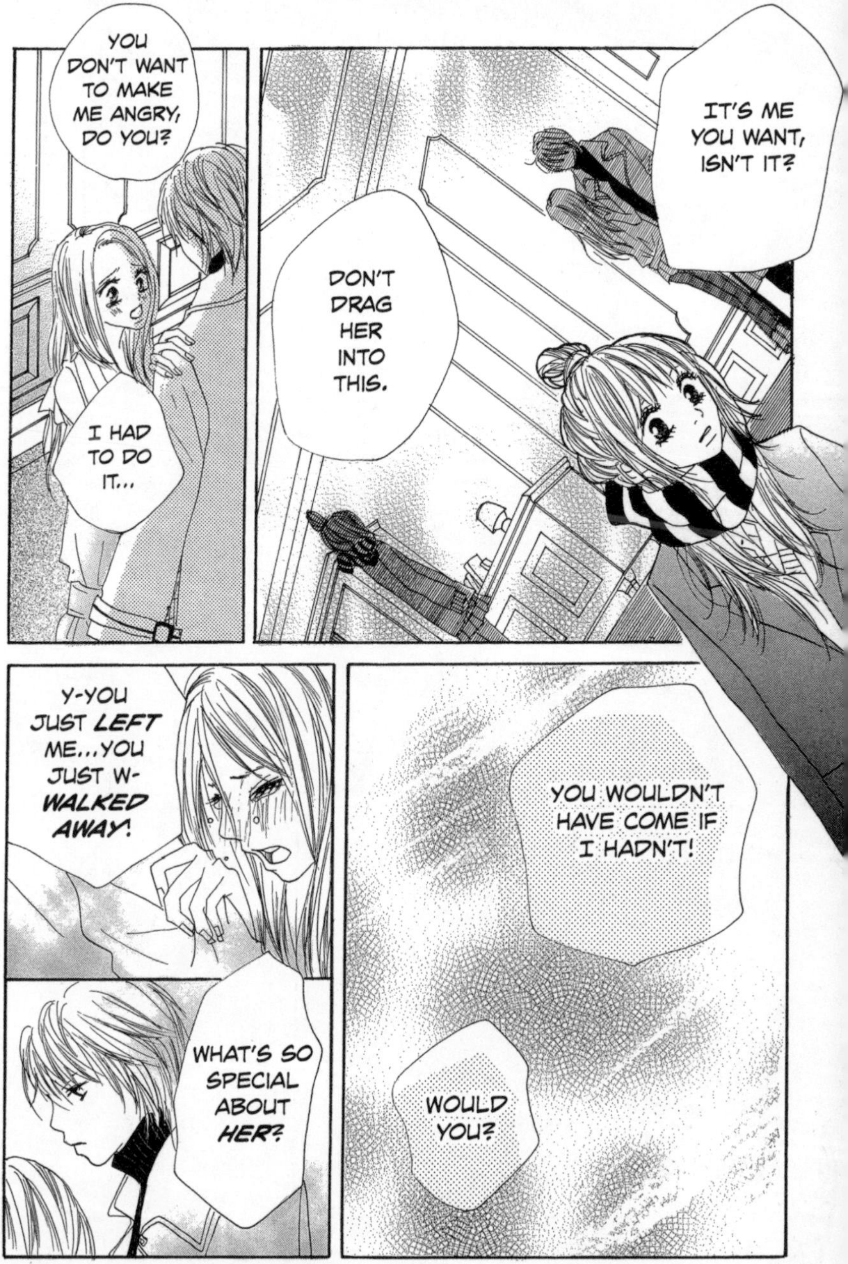
IT'S ME YOU WANT, ISN'T IT?
DON'T DRAG HER INTO THIS.
YOU DON'T WANT TO MAKE ME ANGRY, DO YOU?
I HAD TO DO IT...
YOU WOULDN'T HAVE COME IF I HADN'T!
WOULD YOU?
Y-YOU JUST *LEFT* ME...YOU JUST W-*WALKED AWAY*!
WHAT'S SO SPECIAL ABOUT *HER*?

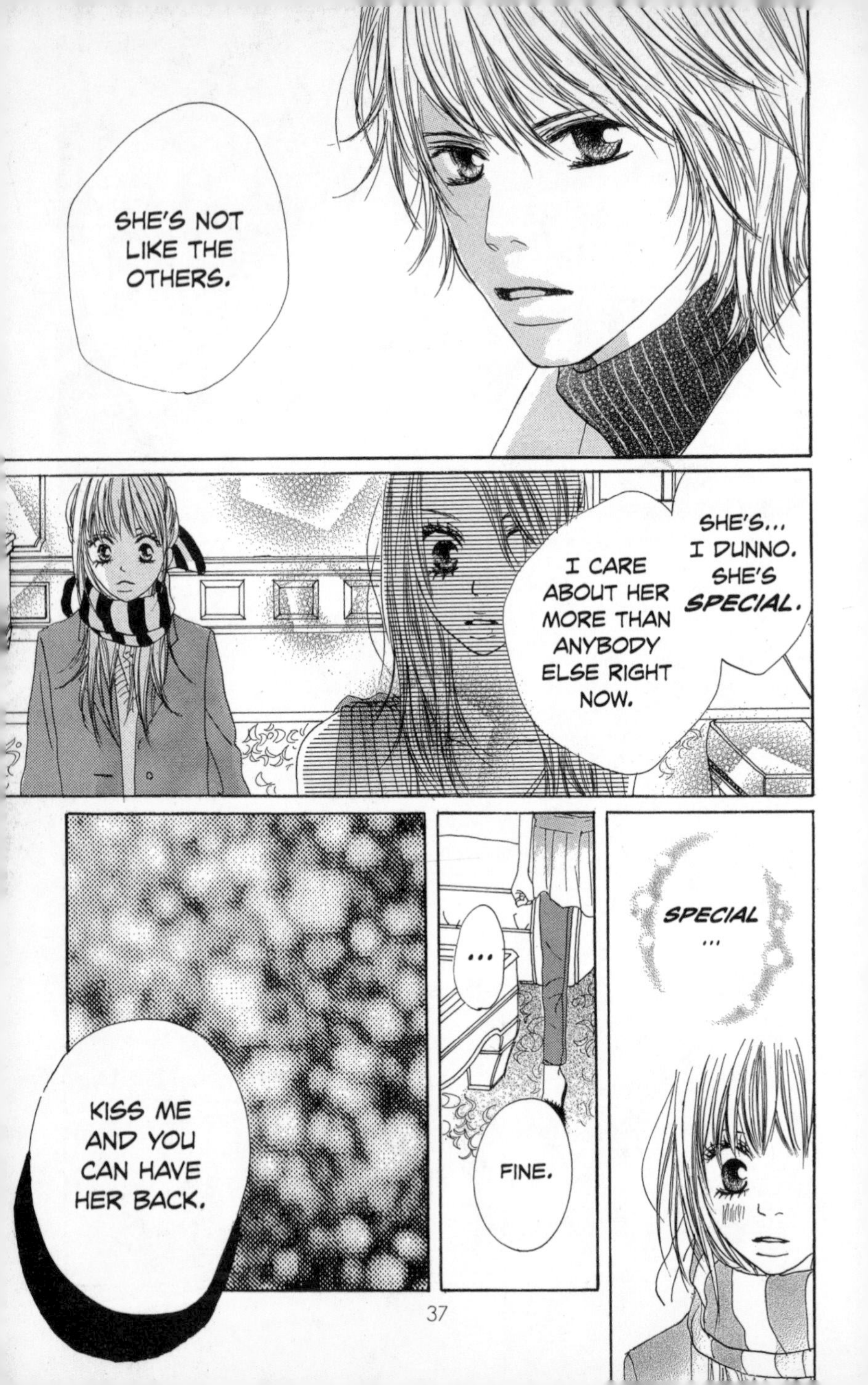
SHE'S NOT LIKE THE OTHERS.
SHE'S... I DUNNO. SHE'S *SPECIAL*.
I CARE ABOUT HER MORE THAN ANYBODY ELSE RIGHT NOW.
SPECIAL ...
...
FINE.
KISS ME AND YOU CAN HAVE HER BACK.

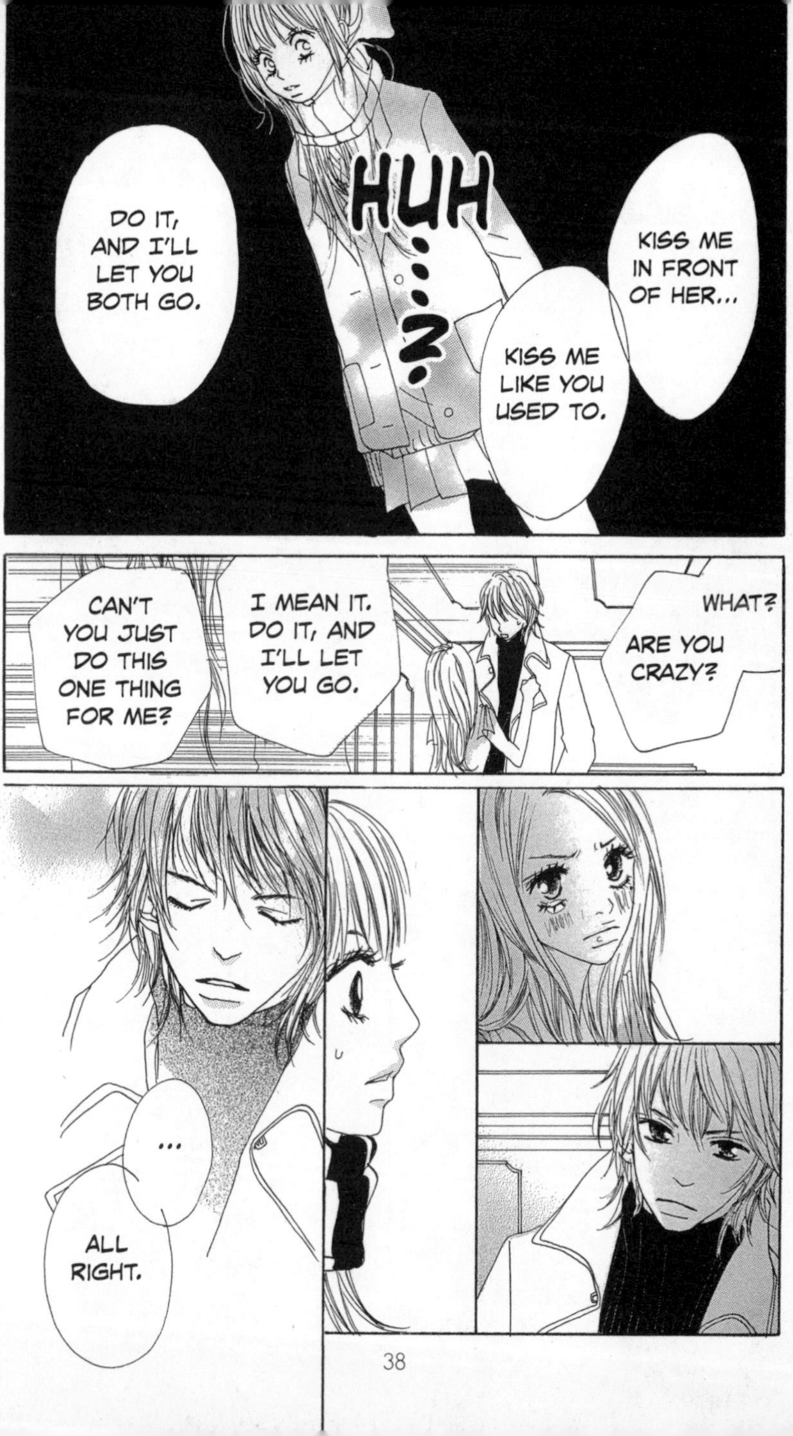
KISS ME IN FRONT OF HER...
HUH...?
KISS ME LIKE YOU USED TO.
DO IT, AND I'LL LET YOU BOTH GO.
WHAT?
ARE YOU CRAZY?
I MEAN IT. DO IT, AND I'LL LET YOU GO.
CAN'T YOU JUST DO THIS ONE THING FOR ME?
...
ALL RIGHT.

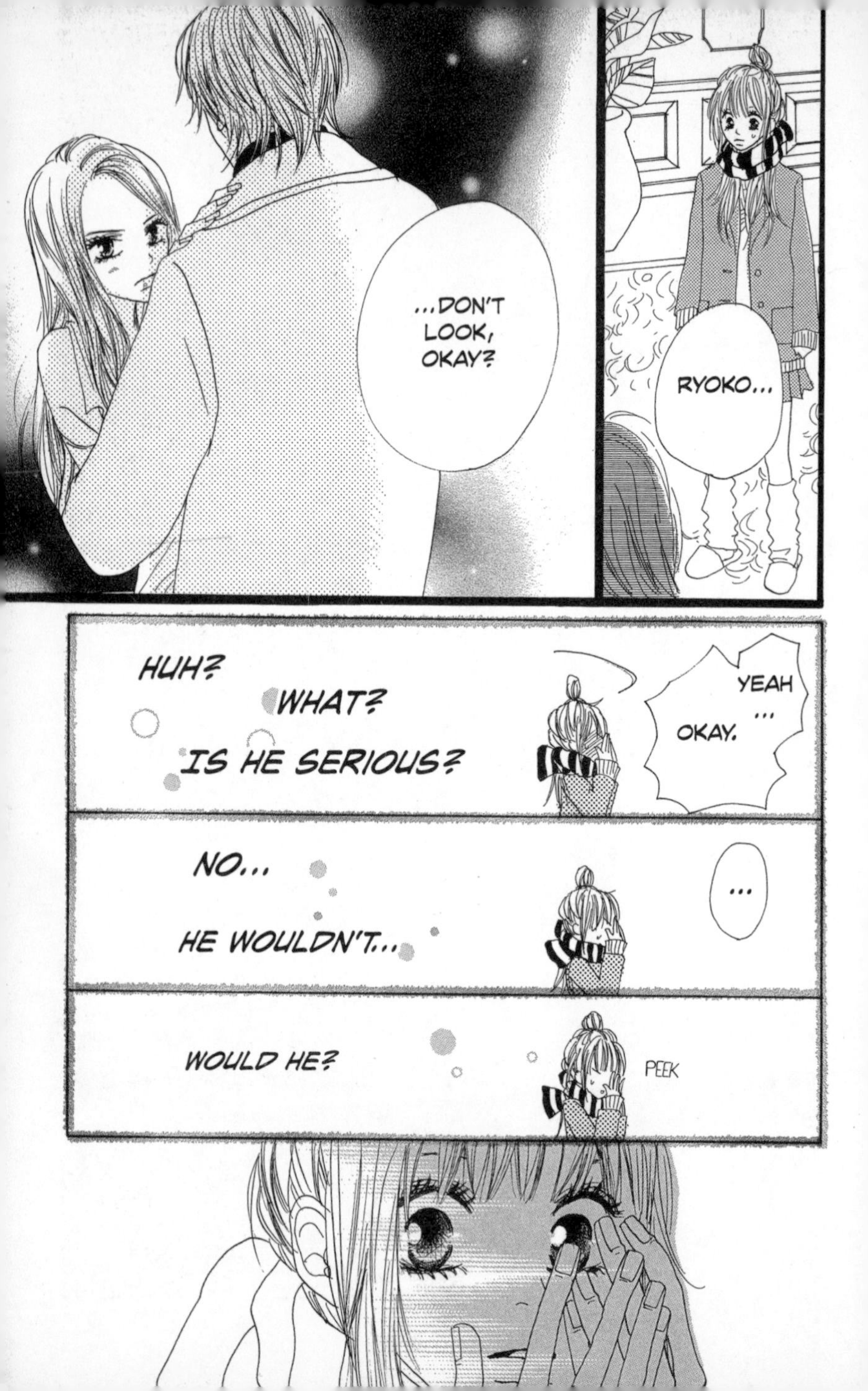
RYOKO...
...DON'T LOOK, OKAY?
YEAH... OKAY.
HUH?
WHAT?
IS HE SERIOUS?
...
NO...
HE WOULDN'T...
PEEK
WOULD HE?

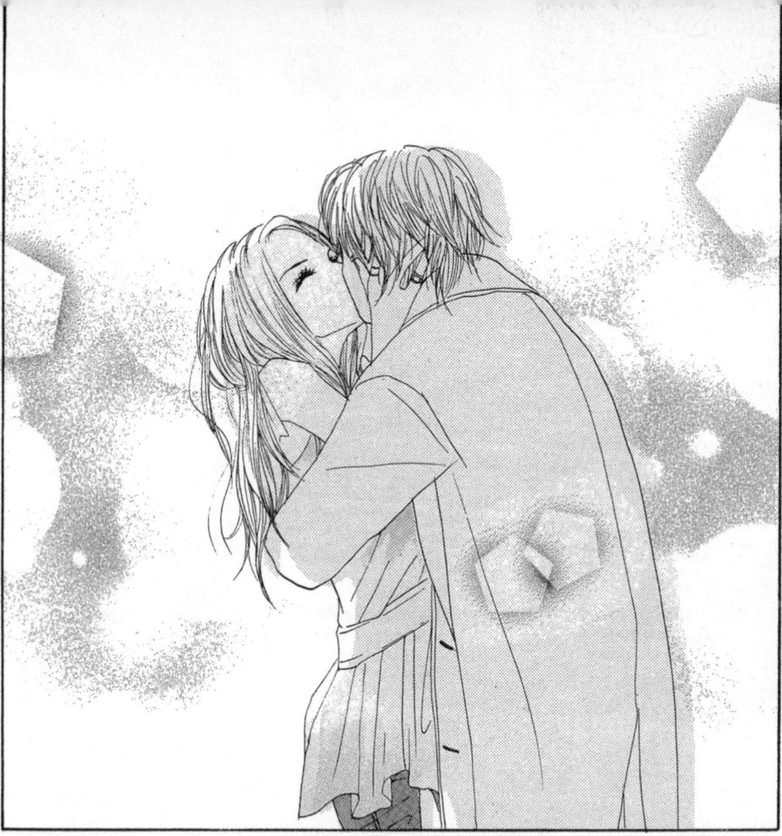
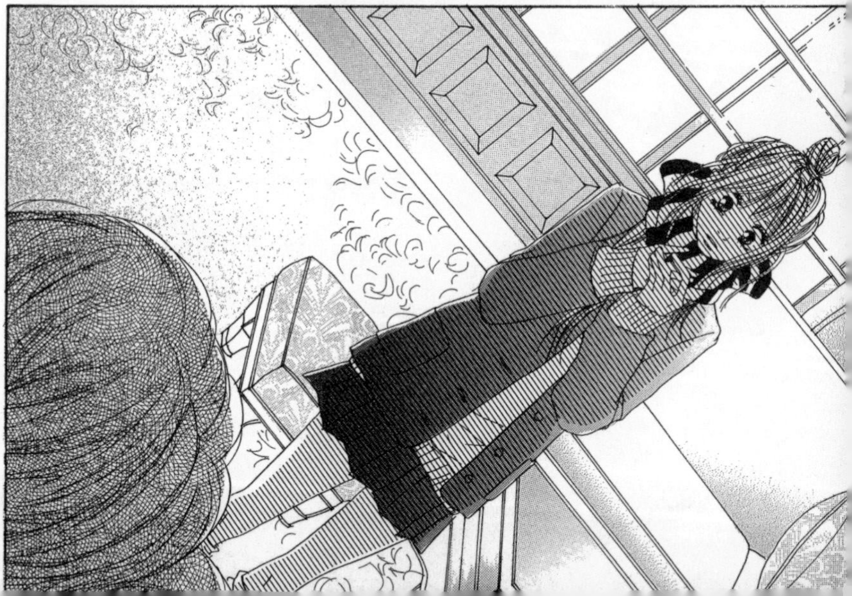

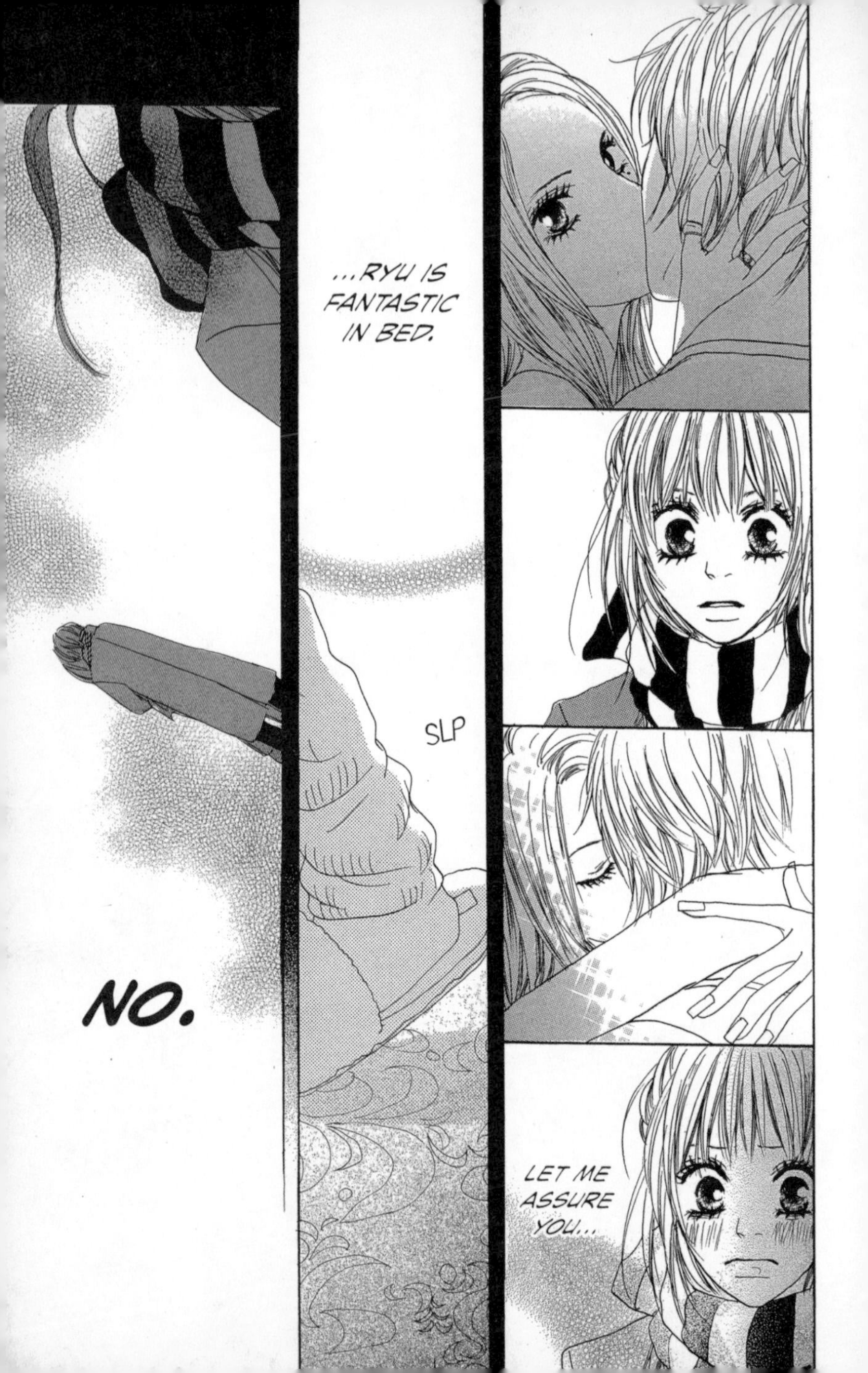
LET ME ASSURE YOU...
...RYU IS FANTASTIC IN BED.
SLP
NO.

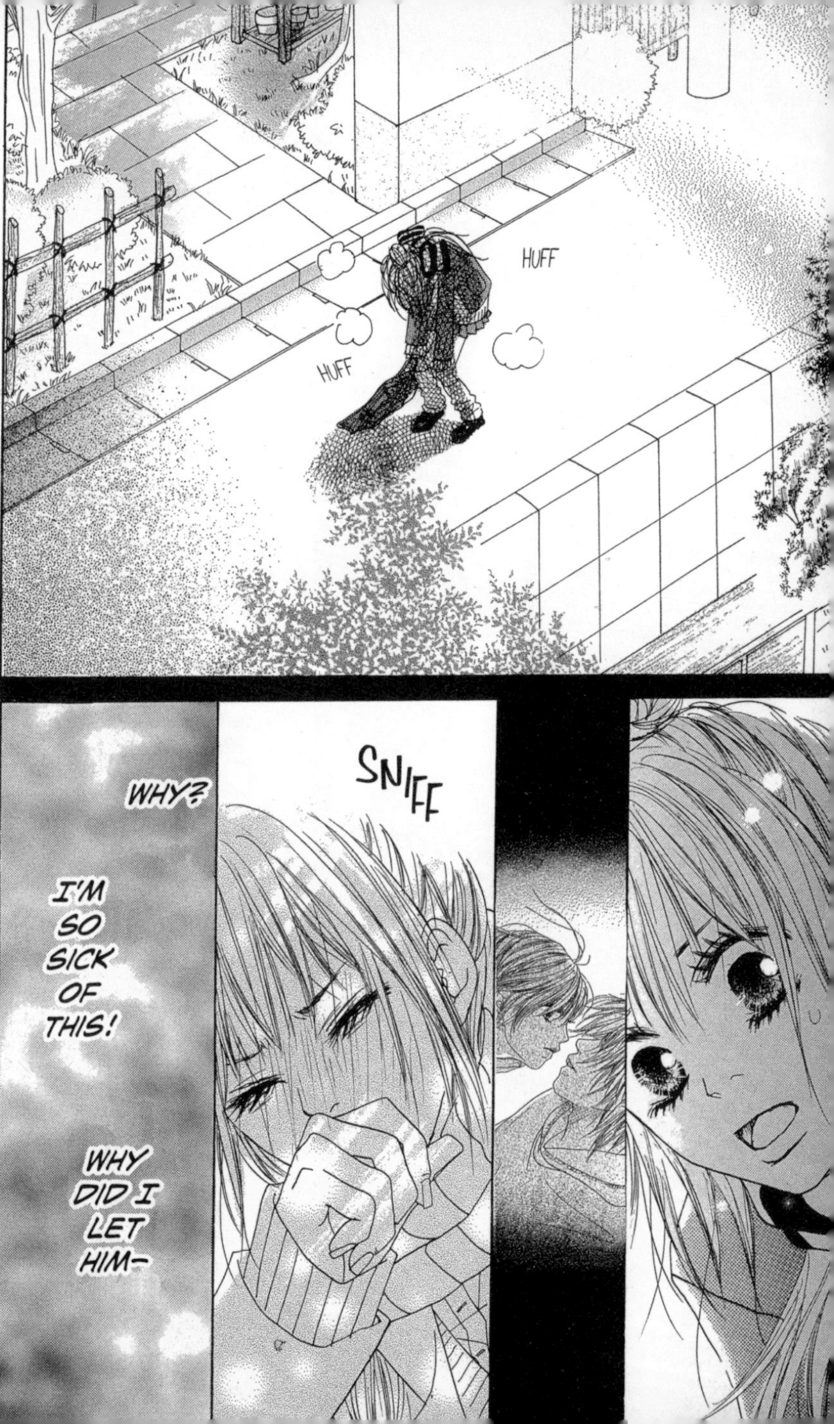
HUFF
HUFF
SNIFF
WHY?
I'M SO SICK OF THIS!
WHY DID I LET HIM-

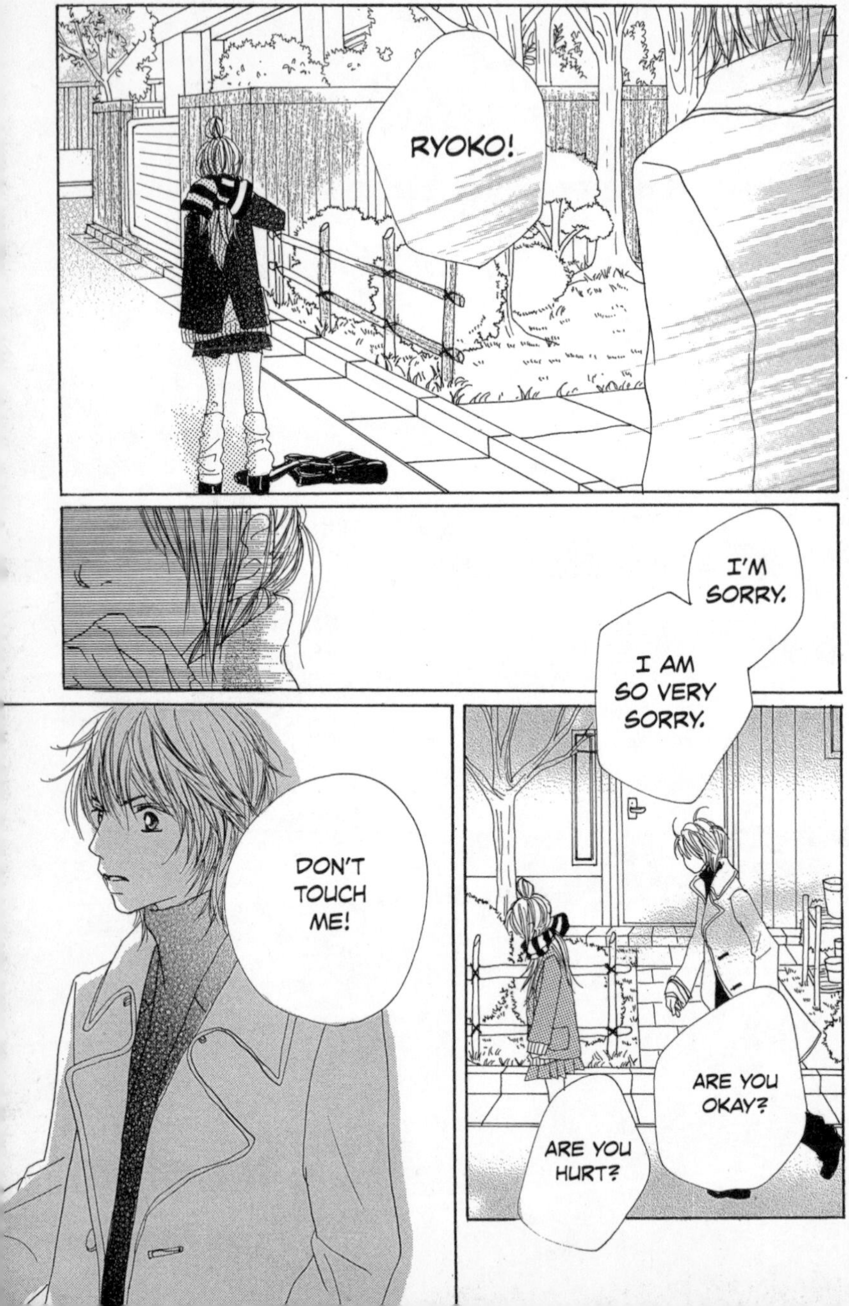
RYOKO!
I'M SORRY.
I AM SO VERY SORRY.
ARE YOU OKAY?
ARE YOU HURT?
DON'T TOUCH ME!

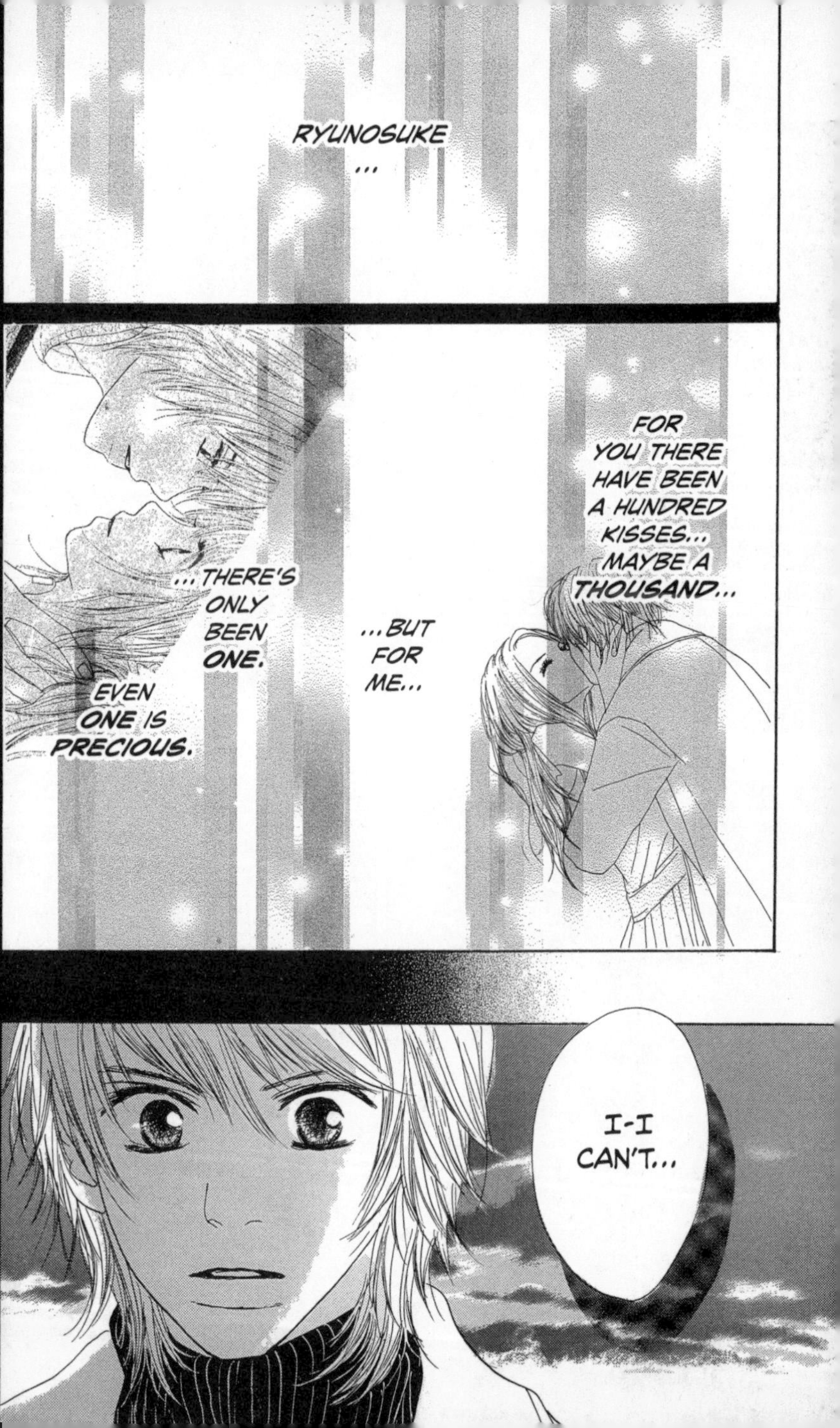
RYUNOSUKE ...
FOR YOU THERE HAVE BEEN A HUNDRED KISSES... MAYBE A THOUSAND...
...BUT FOR ME...
...THERE'S ONLY BEEN ONE.
EVEN ONE IS PRECIOUS.
I-I CAN'T...

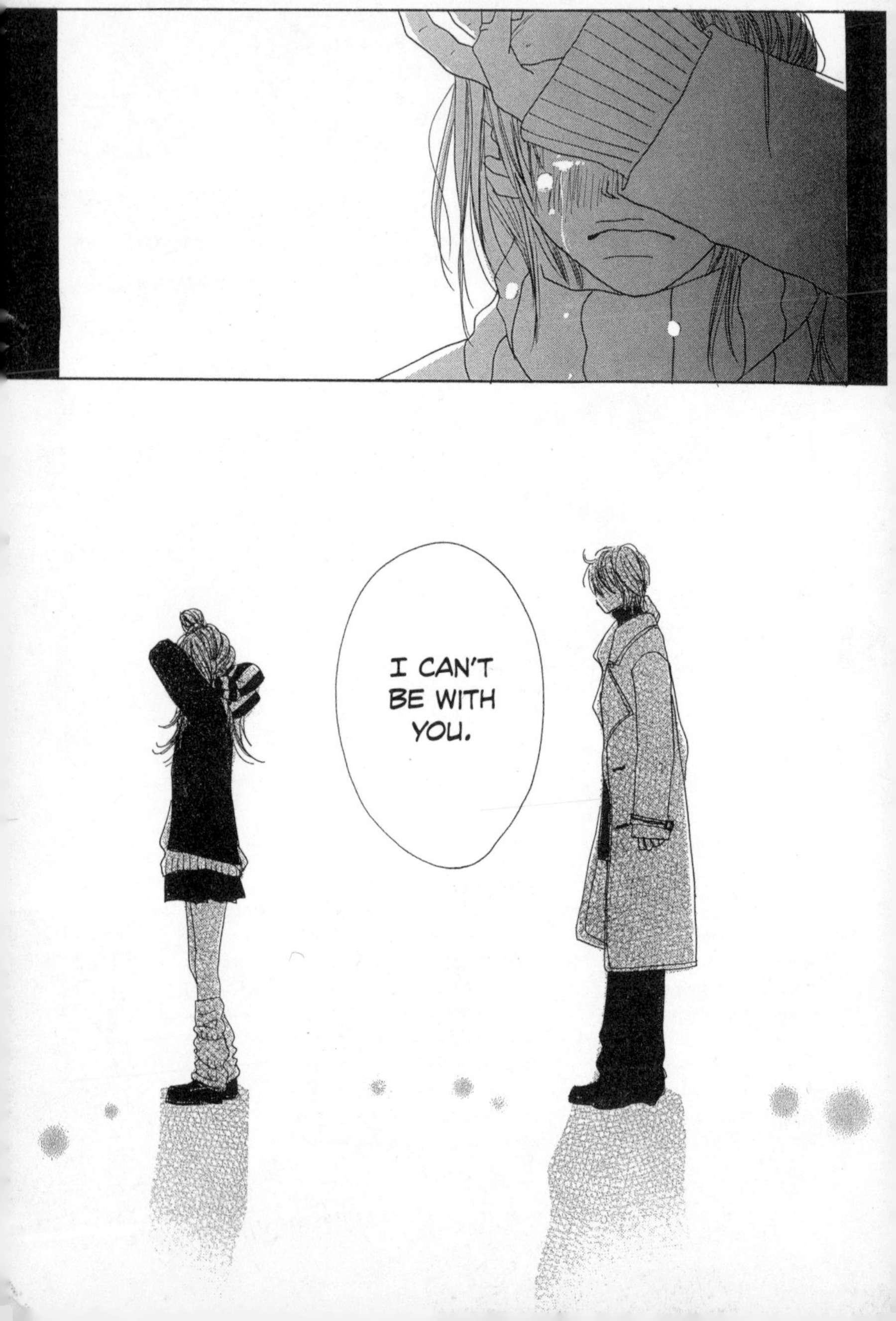
I CAN'T BE WITH YOU.

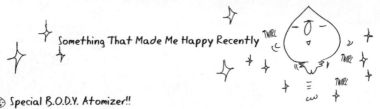

Something That Made Me Happy Recently

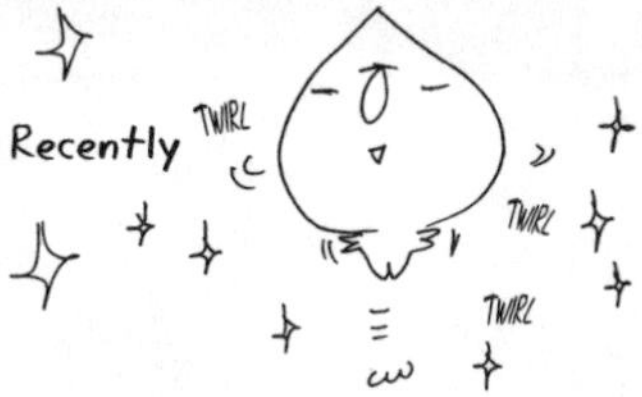
TWIRL
TWIRL
TWIRL

Special B.O.D.Y. Atomizer!!

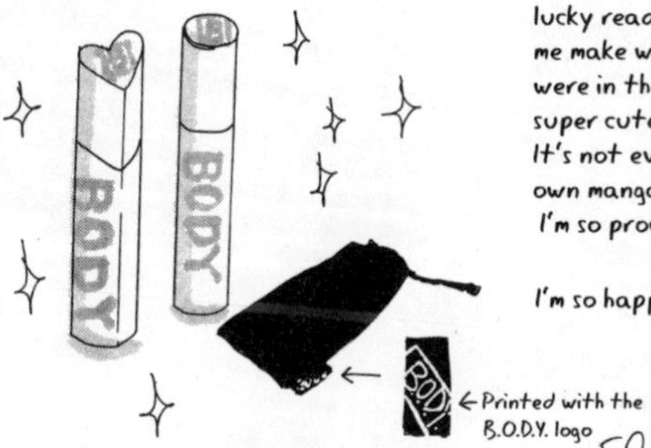
BODY
BODY
BODY
←Printed with the B.O.D.Y. logo

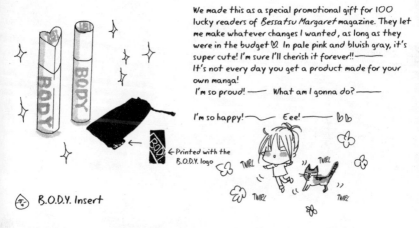

We made this as a special promotional gift for 100 lucky readers of *Bessatsu Margaret* magazine. They let me make whatever changes I wanted, as long as they were in the budget ♡. In pale pink and bluish gray, it's super cute! I'm sure I'll cherish it forever!!———
It's not every day you get a product made for your own manga!
I'm so proud!—— What am I gonna do?———

I'm so happy!~—— Eee!——— bb

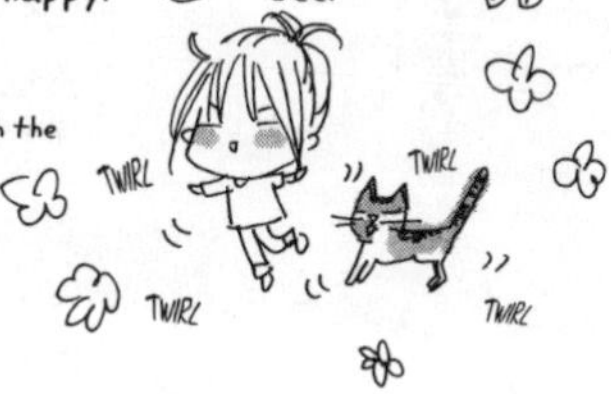
TWIRL
TWIRL
TWIRL
TWIRL

B.O.D.Y. Insert

Bessatsu Margaret's September issue included a B.O.D.Y. insert. It was done for the same promotional event as the atomizer. It contained a character chart and a psychology test. The character chart has been added to the end of this volume!!

I got to teach manga!

Every once in a while, aspiring manga artists gather for a class and they get a chance to ask questions of established professionals. I recently had the honor of being one of the instructors!! Eee! I've attended those classes before, but this was my first time as a teacher. (Kaoru Tada and Kazune Kawahara were my instructors when I went. They were so friendly with each other. I remember thinking how much I wanted my life to be like theirs...My dream finally came true!! Hard work pays off!) Of course, I was so nervous I couldn't draw very well. My hands were shaking! Akemi Fujii and I were the instructors, and we were both like, "What do we do?" We ended up having a lot of fun. Even so, we're not sure we helped anyone. Waaah! What was the point?

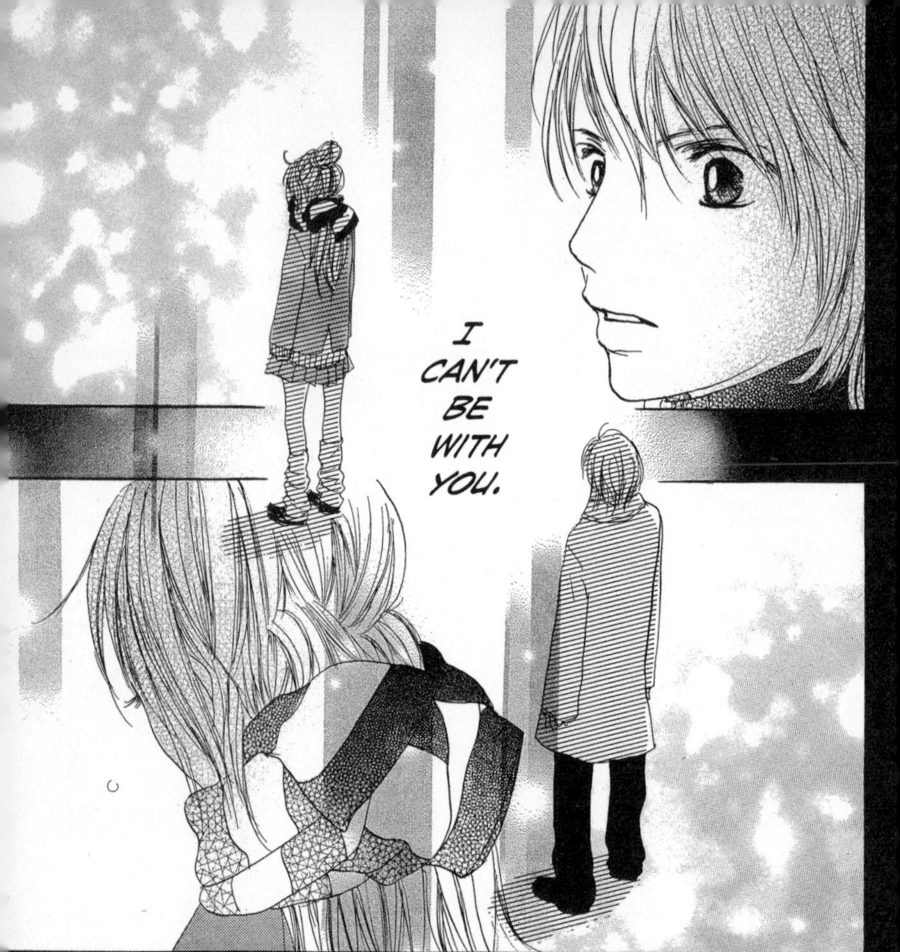
I CAN'T BE WITH YOU.

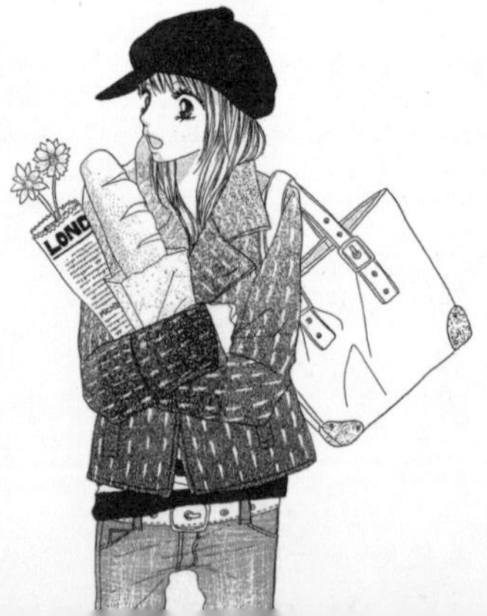

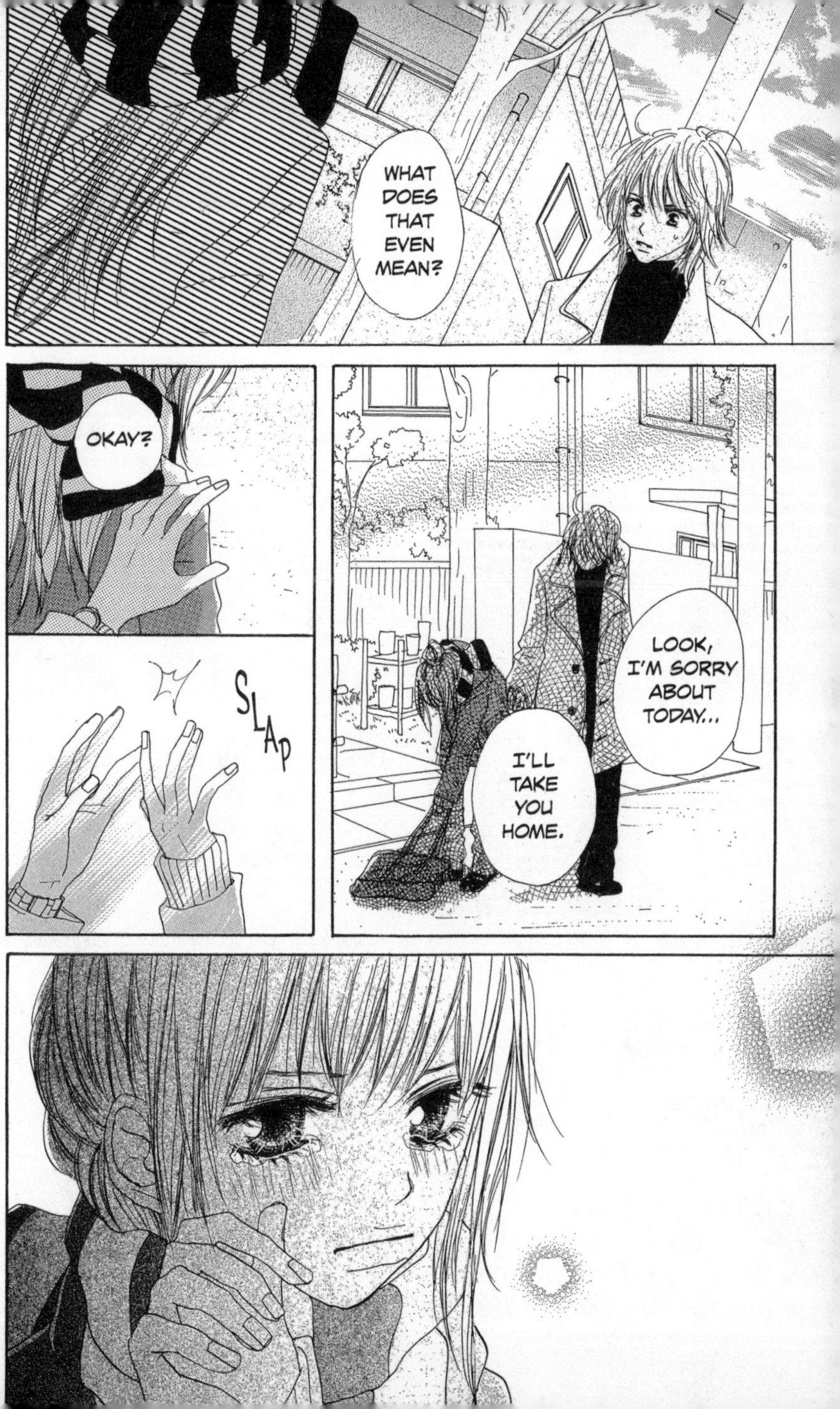
WHAT DOES THAT EVEN MEAN?
LOOK, I'M SORRY ABOUT TODAY...
I'LL TAKE YOU HOME.
OKAY?
SLAP

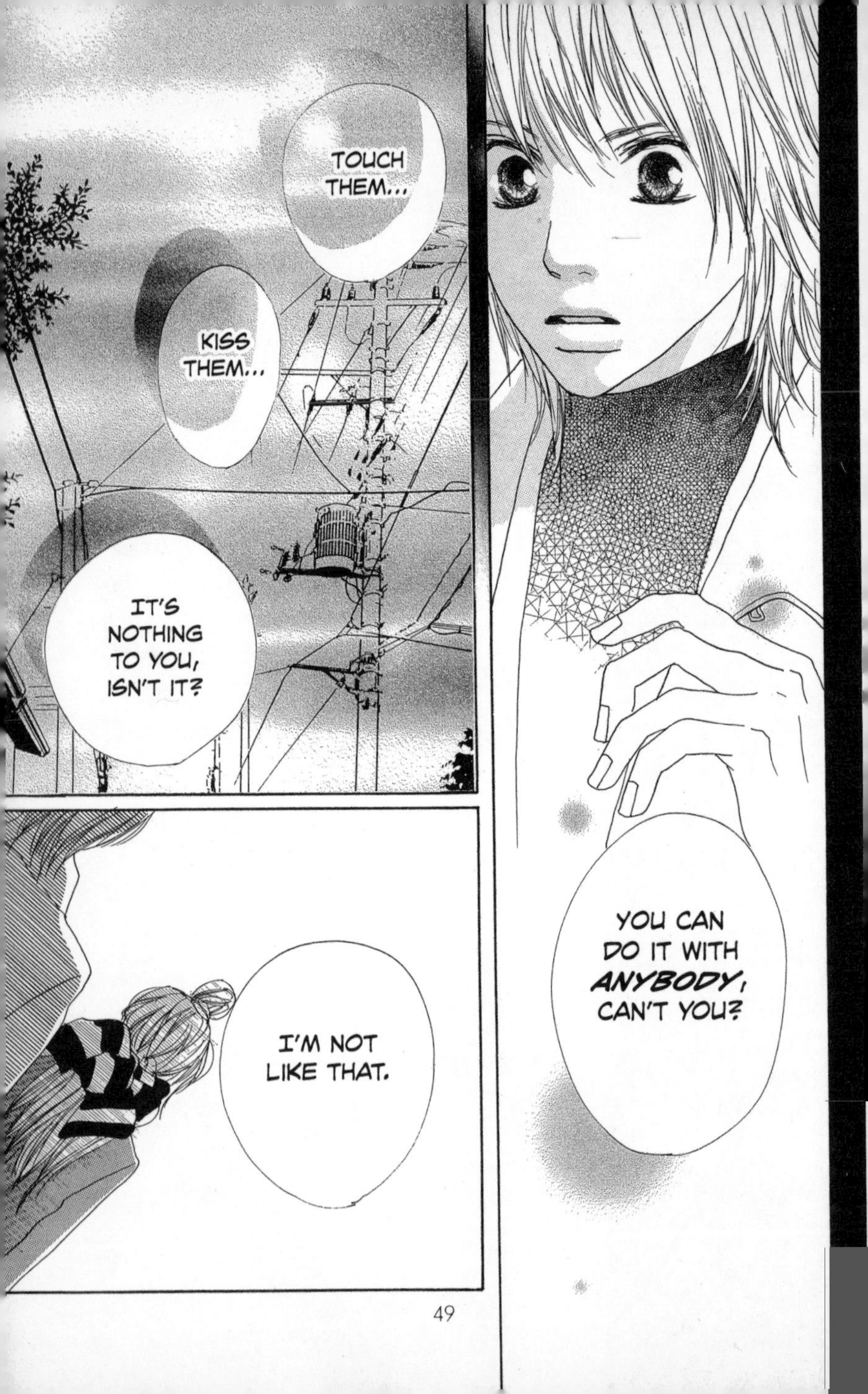
YOU CAN DO IT WITH *ANYBODY*, CAN'T YOU?
TOUCH THEM...
KISS THEM...
IT'S NOTHING TO YOU, ISN'T IT?
I'M NOT LIKE THAT.

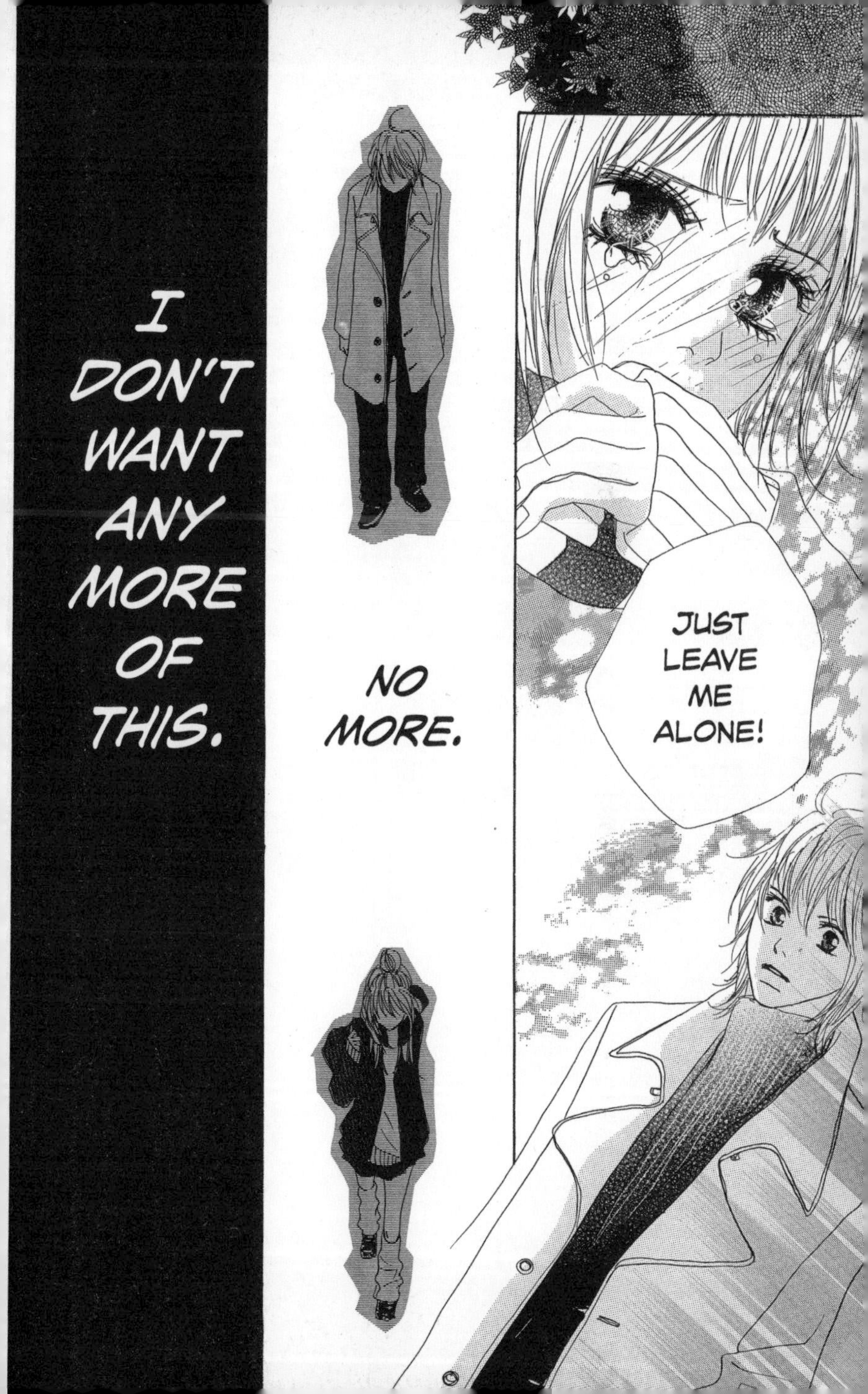
JUST LEAVE ME ALONE!
NO MORE.
I DON'T WANT ANY MORE OF THIS.

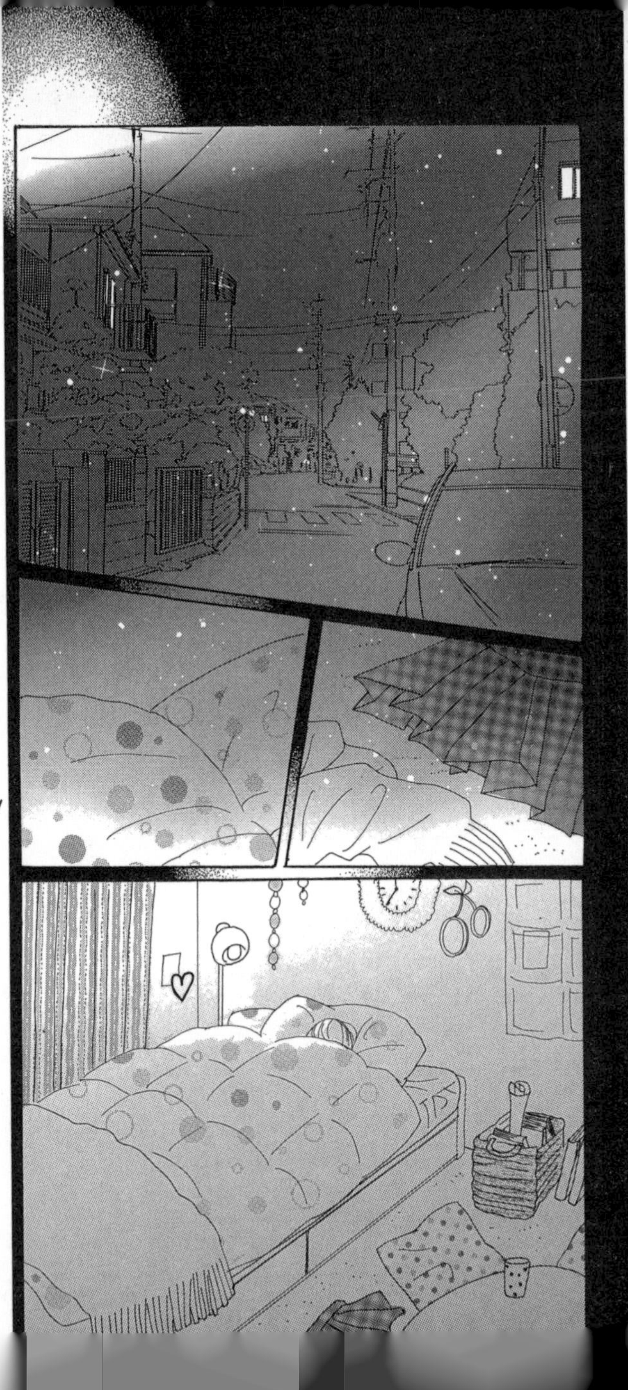

②

My greatest joy these days is running. Ha ha ha! It's kind of funny, isn't it? I started running because I was worried about my health. I'd start off along the river in the late afternoon and just keep going. Every-thing is so beautiful. It's really soothing!! I can hear the change of seasons in the song of the cicadas!! I get excited knowing the leaves are gonna change color soon. I ride my bike a lot too.

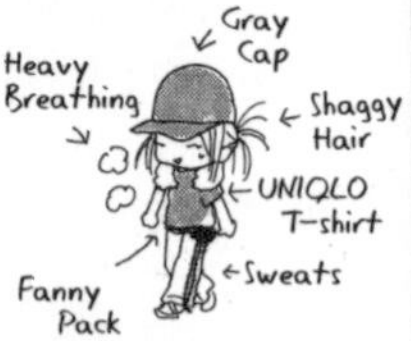
Gray Cap
Heavy Breathing
Shaggy Hair
UNIQLO T-shirt
Fanny Pack
Sweats

If you see a woman running like this, it's probably me! Please pretend you didn't see me. If you try to talk to me, I'll get embar-rassed and run away—really fast!!

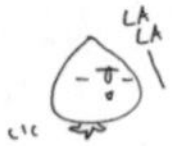
LA LA

Continued in 3—

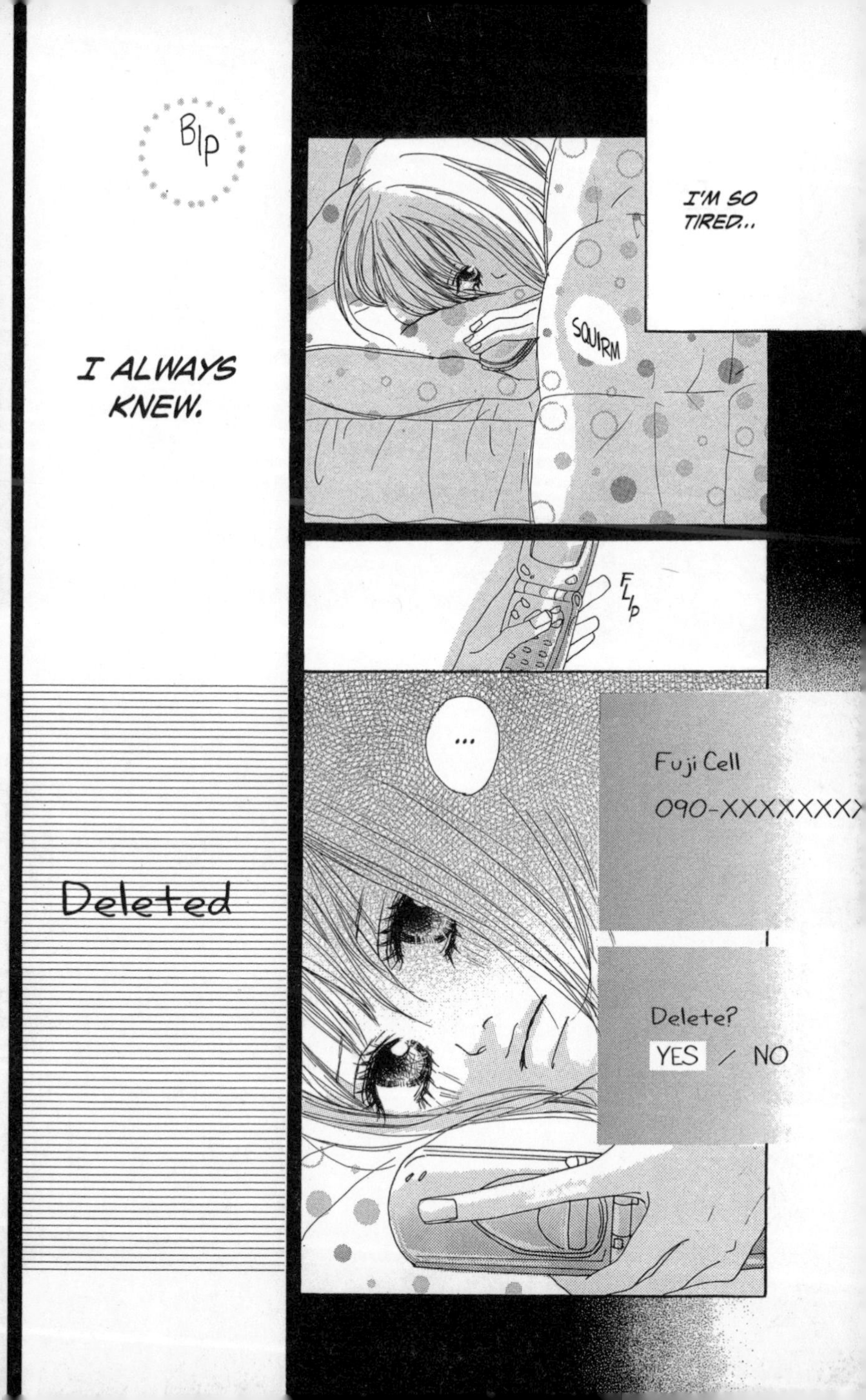
I'M SO TIRED...
SQUIRM
FLIP
...
Fuji Cell
090-XXXXXXX
Delete?
YES / NO
BLIP
I ALWAYS KNEW.
Deleted

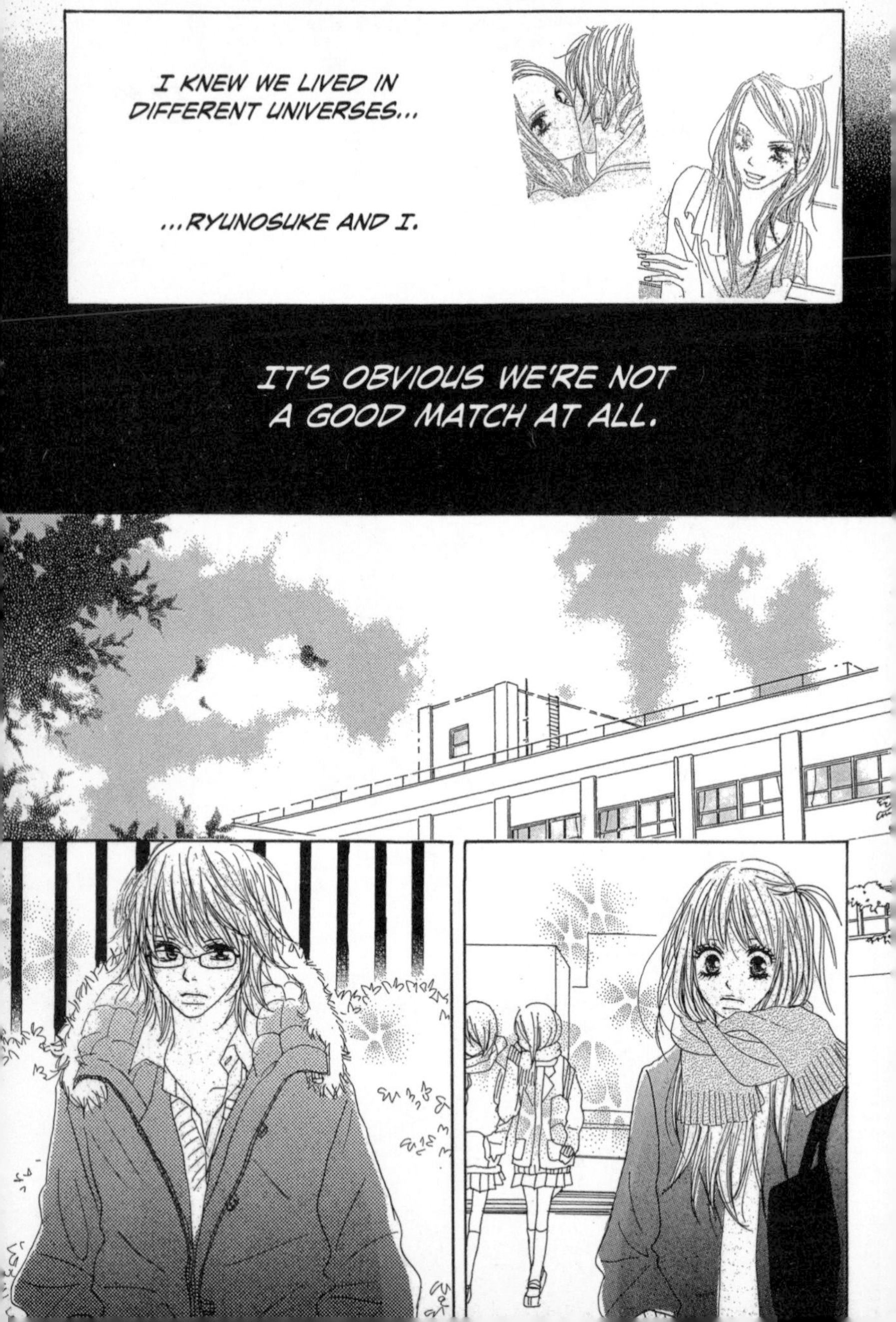
I KNEW WE LIVED IN DIFFERENT UNIVERSES...
...RYUNOSUKE AND I.
IT'S OBVIOUS WE'RE NOT A GOOD MATCH AT ALL.

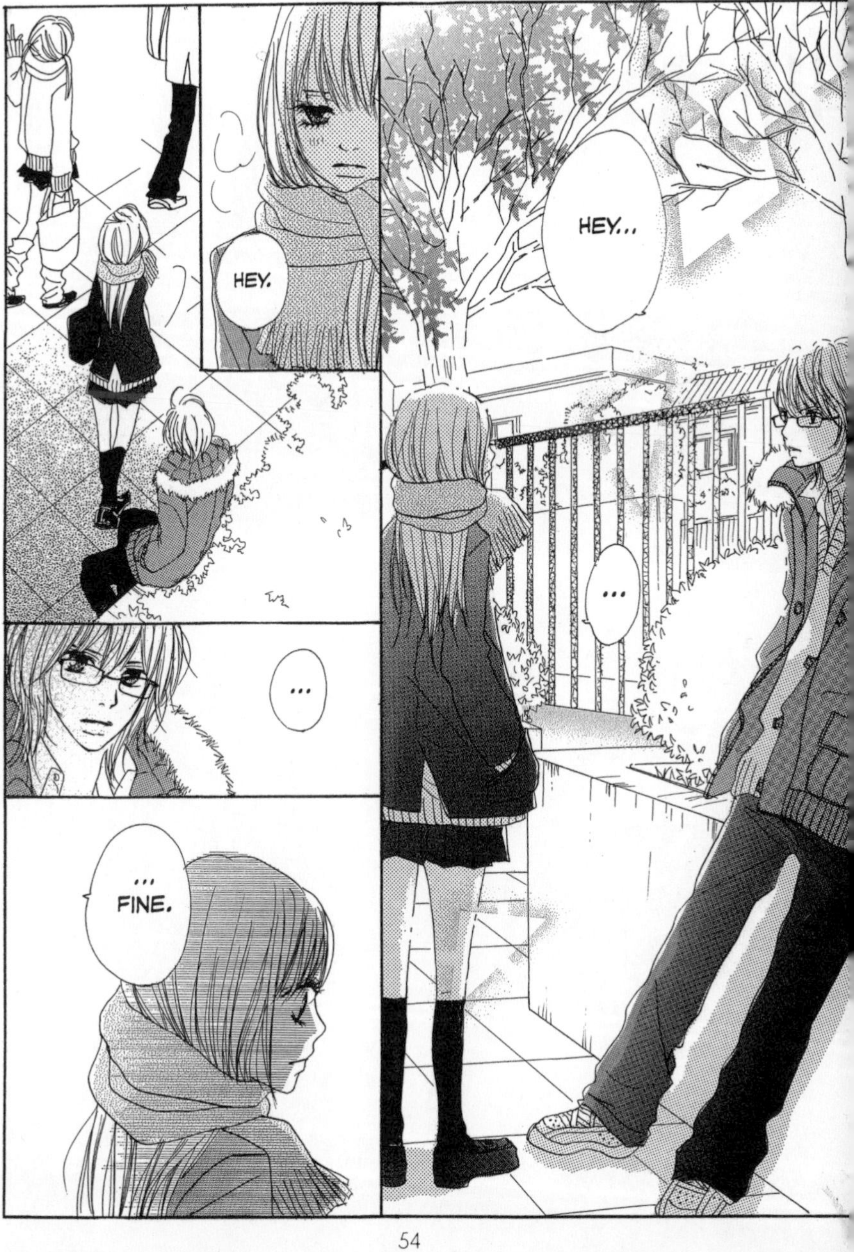
HEY...
...
HEY.
...
... FINE.

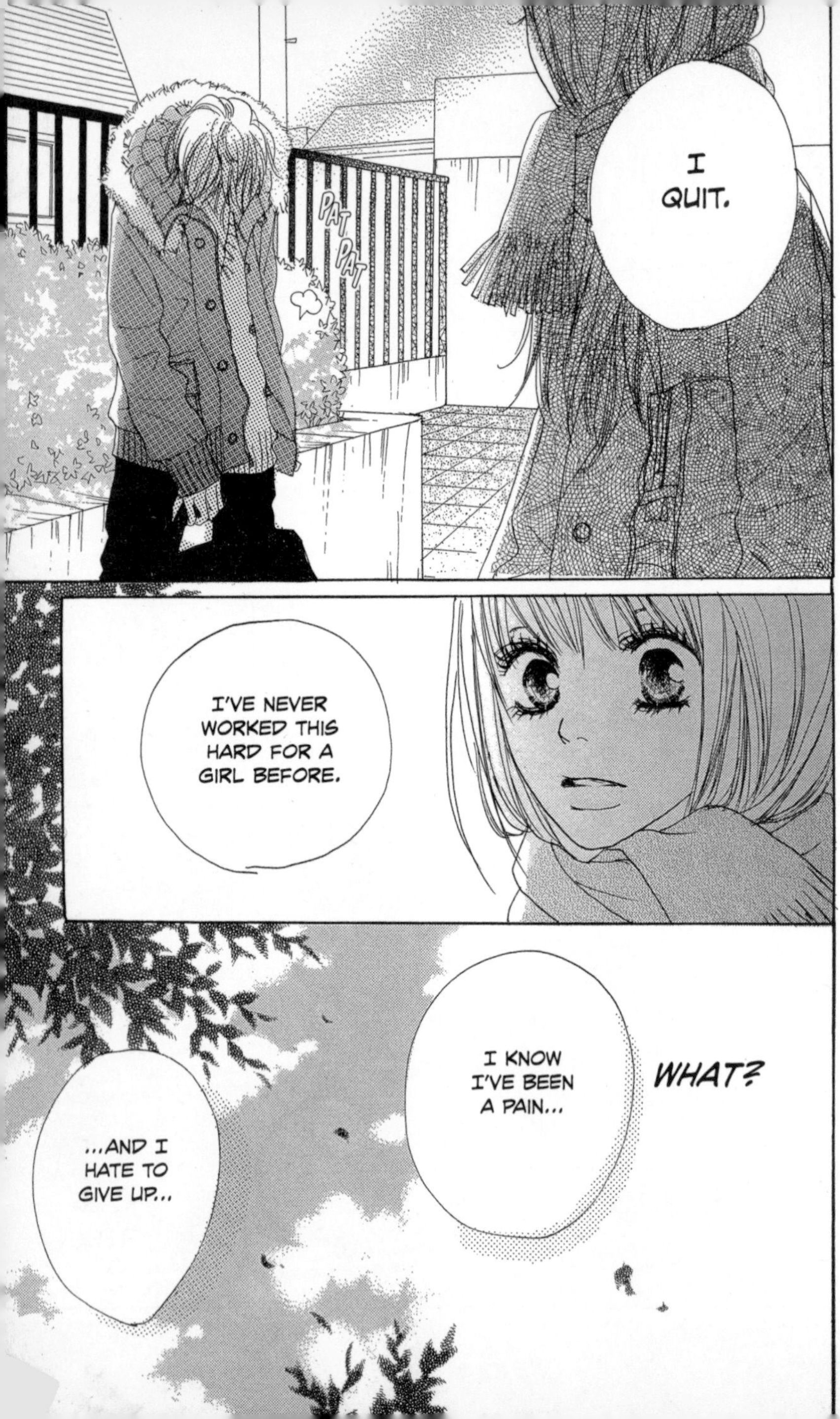
I QUIT.
PAT PAT
I'VE NEVER WORKED THIS HARD FOR A GIRL BEFORE.
WHAT?
I KNOW I'VE BEEN A PAIN...
...AND I HATE TO GIVE UP...

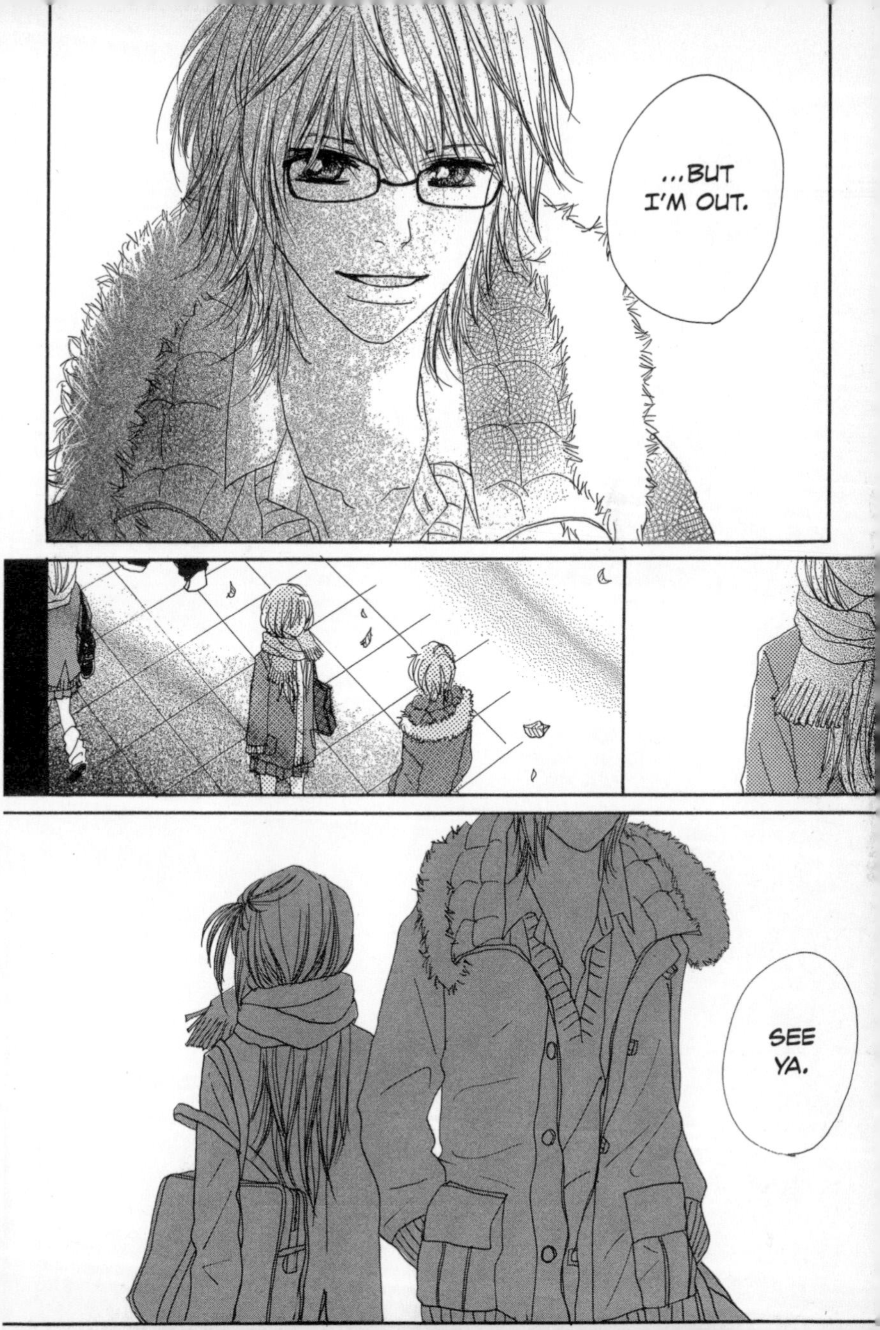
...BUT I'M OUT.
SEE YA.

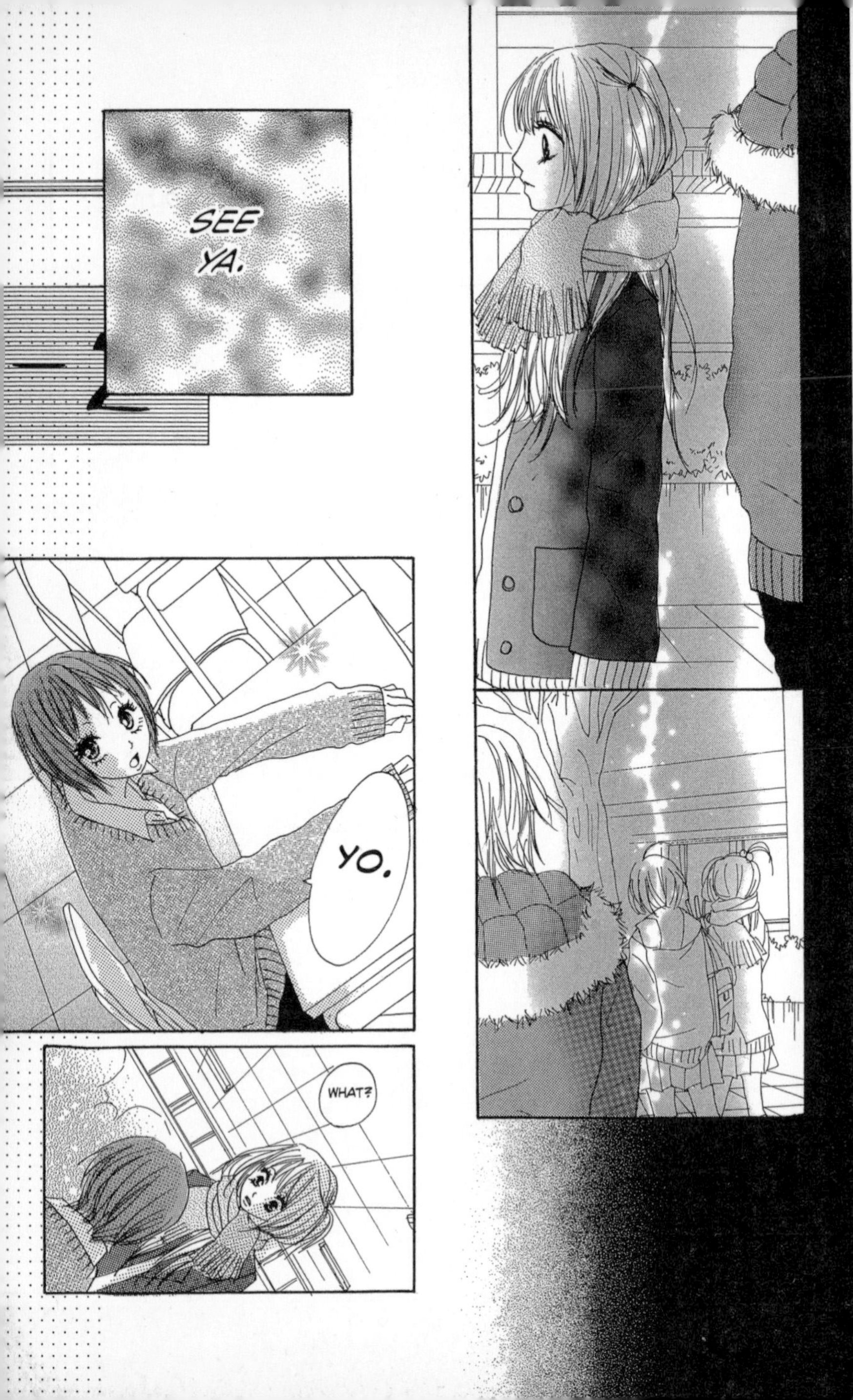
SEE YA.
YO.
WHAT?

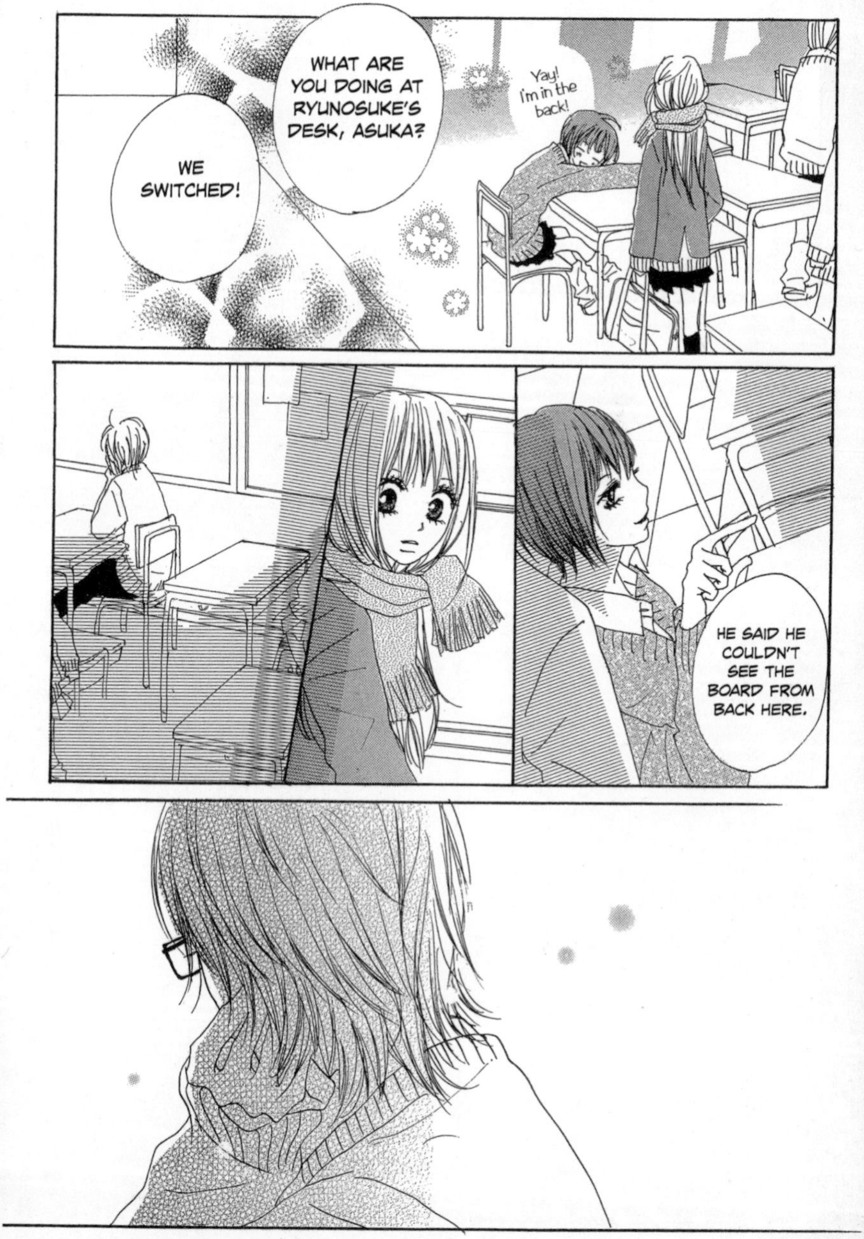
Yay! I'm in the back!
WHAT ARE YOU DOING AT RYUNOSUKE'S DESK, ASUKA?
WE SWITCHED!
HE SAID HE COULDN'T SEE THE BOARD FROM BACK HERE.

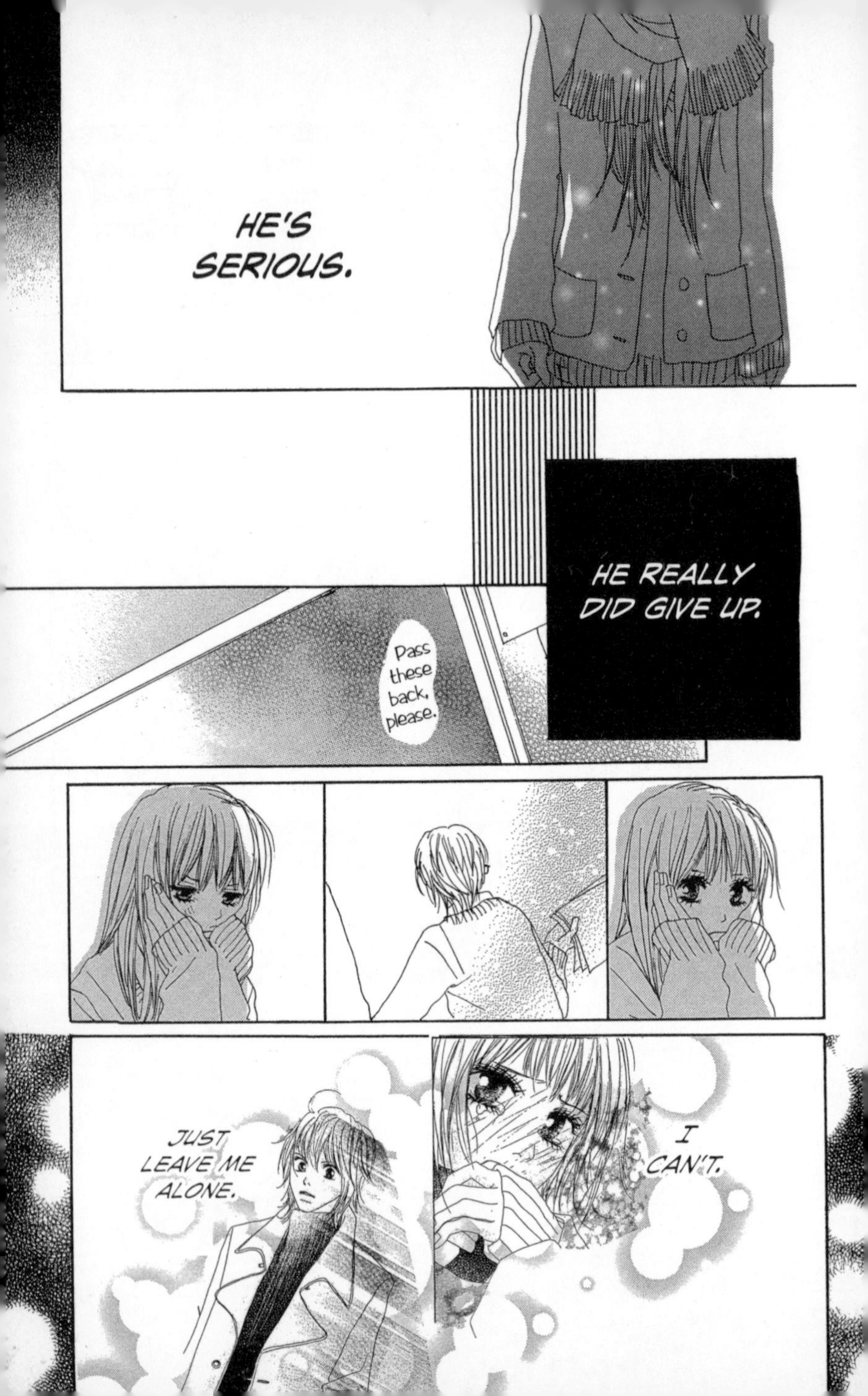
HE'S SERIOUS.
HE REALLY DID GIVE UP.
Pass these back, please.
I CAN'T.
JUST LEAVE ME ALONE.

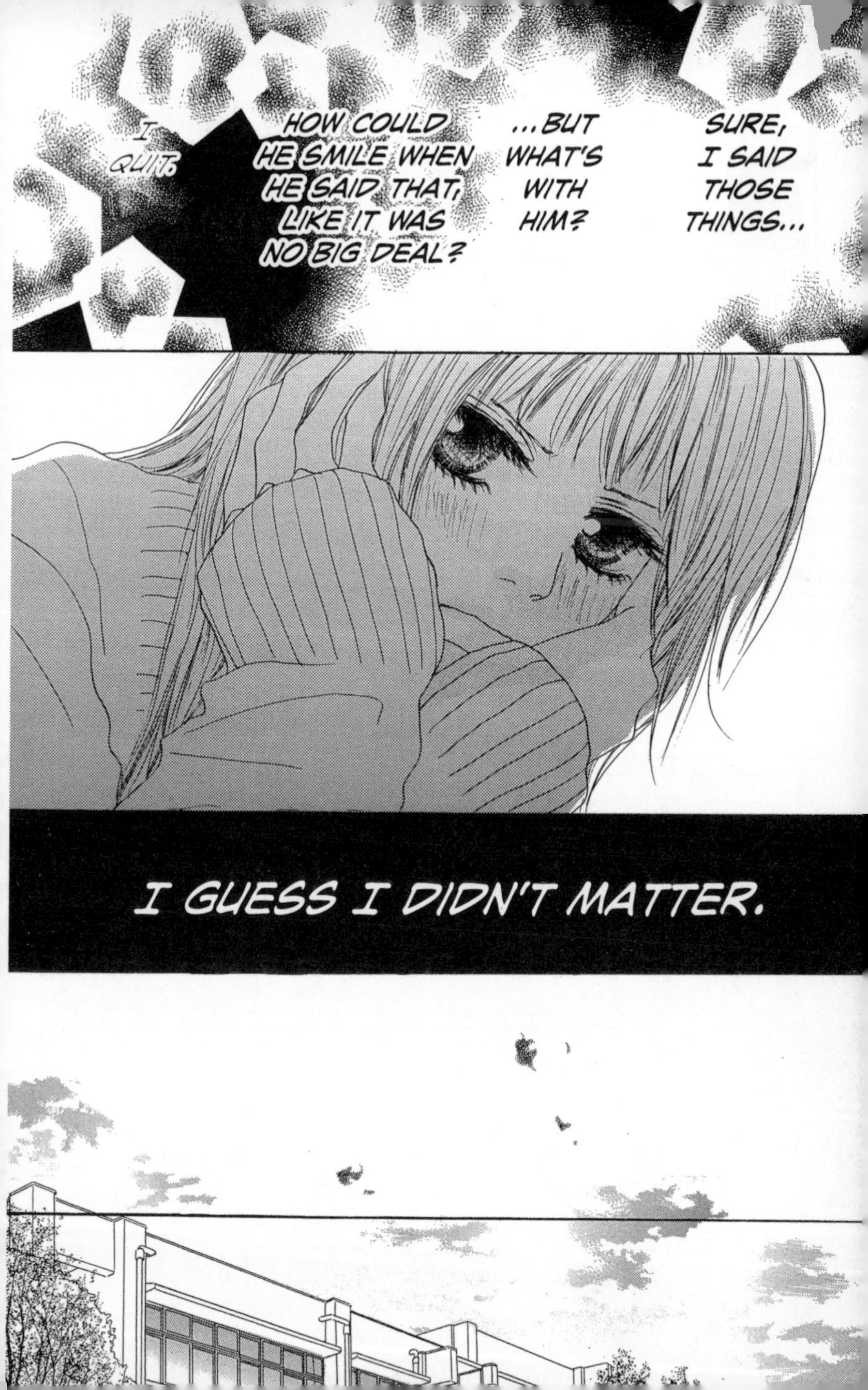
SURE, I SAID THOSE THINGS...
...BUT WHAT'S WITH HIM?
HOW COULD HE SMILE WHEN HE SAID THAT, LIKE IT WAS NO BIG DEAL?
I QUIT.
I GUESS I DIDN'T MATTER.

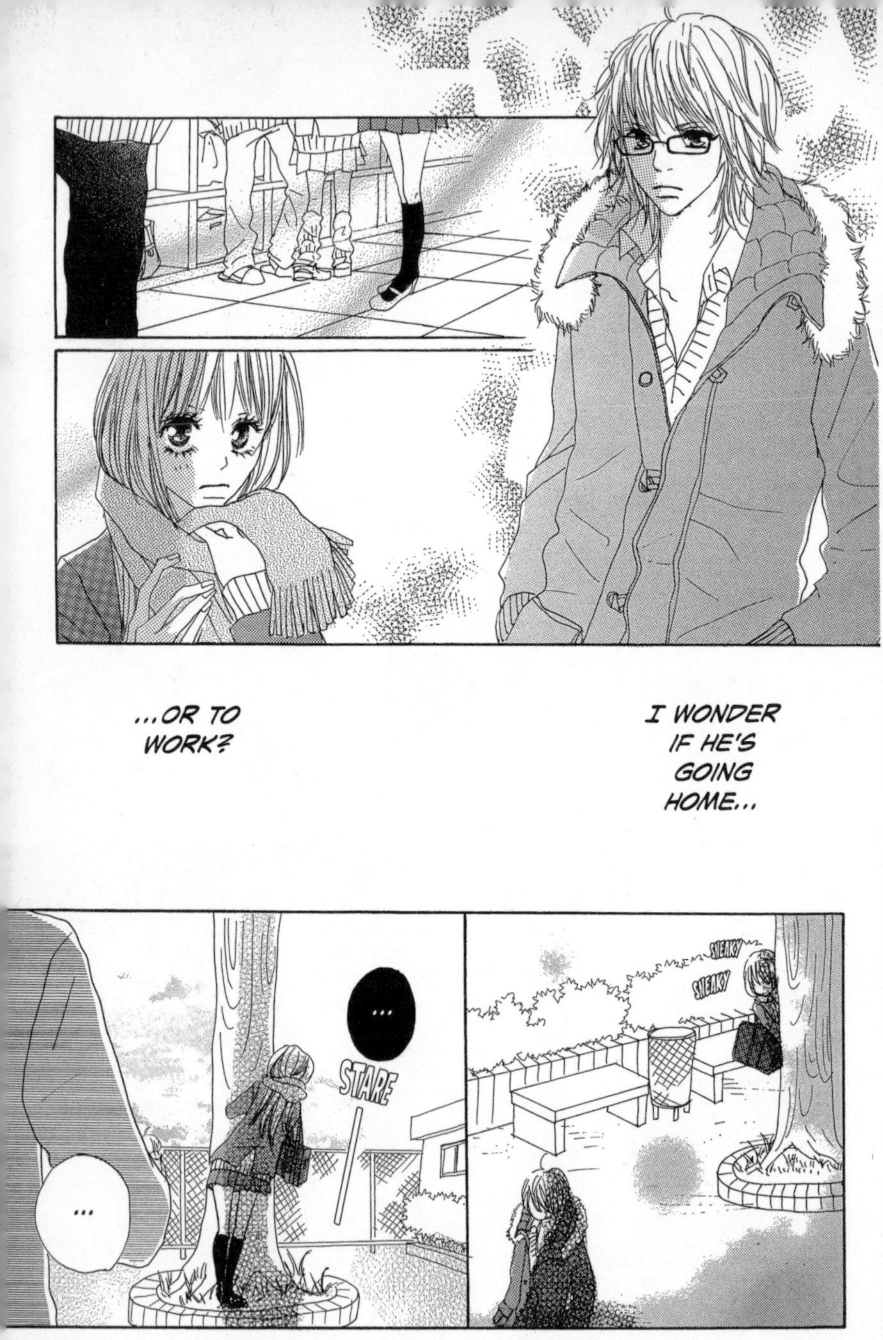
I WONDER IF HE'S GOING HOME...
...OR TO WORK?
SNEAKY
SNEAKY
...
STARE
...

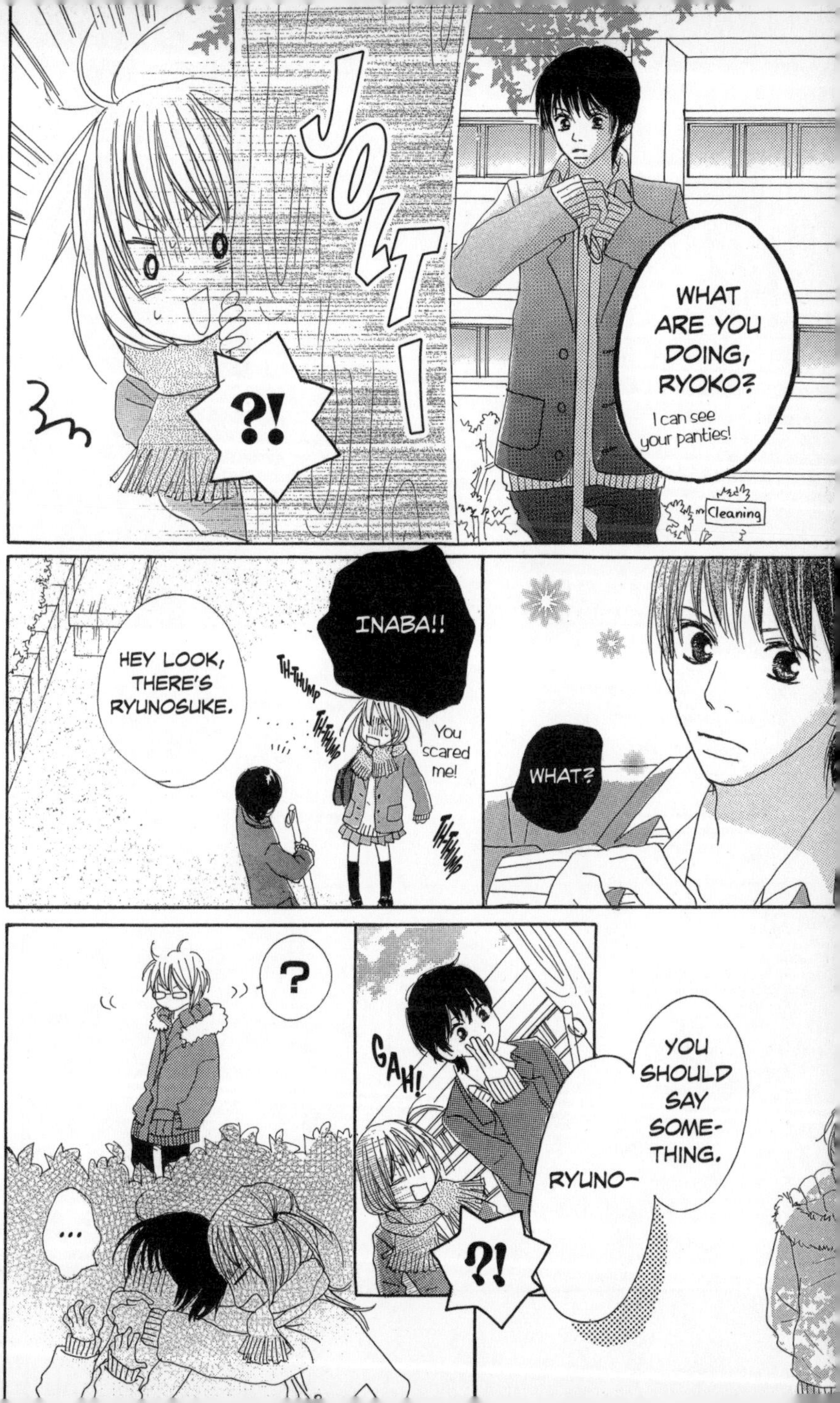
WHAT ARE YOU DOING, RYOKO?
I can see your panties!
Cleaning
JOLT!
?!
WHAT?
INABA!!
TH-THUMP
TH-THUMP
You scared me!
HEY LOOK, THERE'S RYUNOSUKE.
TH-THUMP
YOU SHOULD SAY SOME-THING.
RYUNO-
GAH!
?!
?
...

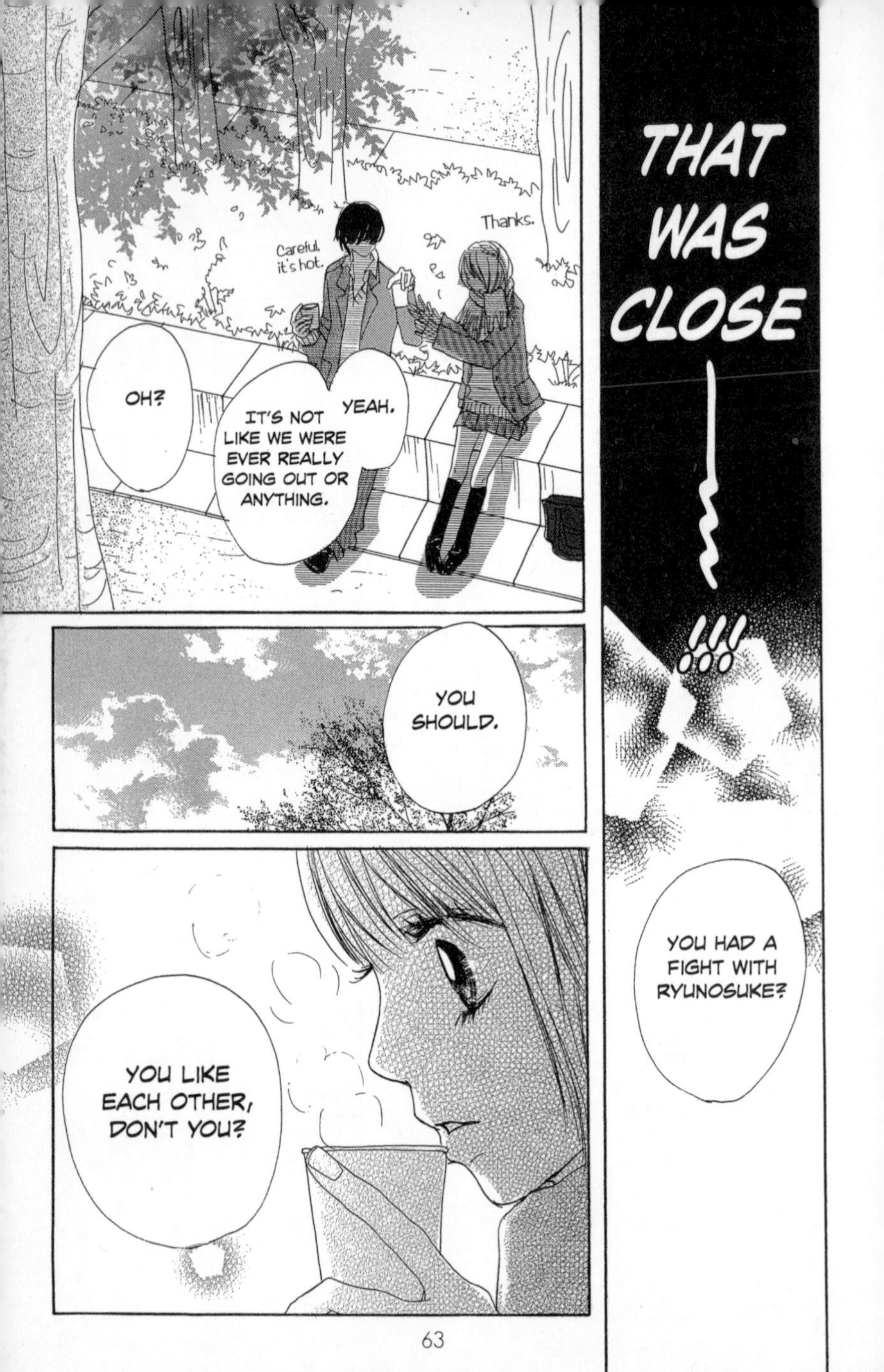
THAT WAS CLOSE—!!!
YOU HAD A FIGHT WITH RYUNOSUKE?
Thanks.
Careful. it's hot.
YEAH.
IT'S NOT LIKE WE WERE EVER REALLY GOING OUT OR ANYTHING.
OH?
YOU SHOULD.
YOU LIKE EACH OTHER, DON'T YOU?

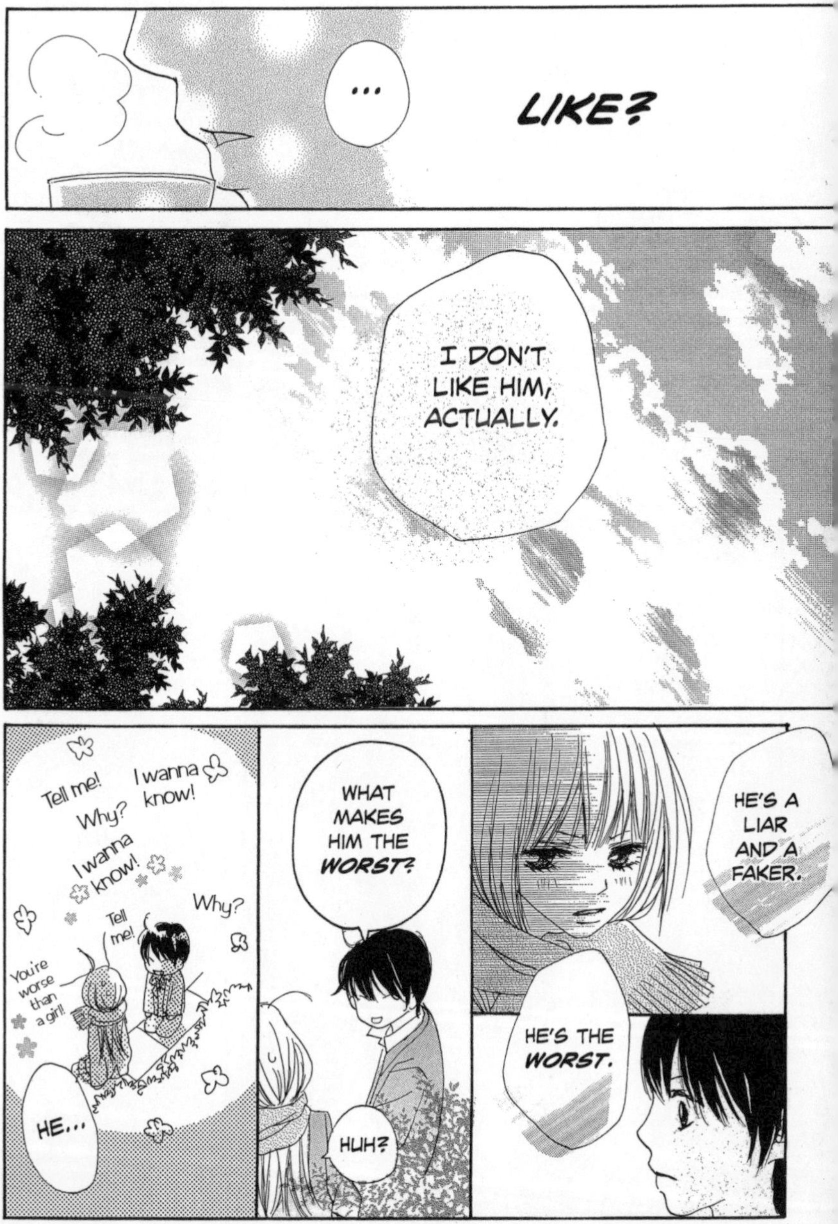
LIKE?
...
I DON'T LIKE HIM, ACTUALLY.
HE'S A LIAR AND A FAKER.
HE'S THE WORST.
WHAT MAKES HIM THE WORST?
HUH?
I wanna know!
Tell me!
Why?
I wanna know!
Why?
Tell me!
You're worse than a girl!
HE...

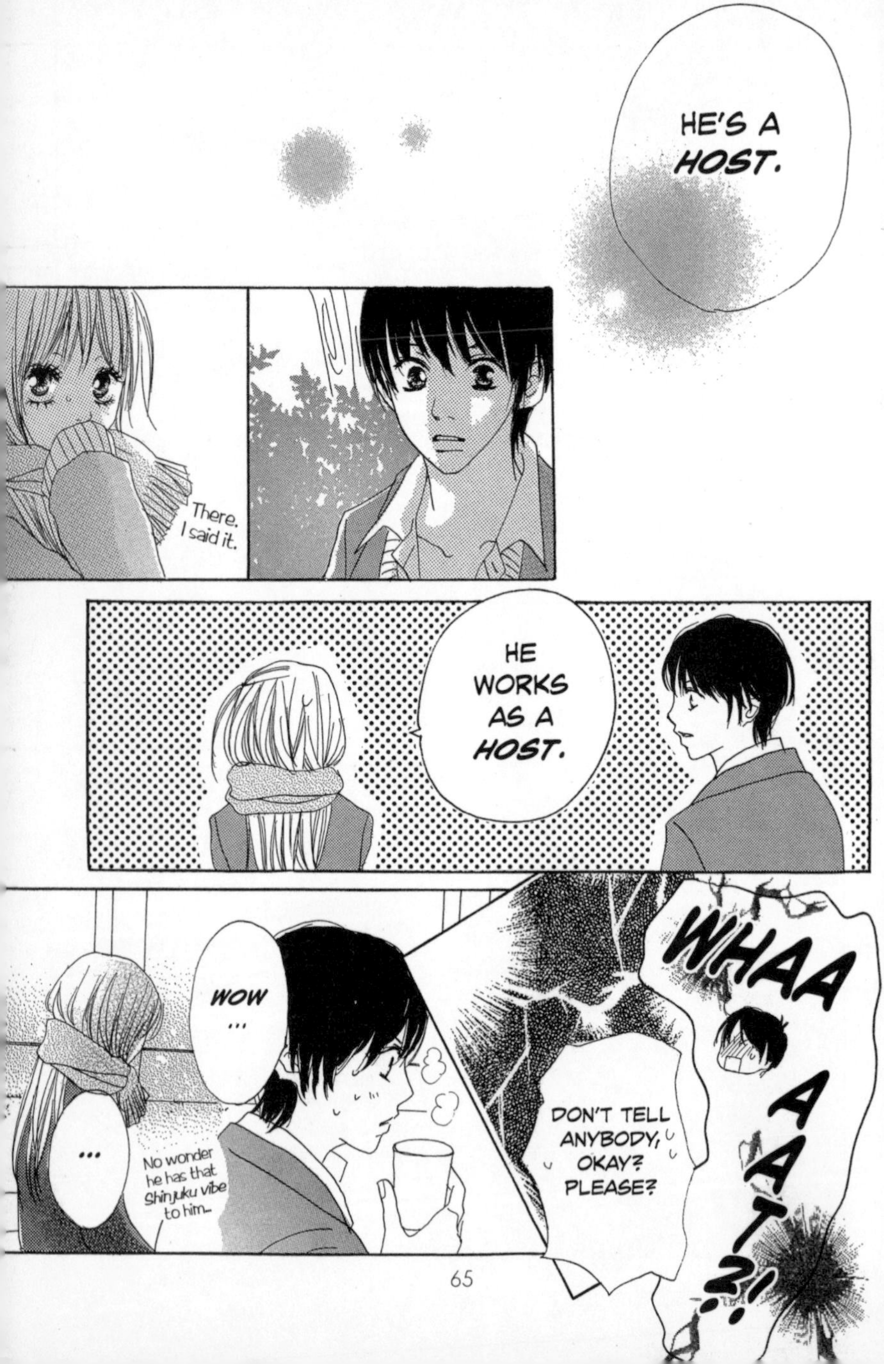
HE'S A HOST.
There. I said it.
HE WORKS AS A HOST.
WHAA AAAT?!
DON'T TELL ANYBODY, OKAY? PLEASE?
WOW...
...
No wonder he has that Shinjuku vibe to him...

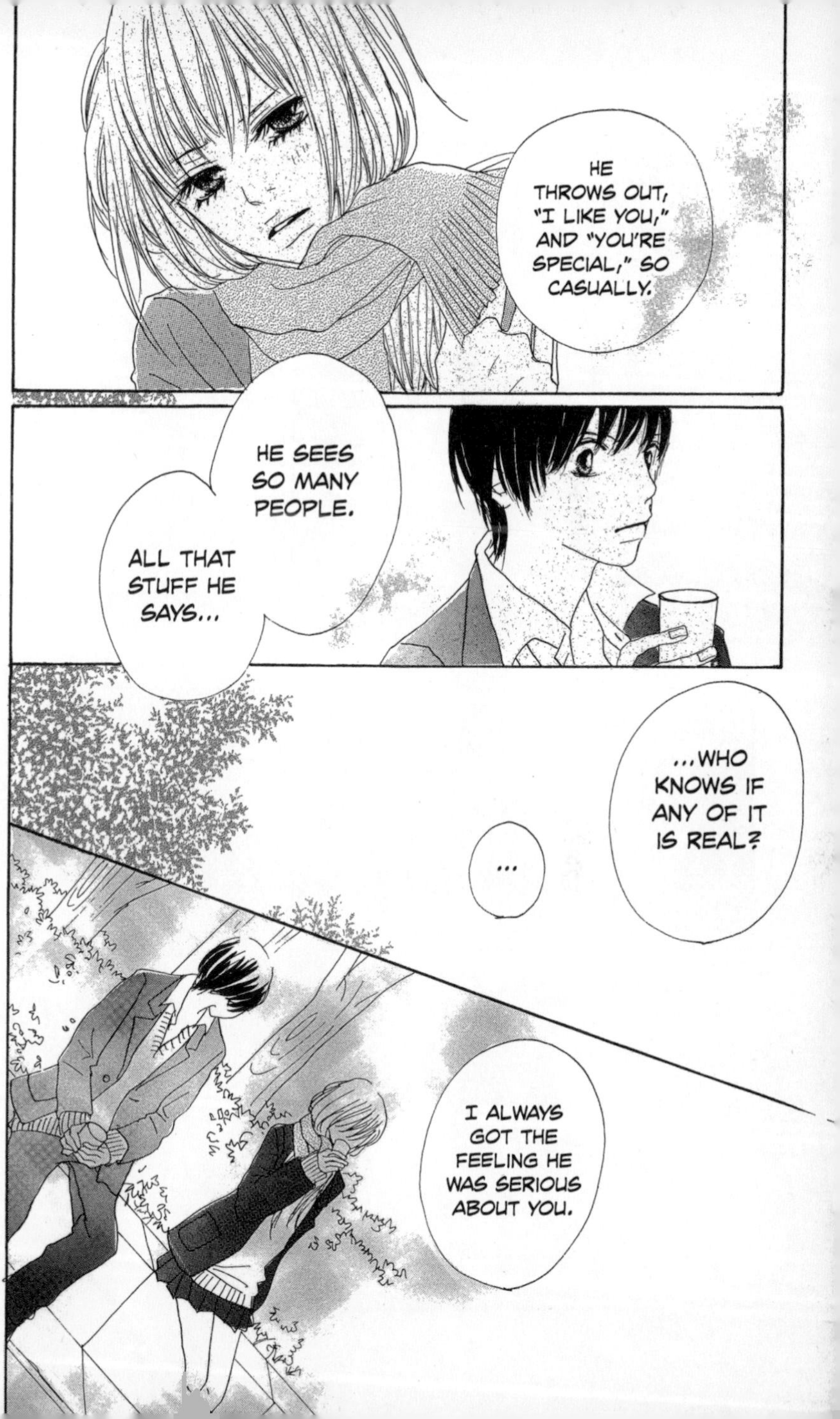
HE THROWS OUT, "I LIKE YOU," AND "YOU'RE SPECIAL," SO CASUALLY.
HE SEES SO MANY PEOPLE.
ALL THAT STUFF HE SAYS...
...WHO KNOWS IF ANY OF IT IS REAL?
...
I ALWAYS GOT THE FEELING HE WAS SERIOUS ABOUT YOU.

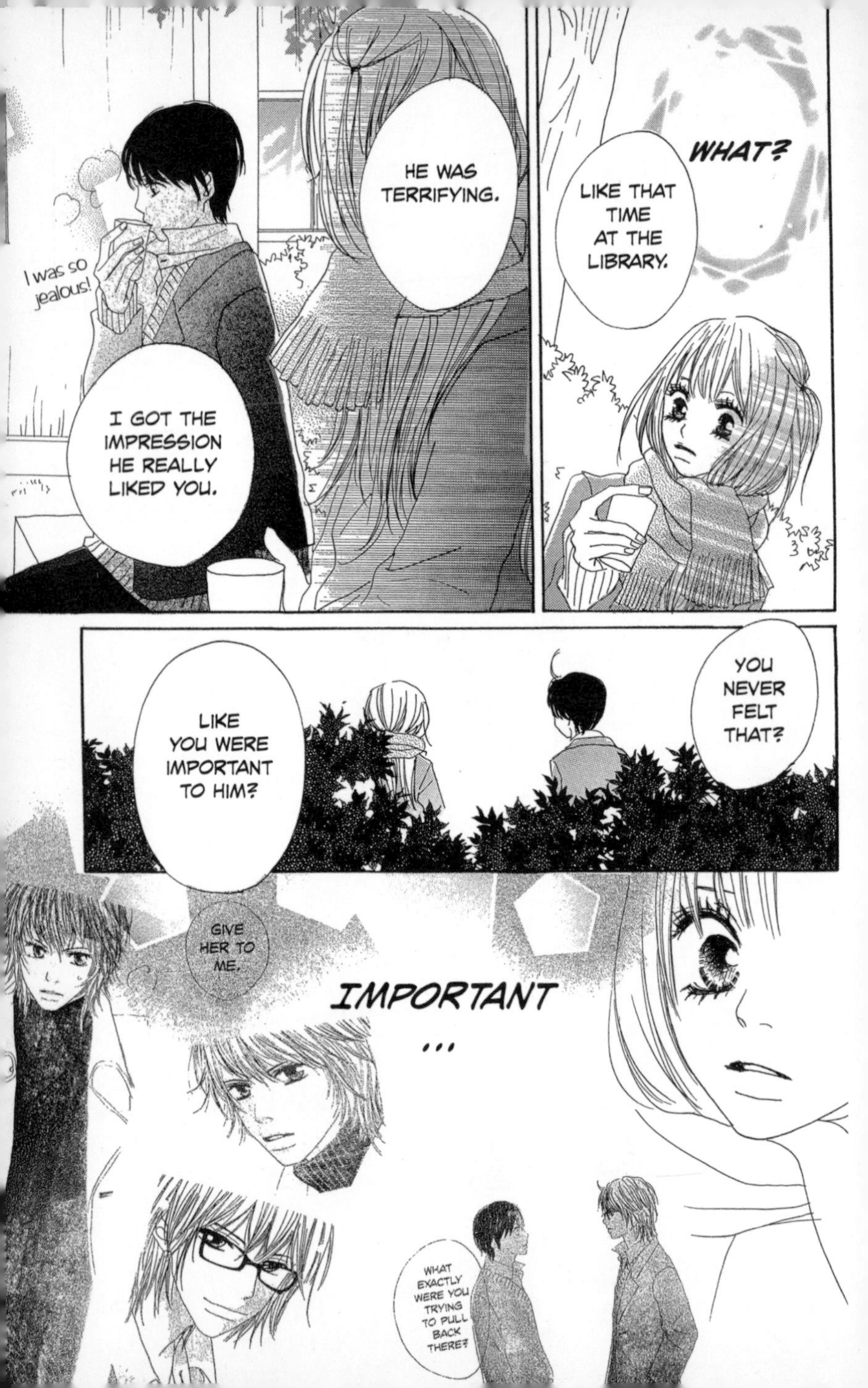
WHAT?
LIKE THAT TIME AT THE LIBRARY.
HE WAS TERRIFYING.
I was so jealous!
I GOT THE IMPRESSION HE REALLY LIKED YOU.
YOU NEVER FELT THAT?
LIKE YOU WERE IMPORTANT TO HIM?
IMPORTANT ...
GIVE HER TO ME.
WHAT EXACTLY WERE YOU TRYING TO PULL BACK THERE?

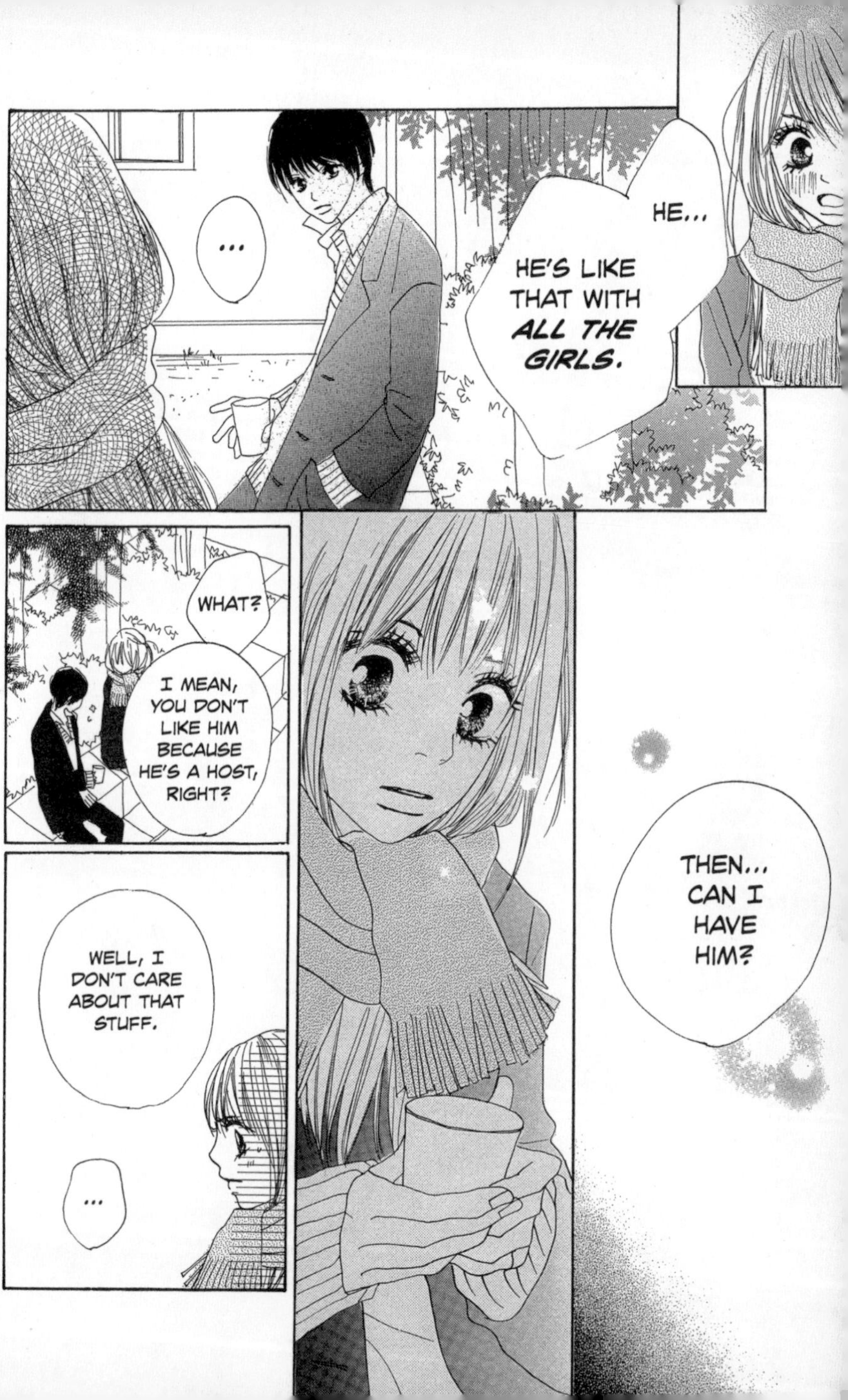
HE...
HE'S LIKE THAT WITH ALL THE GIRLS.
...
WHAT?
I MEAN, YOU DON'T LIKE HIM BECAUSE HE'S A HOST, RIGHT?
WELL, I DON'T CARE ABOUT THAT STUFF.
...
THEN... CAN I HAVE HIM?

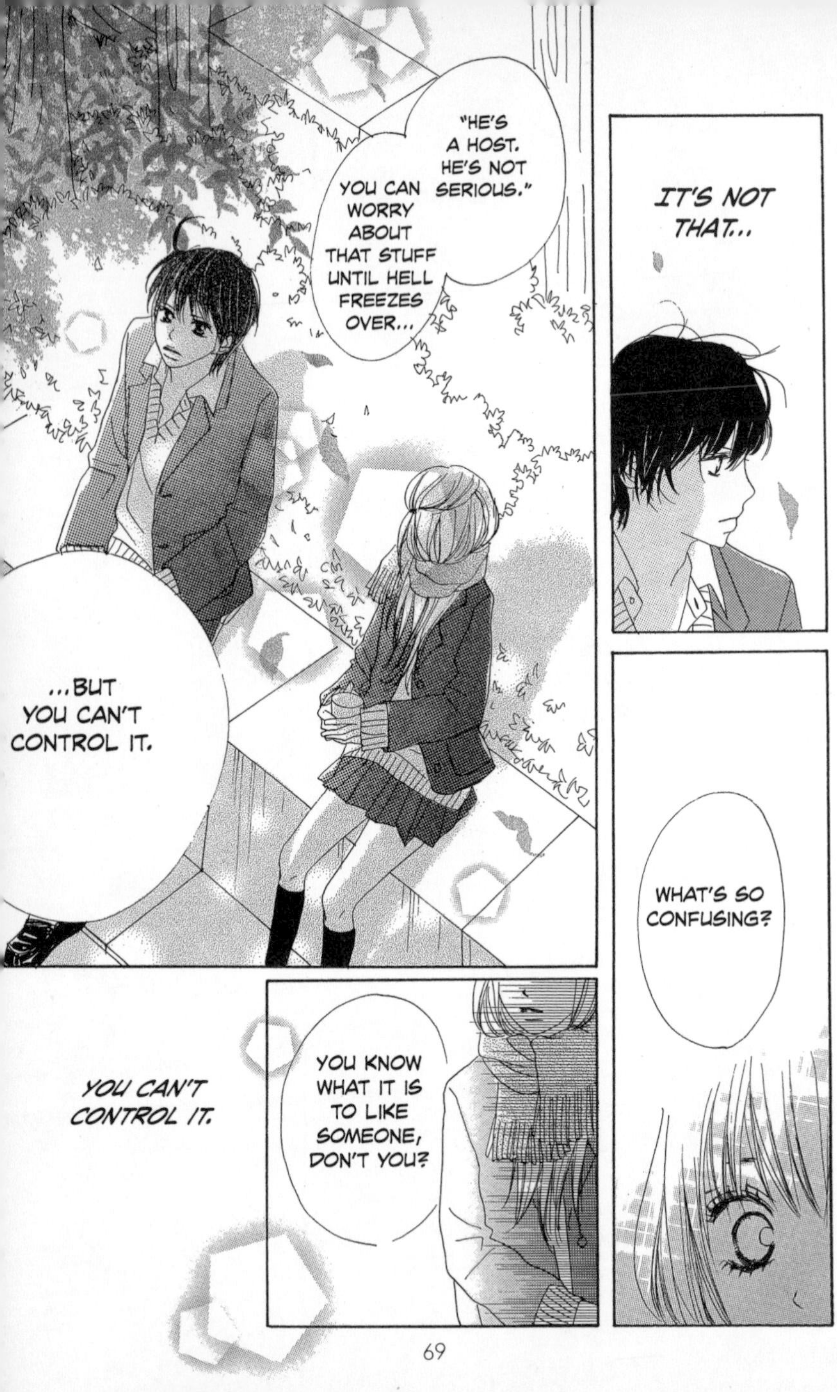
IT'S NOT THAT...
WHAT'S SO CONFUSING?
"HE'S A HOST. HE'S NOT SERIOUS." YOU CAN WORRY ABOUT THAT STUFF UNTIL HELL FREEZES OVER...
...BUT YOU CAN'T CONTROL IT.
YOU KNOW WHAT IT IS TO LIKE SOMEONE, DON'T YOU?
YOU CAN'T CONTROL IT.

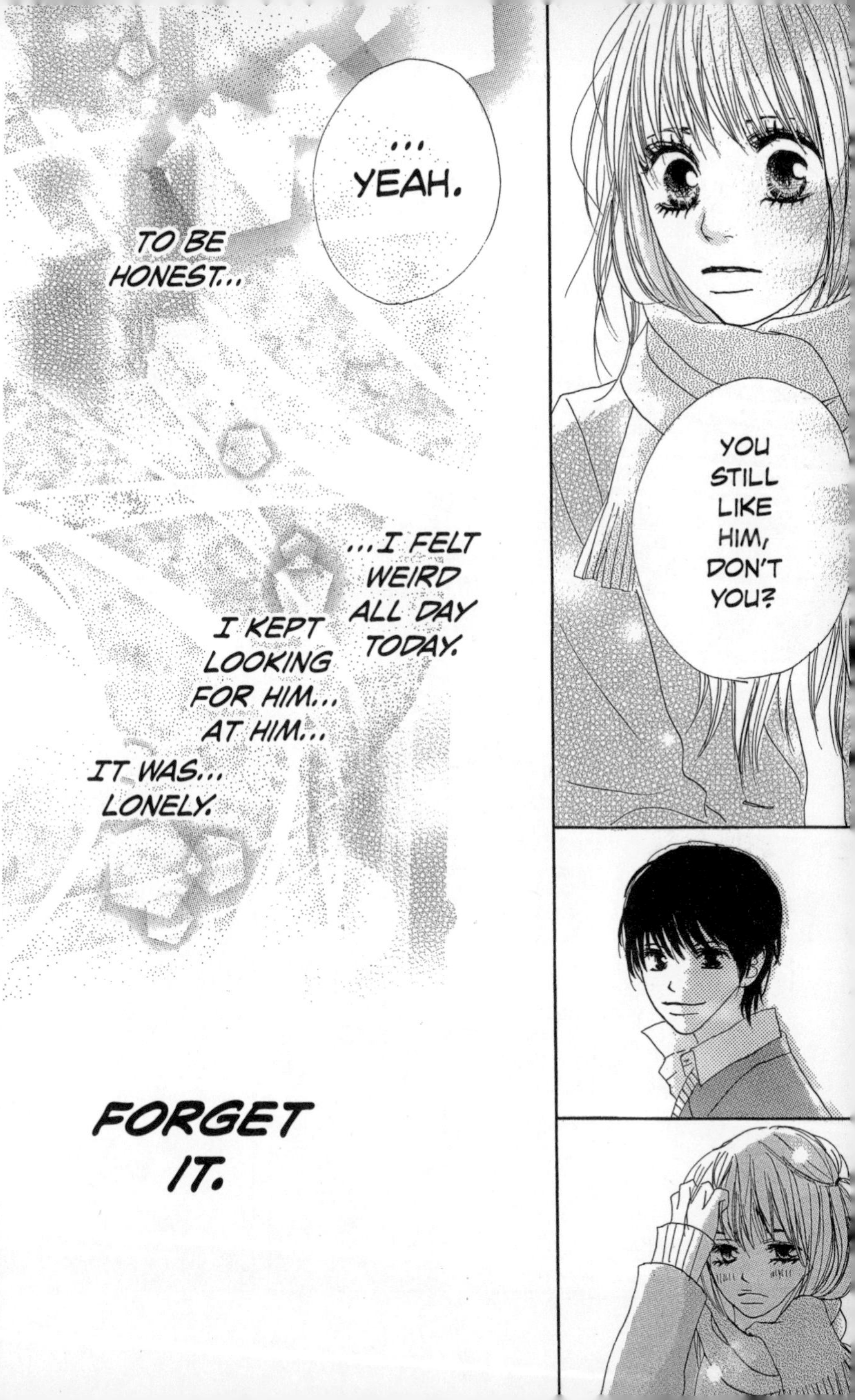
YOU STILL LIKE HIM, DON'T YOU?
...YEAH.
TO BE HONEST...
...I FELT WEIRD ALL DAY TODAY.
I KEPT LOOKING FOR HIM... AT HIM...
IT WAS... LONELY.
FORGET IT.

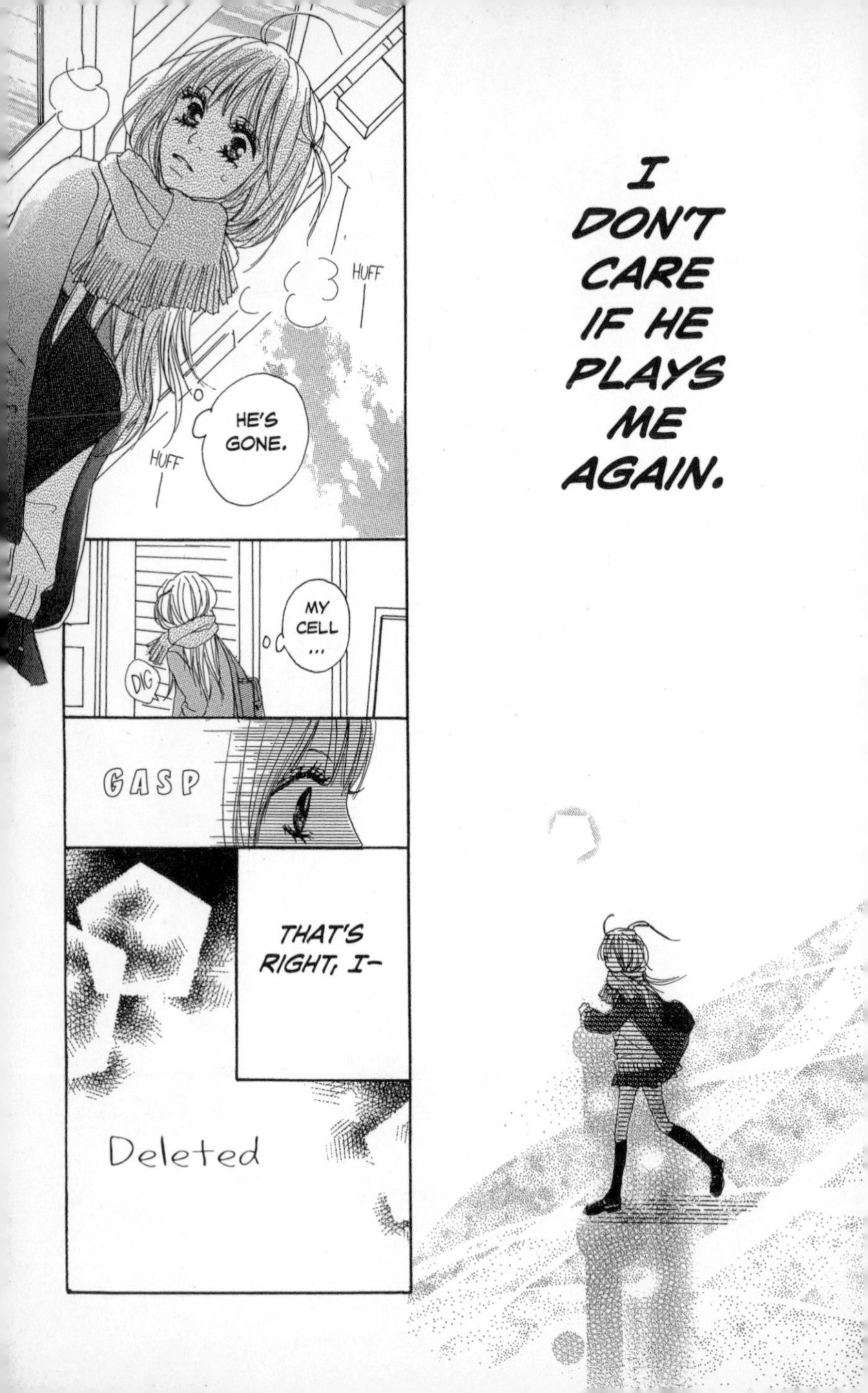
I DON'T CARE IF HE PLAYS ME AGAIN.
HUFF
HE'S GONE.
HUFF
MY CELL ...
DIG
GASP
THAT'S RIGHT, I-
Deleted

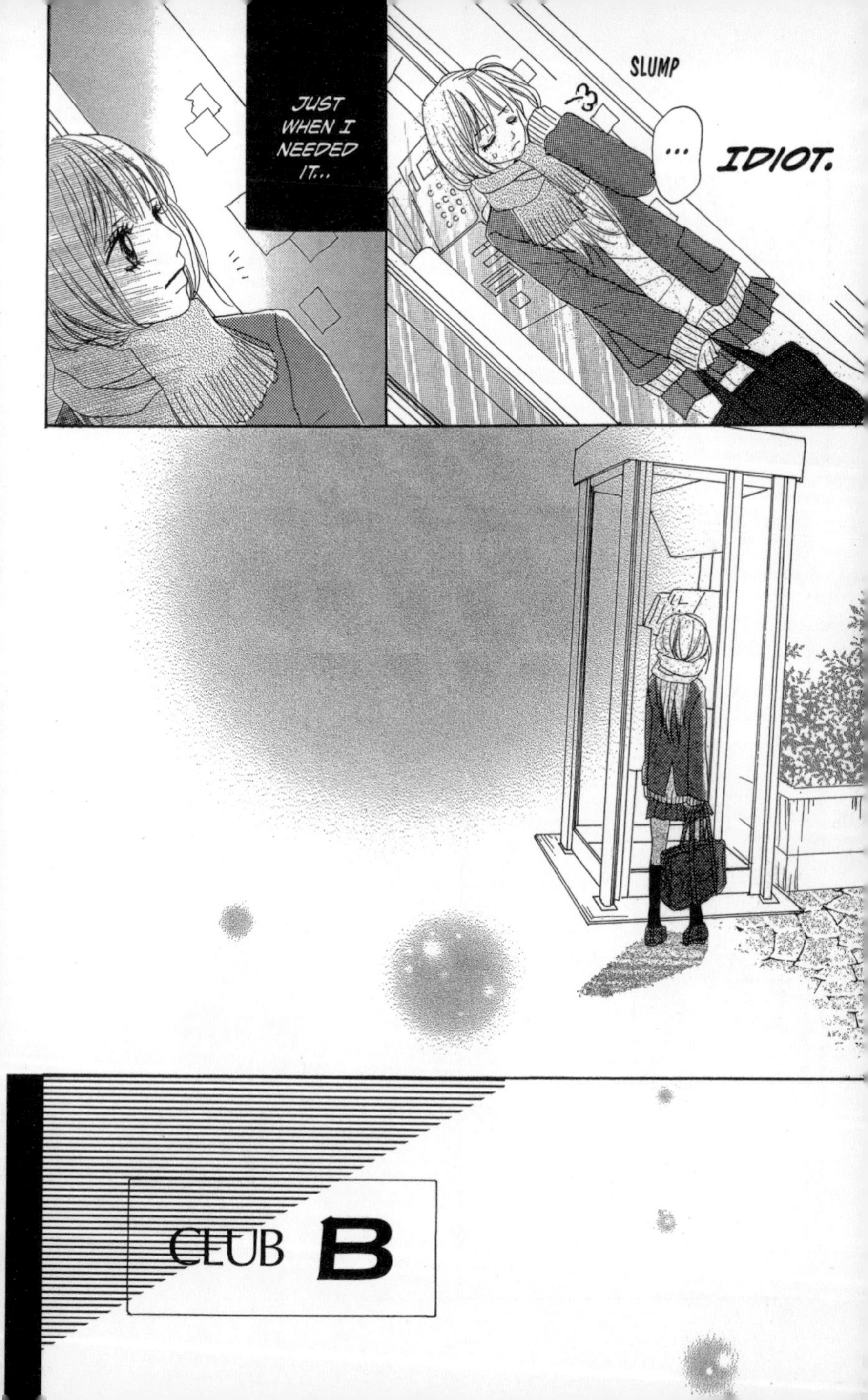
SLUMP
...
IDIOT.
JUST WHEN I NEEDED IT...
CLUB B

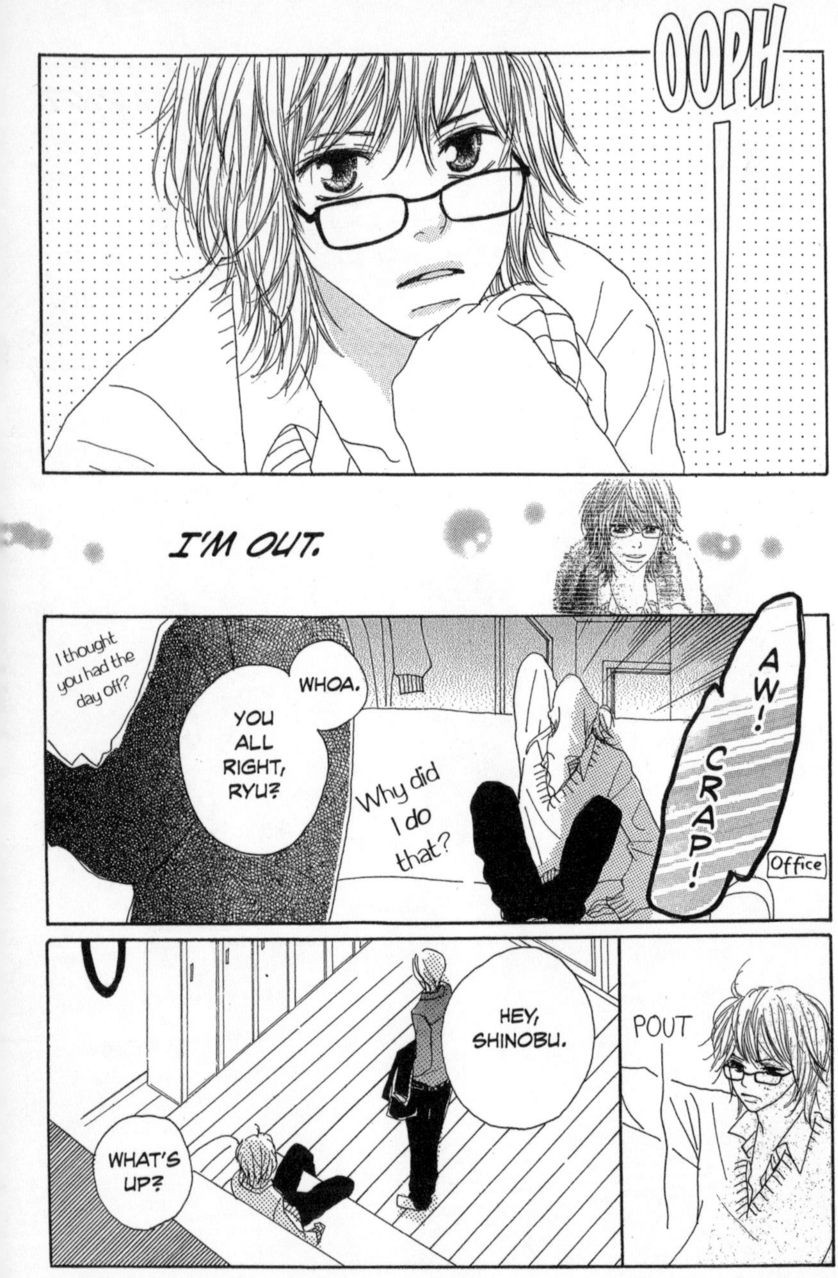
OOPH
I'M OUT.
AW! CRAP!
Office
Why did I do that?
WHOA.
YOU ALL RIGHT, RYU?
I thought you had the day off?
POUT
HEY, SHINOBU.
WHAT'S UP?

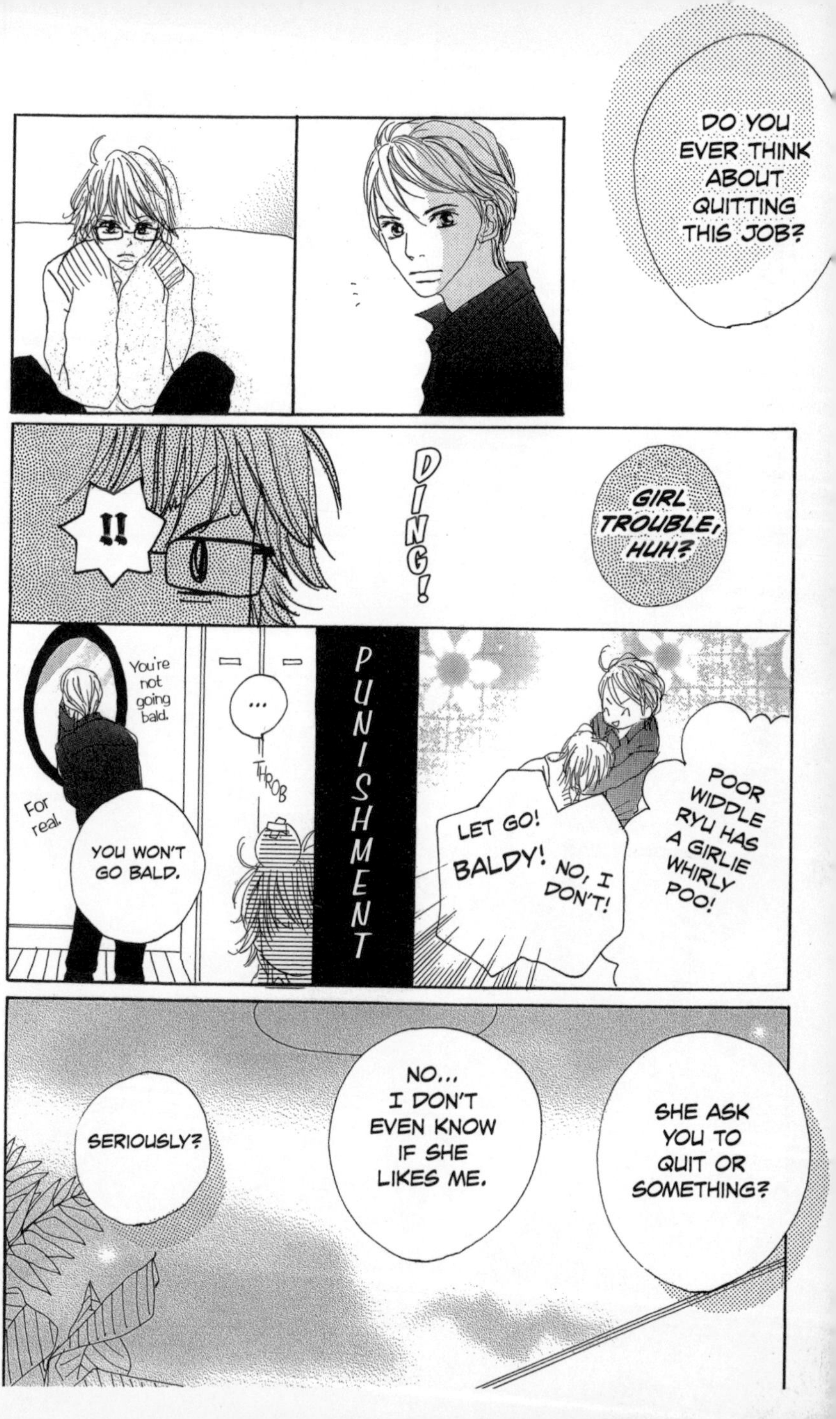
DO YOU EVER THINK ABOUT QUITTING THIS JOB?
GIRL TROUBLE, HUH?
DING!
!!
POOR WIDDLE RYU HAS A GIRLIE WHIRLY POO!
LET GO!
BALDY!
NO, I DON'T!
PUNISHMENT
...
THROB
You're not going bald.
YOU WON'T GO BALD.
For real.
SHE ASK YOU TO QUIT OR SOMETHING?
NO... I DON'T EVEN KNOW IF SHE LIKES ME.
SERIOUSLY?

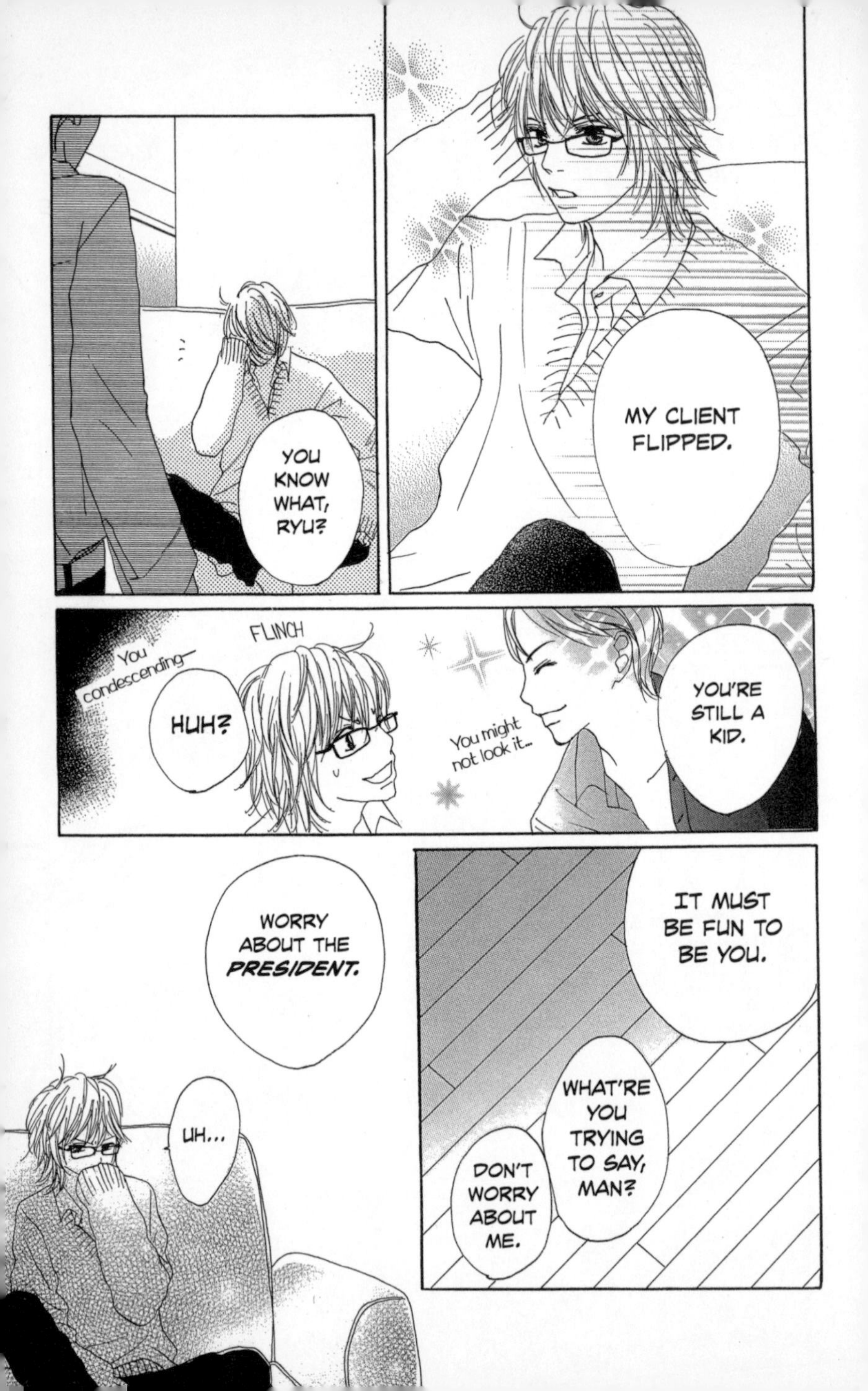
MY CLIENT FLIPPED.
YOU KNOW WHAT, RYU?
YOU'RE STILL A KID.
You might not look it...
FLINCH
HUH?
You condescending—
IT MUST BE FUN TO BE YOU.
WHAT'RE YOU TRYING TO SAY, MAN?
DON'T WORRY ABOUT ME.
WORRY ABOUT THE PRESIDENT.
UH...

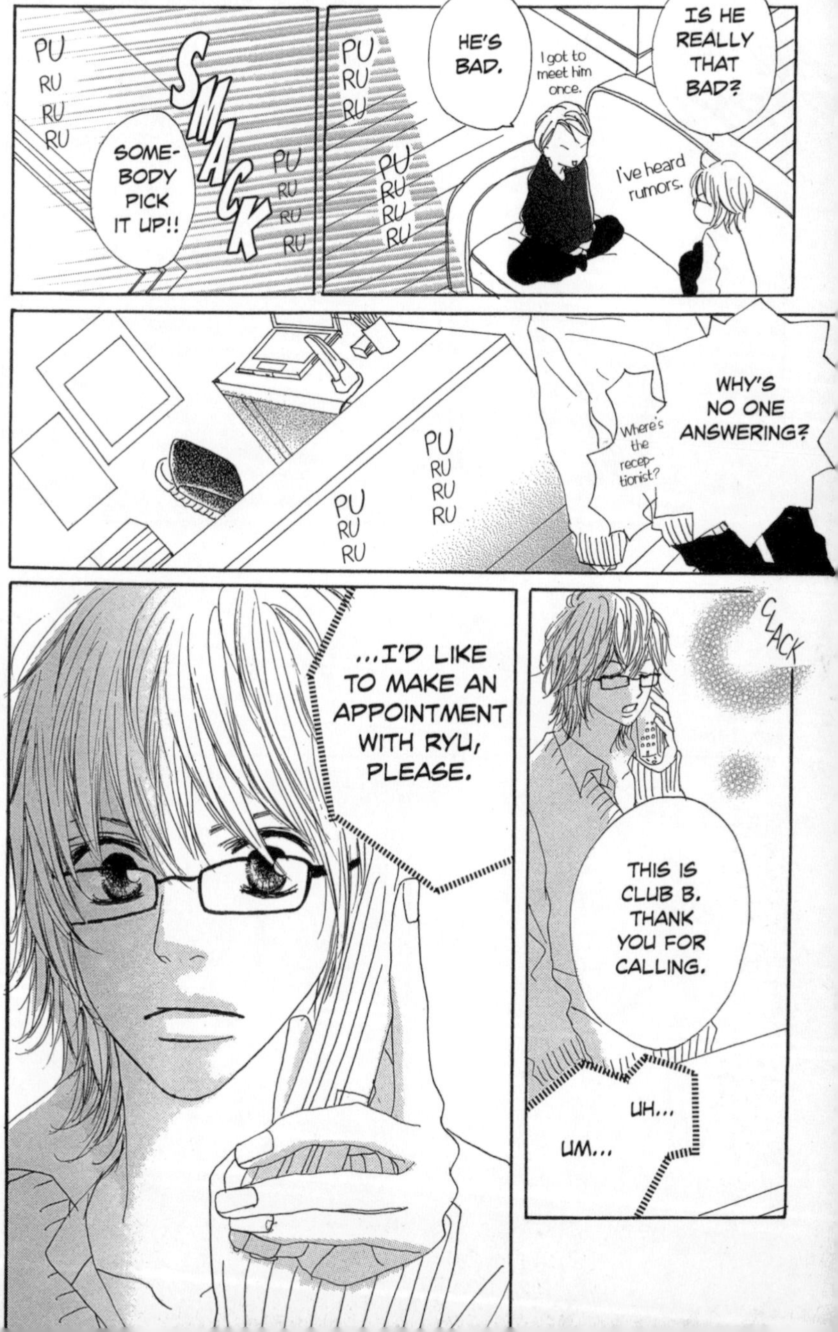
IS HE REALLY THAT BAD?
HE'S BAD.
I got to meet him once.
PU RU RU
I've heard rumors.
PU RU RU RU
PU RU RU RU
SMACK
SOMEBODY PICK IT UP!!
PU RU RU RU
WHY'S NO ONE ANSWERING?
Where's the receptionist?
PU RU RU RU
PU RU RU
CLACK
THIS IS CLUB B. THANK YOU FOR CALLING.
UH...
UM...
...I'D LIKE TO MAKE AN APPOINTMENT WITH RYU, PLEASE.

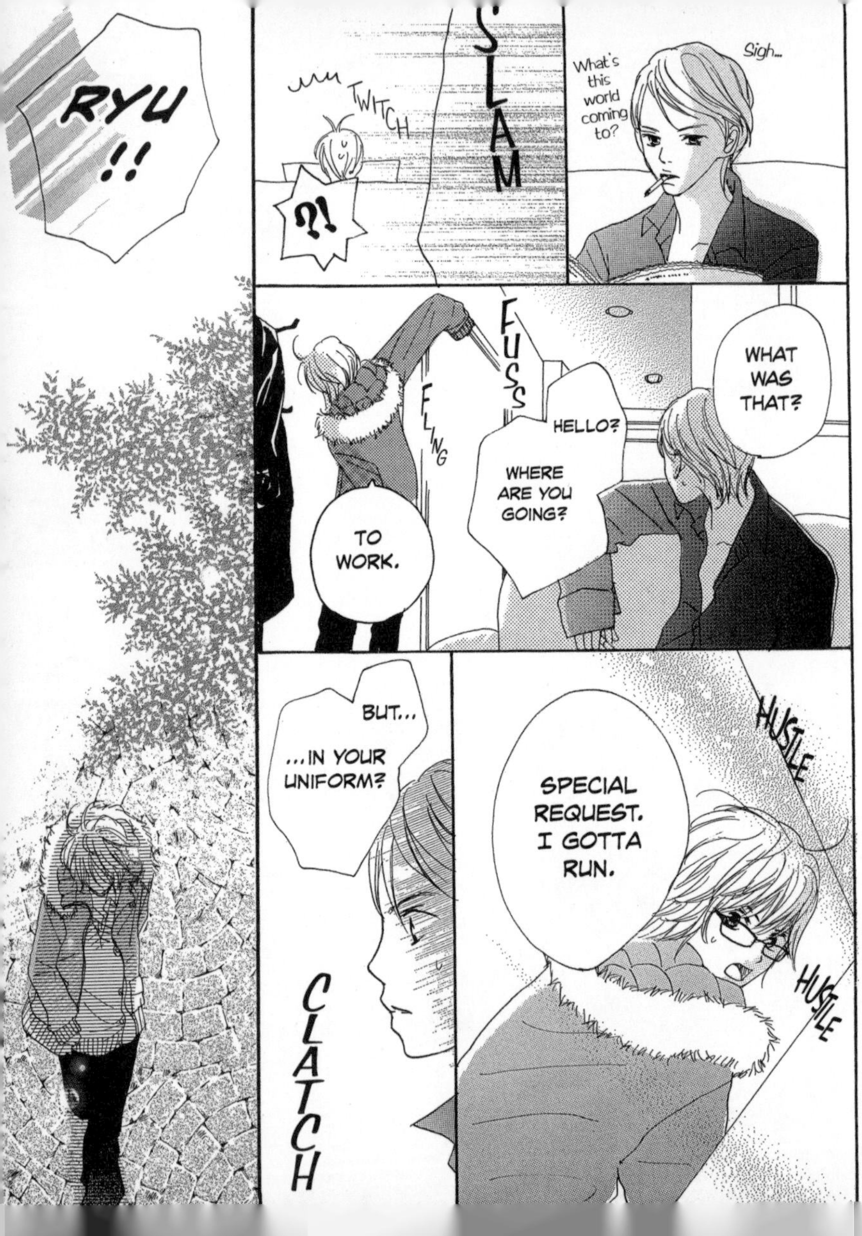

Sigh...
What's this world coming to?
SLAM
TWITCH
?!
WHAT WAS THAT?
HELLO?
WHERE ARE YOU GOING?
FUSS
FLING
TO WORK.
HUSTLE
SPECIAL REQUEST. I GOTTA RUN.
HUSTLE
BUT...
...IN YOUR UNIFORM?
CLATCH
RYU!!

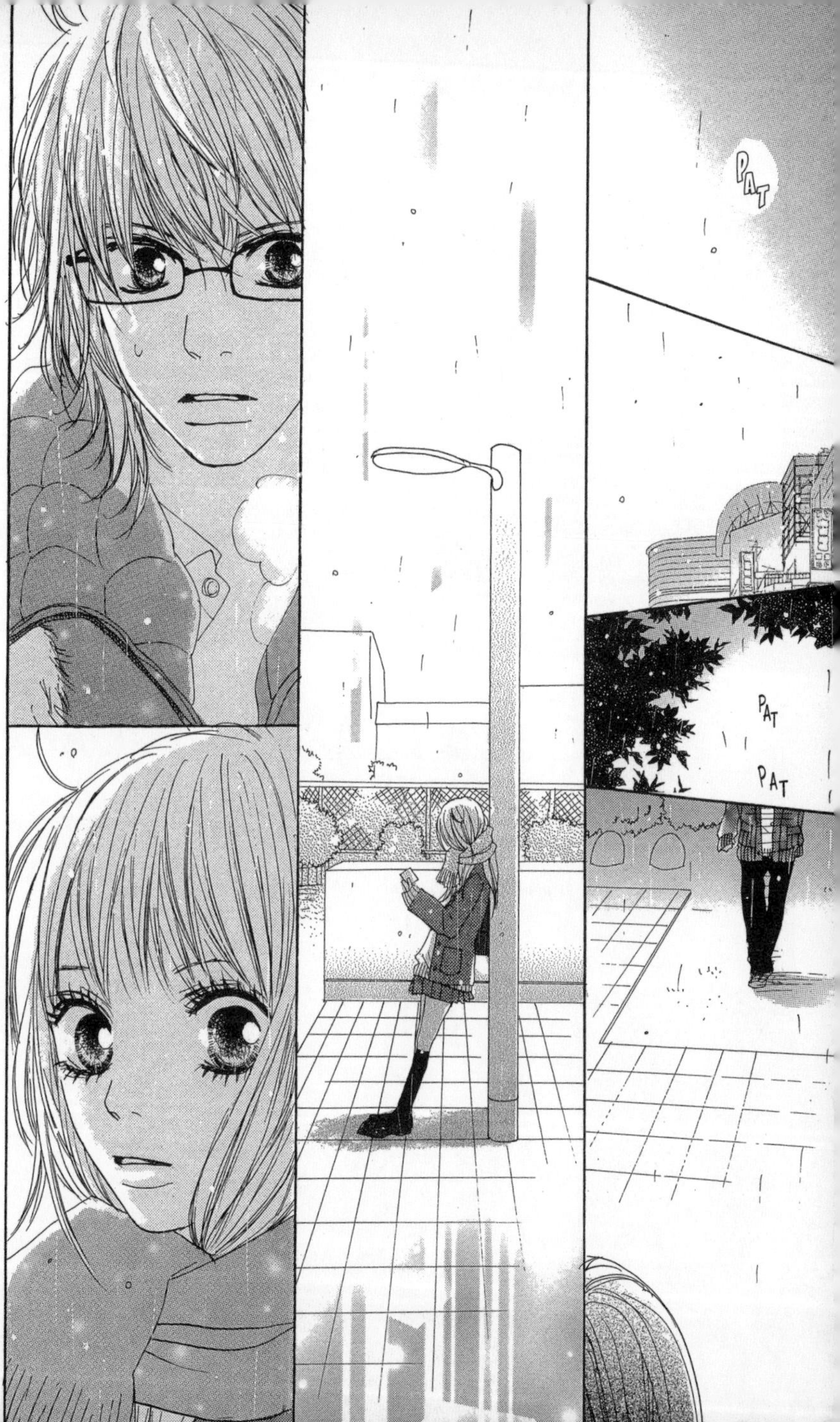
PAT
PAT
PAT

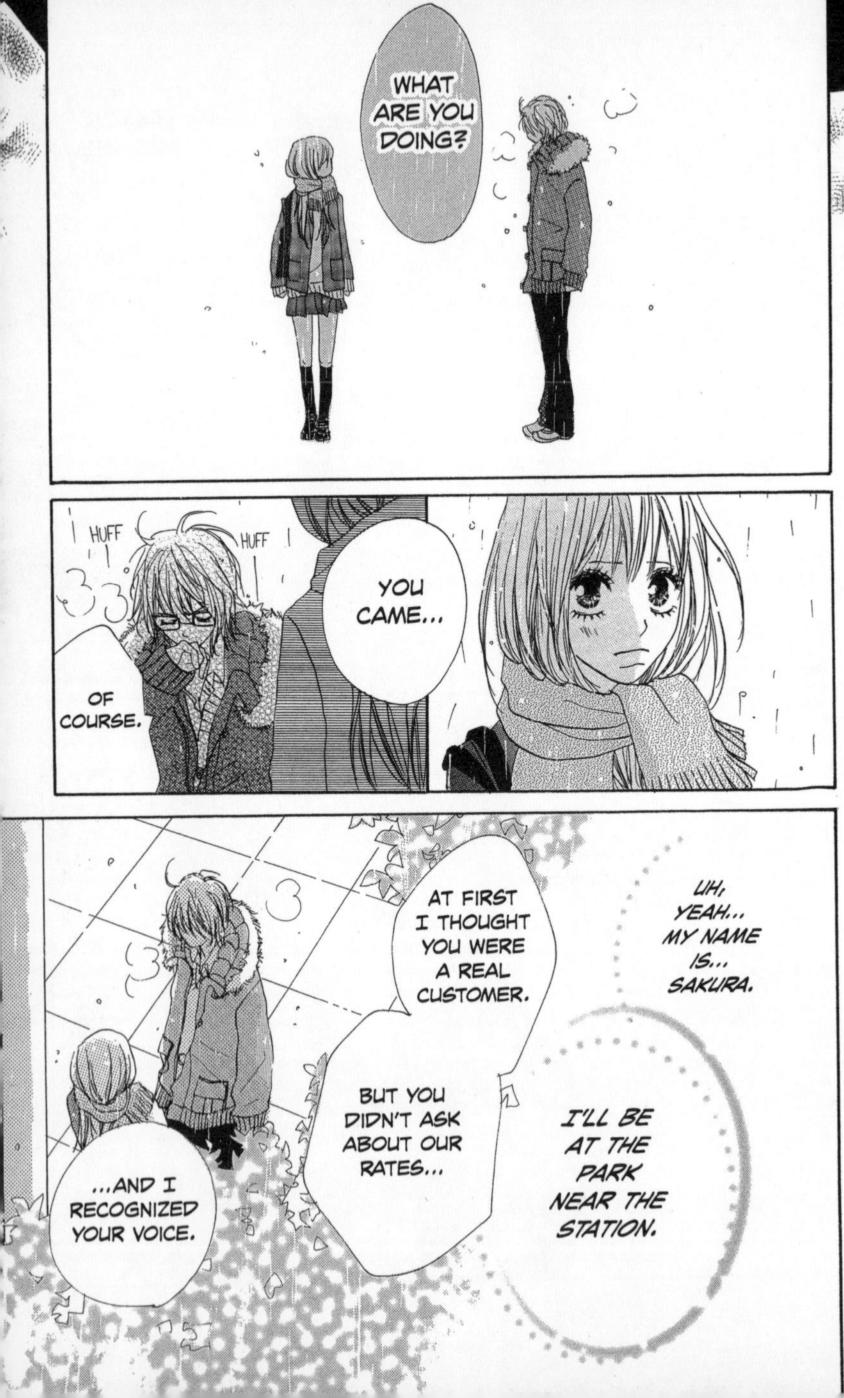
WHAT ARE YOU DOING?
YOU CAME...
HUFF
HUFF
OF COURSE.
UH, YEAH... MY NAME IS... SAKURA.
I'LL BE AT THE PARK NEAR THE STATION.
AT FIRST I THOUGHT YOU WERE A REAL CUSTOMER.
BUT YOU DIDN'T ASK ABOUT OUR RATES...
...AND I RECOGNIZED YOUR VOICE.

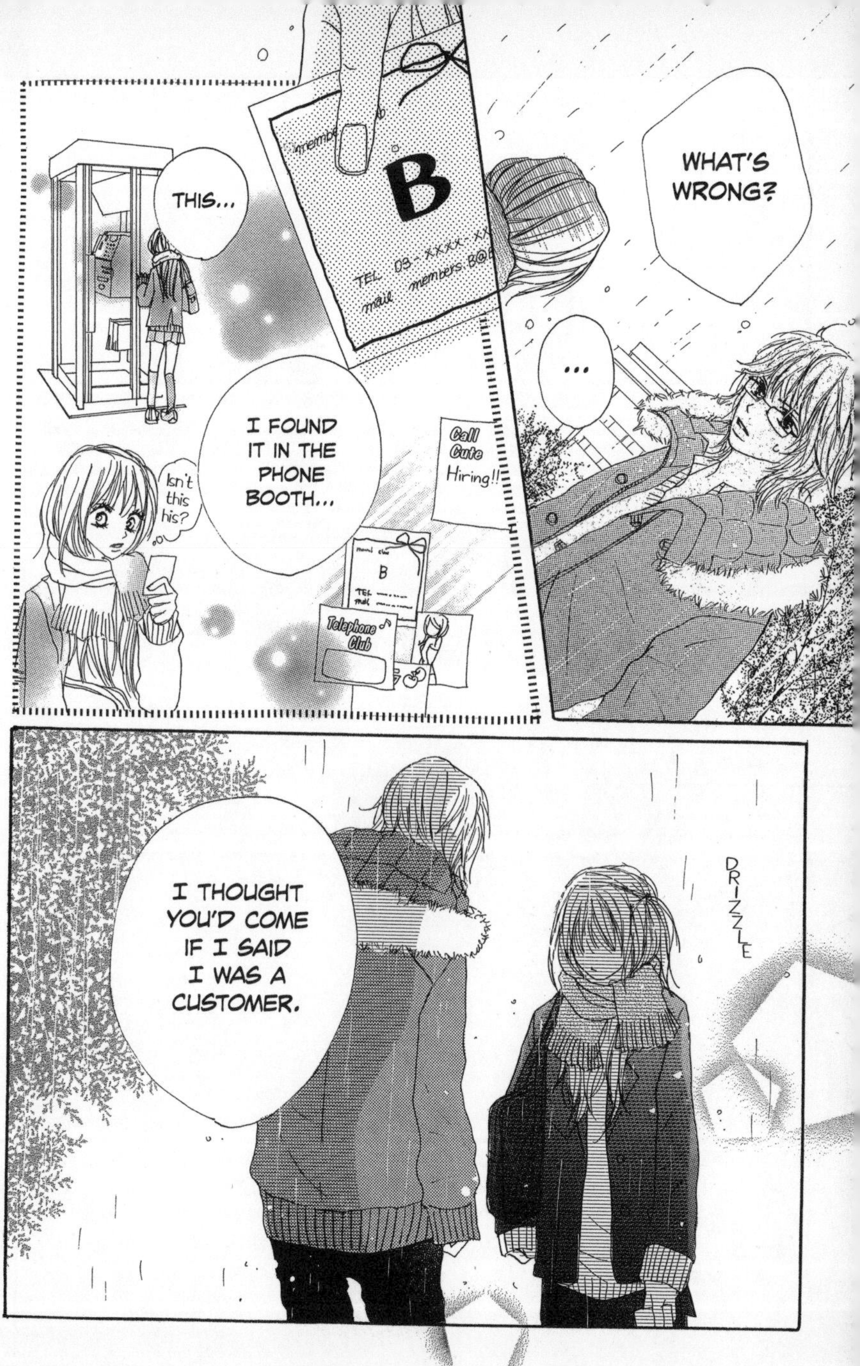
WHAT'S WRONG?
...
THIS...
B
I FOUND IT IN THE PHONE BOOTH...
Isn't this his?
Call Cute Hiring!!
Telephone Club
I THOUGHT YOU'D COME IF I SAID I WAS A CUSTOMER.
DRIZZLE

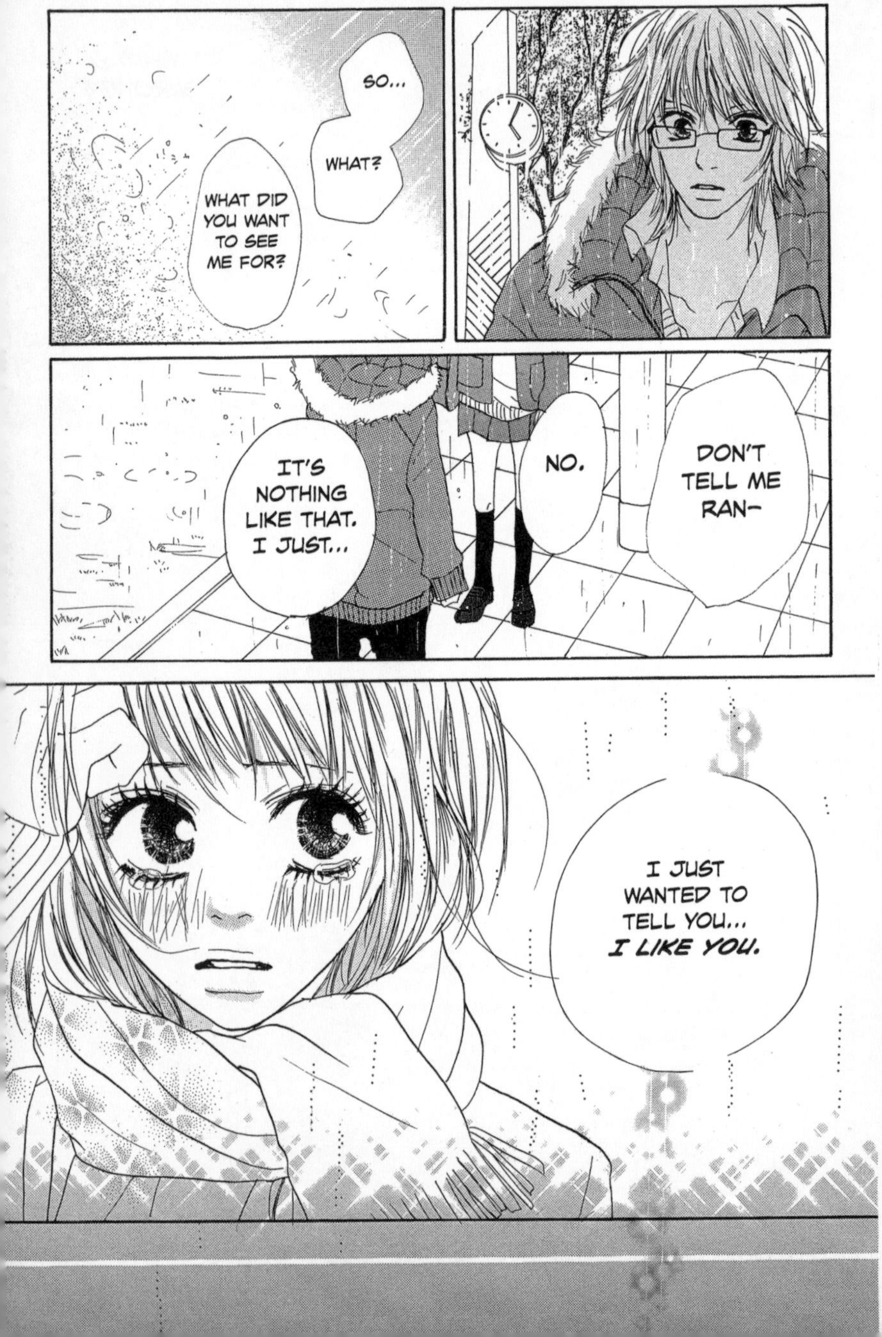
SO...
WHAT?
WHAT DID YOU WANT TO SEE ME FOR?
DON'T TELL ME RAN-
NO.
IT'S NOTHING LIKE THAT. I JUST...
I JUST WANTED TO TELL YOU... *I LIKE YOU.*

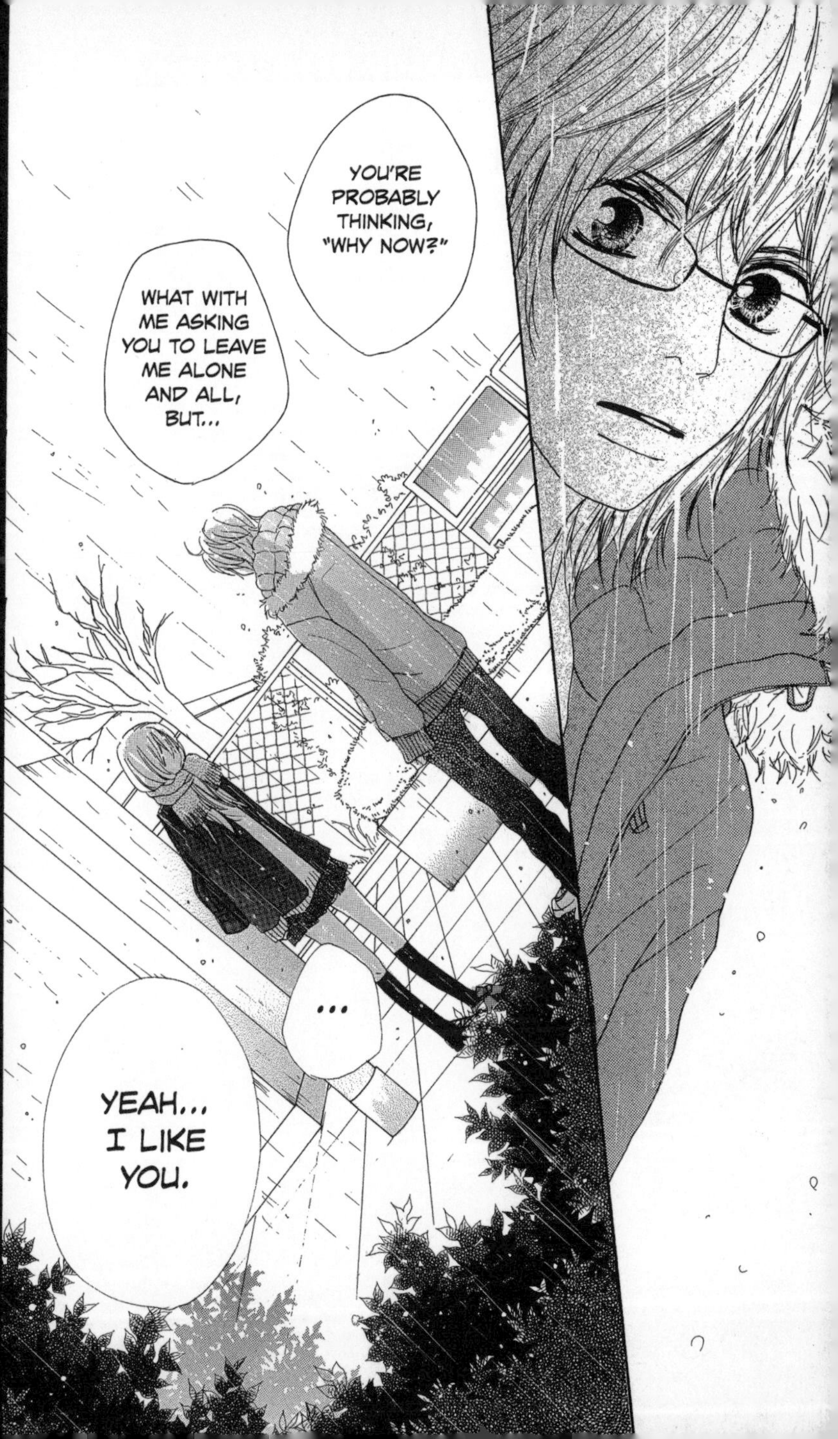
YOU'RE PROBABLY THINKING, "WHY NOW?"
WHAT WITH ME ASKING YOU TO LEAVE ME ALONE AND ALL, BUT...
...
YEAH... I LIKE YOU.

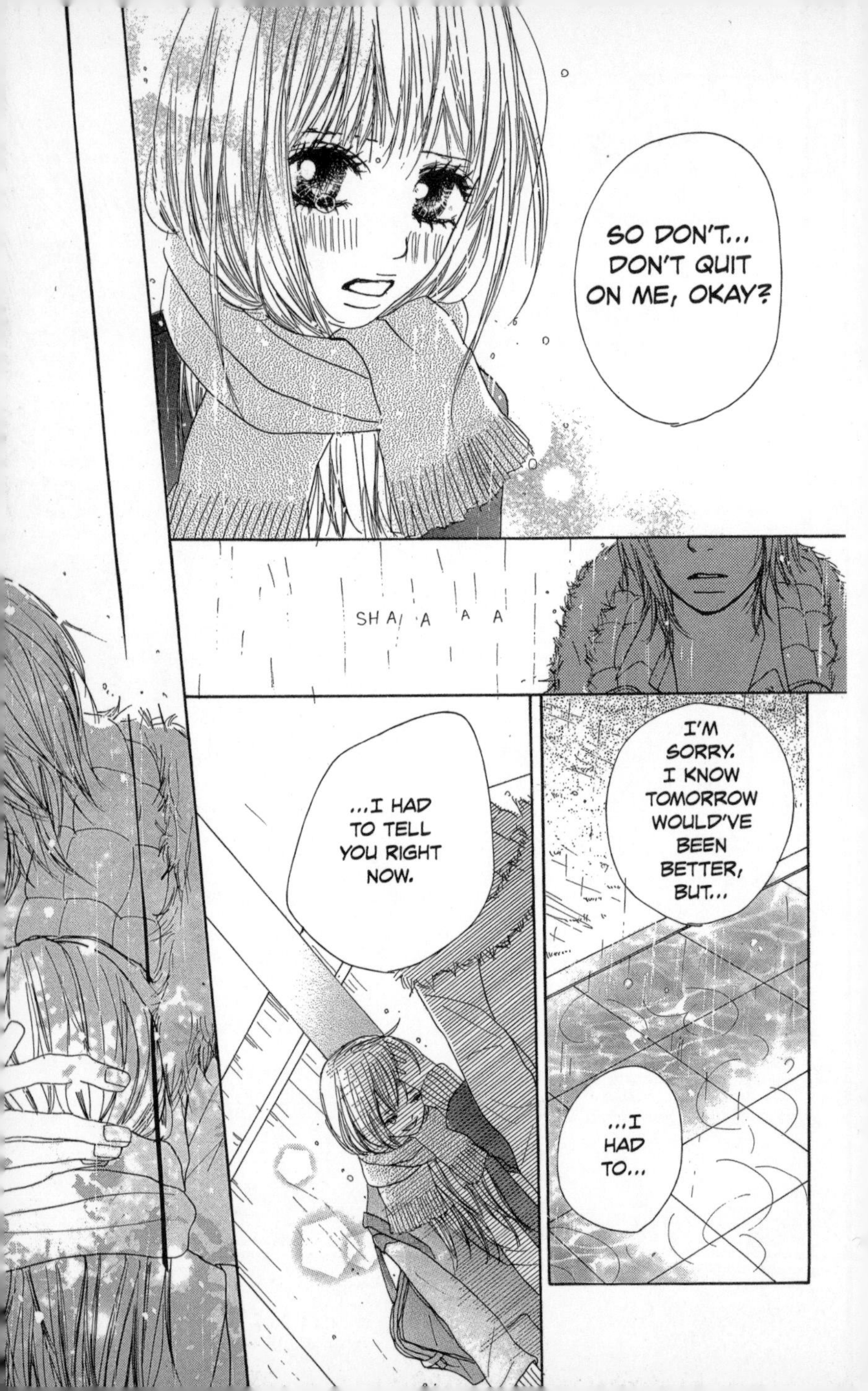
SO DON'T... DON'T QUIT ON ME, OKAY?
SHAAAA
I'M SORRY. I KNOW TOMORROW WOULD'VE BEEN BETTER, BUT...
...I HAD TO...
...I HAD TO TELL YOU RIGHT NOW.

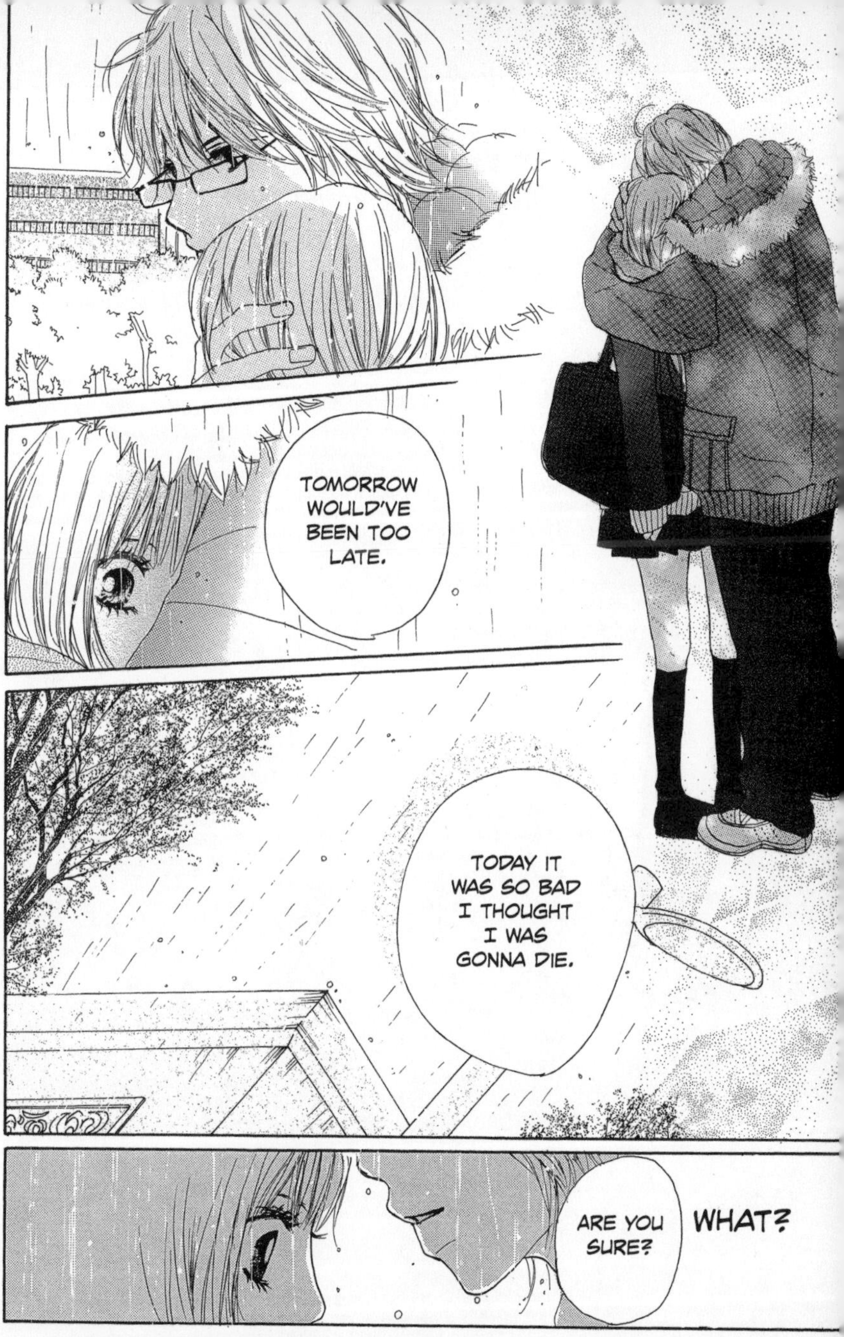
TOMORROW WOULD'VE BEEN TOO LATE.
TODAY IT WAS SO BAD I THOUGHT I WAS GONNA DIE.
WHAT?
ARE YOU SURE?

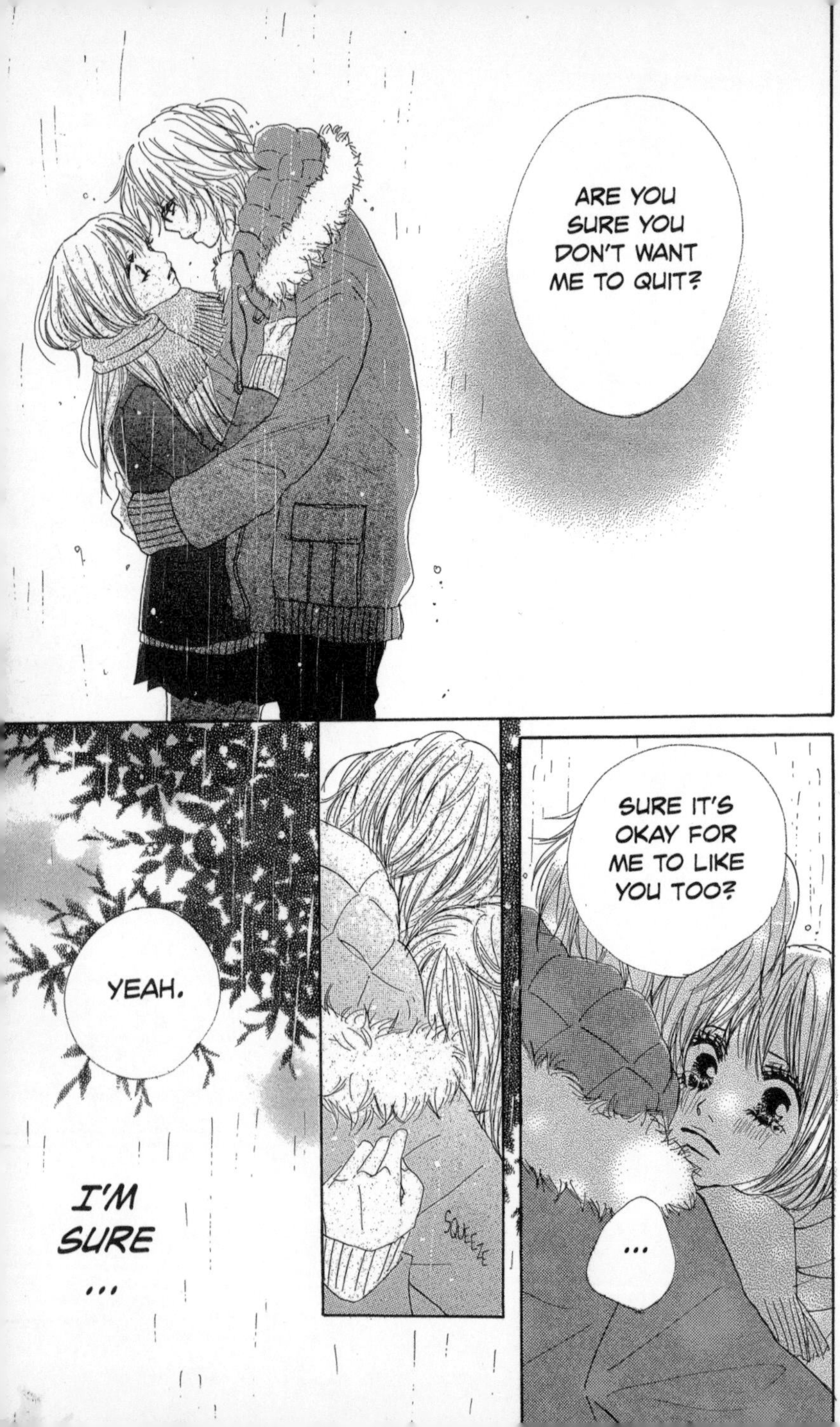
ARE YOU SURE YOU DON'T WANT ME TO QUIT?
SURE IT'S OKAY FOR ME TO LIKE YOU TOO?
...
SQUEEZE
YEAH.
I'M SURE ...

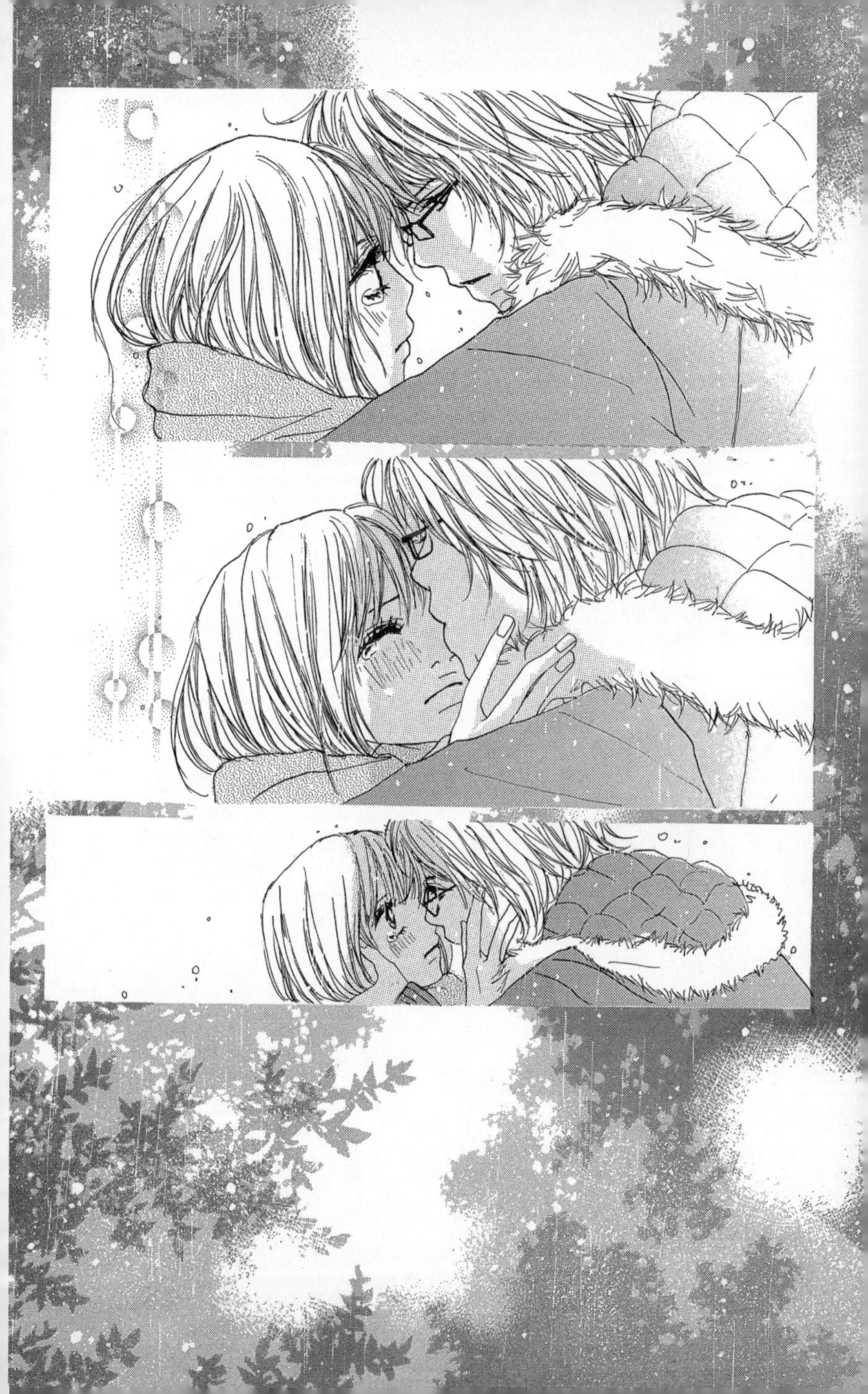

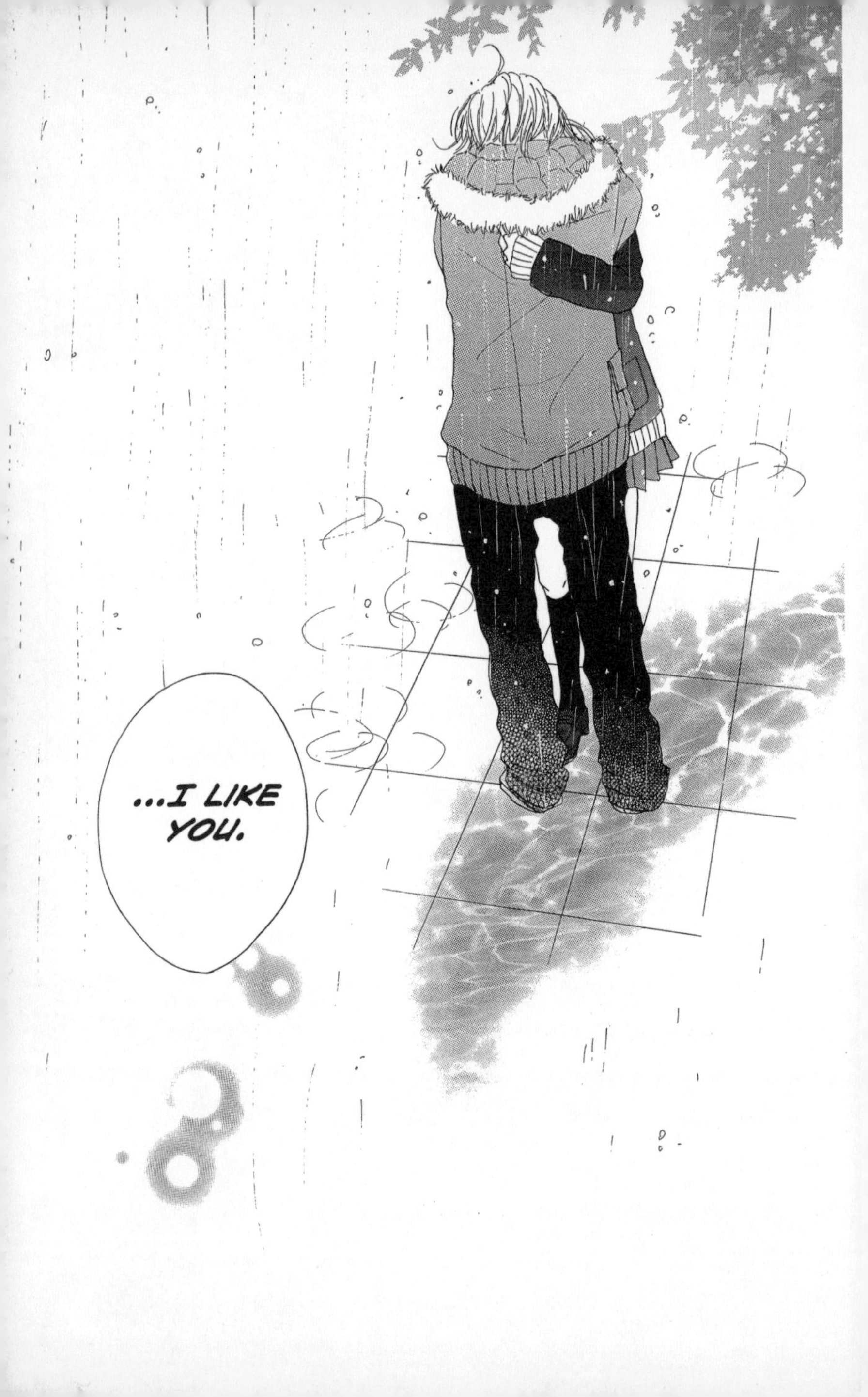
...I LIKE YOU.

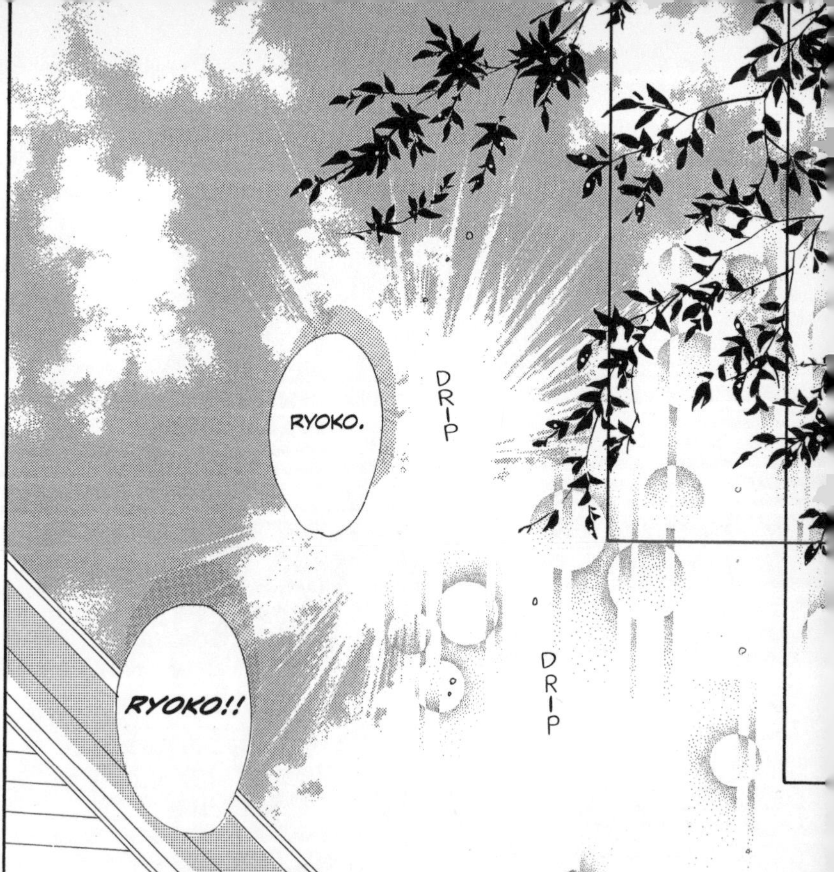
DRIP
RYOKO.
DRIP
RYOKO!!
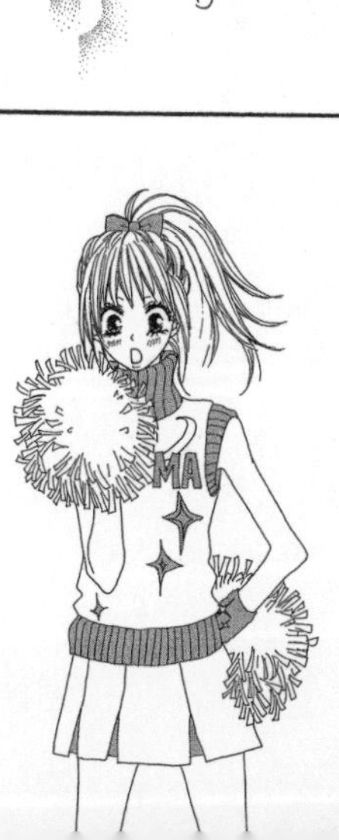

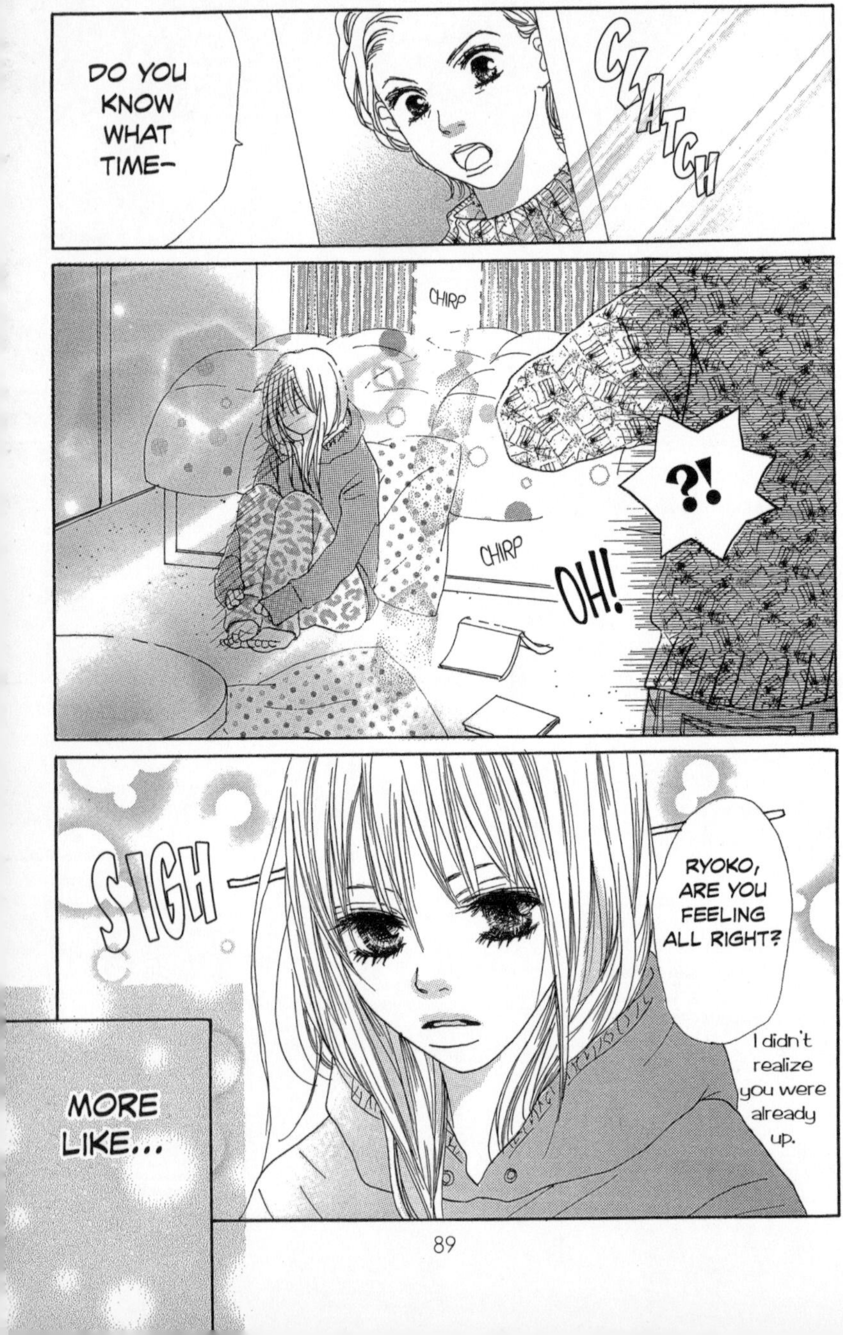
CLATCH
DO YOU KNOW WHAT TIME–
?!
OH!
CHIRP
CHIRP
RYOKO, ARE YOU FEELING ALL RIGHT?
I didn't realize you were already up.
SIGH
MORE LIKE...

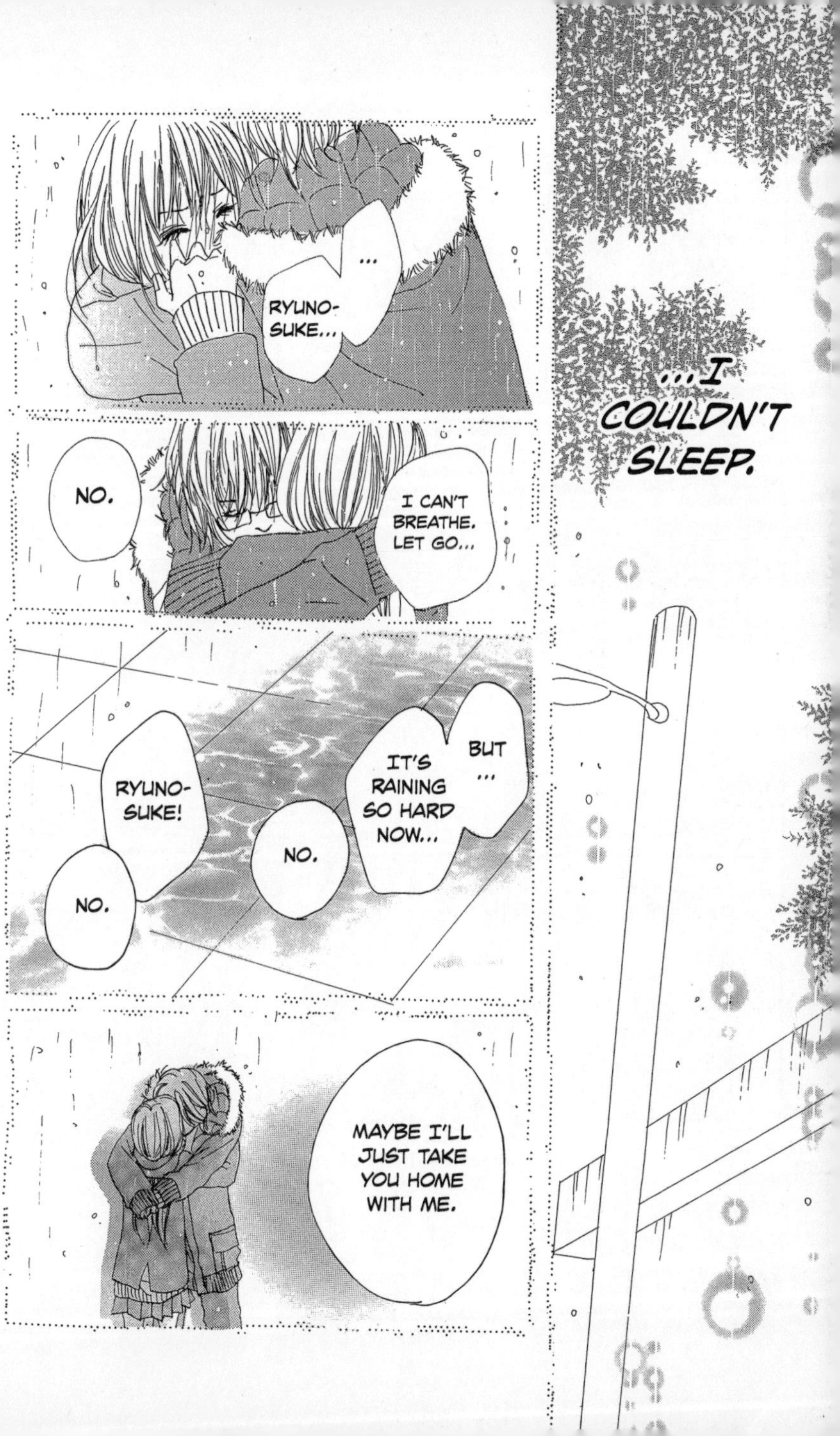
...I COULDN'T SLEEP.
...
RYUNO-SUKE...
I CAN'T BREATHE. LET GO...
NO.
BUT ...
IT'S RAINING SO HARD NOW...
NO.
RYUNO-SUKE!
NO.
MAYBE I'LL JUST TAKE YOU HOME WITH ME.

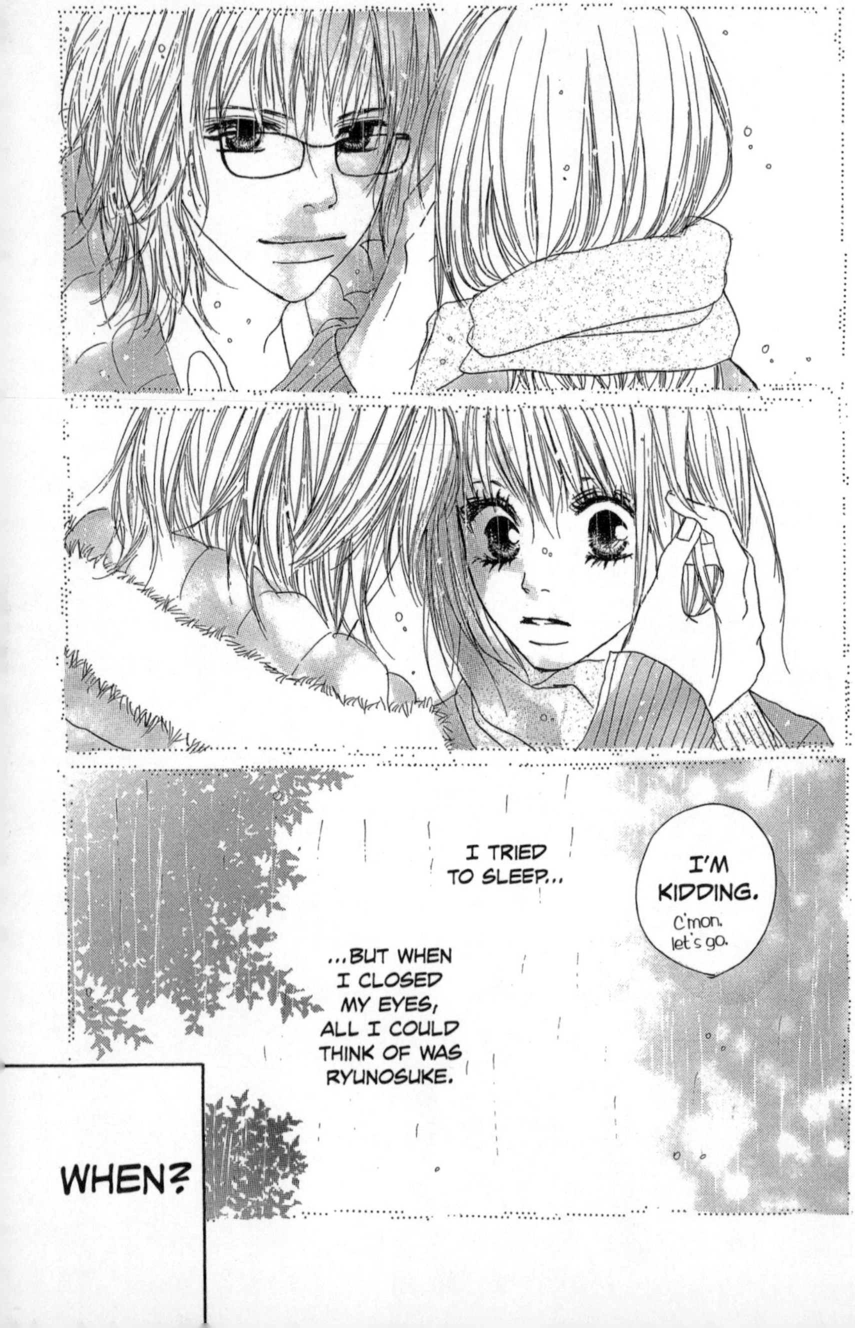
I'M KIDDING.
C'mon, let's go.
I TRIED TO SLEEP...
...BUT WHEN I CLOSED MY EYES, ALL I COULD THINK OF WAS RYUNOSUKE.
WHEN?

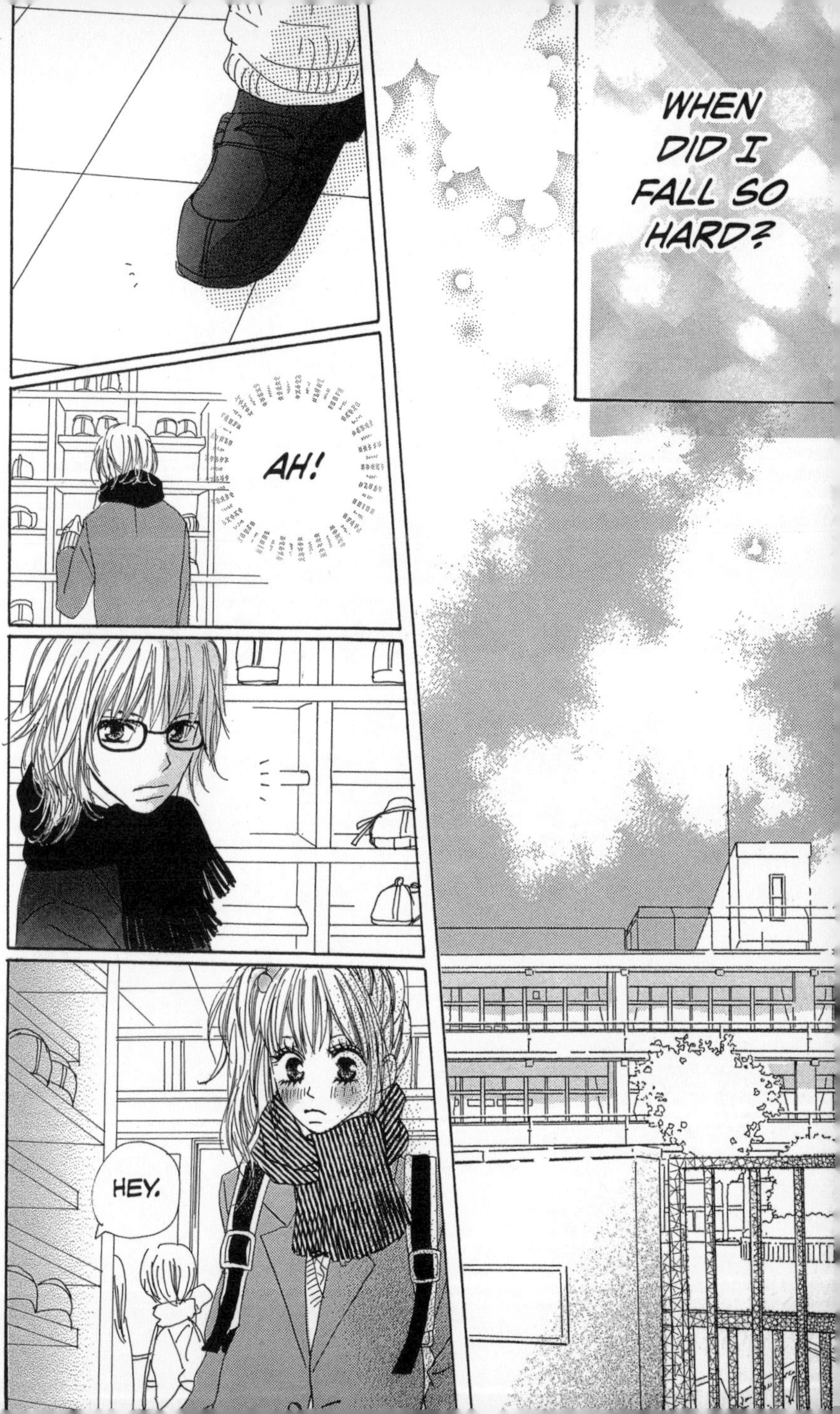
WHEN DID I FALL SO HARD?
AH!
HEY.

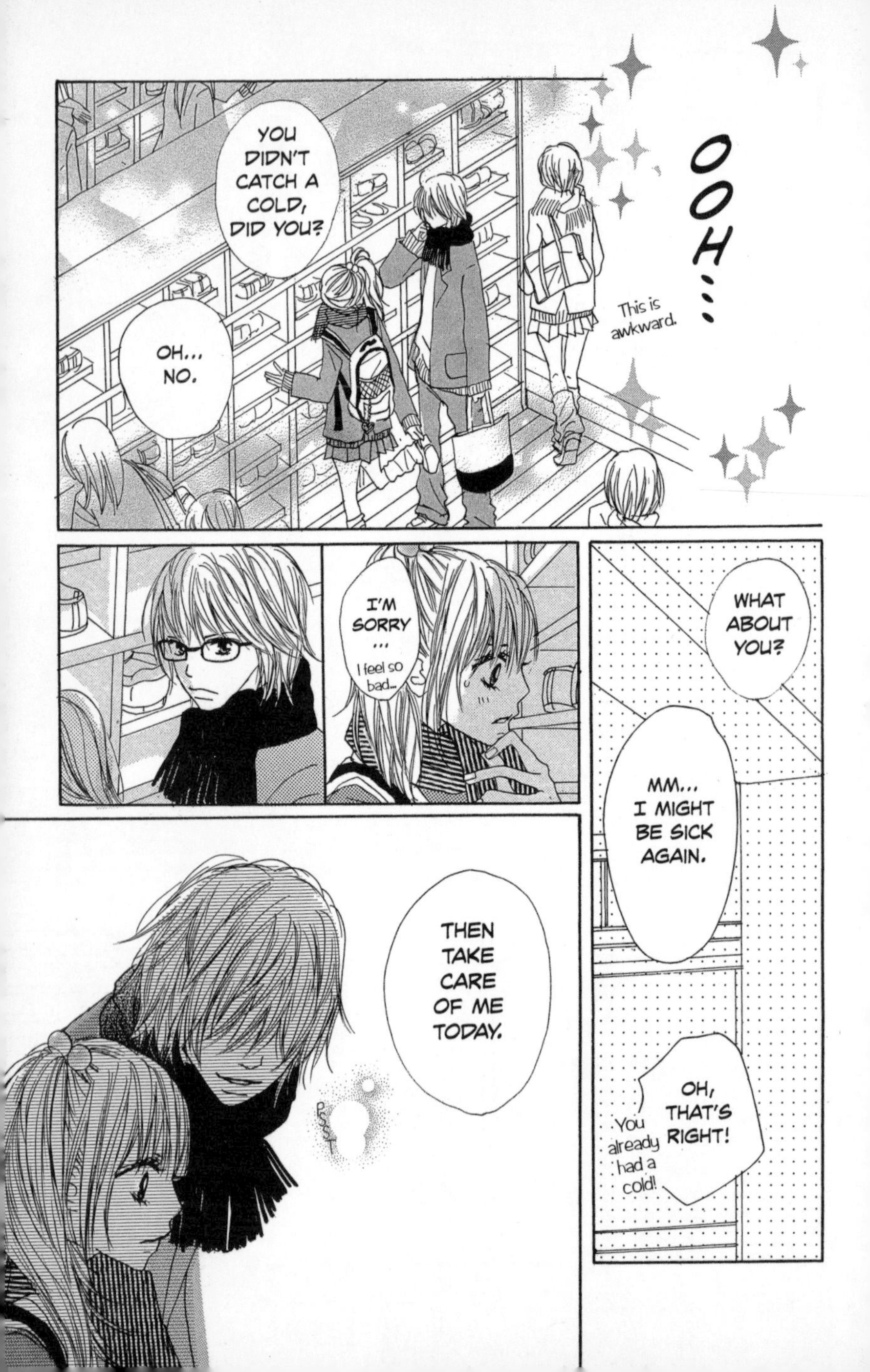
OOH...
This is awkward.
YOU DIDN'T CATCH A COLD, DID YOU?
OH... NO.
WHAT ABOUT YOU?
MM... I MIGHT BE SICK AGAIN.
OH, THAT'S RIGHT!
You already had a cold!
I'M SORRY...
I feel so bad...
THEN TAKE CARE OF ME TODAY.
PSST

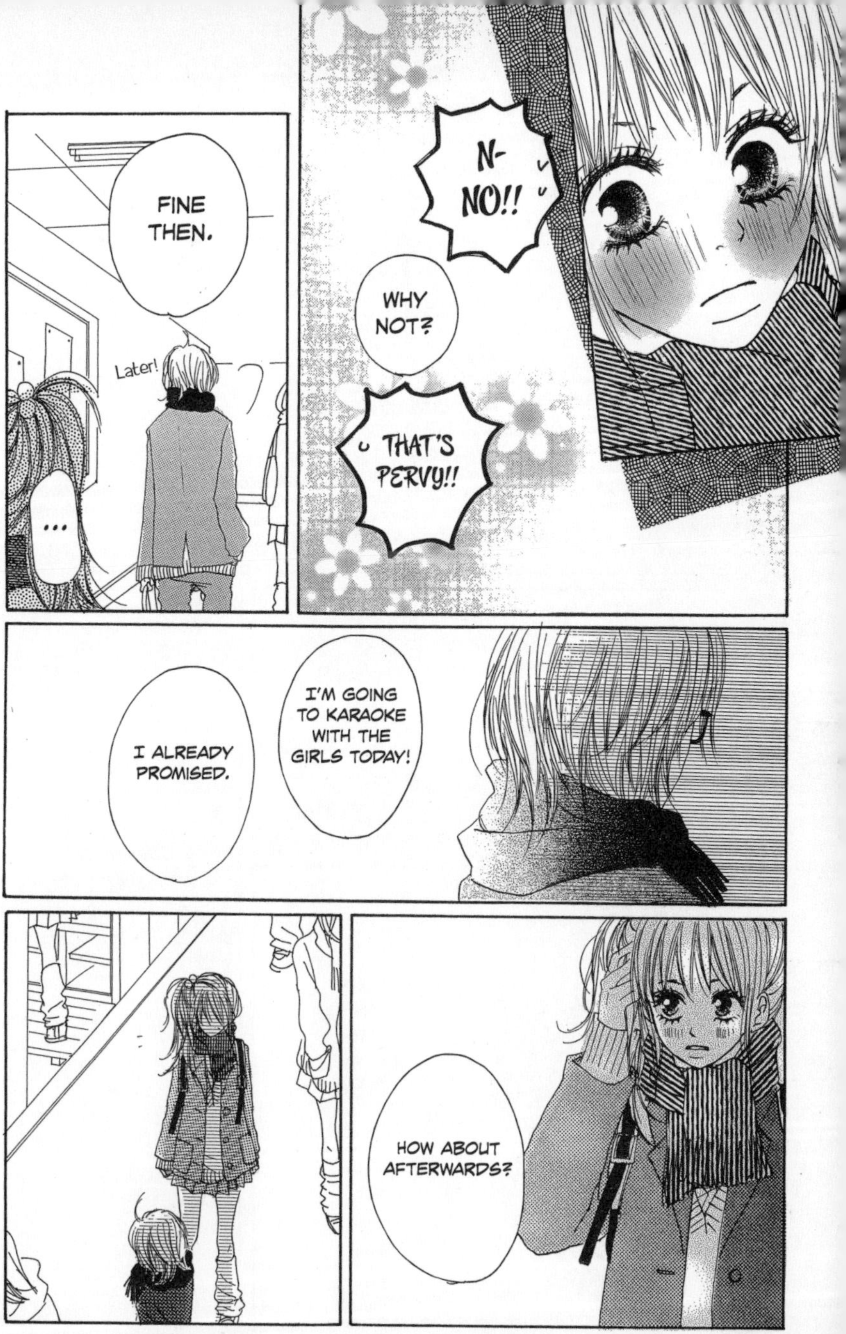
N-NO!!
WHY NOT?
THAT'S PERVY!!
FINE THEN.
Later!
...
I'M GOING TO KARAOKE WITH THE GIRLS TODAY!
I ALREADY PROMISED.
HOW ABOUT AFTERWARDS?

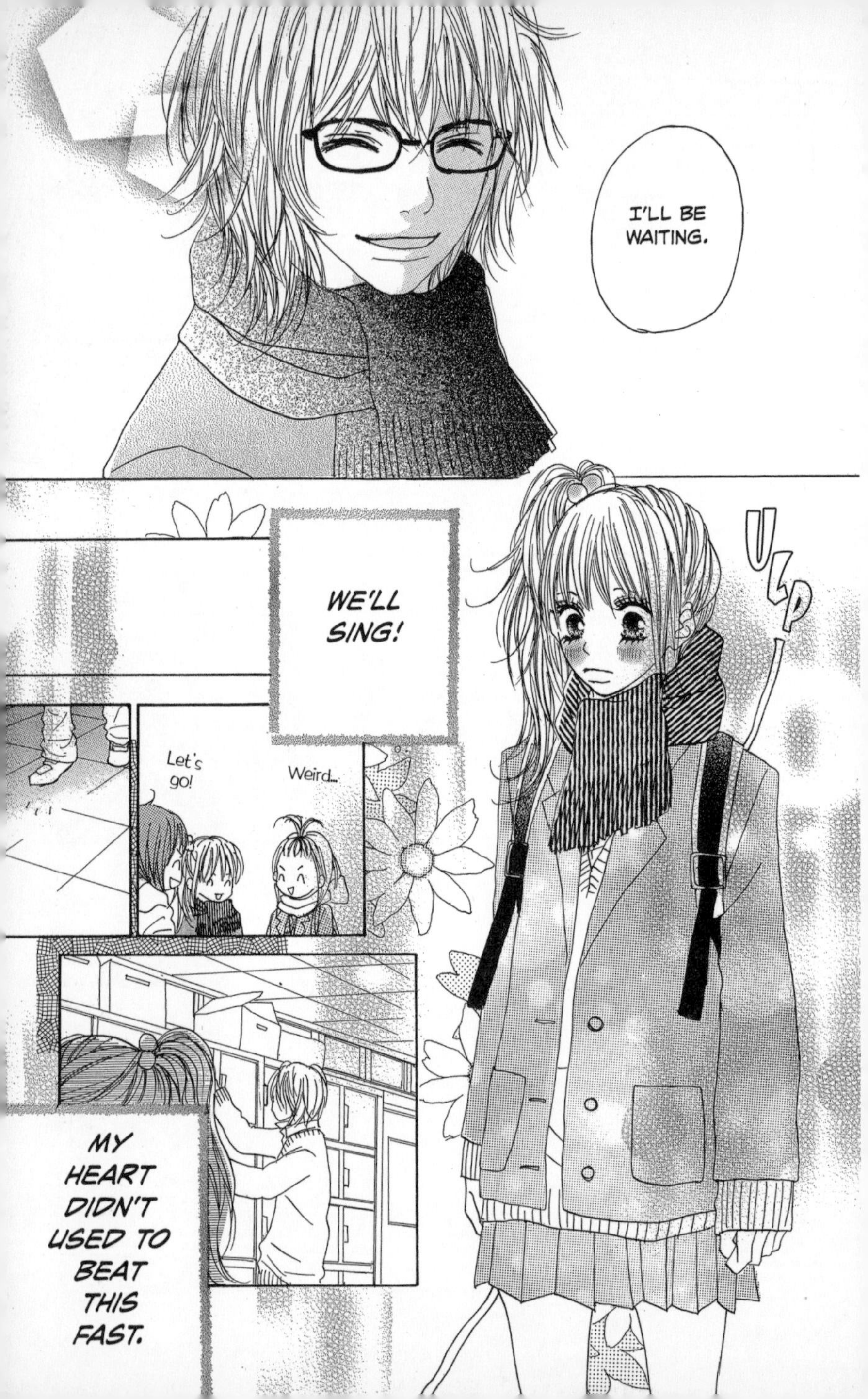
I'LL BE WAITING.
ULP
WE'LL SING!
Weird...
Let's go!
MY HEART DIDN'T USED TO BEAT THIS FAST.

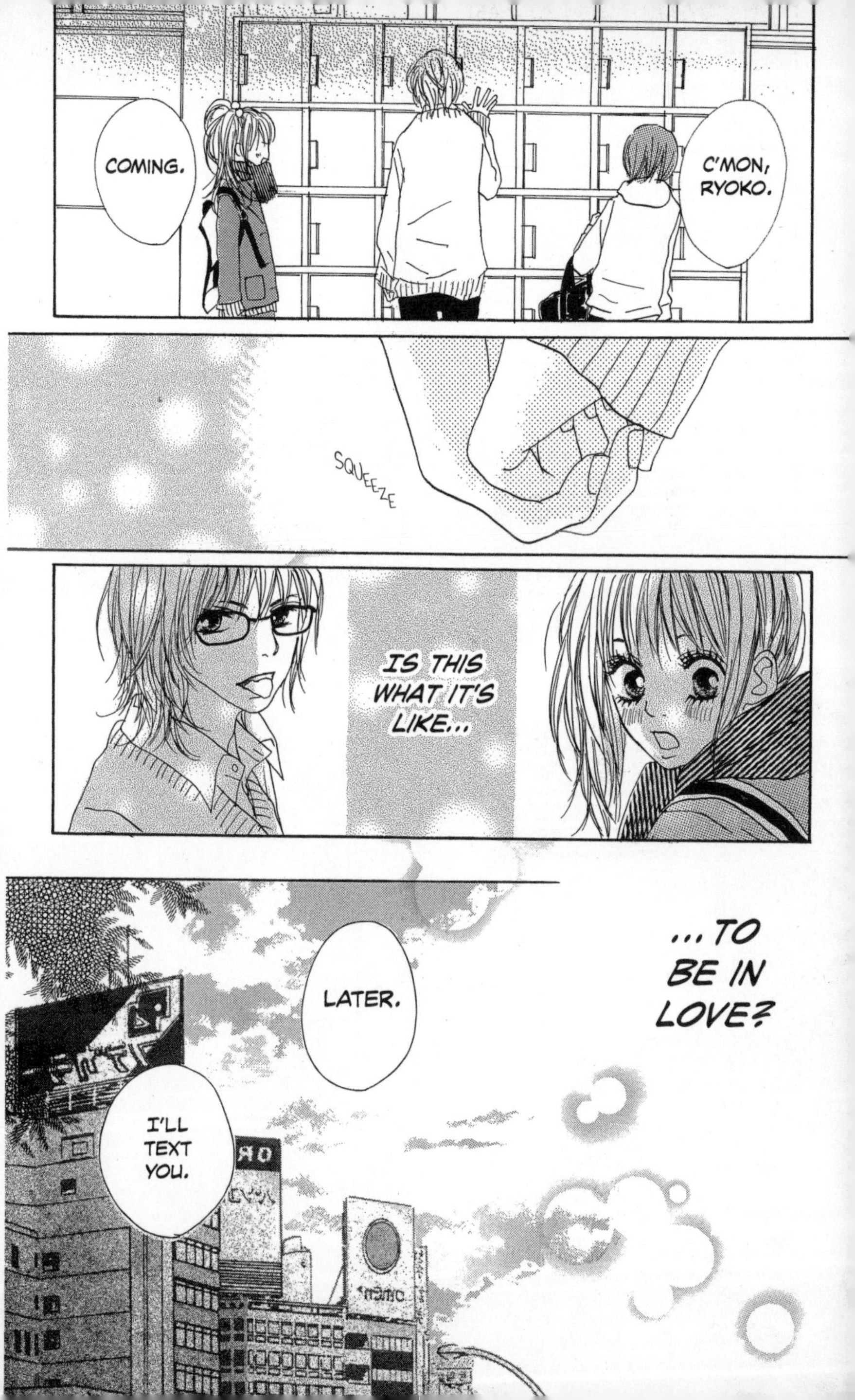
C'MON, RYOKO.
COMING.
SQUEEZE
IS THIS WHAT IT'S LIKE...
...TO BE IN LOVE?
LATER.
I'LL TEXT YOU.

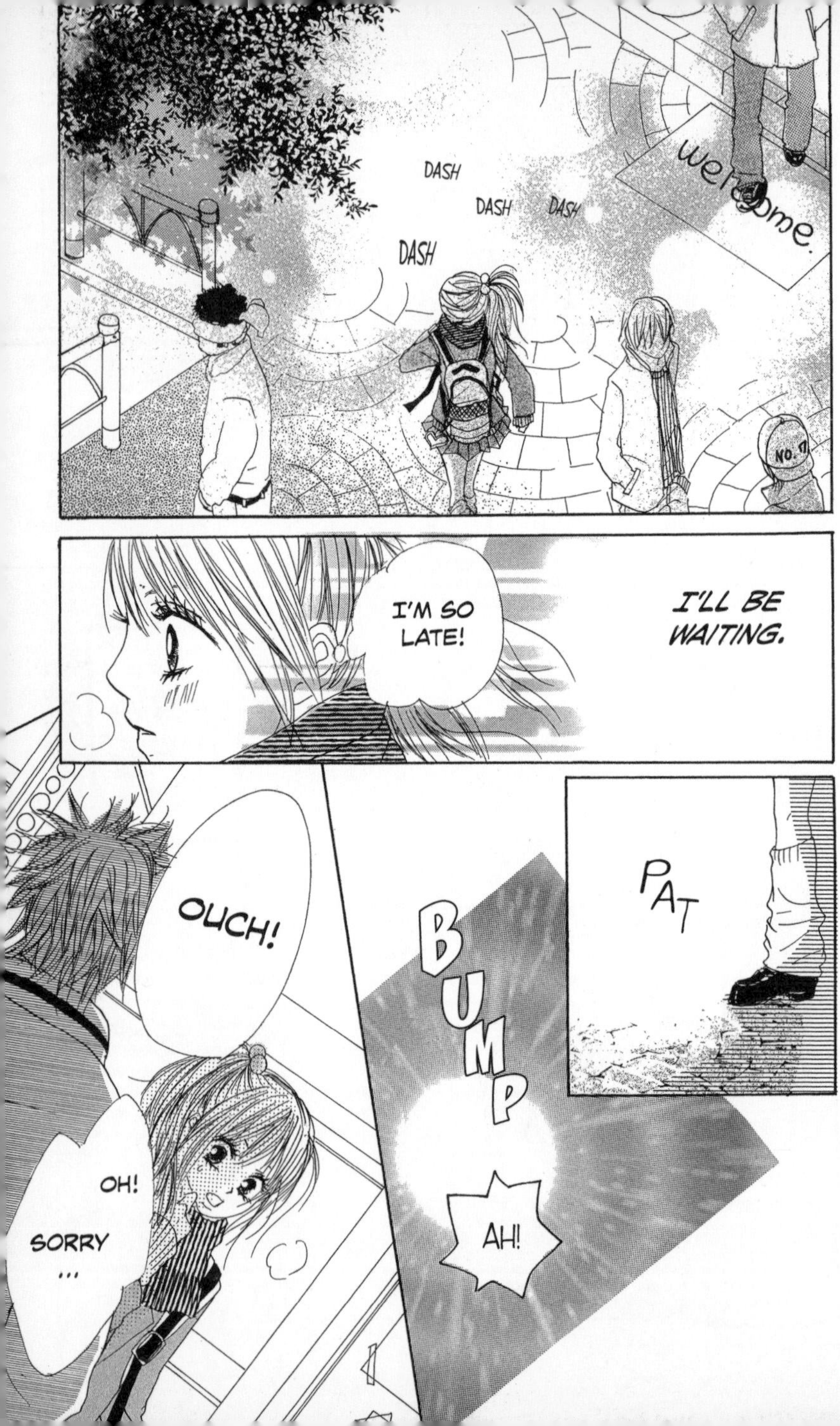
welcome.
DASH
DASH
DASH
DASH
NO. 17
I'LL BE WAITING.
I'M SO LATE!
PAT
BUMP
AH!
OUCH!
OH!
SORRY ...

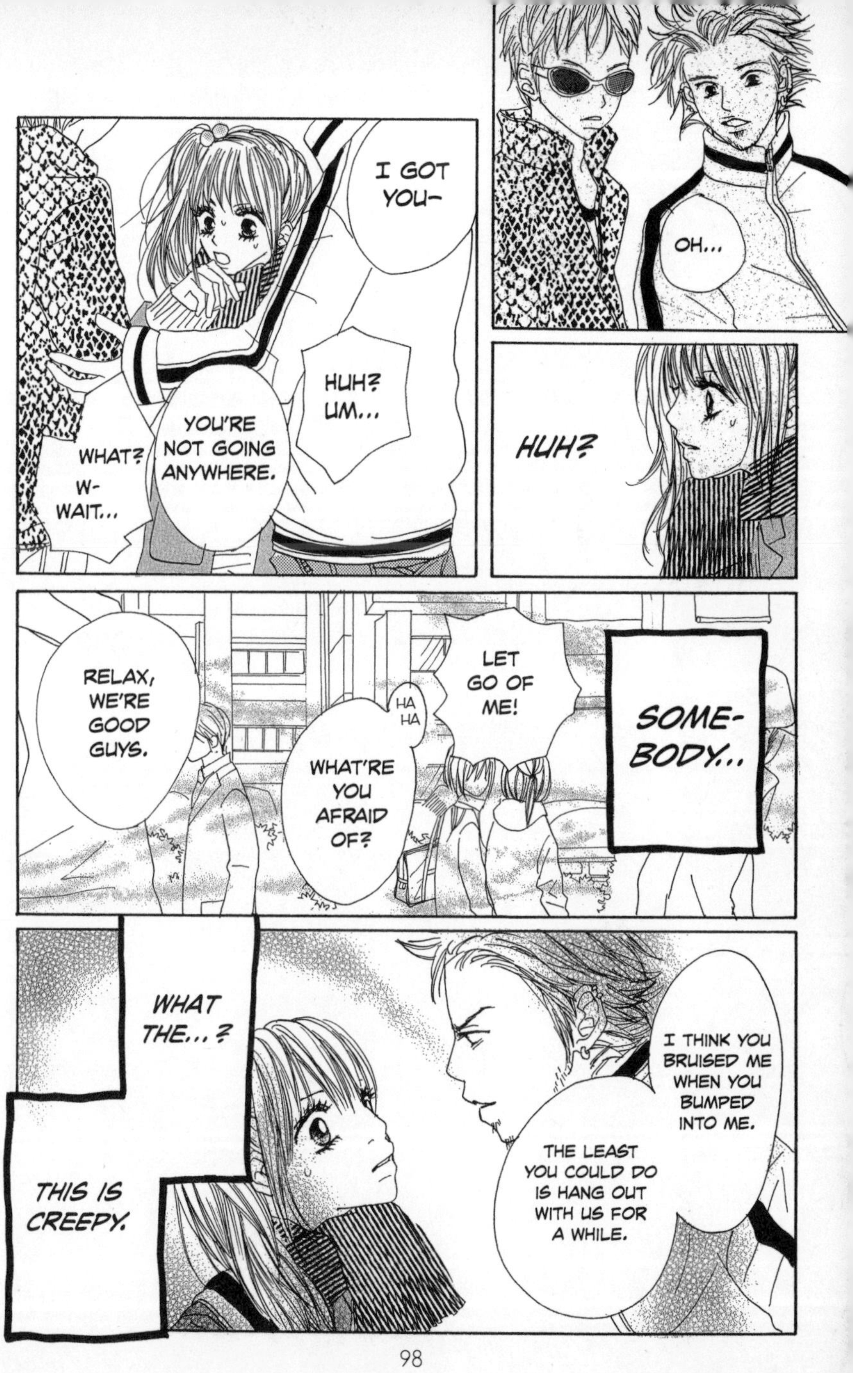
OH...
HUH?
I GOT YOU-
HUH? UM...
YOU'RE NOT GOING ANYWHERE.
WHAT? W- WAIT...
SOME-BODY...
LET GO OF ME!
HA HA
WHAT'RE YOU AFRAID OF?
RELAX, WE'RE GOOD GUYS.
I THINK YOU BRUISED ME WHEN YOU BUMPED INTO ME.
THE LEAST YOU COULD DO IS HANG OUT WITH US FOR A WHILE.
WHAT THE...?
THIS IS CREEPY.

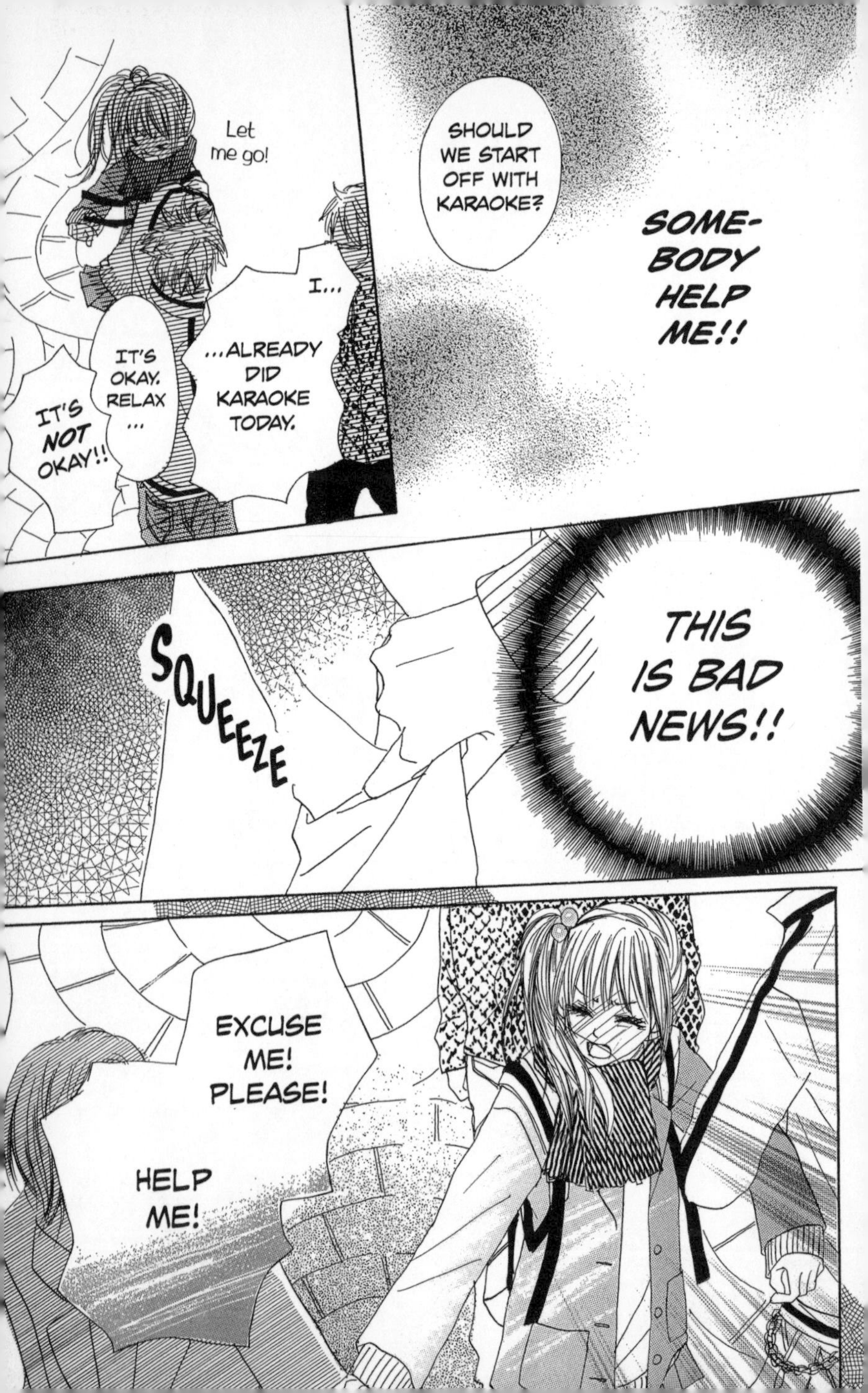
SHOULD WE START OFF WITH KARAOKE?
SOME-BODY HELP ME!!
Let me go!
I...
...ALREADY DID KARAOKE TODAY.
IT'S OKAY. RELAX...
IT'S NOT OKAY!!
THIS IS BAD NEWS!!
SQUEEEZE
EXCUSE ME! PLEASE!
HELP ME!

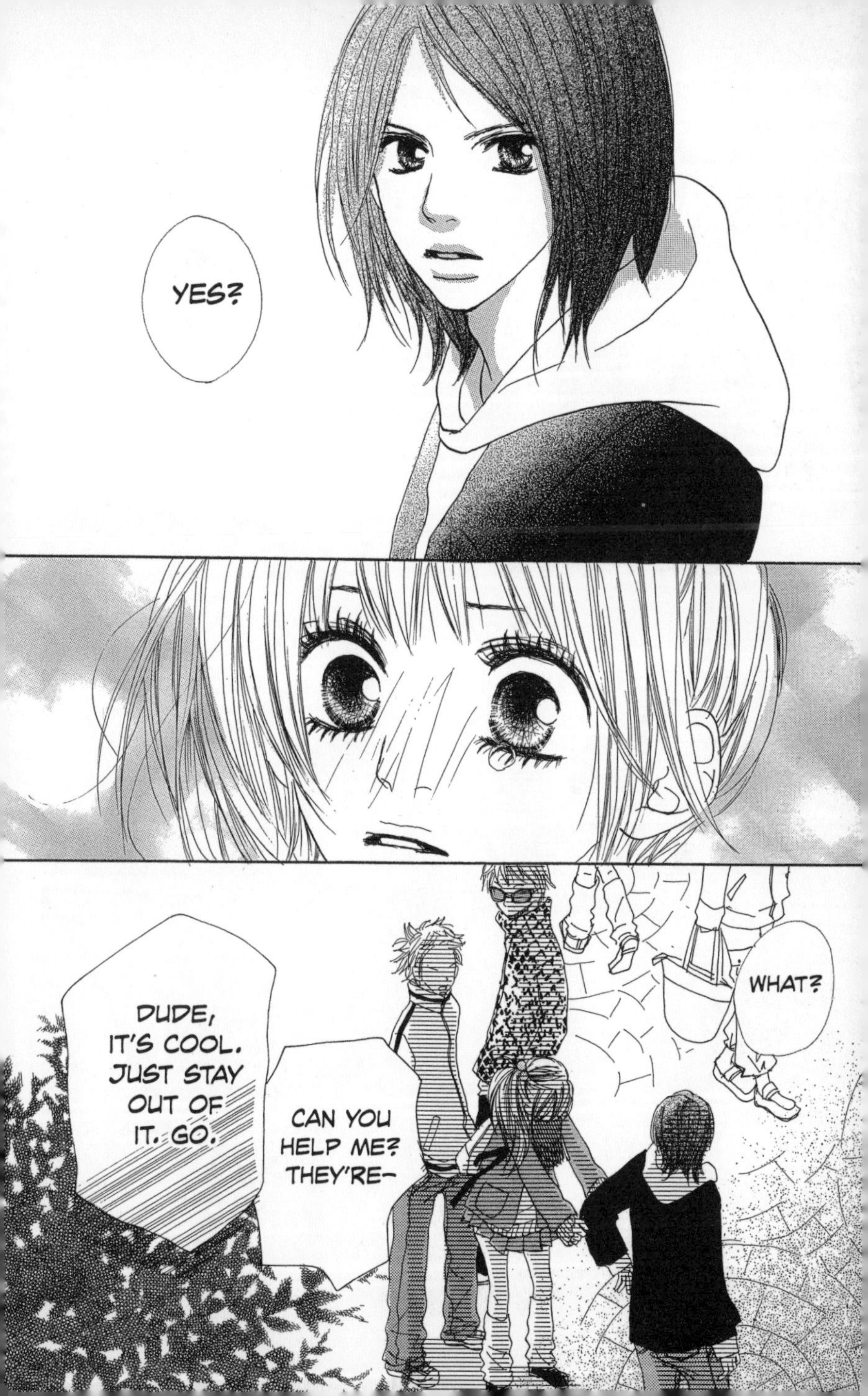
YES?
WHAT?
CAN YOU HELP ME? THEY'RE-
DUDE, IT'S COOL. JUST STAY OUT OF IT. GO.

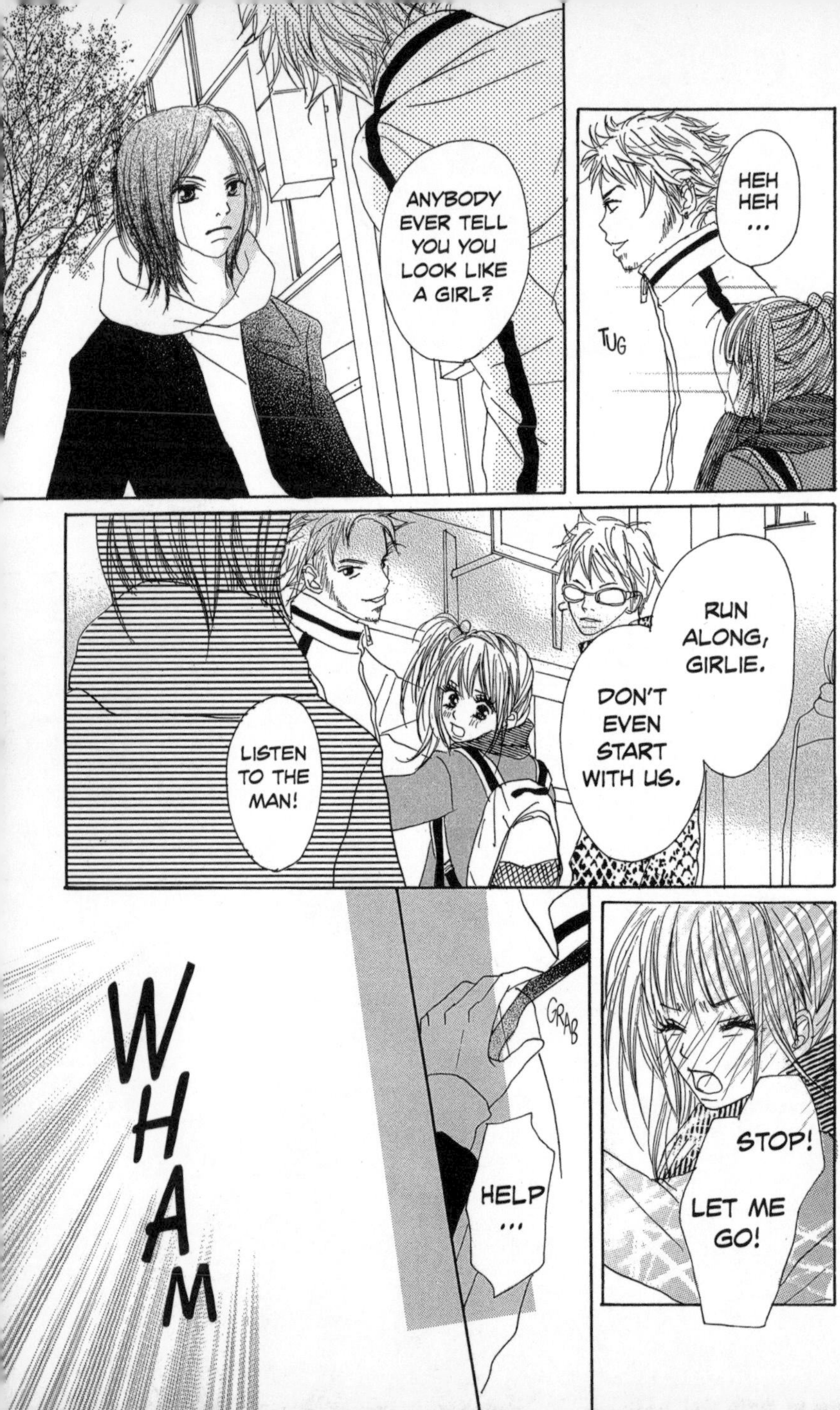
HEH HEH ...
TUG
ANYBODY EVER TELL YOU YOU LOOK LIKE A GIRL?
RUN ALONG, GIRLIE.
DON'T EVEN START WITH US.
LISTEN TO THE MAN!
STOP!
LET ME GO!
GRAB
HELP ...
WHAM

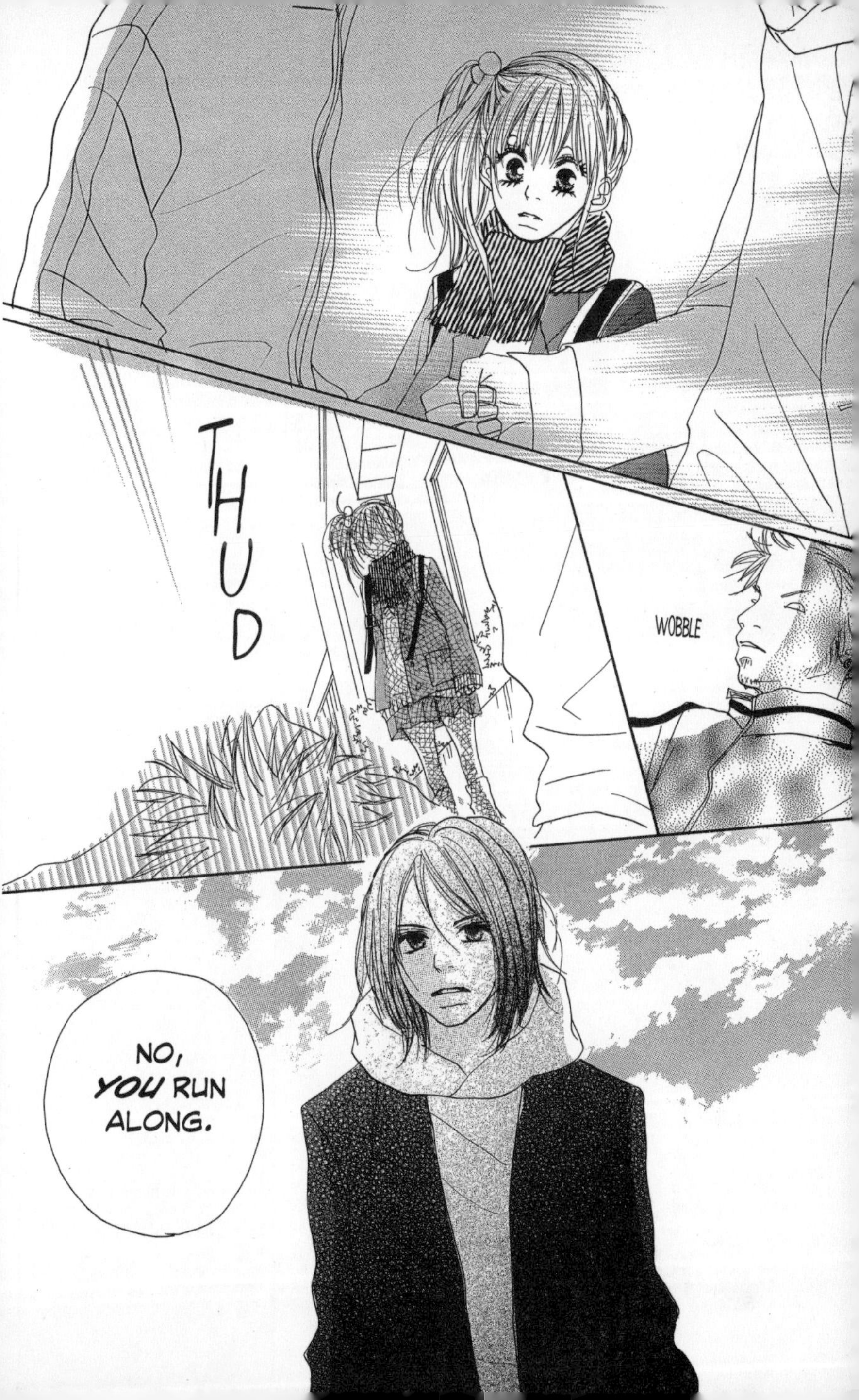
THUD
WOBBLE
NO, *YOU* RUN ALONG.

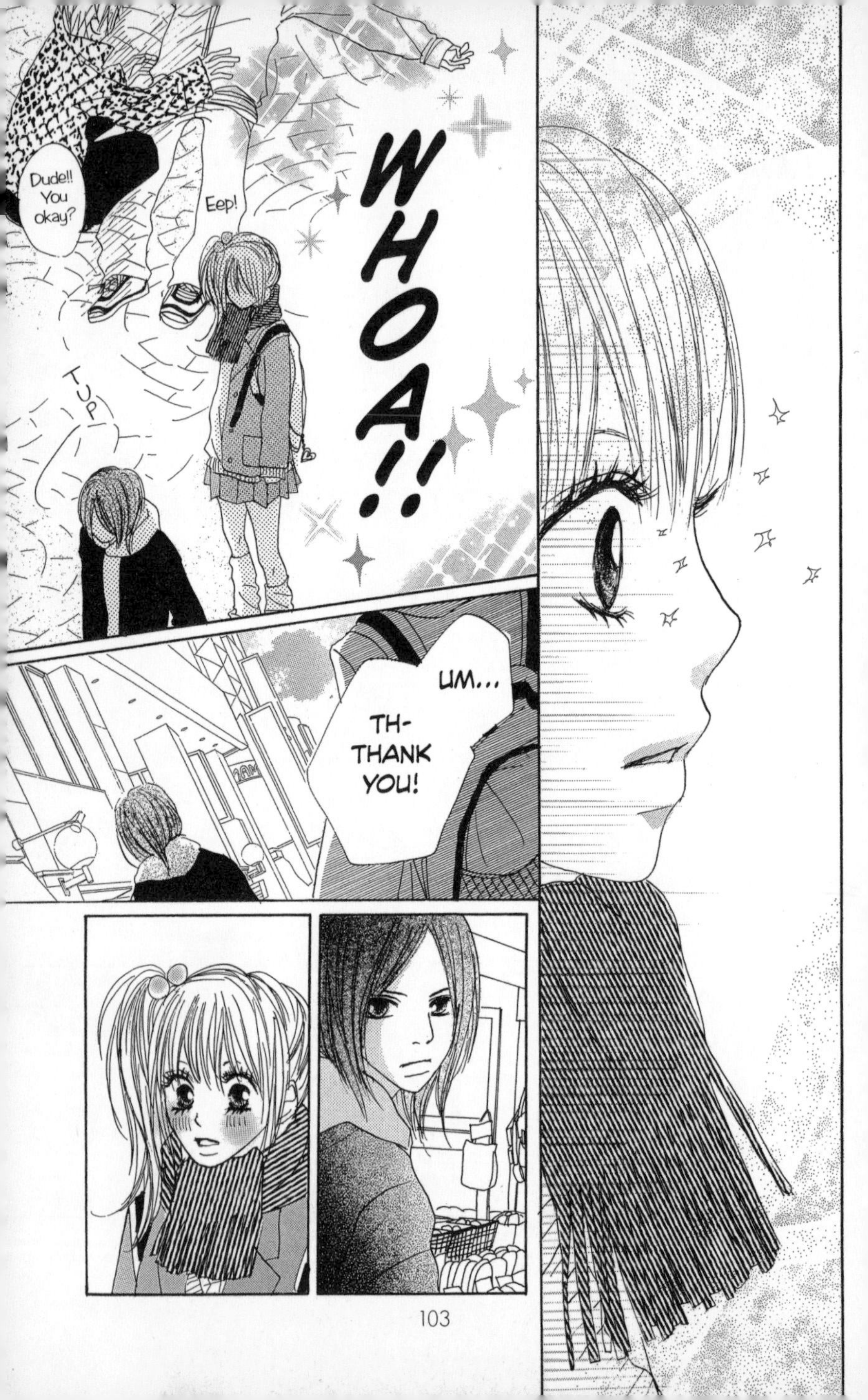
WHOA!!
Eep!
Dude!! You okay?
TUP
UM...
TH-THANK YOU!

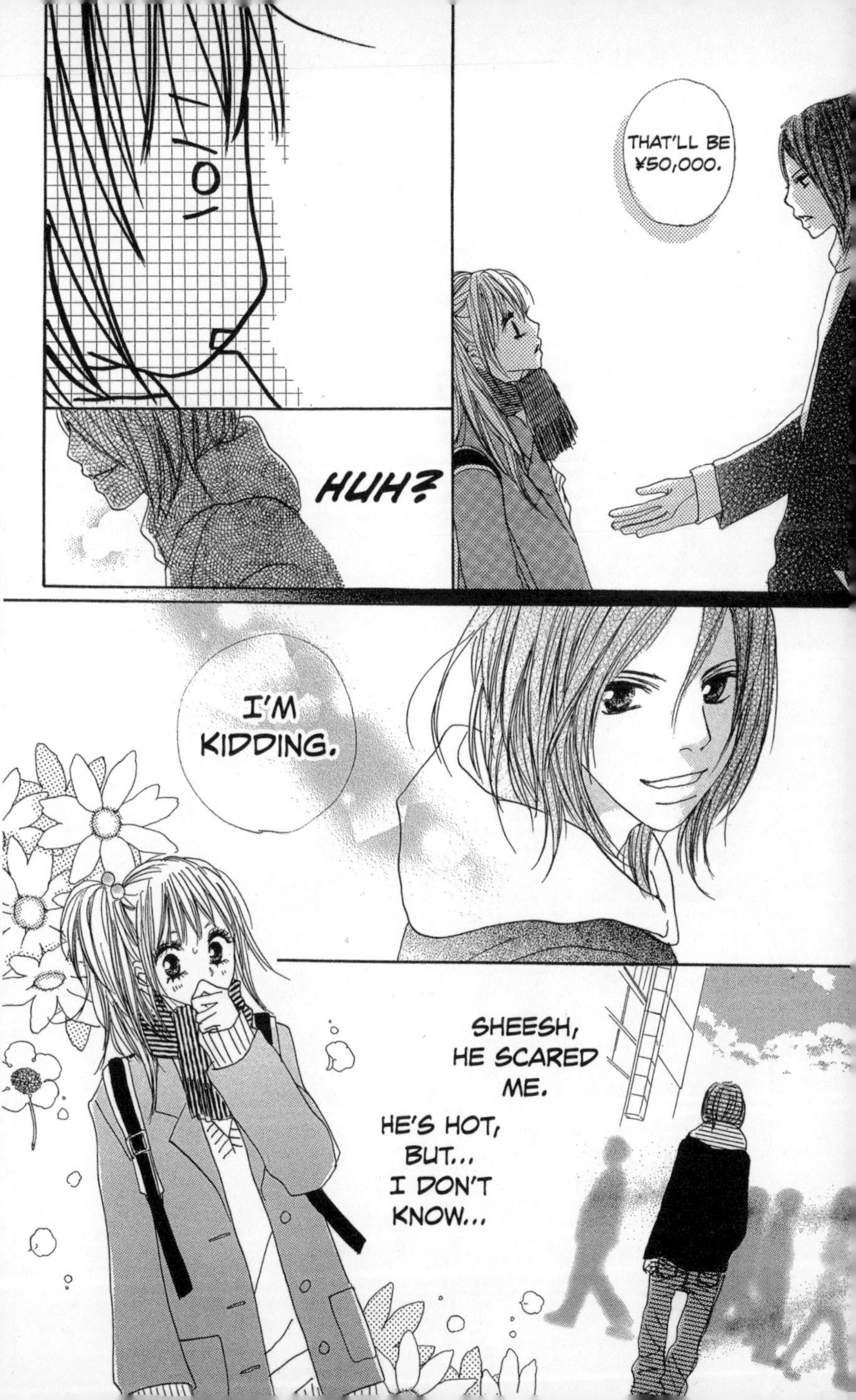
THAT'LL BE ¥50,000.
HUH?
I'M KIDDING.
SHEESH, HE SCARED ME.
HE'S HOT, BUT... I DON'T KNOW...

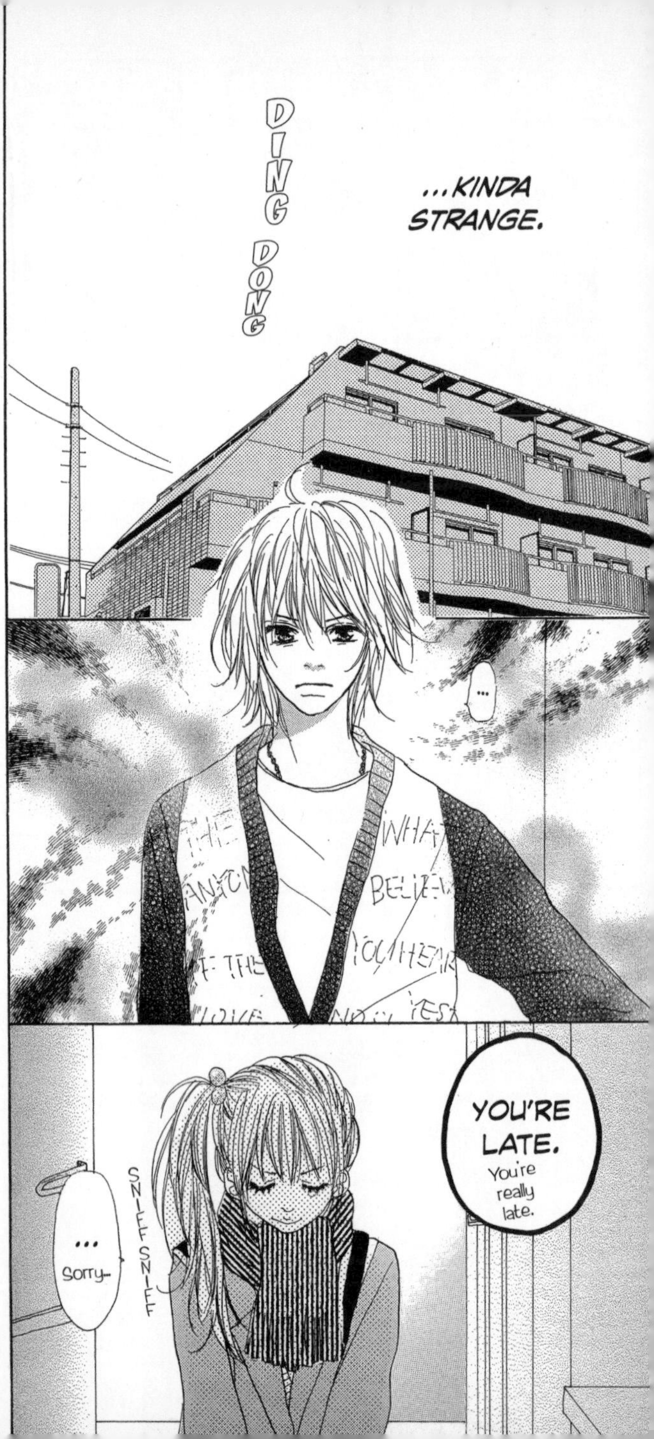
...KINDA STRANGE.
DING DONG
...
YOU'RE LATE.
You're really late.
SNIFF SNIFF
... Sorry...

③

Speaking of running, why is it that whenever I go outside, I get attacked by mosquitoes? I'm waiting at a stoplight, I get bitten. I look inside my mailbox, one lands on my hand...What is it with me and mosquitoes? Is it some kind of curse? The Pharaoh's Mosquito Curse? Am I not allowed to stand outside unmolested? And those little suckers...they drink so much!! They get all bloated!! On the rare occasion when I can catch them, they're so dead! I demolish them. Then, of course, I get blood all over my hands...Ugh! It's so gross. People with type O blood get stung a lot. They seek us out—even in a crowd! Of all my random "whatever" stories, this is the most random— the whatever-est! I'm so sorry. To those of you who are wishing I had something more interesting to say, my apologies!

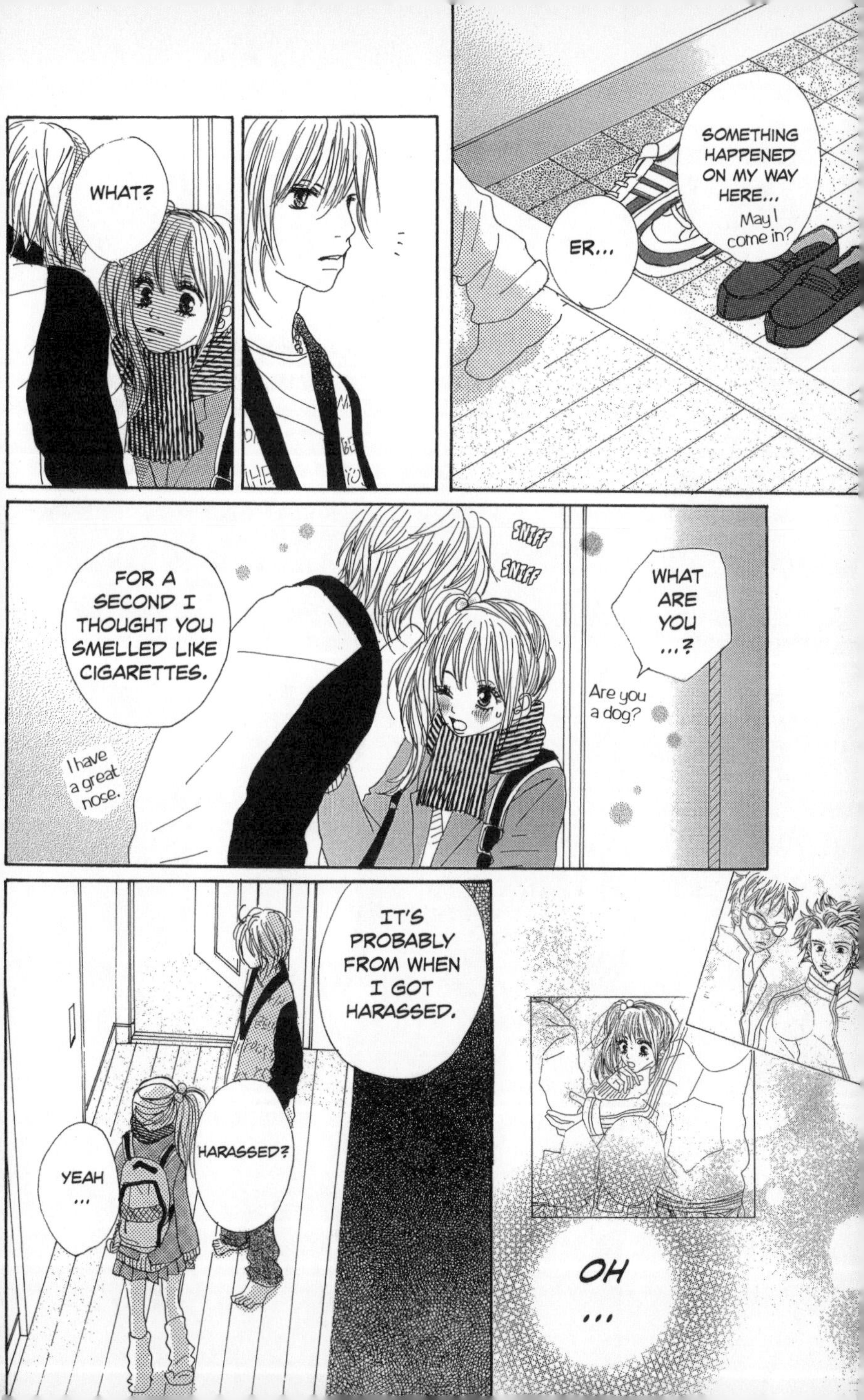
ER...
SOMETHING HAPPENED ON MY WAY HERE...
May I come in?
WHAT?
WHAT ARE YOU ...?
Are you a dog?
SNIFF
SNIFF
FOR A SECOND I THOUGHT YOU SMELLED LIKE CIGARETTES.
I have a great nose.
IT'S PROBABLY FROM WHEN I GOT HARASSED.
HARASSED?
YEAH ...
OH ...

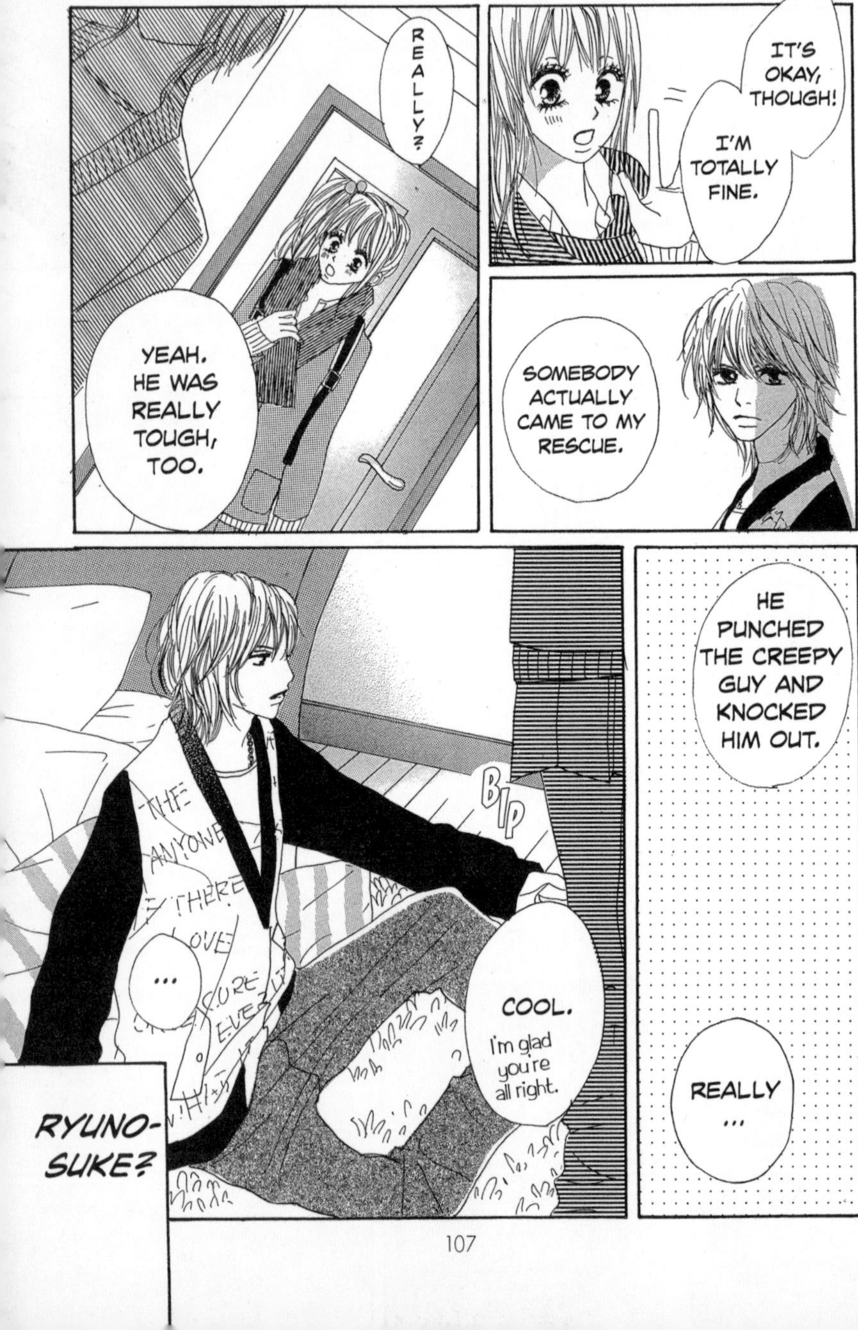
IT'S OKAY, THOUGH!
I'M TOTALLY FINE.
SOMEBODY ACTUALLY CAME TO MY RESCUE.
REALLY?
YEAH. HE WAS REALLY TOUGH, TOO.
HE PUNCHED THE CREEPY GUY AND KNOCKED HIM OUT.
REALLY...
BIP
COOL.
I'm glad you're all right.
...
RYUNO-SUKE?

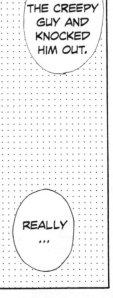

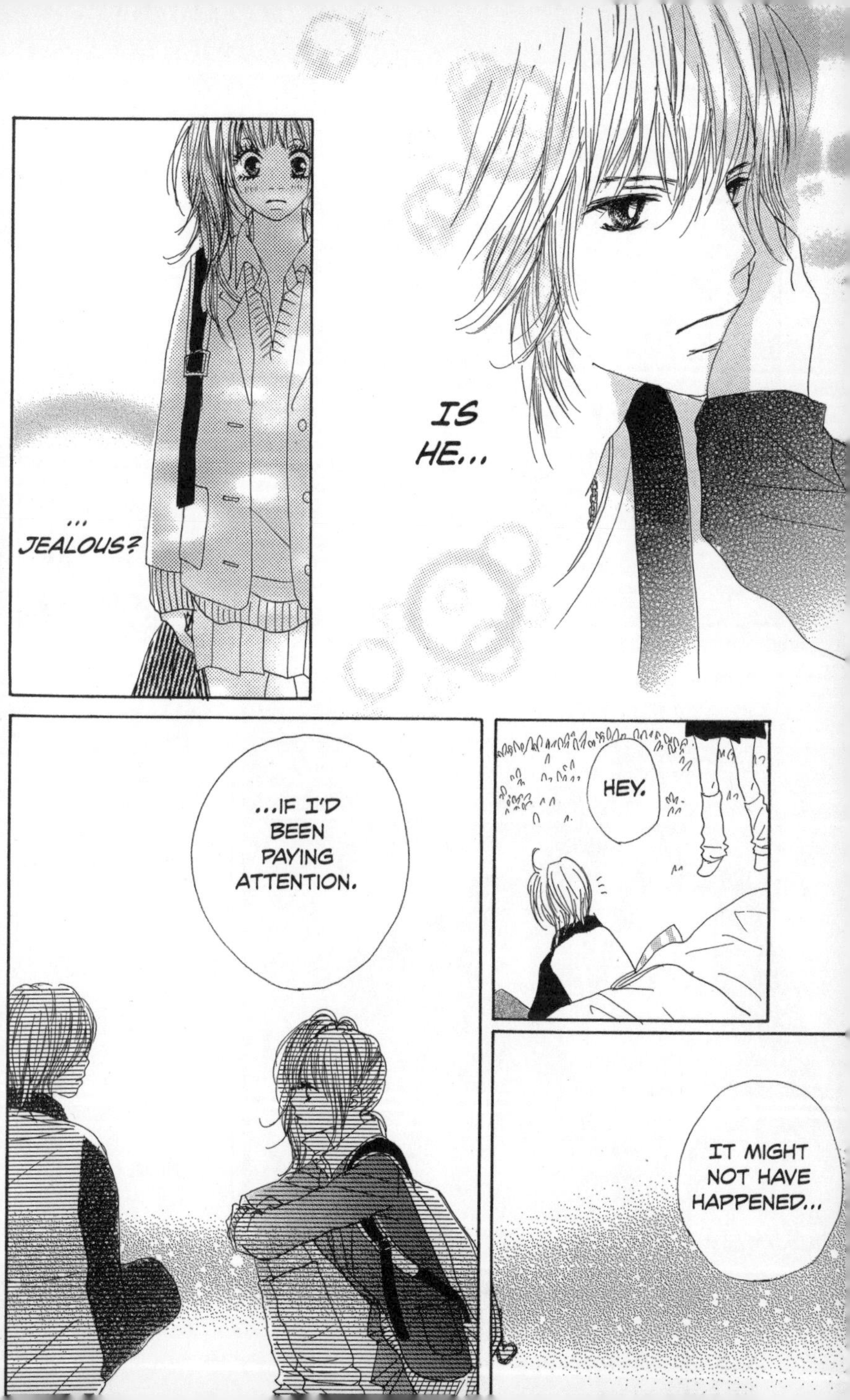
IS HE...
... JEALOUS?
HEY.
IT MIGHT NOT HAVE HAPPENED...
...IF I'D BEEN PAYING ATTENTION.

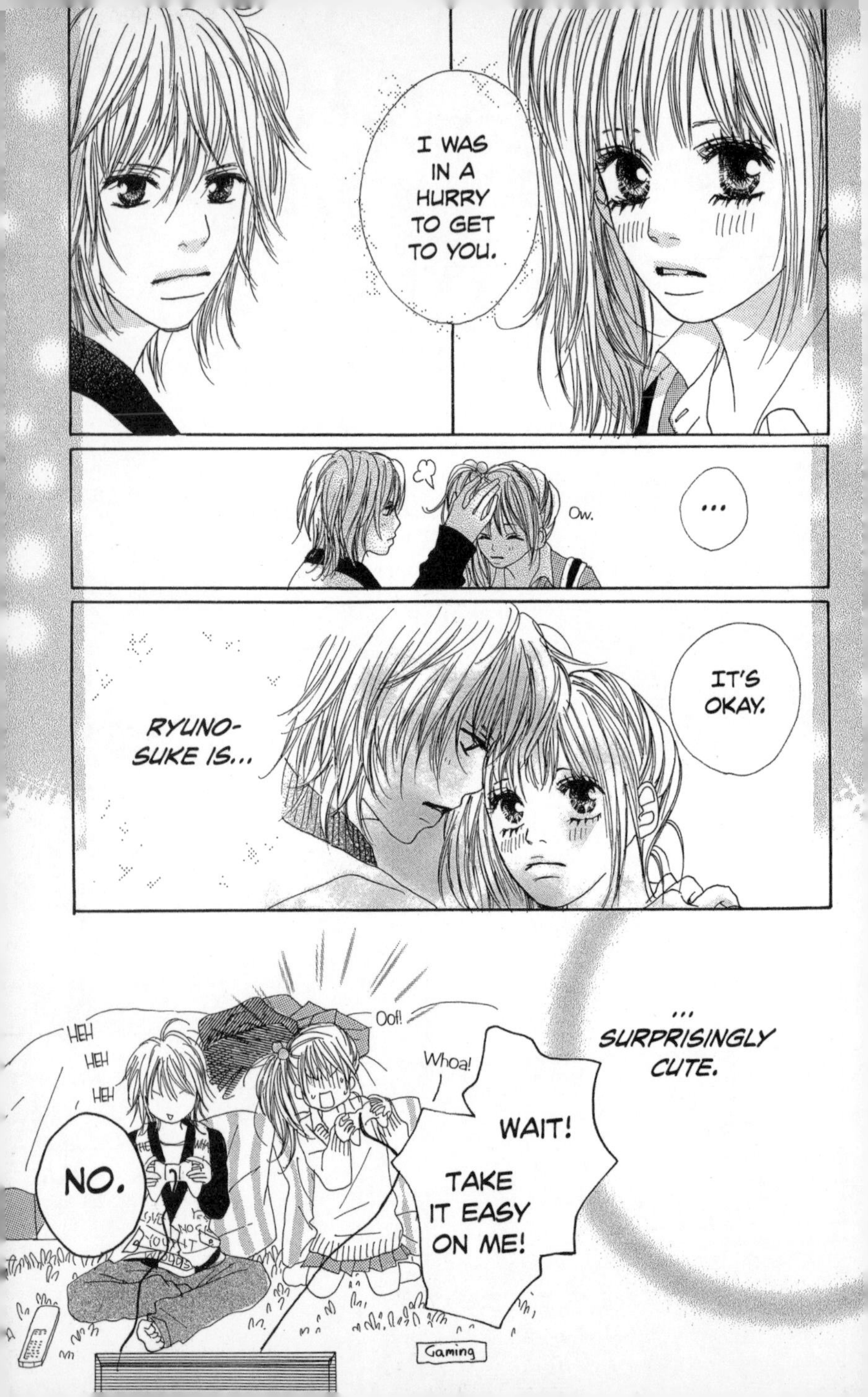
I WAS IN A HURRY TO GET TO YOU.
...
Ow.
IT'S OKAY.
RYUNO-SUKE IS...
... SURPRISINGLY CUTE.
Oof!
Whoa!
WAIT!
TAKE IT EASY ON ME!
HEH HEH HEH
NO.
Gaming

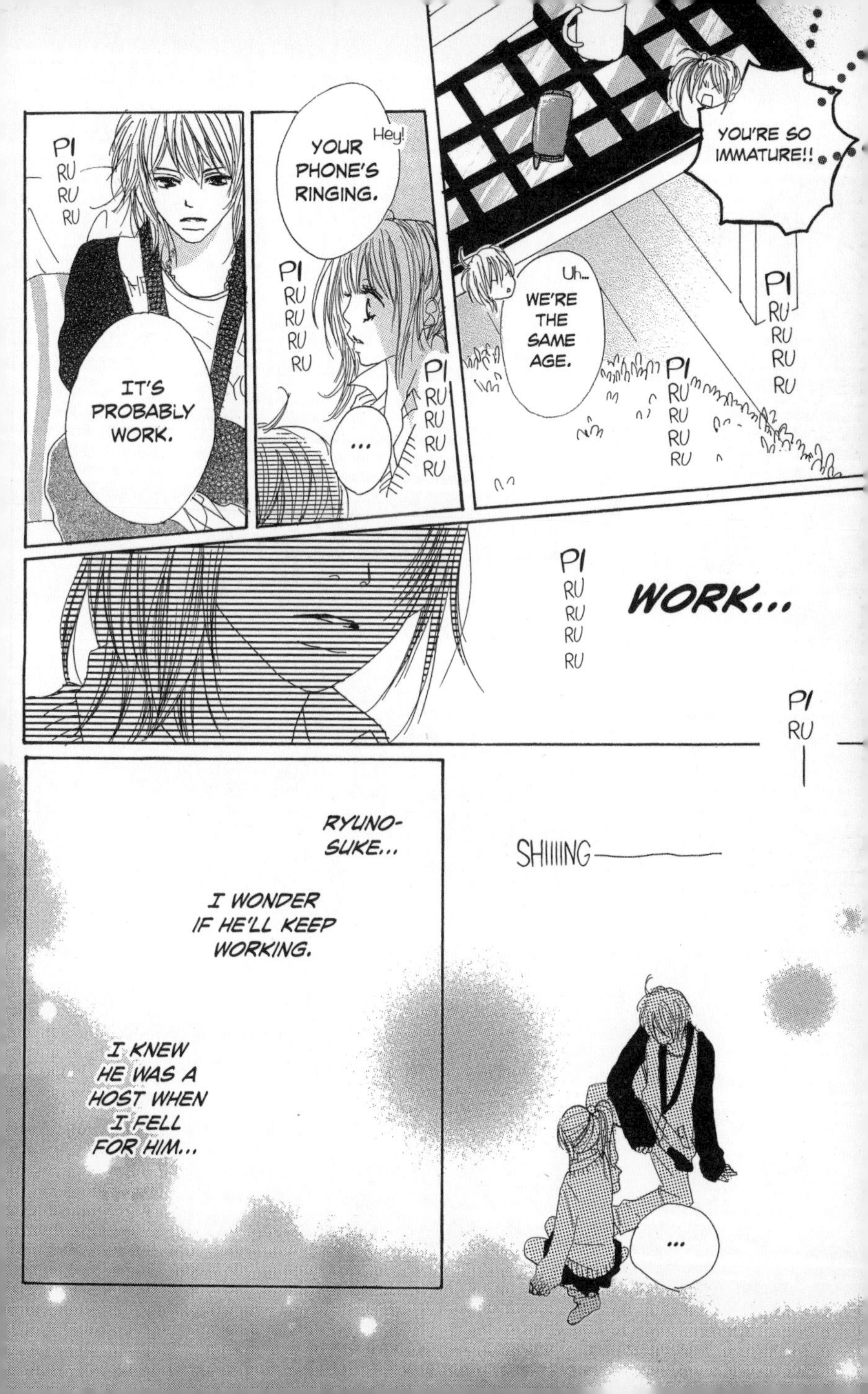
YOU'RE SO IMMATURE!!
Uh... WE'RE THE SAME AGE.
PI RU RU RU RU
PI RU RU RU RU
Hey! YOUR PHONE'S RINGING.
PI RU RU RU RU
PI RU RU RU RU
...
PI RU RU RU
IT'S PROBABLY WORK.
WORK...
PI RU RU RU RU
PI RU—
SHIIIING—
...
RYUNO-SUKE...
I WONDER IF HE'LL KEEP WORKING.
I KNEW HE WAS A HOST WHEN I FELL FOR HIM...

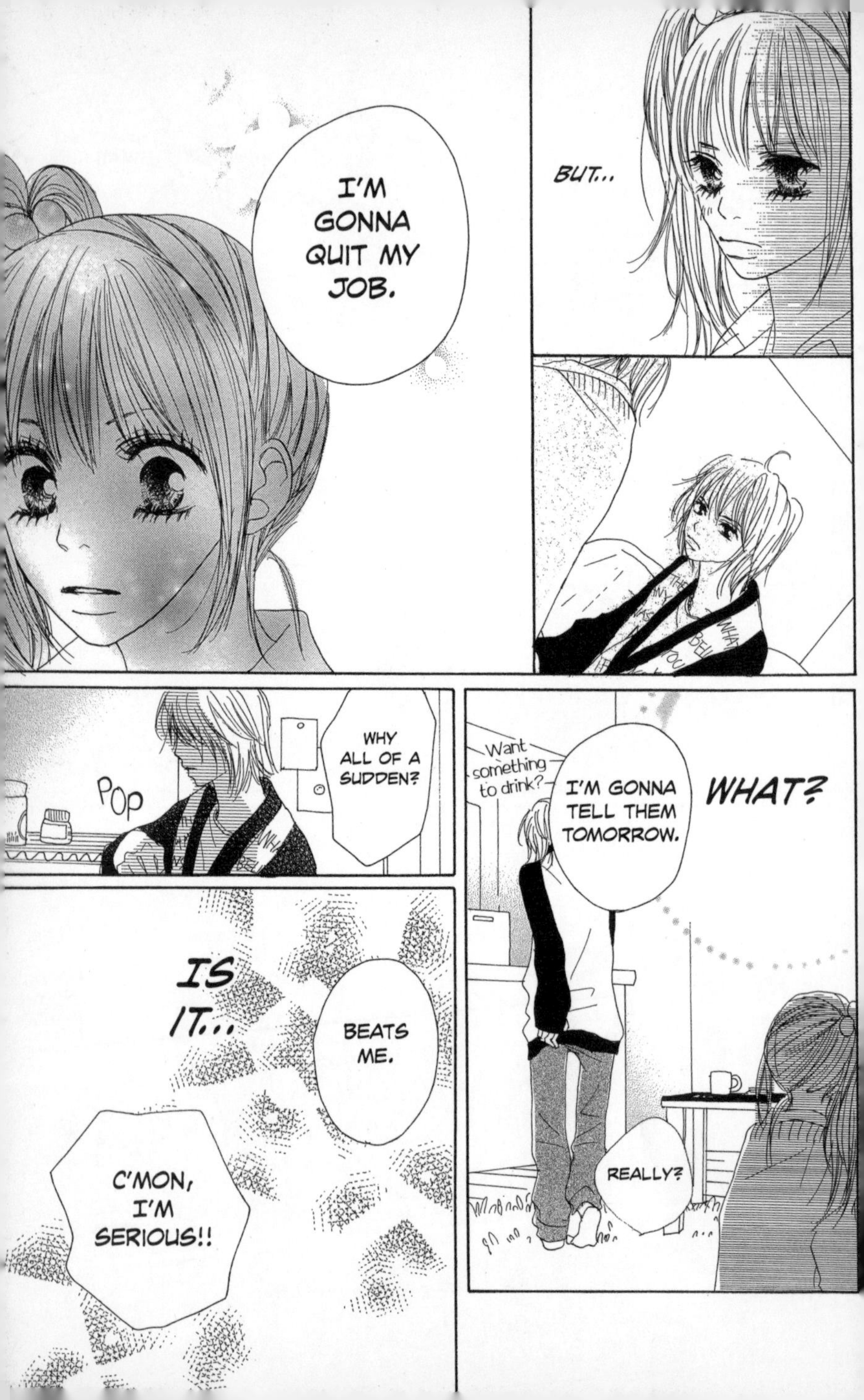
BUT...
I'M GONNA QUIT MY JOB.
WHAT?
I'M GONNA TELL THEM TOMORROW.
Want something to drink?
REALLY?
WHY ALL OF A SUDDEN?
POP
BEATS ME.
IS IT...
C'MON, I'M SERIOUS!!

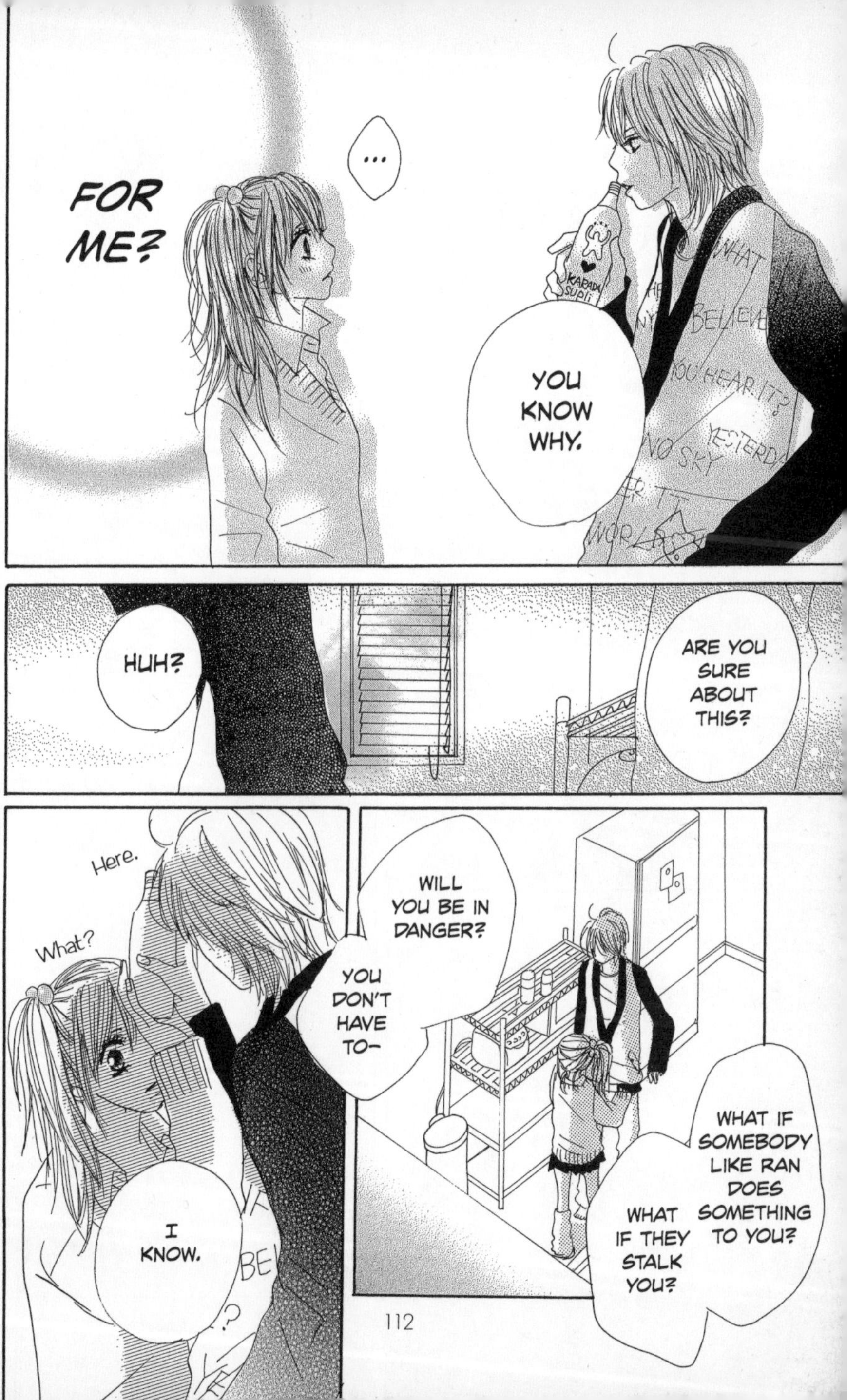
...
FOR ME?
YOU KNOW WHY.
ARE YOU SURE ABOUT THIS?
HUH?
WILL YOU BE IN DANGER?
WHAT IF SOMEBODY LIKE RAN DOES SOMETHING TO YOU?
WHAT IF THEY STALK YOU?
YOU DON'T HAVE TO—
Here.
What?
I KNOW.

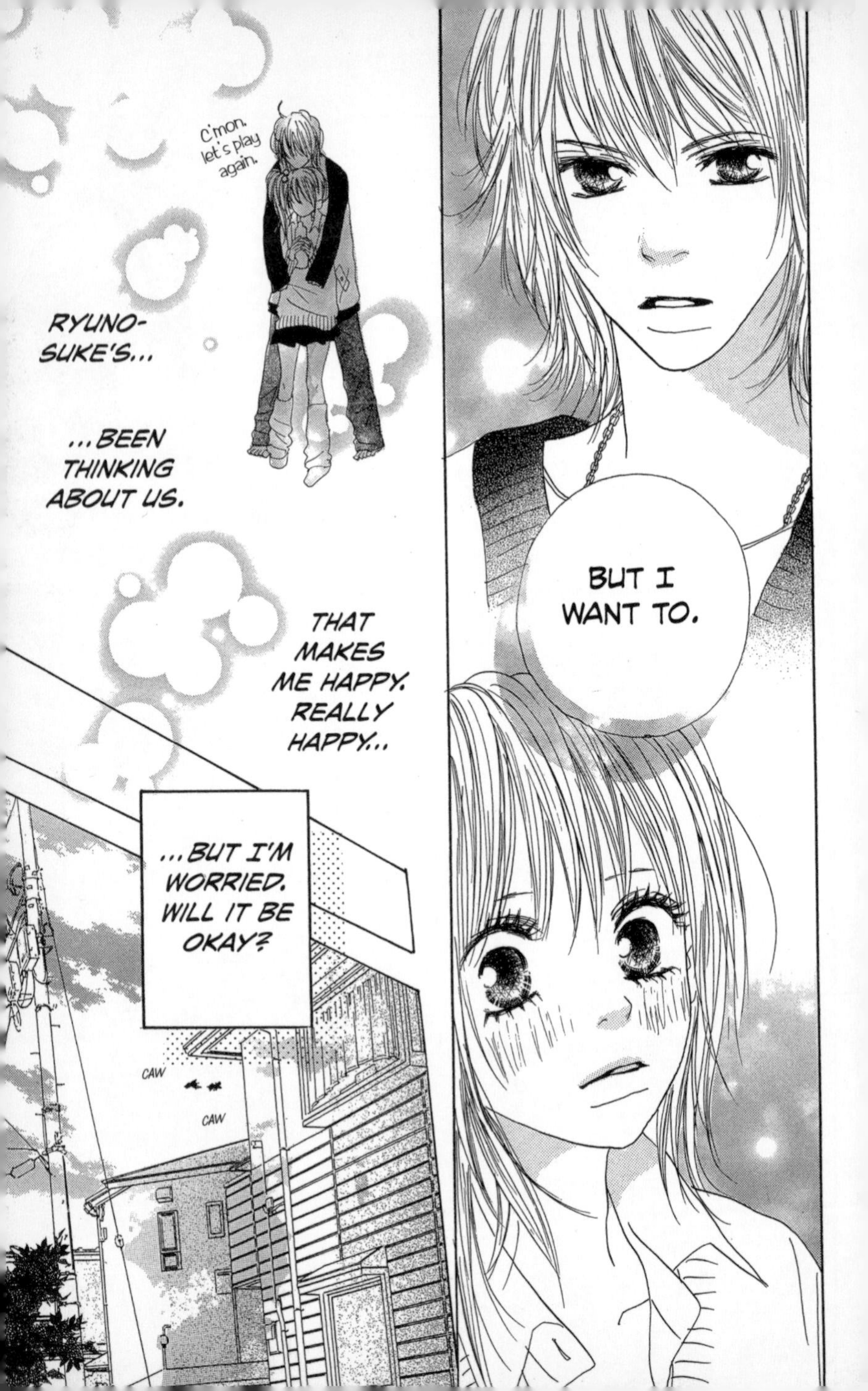
BUT I WANT TO.
C'mon, let's play again.
RYUNO-SUKE'S...
...BEEN THINKING ABOUT US.
THAT MAKES ME HAPPY. REALLY HAPPY...
...BUT I'M WORRIED. WILL IT BE OKAY?
CAW
CAW

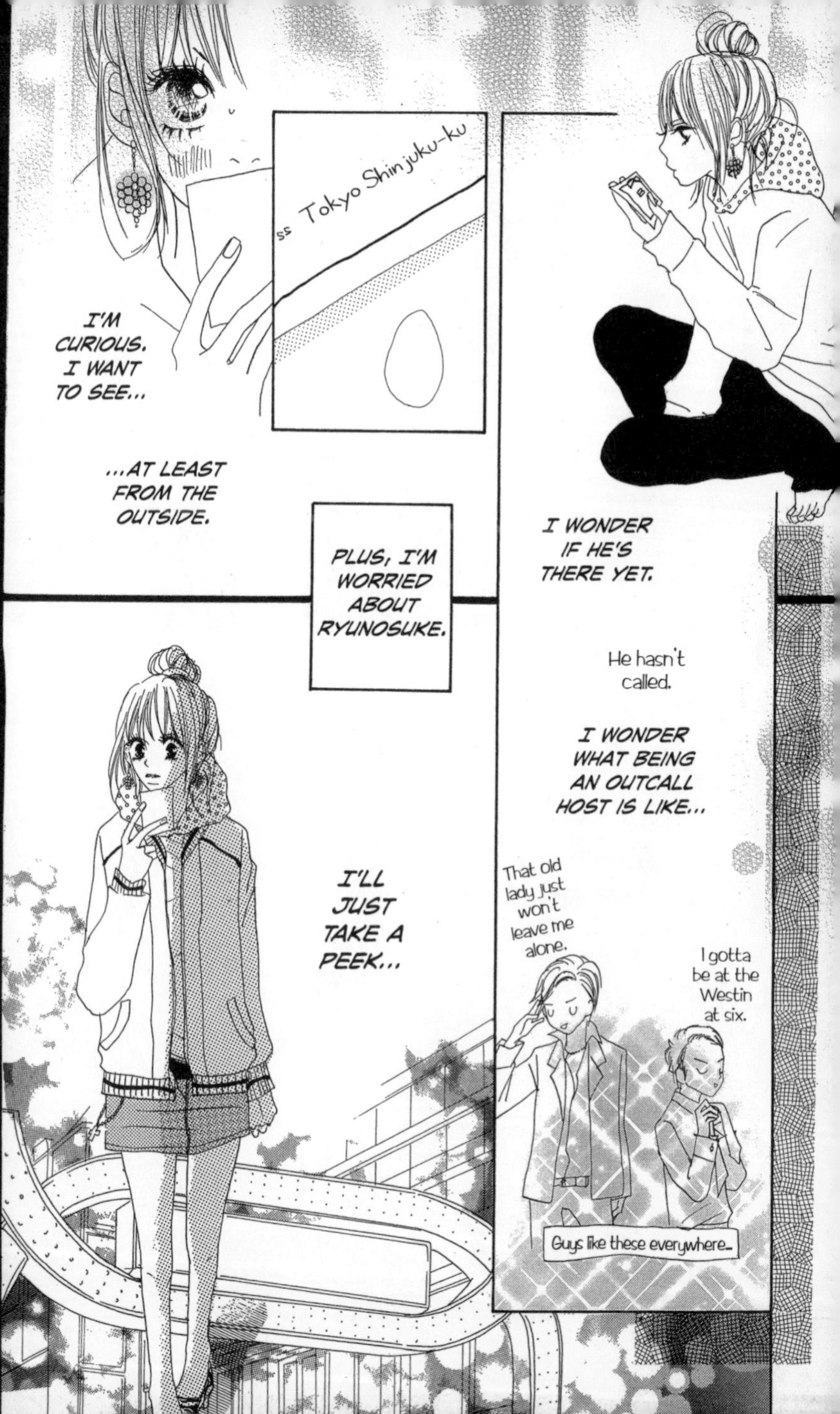
I WONDER IF HE'S THERE YET.
ss Tokyo Shinjuku-ku
I'M CURIOUS. I WANT TO SEE...
...AT LEAST FROM THE OUTSIDE.
PLUS, I'M WORRIED ABOUT RYUNOSUKE.
He hasn't called.
I WONDER WHAT BEING AN OUTCALL HOST IS LIKE...
That old lady just won't leave me alone.
I gotta be at the Westin at six.
Guys like these everywhere...
I'LL JUST TAKE A PEEK...

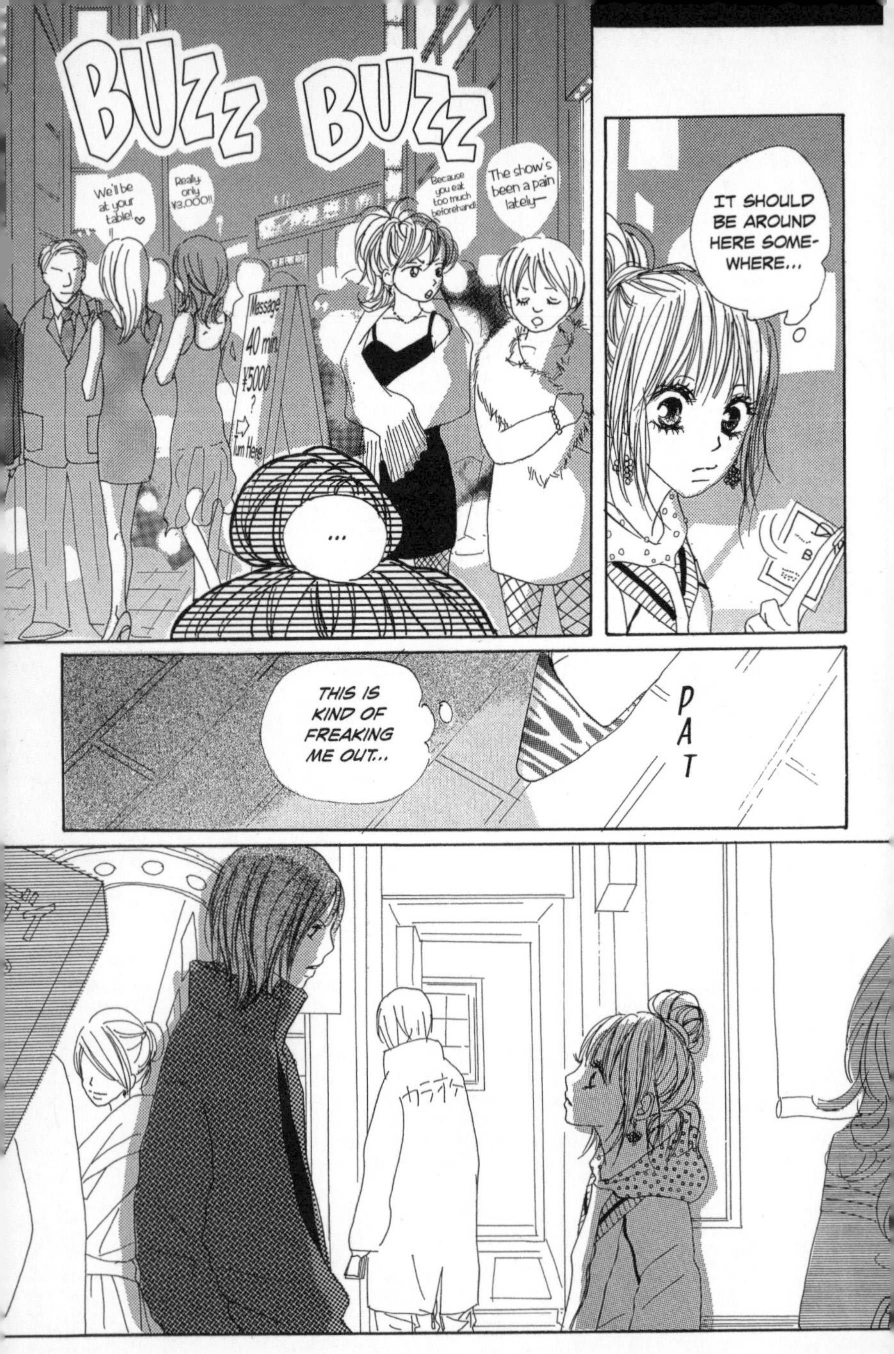
IT SHOULD BE AROUND HERE SOME-WHERE...
The show's been a pain lately—
Because you eat too much beforehand!!
BUZZ BUZZ
Really, only ¥3,000!!
We'll be at your table!♡
Message 40 min. ¥5000 ? Turn Here
...
PAT
THIS IS KIND OF FREAKING ME OUT...
カラオケ

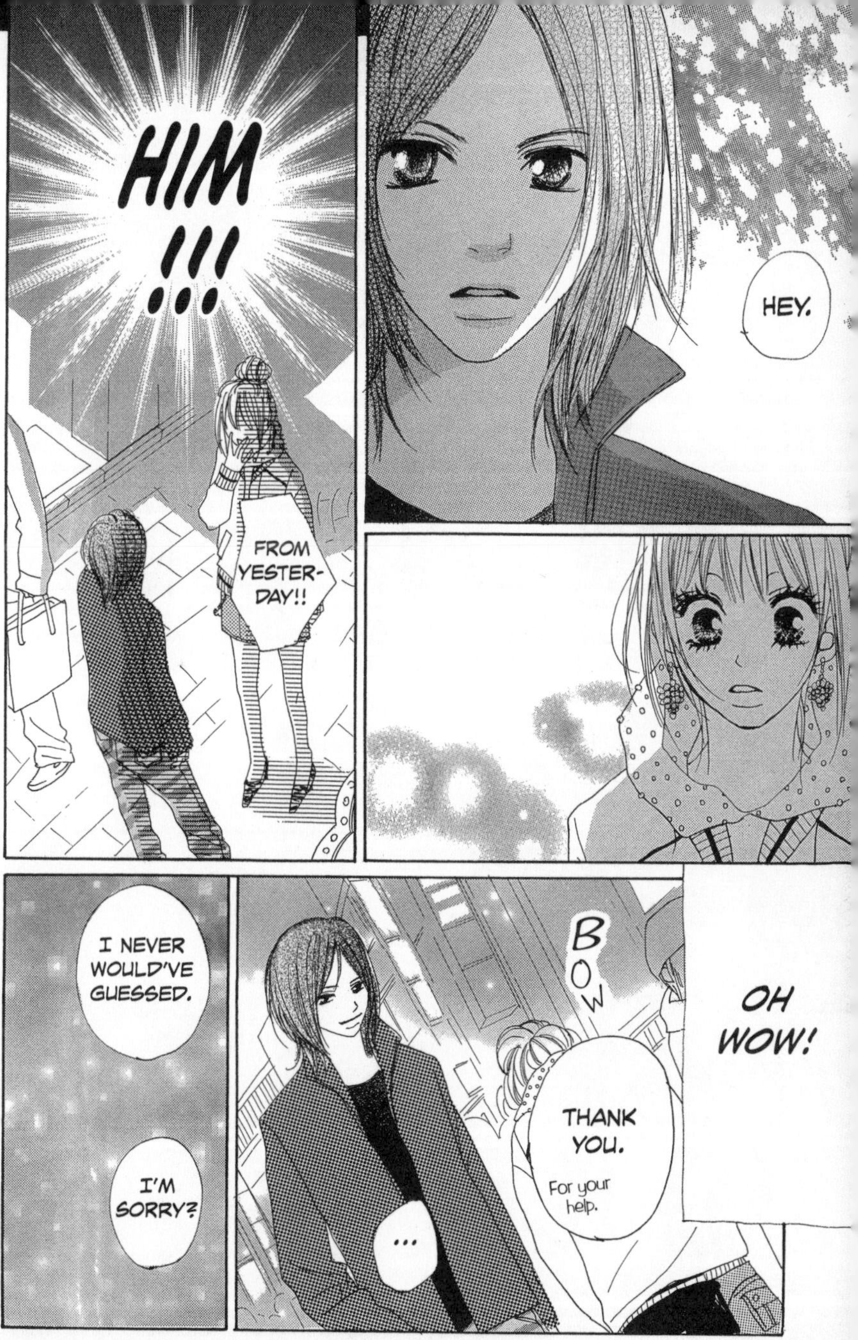
HEY.
HIM !!!
FROM YESTER-DAY!!
OH WOW!
BOW
THANK YOU.
For your help.
...
I NEVER WOULD'VE GUESSED.
I'M SORRY?

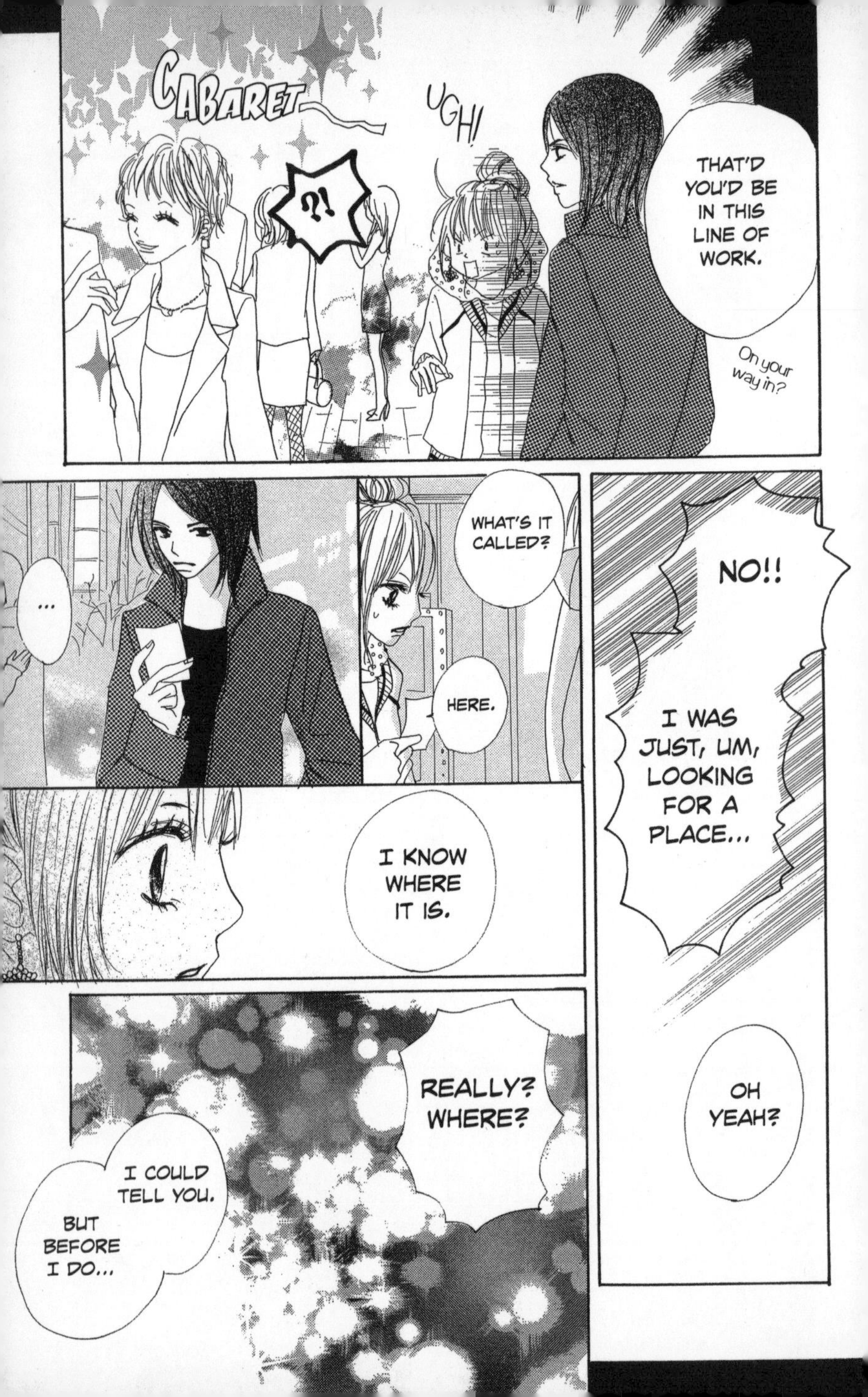
THAT'D YOU'D BE IN THIS LINE OF WORK.
On your way in?
UGH!
?!
CABARET
NO!!
I WAS JUST, UM, LOOKING FOR A PLACE...
OH YEAH?
WHAT'S IT CALLED?
HERE.
...
I KNOW WHERE IT IS.
REALLY? WHERE?
I COULD TELL YOU.
BUT BEFORE I DO...

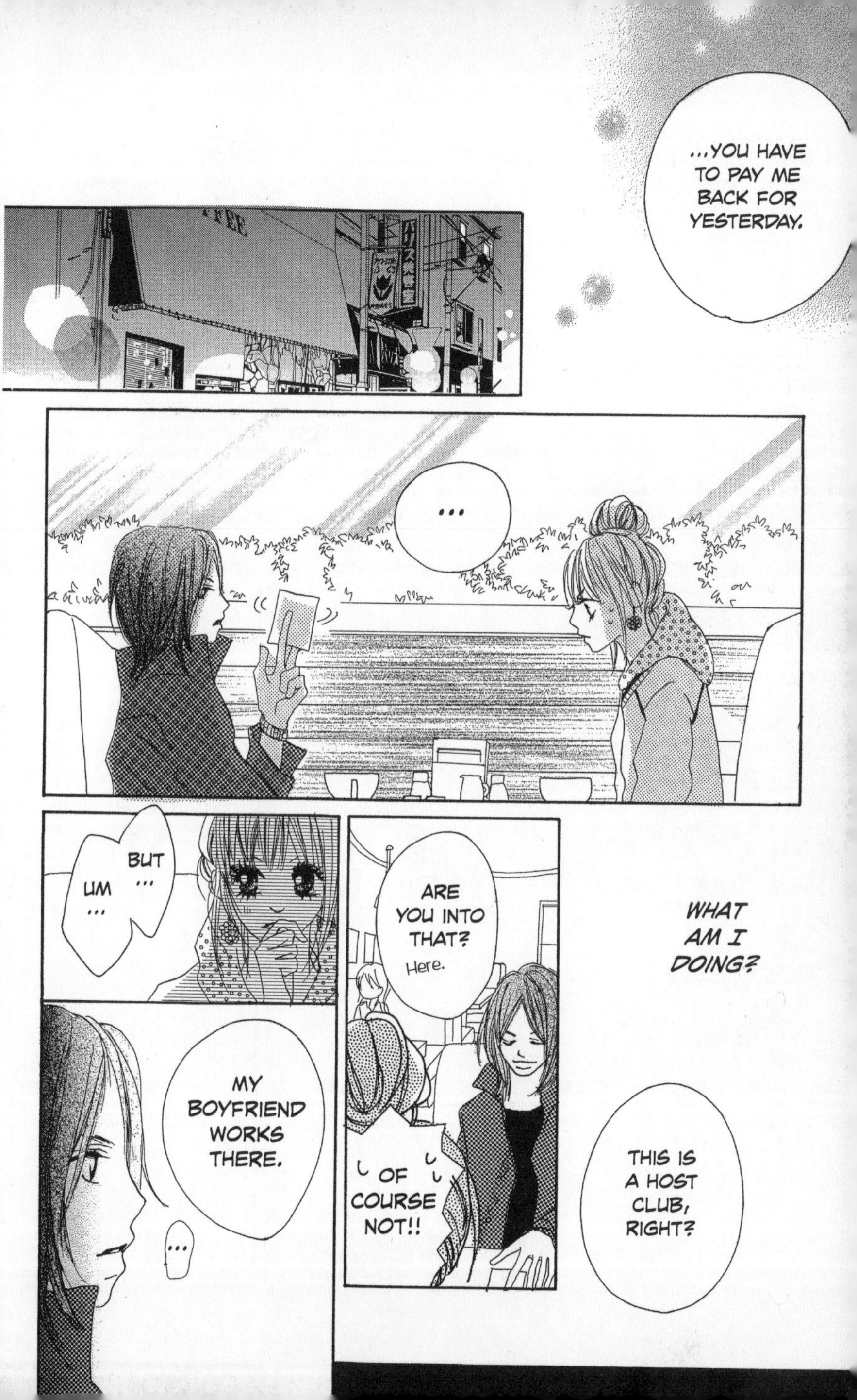
...YOU HAVE TO PAY ME BACK FOR YESTERDAY.
...
WHAT AM I DOING?
THIS IS A HOST CLUB, RIGHT?
ARE YOU INTO THAT?
Here.
OF COURSE NOT!!
UM...
BUT...
MY BOYFRIEND WORKS THERE.
...

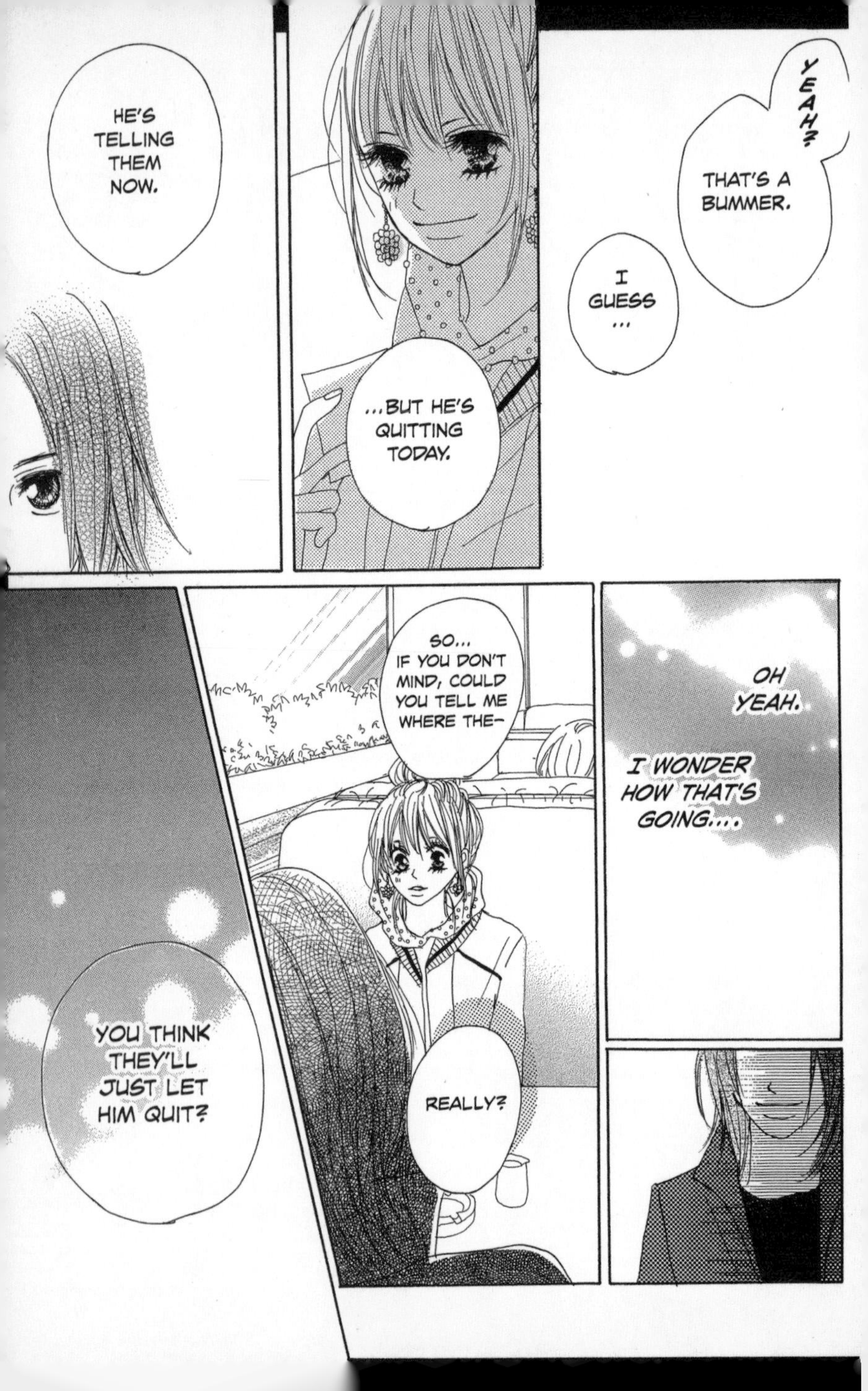
YEAH?
THAT'S A BUMMER.
I GUESS...
...BUT HE'S QUITTING TODAY.
HE'S TELLING THEM NOW.
OH YEAH.
I WONDER HOW THAT'S GOING....
SO... IF YOU DON'T MIND, COULD YOU TELL ME WHERE THE-
REALLY?
YOU THINK THEY'LL JUST LET HIM QUIT?

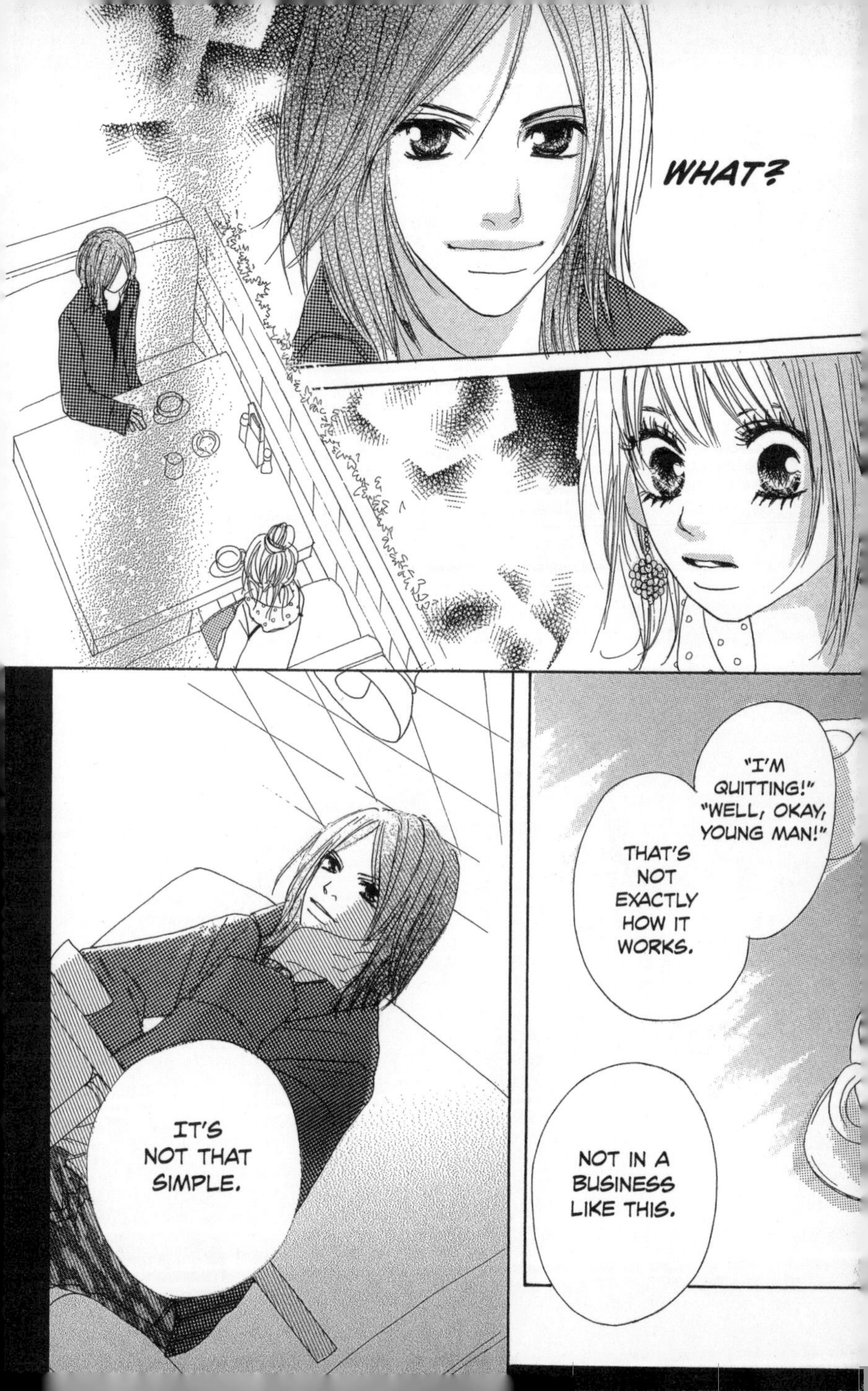
WHAT?
"I'M QUITTING!" "WELL, OKAY, YOUNG MAN!"
THAT'S NOT EXACTLY HOW IT WORKS.
NOT IN A BUSINESS LIKE THIS.
IT'S NOT THAT SIMPLE.

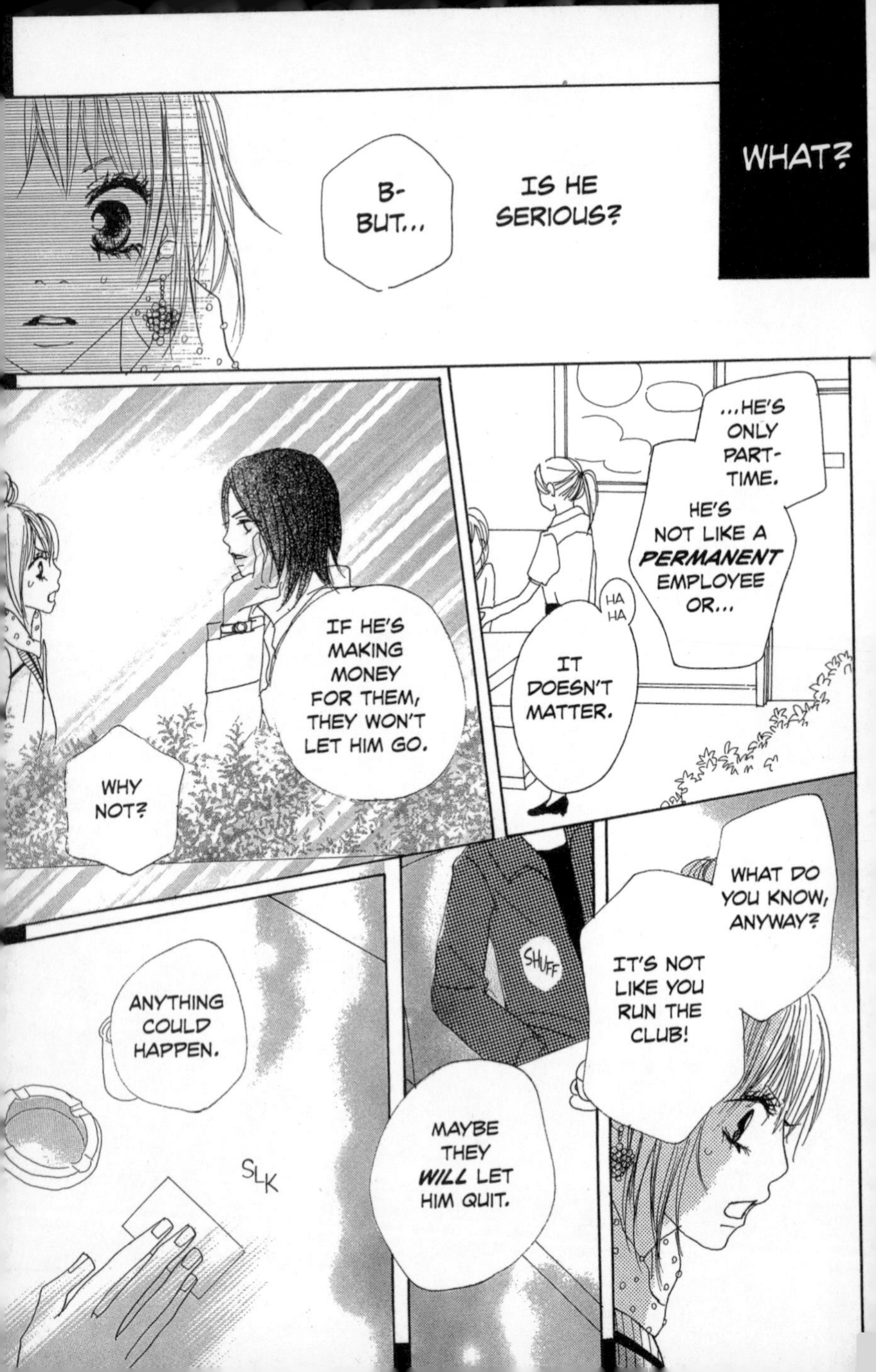

WHAT?
IS HE SERIOUS?
B-BUT...
...HE'S ONLY PART-TIME.
HE'S NOT LIKE A *PERMANENT* EMPLOYEE OR...
HA HA
IT DOESN'T MATTER.
IF HE'S MAKING MONEY FOR THEM, THEY WON'T LET HIM GO.
WHY NOT?
WHAT DO YOU KNOW, ANYWAY?
IT'S NOT LIKE YOU RUN THE CLUB!
SHUFF
ANYTHING COULD HAPPEN.
SLK
MAYBE THEY *WILL* LET HIM QUIT.

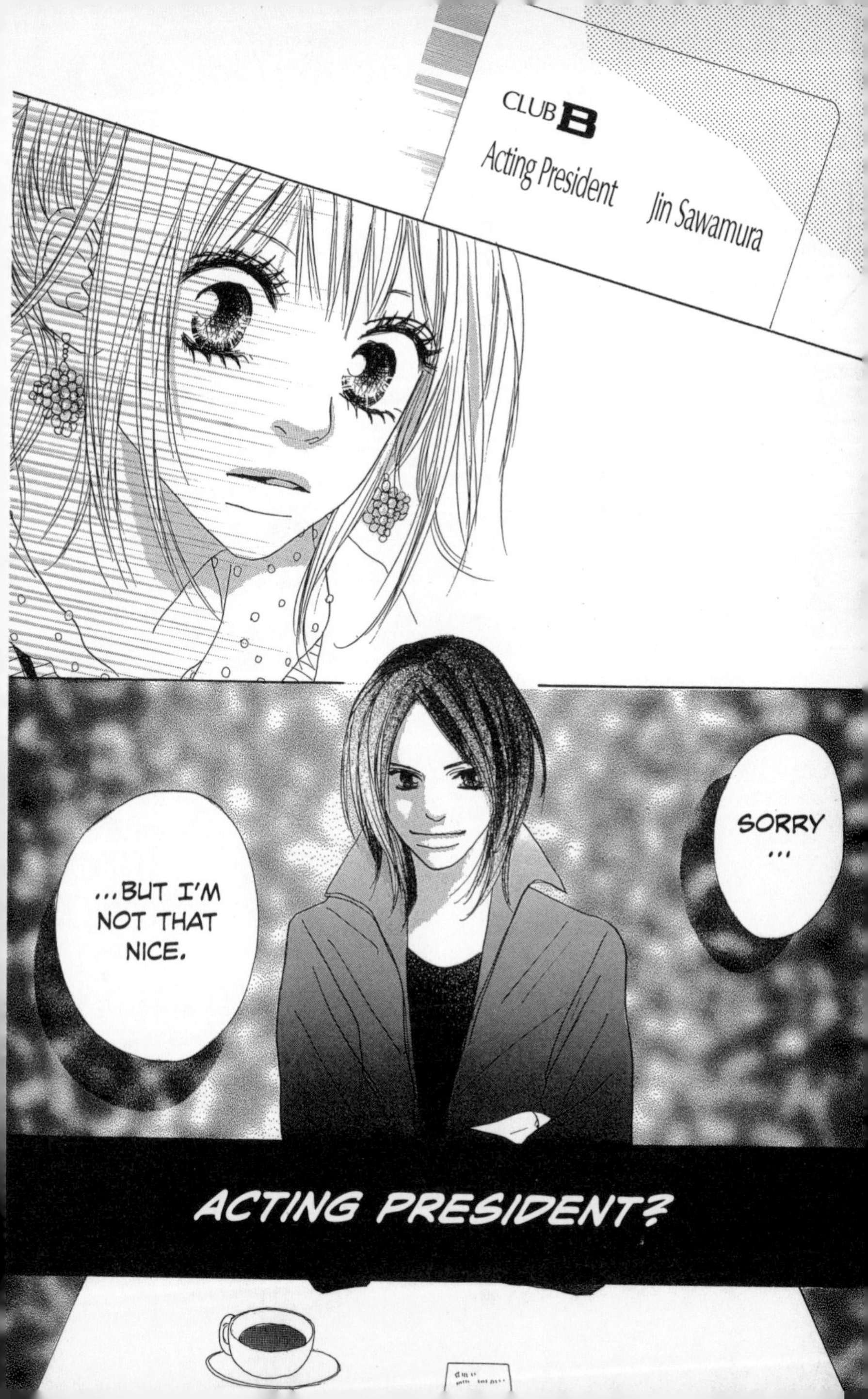
CLUB B
Acting President Jin Sawamura
SORRY...
...BUT I'M NOT THAT NICE.
ACTING PRESIDENT?

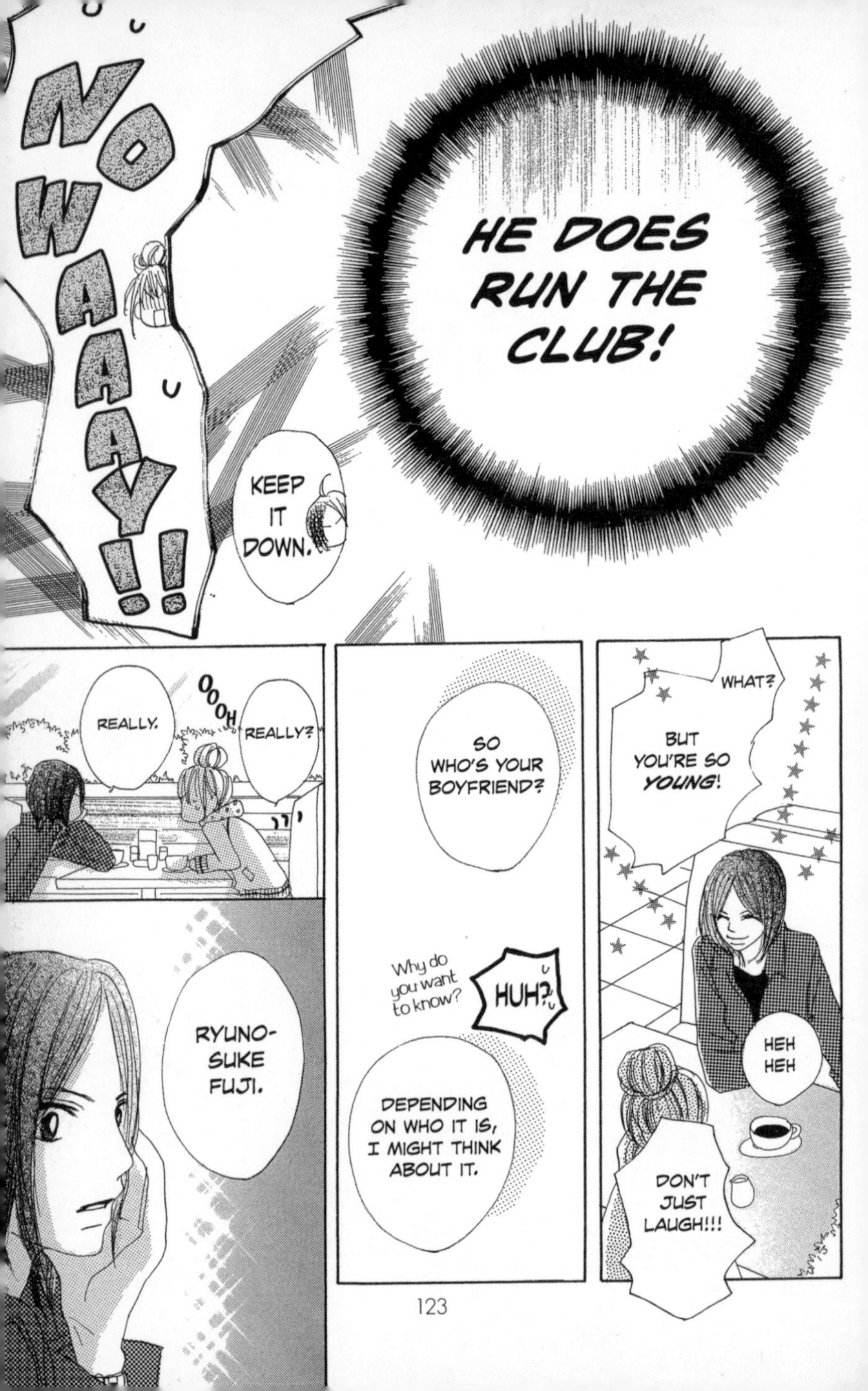
HE DOES RUN THE CLUB!
NO WAAAY!!
KEEP IT DOWN.
WHAT?
BUT YOU'RE SO *YOUNG*!
HEH HEH
DON'T JUST LAUGH!!!
SO WHO'S YOUR BOYFRIEND?
HUH?
Why do you want to know?
DEPENDING ON WHO IT IS, I MIGHT THINK ABOUT IT.
REALLY?
OOOH
REALLY.
RYUNOSUKE FUJI.

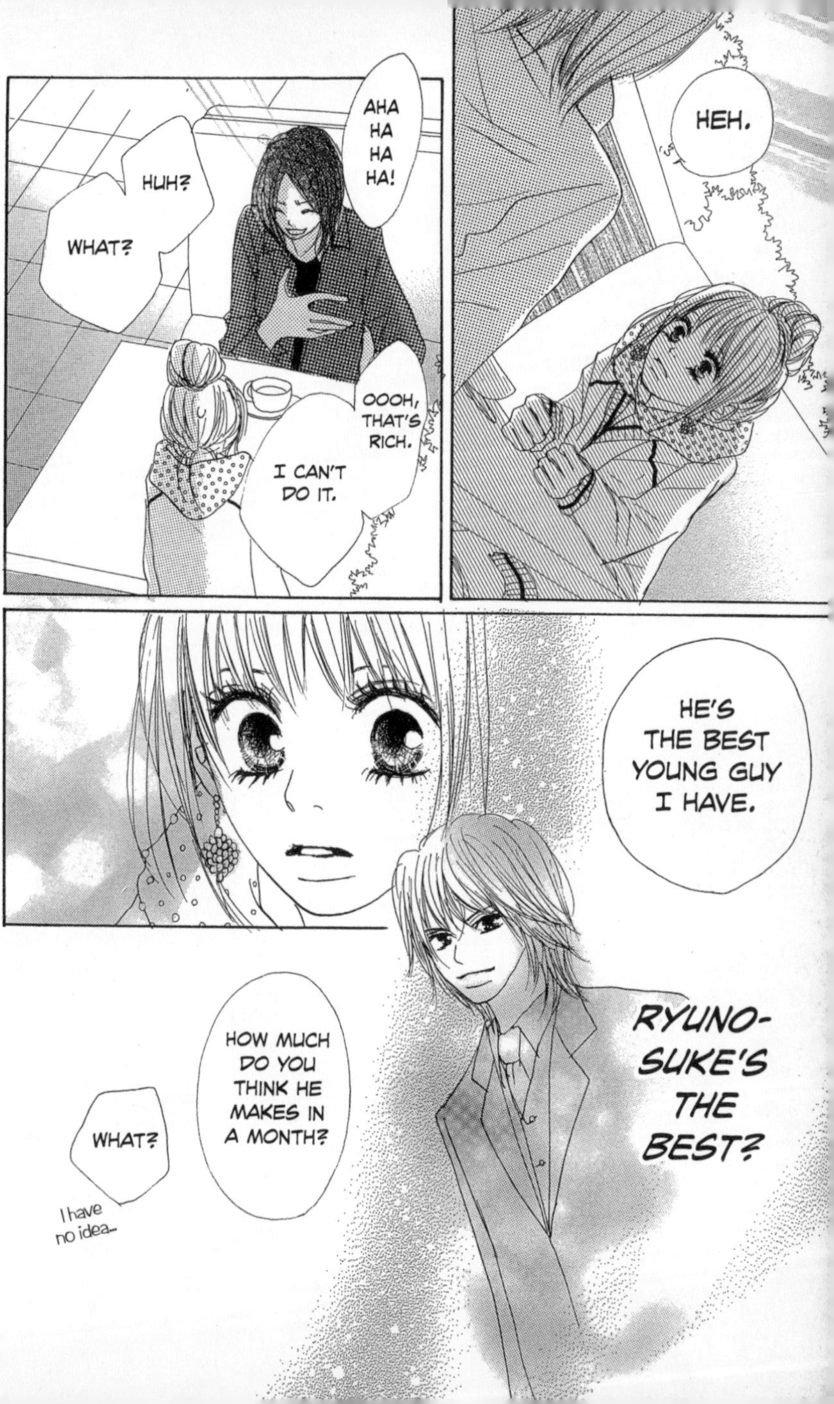
HEH.
AHA HA HA HA!
HUH?
WHAT?
OOOH, THAT'S RICH.
I CAN'T DO IT.
HE'S THE BEST YOUNG GUY I HAVE.
RYUNO-SUKE'S THE BEST?
HOW MUCH DO YOU THINK HE MAKES IN A MONTH?
WHAT?
I have no idea...

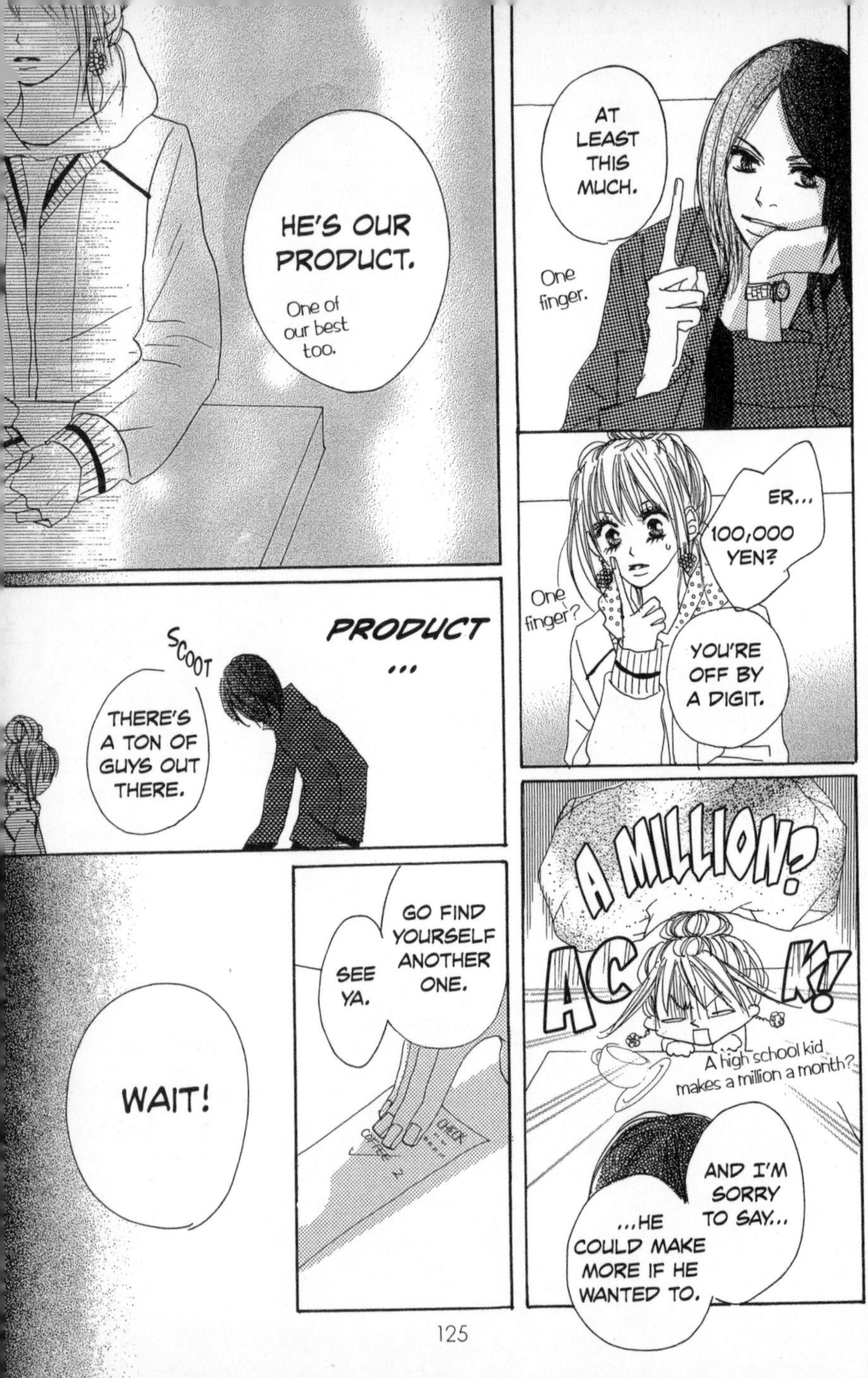
AT LEAST THIS MUCH.
One finger.
ER... 100,000 YEN?
One finger?
YOU'RE OFF BY A DIGIT.
A MILLION?!
ACK!
A high school kid makes a million a month?
AND I'M SORRY TO SAY...
...HE COULD MAKE MORE IF HE WANTED TO.
HE'S OUR PRODUCT.
One of our best too.
PRODUCT ...
SCOOT
THERE'S A TON OF GUYS OUT THERE.
GO FIND YOURSELF ANOTHER ONE.
SEE YA.
WAIT!

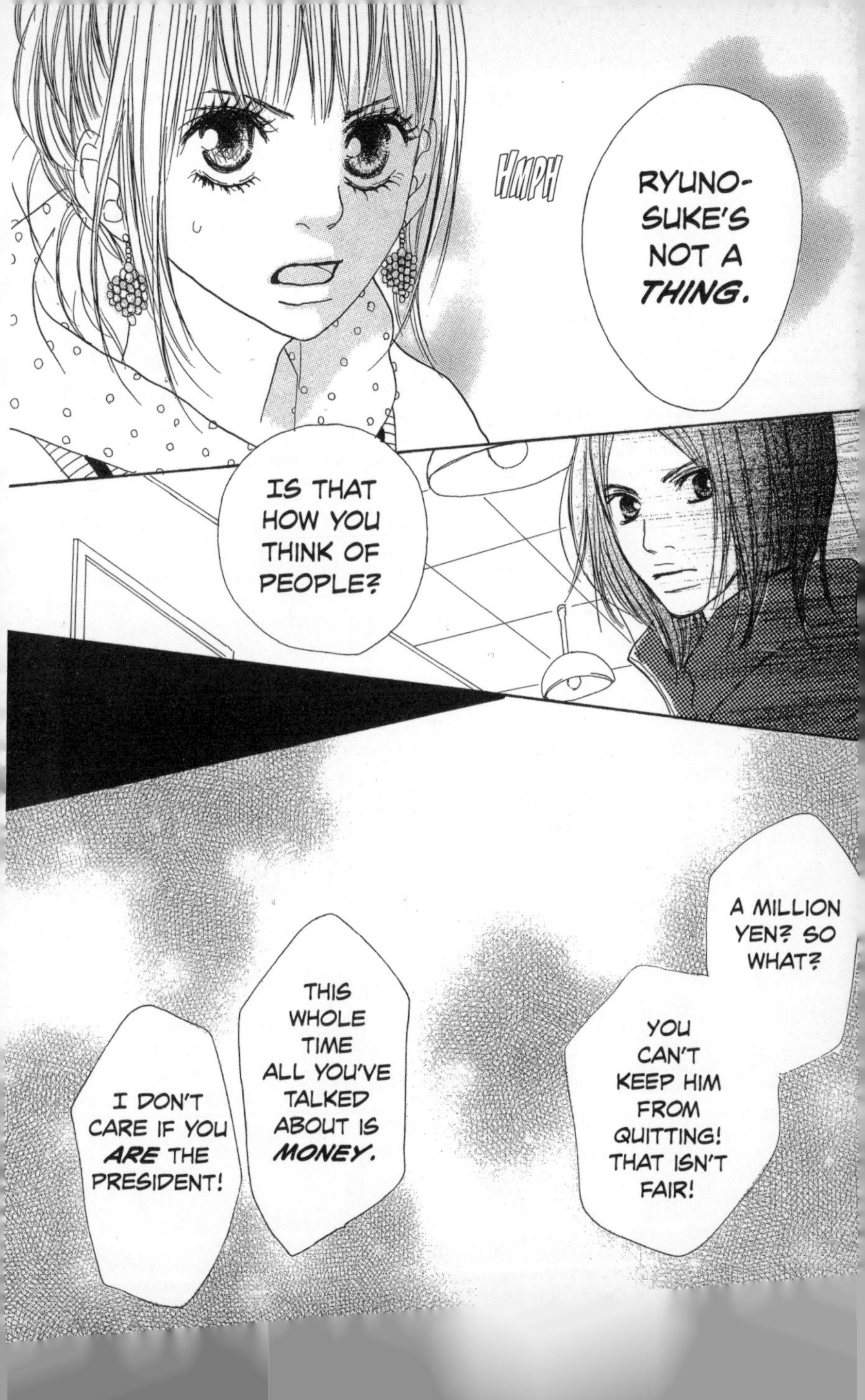
HMPH
RYUNO-SUKE'S NOT A *THING*.
IS THAT HOW YOU THINK OF PEOPLE?
A MILLION YEN? SO WHAT?
YOU CAN'T KEEP HIM FROM QUITTING! THAT ISN'T FAIR!
THIS WHOLE TIME ALL YOU'VE TALKED ABOUT IS *MONEY*.
I DON'T CARE IF YOU *ARE* THE PRESIDENT!

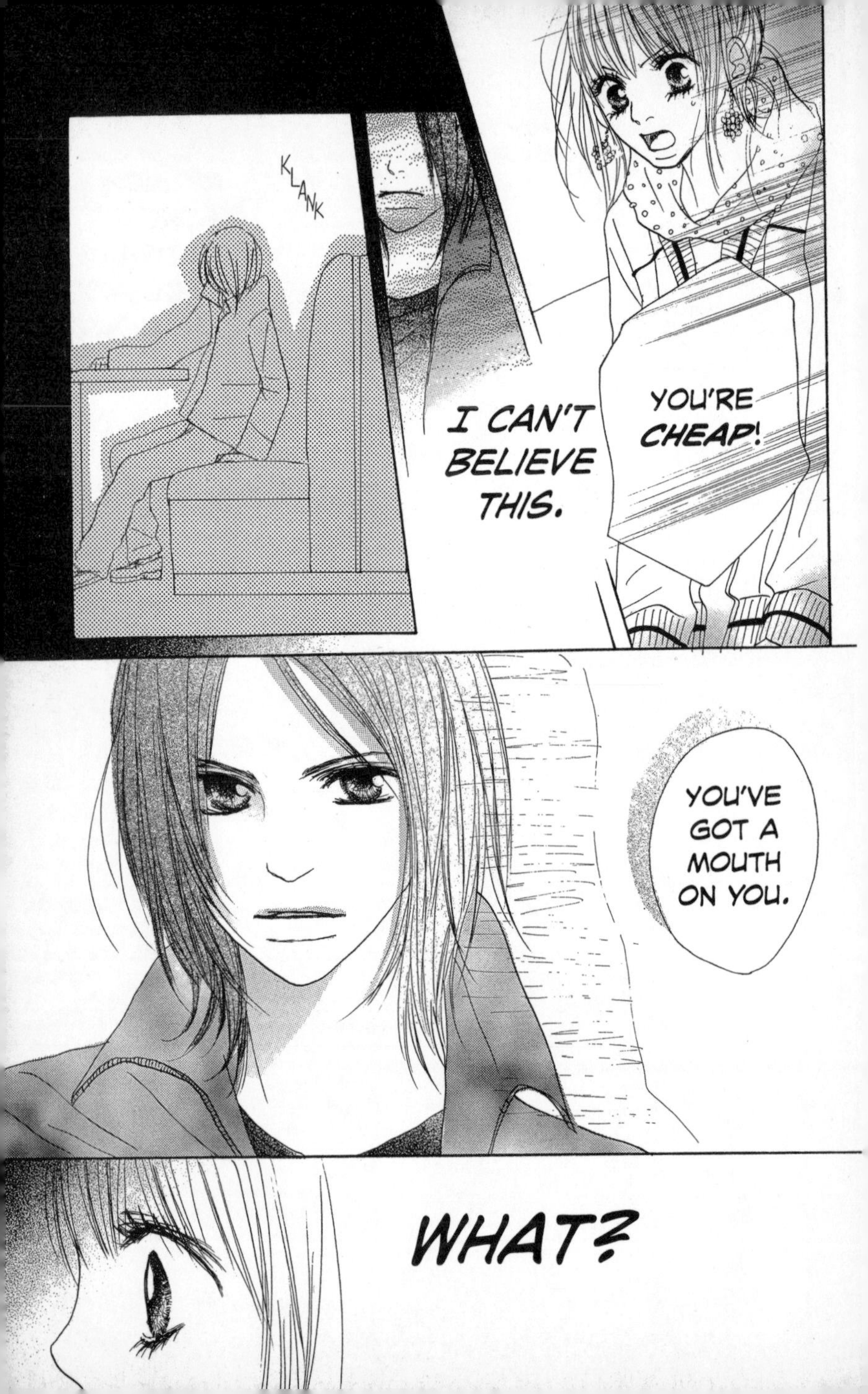
YOU'RE CHEAP!
I CAN'T BELIEVE THIS.
KLANK
YOU'VE GOT A MOUTH ON YOU.
WHAT?

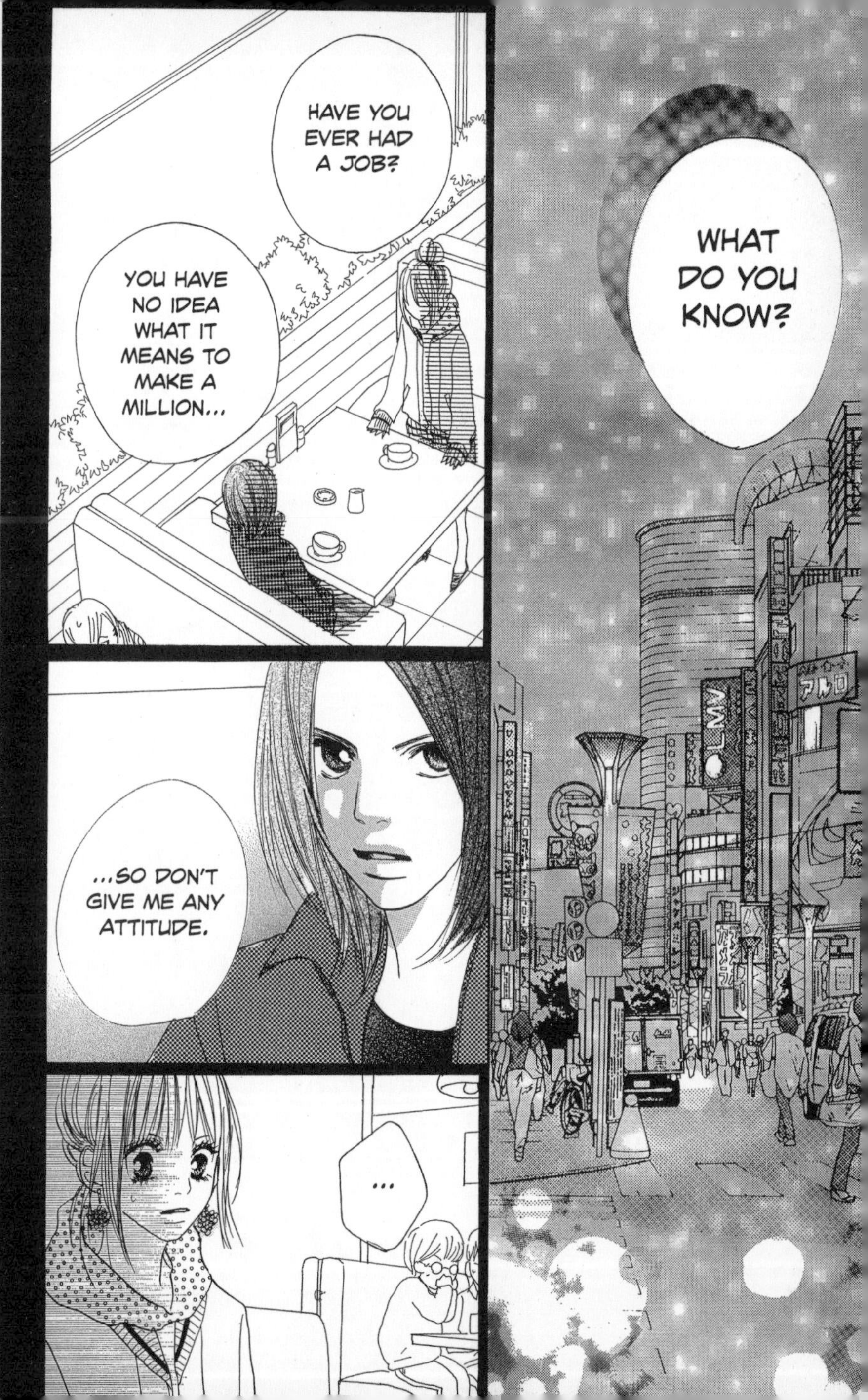
WHAT DO YOU KNOW?
HAVE YOU EVER HAD A JOB?
YOU HAVE NO IDEA WHAT IT MEANS TO MAKE A MILLION...
...SO DON'T GIVE ME ANY ATTITUDE.
...

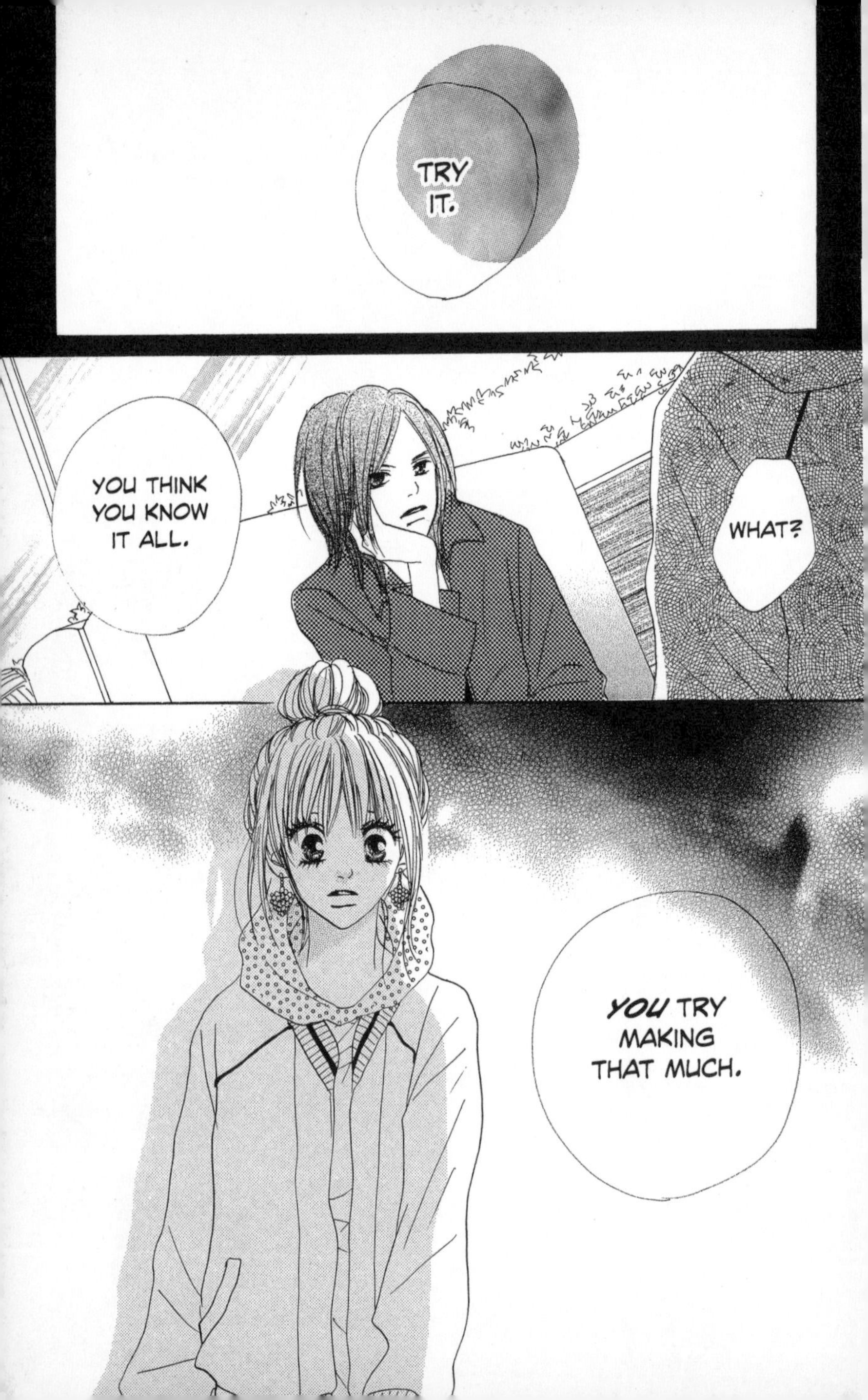
TRY IT.
WHAT?
YOU THINK YOU KNOW IT ALL.
YOU TRY MAKING THAT MUCH.

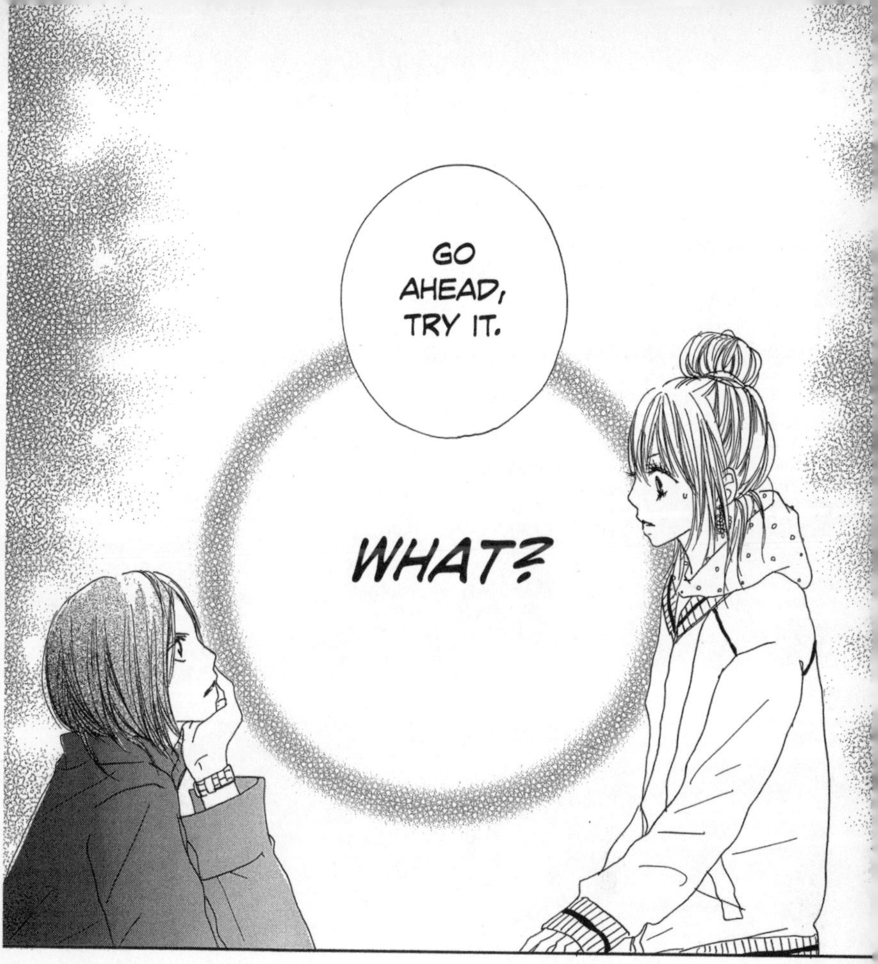
GO AHEAD, TRY IT.
WHAT?

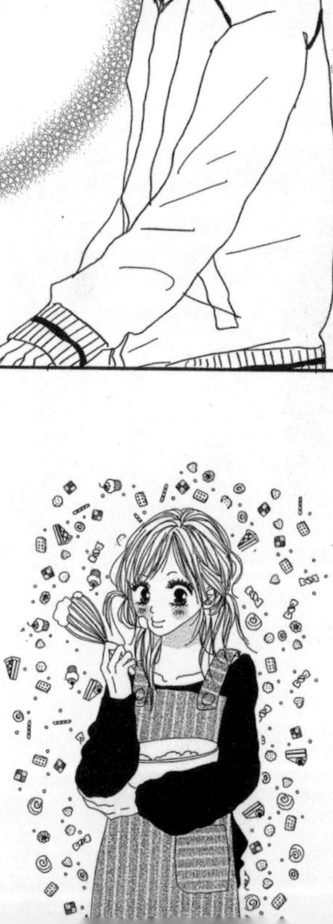

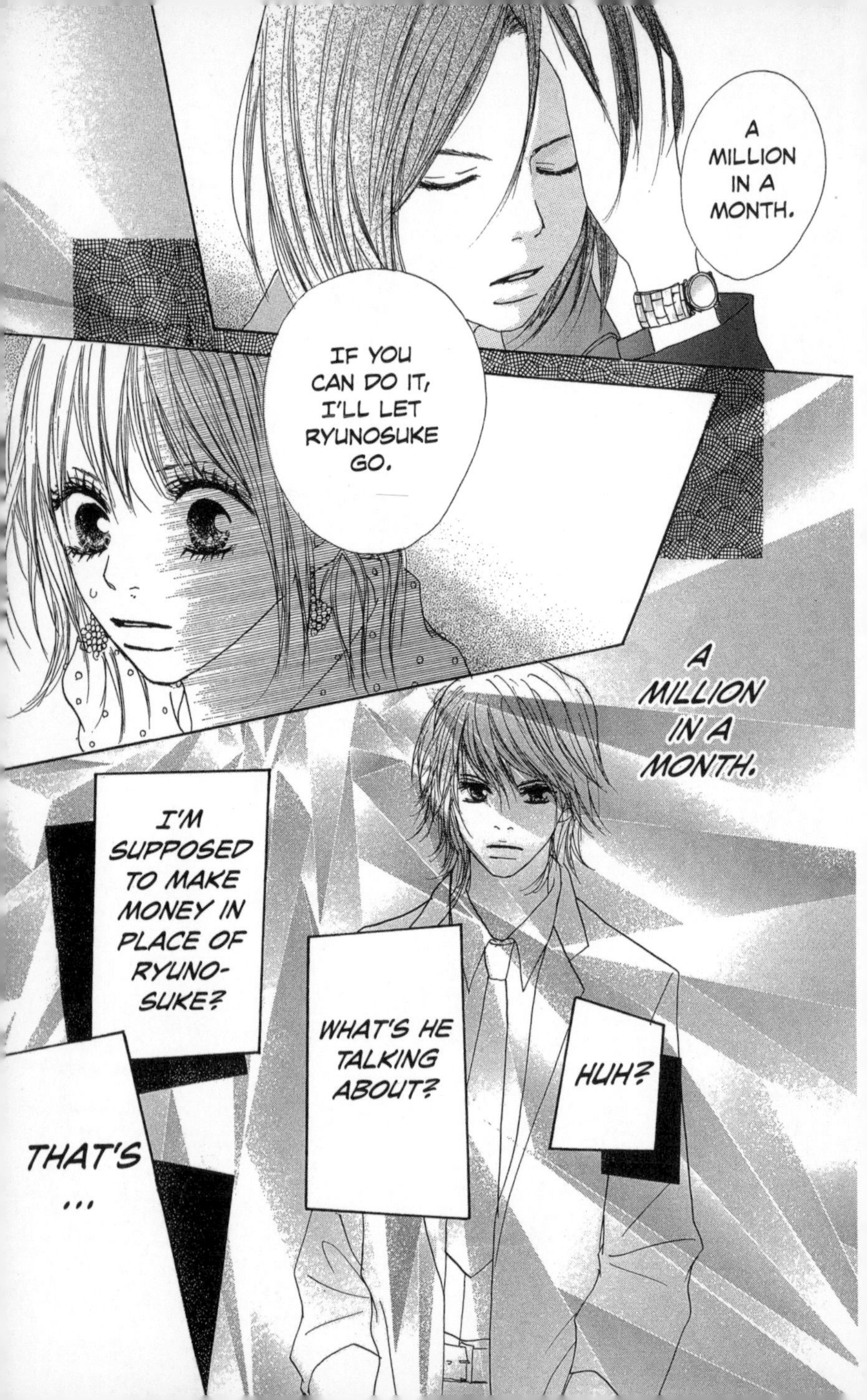
A MILLION IN A MONTH.
IF YOU CAN DO IT, I'LL LET RYUNOSUKE GO.
A MILLION IN A MONTH.
HUH?
WHAT'S HE TALKING ABOUT?
I'M SUPPOSED TO MAKE MONEY IN PLACE OF RYUNO-SUKE?
THAT'S ...

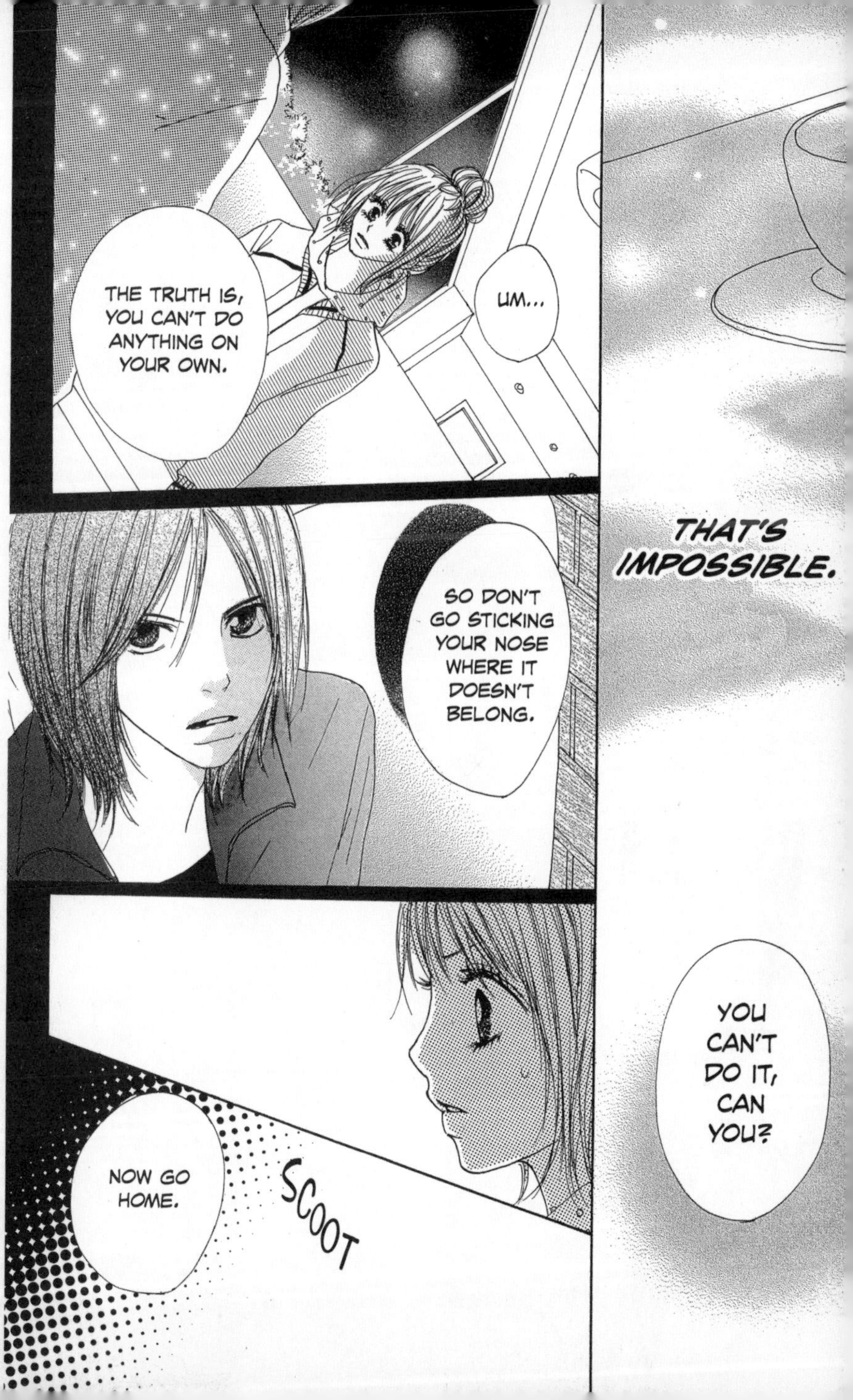
THAT'S IMPOSSIBLE.
YOU CAN'T DO IT, CAN YOU?
UM...
THE TRUTH IS, YOU CAN'T DO ANYTHING ON YOUR OWN.
SO DON'T GO STICKING YOUR NOSE WHERE IT DOESN'T BELONG.
SCOOT
NOW GO HOME.

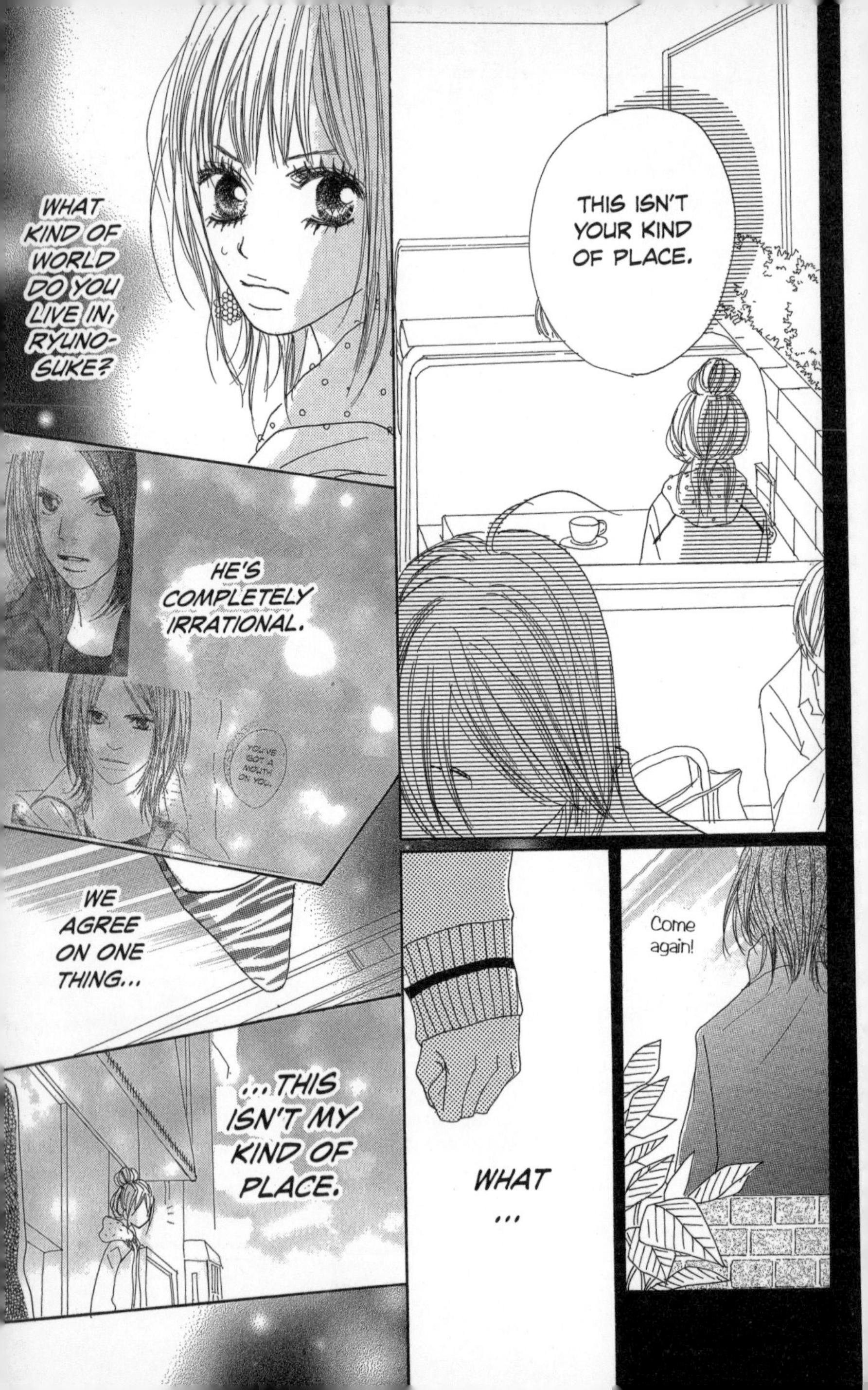
THIS ISN'T YOUR KIND OF PLACE.
WHAT KIND OF WORLD DO YOU LIVE IN, RYUNOSUKE?
HE'S COMPLETELY IRRATIONAL.
YOU'VE GOT A MOUTH ON YOU.
Come again!
WHAT ...
WE AGREE ON ONE THING...
...THIS ISN'T MY KIND OF PLACE.

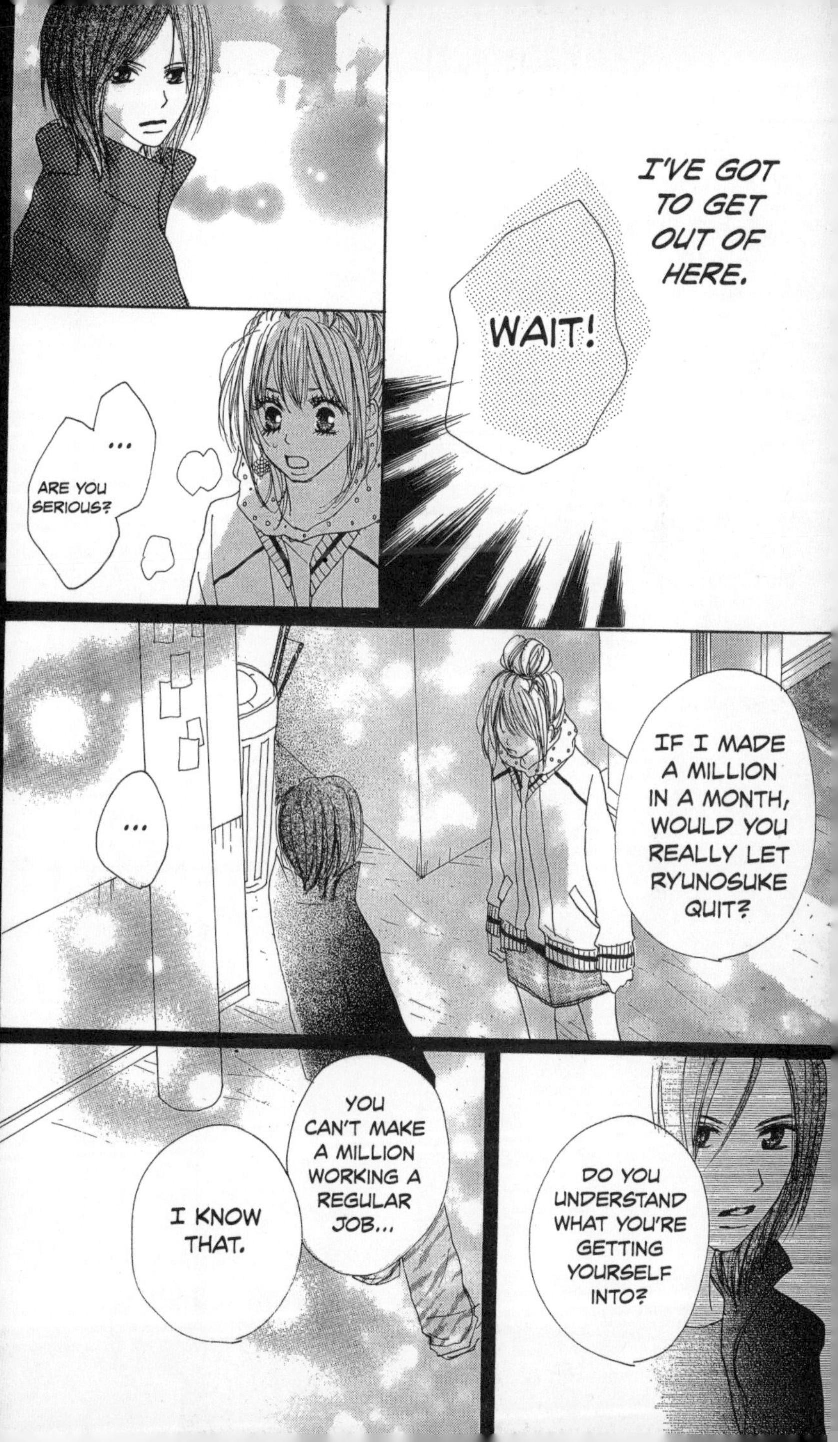
I'VE GOT TO GET OUT OF HERE.
WAIT!
...
ARE YOU SERIOUS?
IF I MADE A MILLION IN A MONTH, WOULD YOU REALLY LET RYUNOSUKE QUIT?
...
DO YOU UNDERSTAND WHAT YOU'RE GETTING YOURSELF INTO?
YOU CAN'T MAKE A MILLION WORKING A REGULAR JOB...
I KNOW THAT.

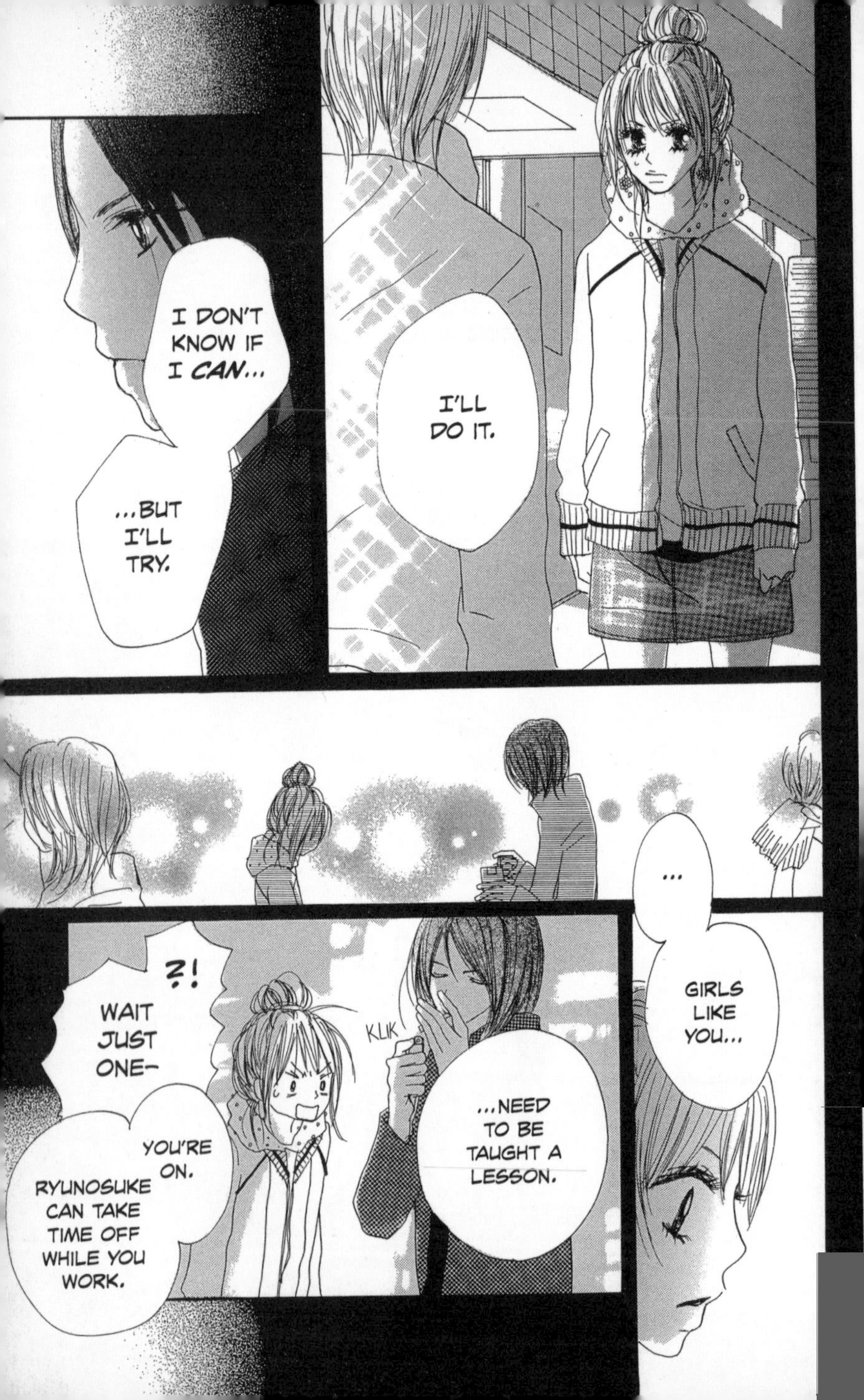
I'LL DO IT.
I DON'T KNOW IF I CAN...
...BUT I'LL TRY.
...
GIRLS LIKE YOU...
...NEED TO BE TAUGHT A LESSON.
KLIK
?!
WAIT JUST ONE-
YOU'RE ON. RYUNOSUKE CAN TAKE TIME OFF WHILE YOU WORK.

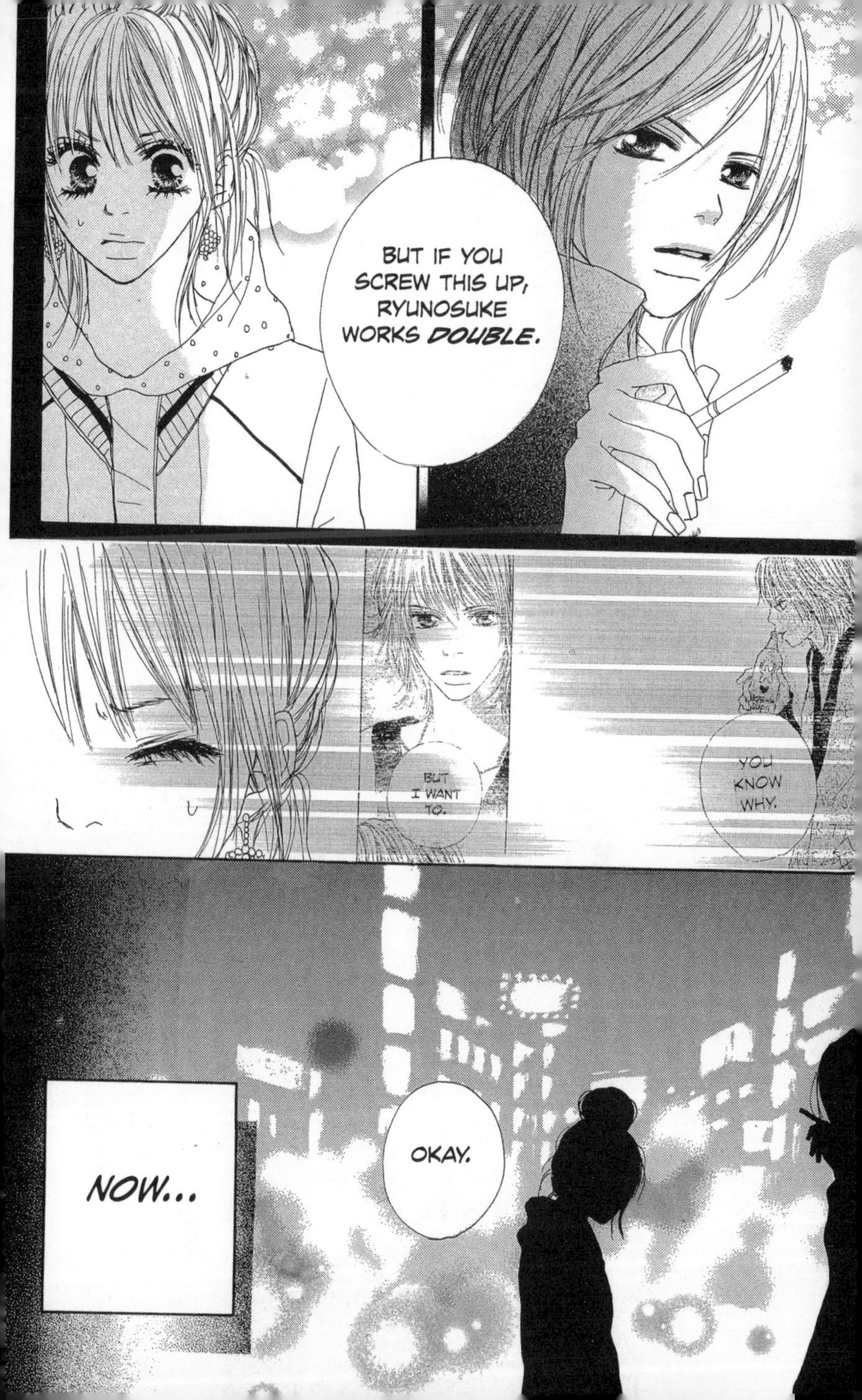
BUT IF YOU SCREW THIS UP, RYUNOSUKE WORKS *DOUBLE.*
YOU KNOW WHY.
BUT I WANT TO.
OKAY.
NOW...

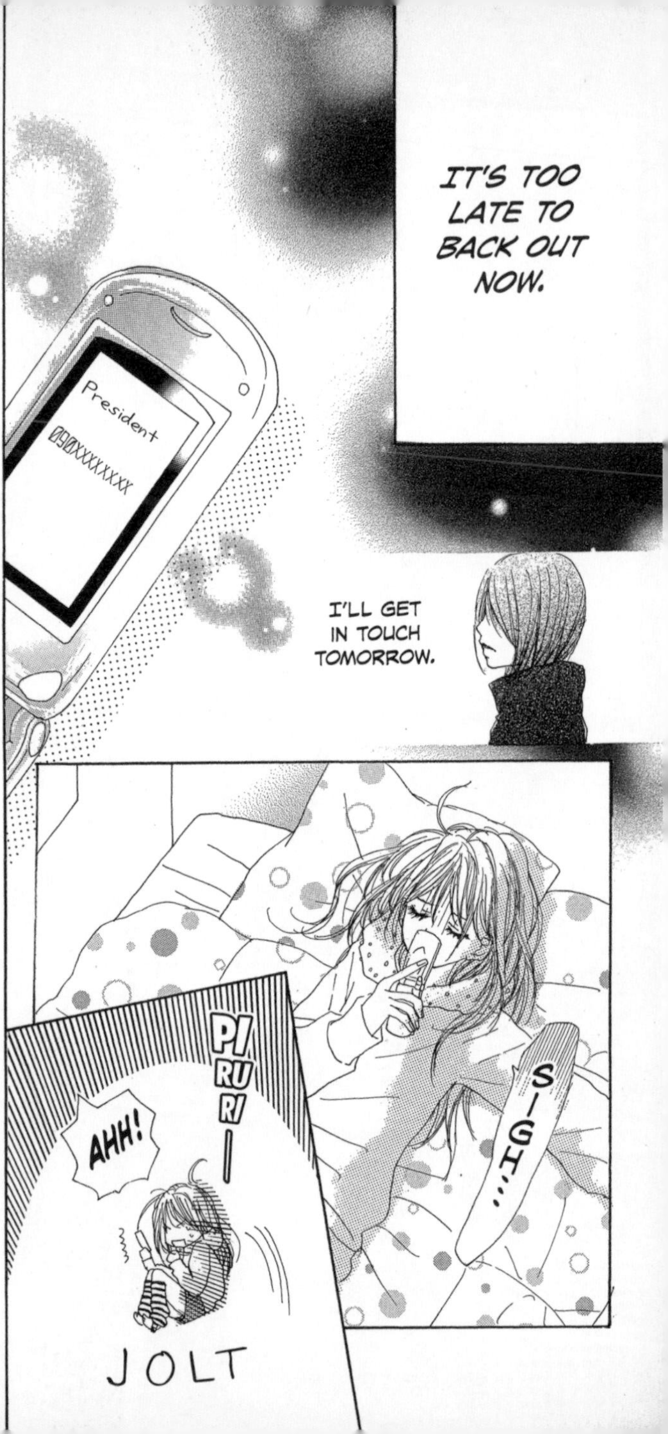
IT'S TOO LATE TO BACK OUT NOW.
President
Ø9ØXXXXXXXX
I'LL GET IN TOUCH TOMORROW.
SIGH...
PIRURI
AHH!
JOLT

④

My love for Karuho Shiina is growing deeper every day.

Karuho Shiina's emoji:

(/¬_¬)/

This little guy usually shows up when I'm having a hard time coming up with a first draft:

(/¬_¬)/ ((((T_T)

Wait— AHHH!

When both of us are motivated, we look like this:

HUFF HUFF
](ˋ~ˊ) (ˋ~ˊ) =3

When we're going through a difficult time:

Waaaaaa
(/ToT)/\(ToT\)

(This is also appropriate when our deadlines have just passed.)

We use a lot of other ones too. It's really fun. I know there have been a lot of cute ones but I can't remember how to make them all right now!

(T_T)
90% of the time before a deadline, it's this guy.

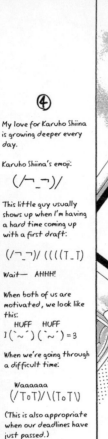

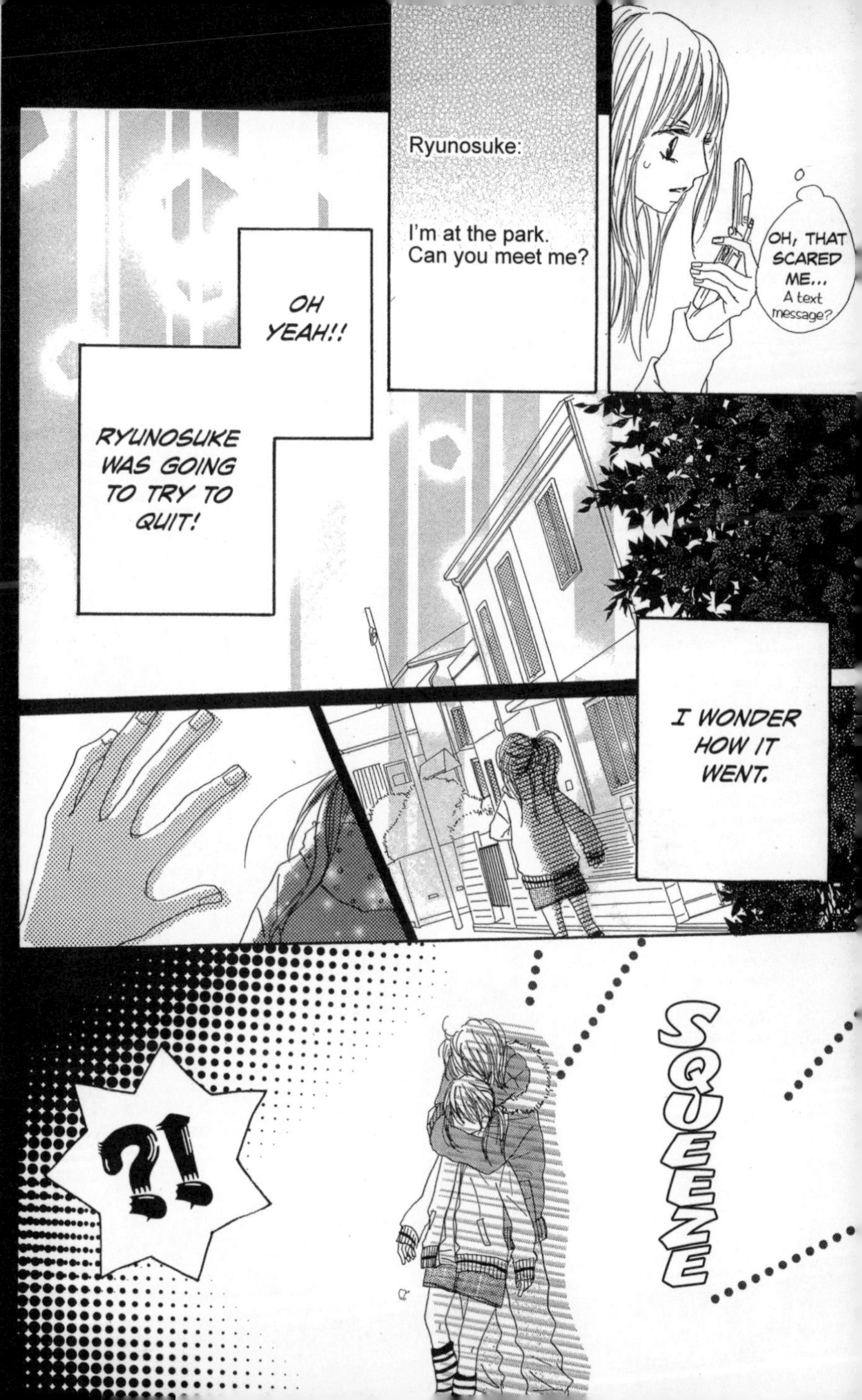
OH, THAT SCARED ME... A text message?
Ryunosuke:
I'm at the park. Can you meet me?
OH YEAH!!
RYUNOSUKE WAS GOING TO TRY TO QUIT!
I WONDER HOW IT WENT.
SQUEEZE
?!

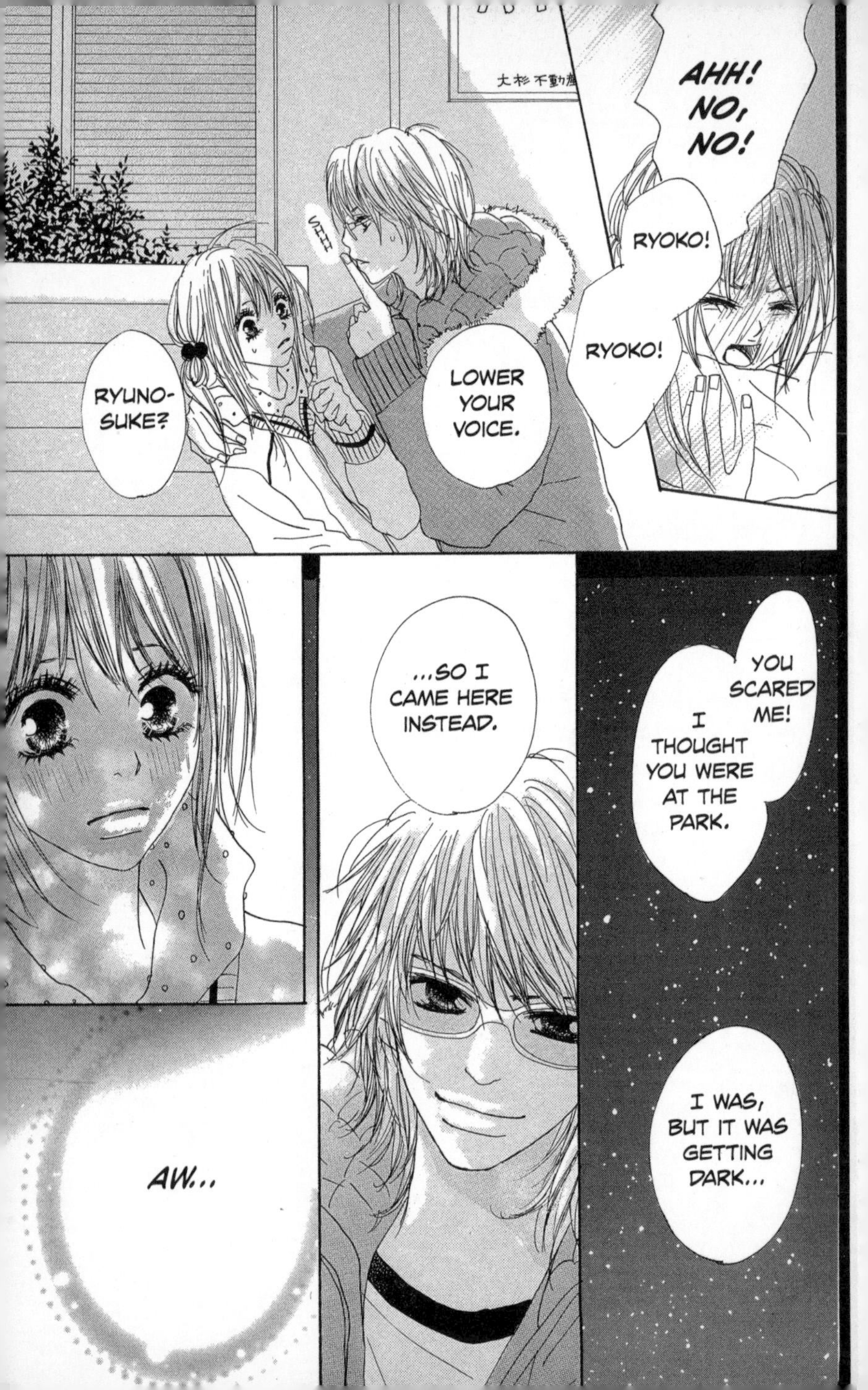
AHH! NO, NO!
RYOKO!
RYOKO!
大杉不動産
SHHH
LOWER YOUR VOICE.
RYUNO-SUKE?
YOU SCARED ME! I THOUGHT YOU WERE AT THE PARK.
I WAS, BUT IT WAS GETTING DARK...
...SO I CAME HERE INSTEAD.
AW...

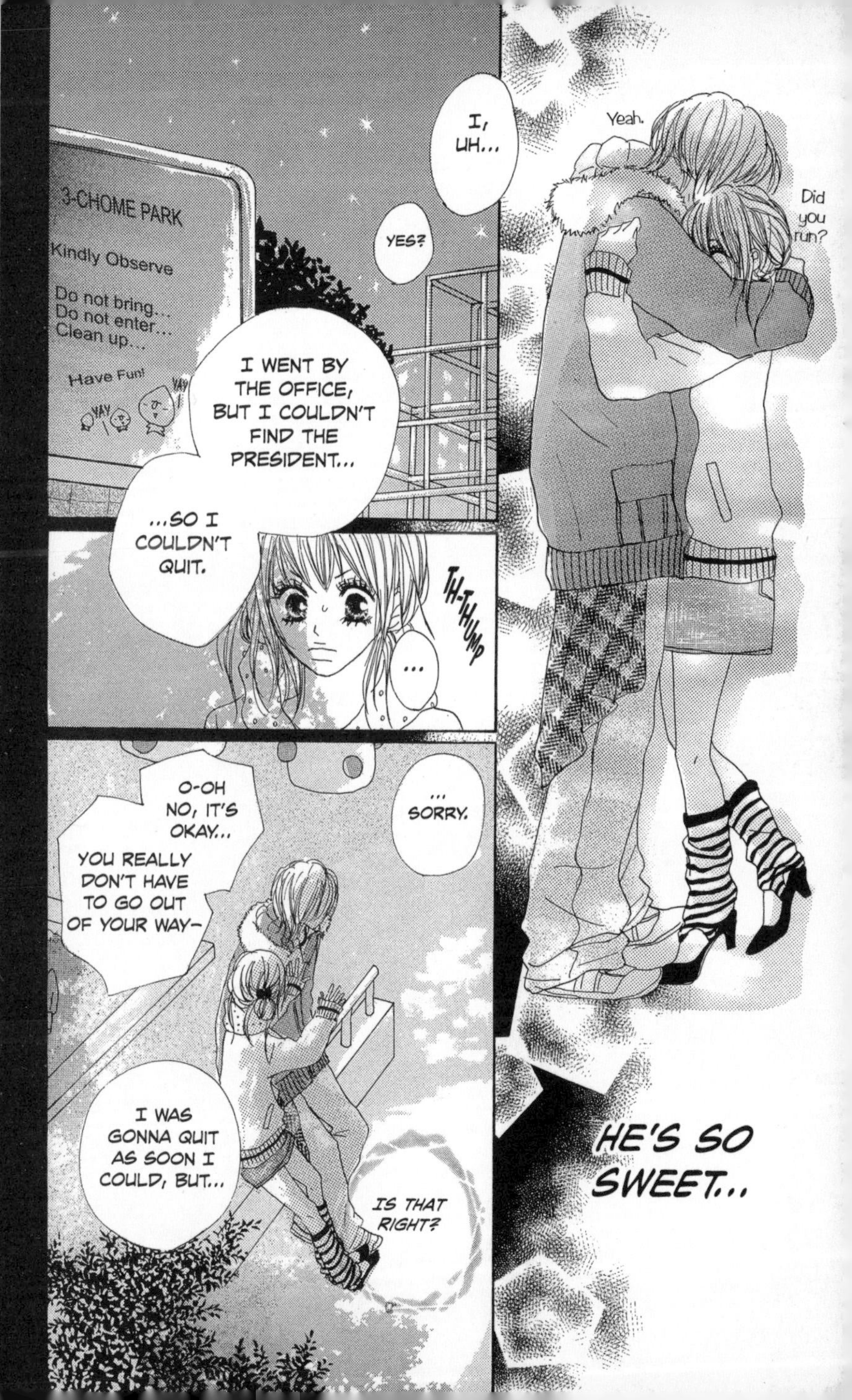
Did you run?
Yeah.
HE'S SO SWEET...
I, UH...
YES?
3-CHOME PARK
Kindly Observe
Do not bring...
Do not enter...
Clean up...
Have Fun!
YAY
YAY
I WENT BY THE OFFICE, BUT I COULDN'T FIND THE PRESIDENT...
...SO I COULDN'T QUIT.
TH-THUMP
...
... SORRY.
O-OH NO, IT'S OKAY...
YOU REALLY DON'T HAVE TO GO OUT OF YOUR WAY–
I WAS GONNA QUIT AS SOON I COULD, BUT...
IS THAT RIGHT?

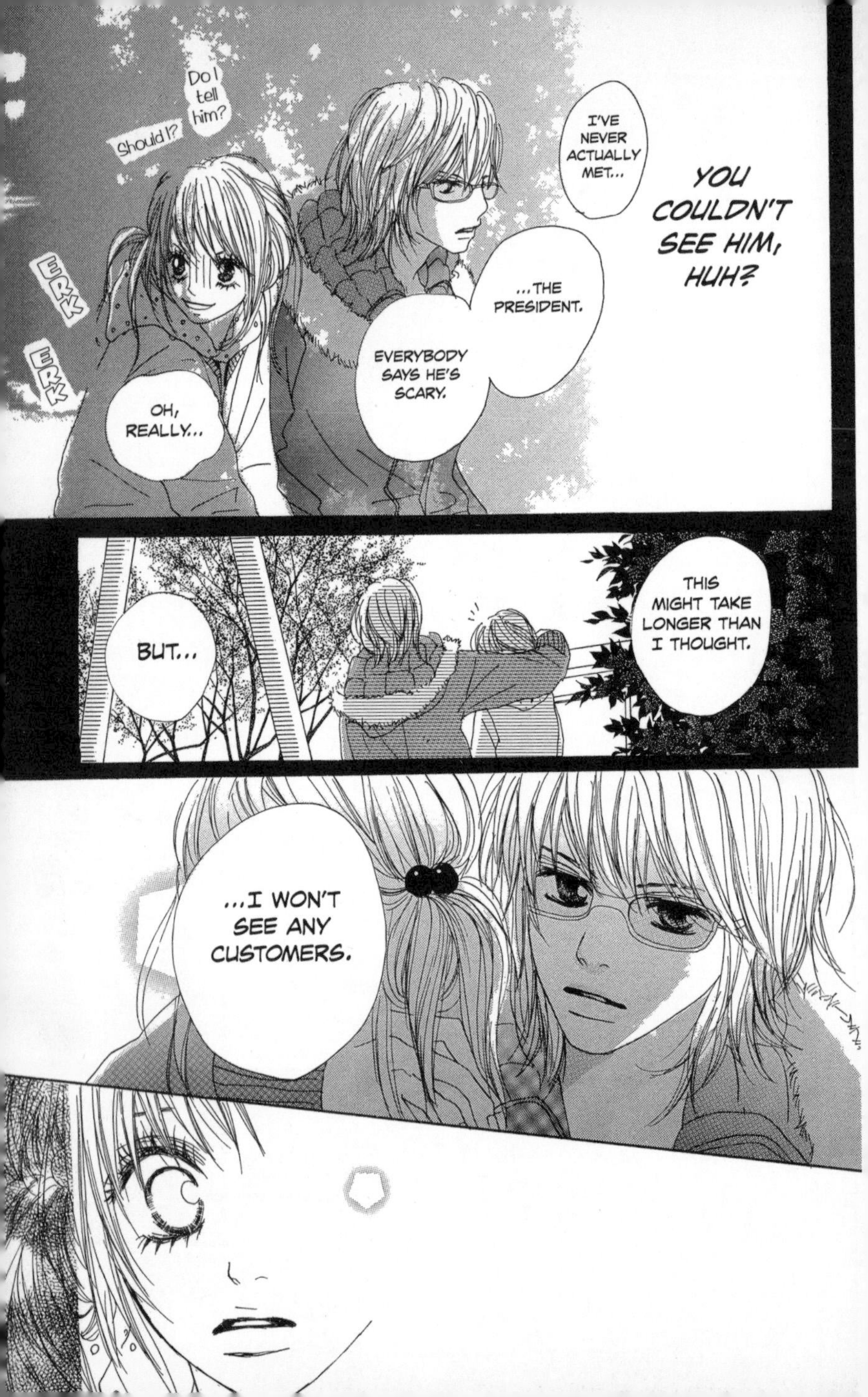
YOU COULDN'T SEE HIM, HUH?
I'VE NEVER ACTUALLY MET...
...THE PRESIDENT.
EVERYBODY SAYS HE'S SCARY.
Do I tell him?
Should I?
ERK
ERK
OH, REALLY...
THIS MIGHT TAKE LONGER THAN I THOUGHT.
BUT...
...I WON'T SEE ANY CUSTOMERS.

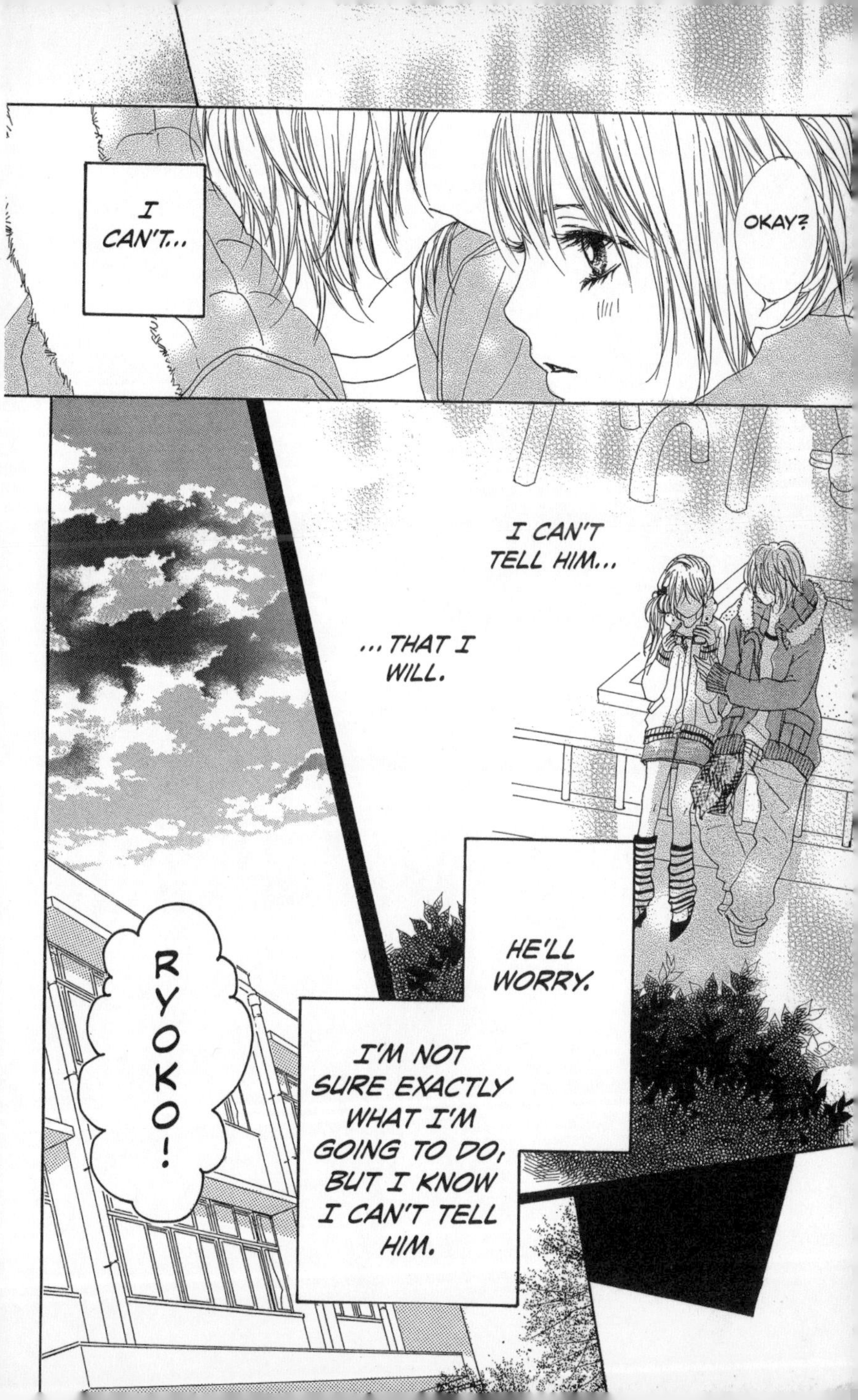
OKAY?
I CAN'T...
I CAN'T TELL HIM...
...THAT I WILL.
HE'LL WORRY.
I'M NOT SURE EXACTLY WHAT I'M GOING TO DO, BUT I KNOW I CAN'T TELL HIM.
RYOKO!

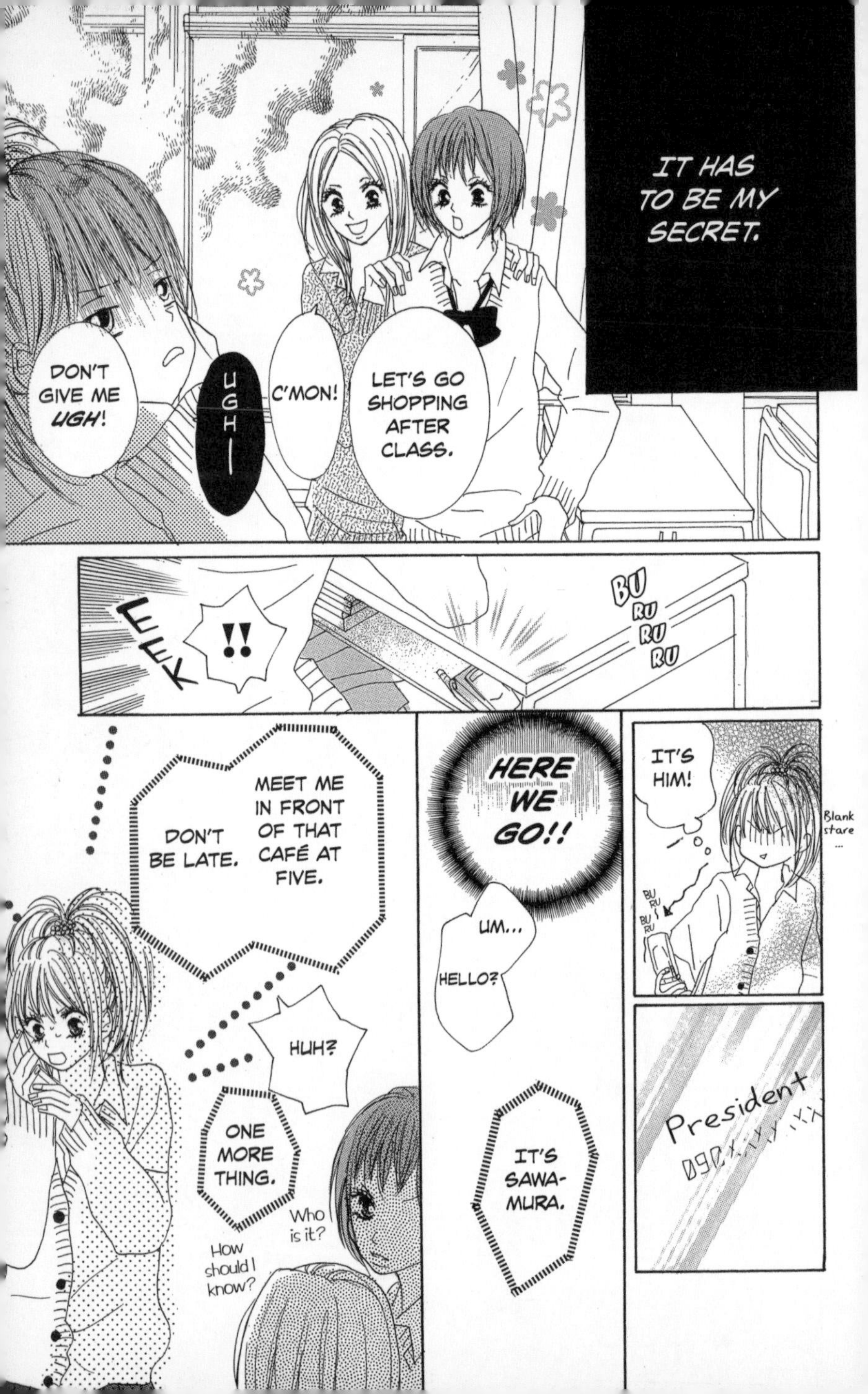
IT HAS TO BE MY SECRET.
LET'S GO SHOPPING AFTER CLASS.
C'MON!
UGH!
DON'T GIVE ME *UGH*!
BU RU RU RU
!!
EEK
IT'S HIM!
Blank stare ...
BU RU BU RU
President
HERE WE GO!!
UM...
HELLO?
IT'S SAWA-MURA.
MEET ME IN FRONT OF THAT CAFÉ AT FIVE.
DON'T BE LATE.
......
HUH?
ONE MORE THING.
Who is it?
How should I know?

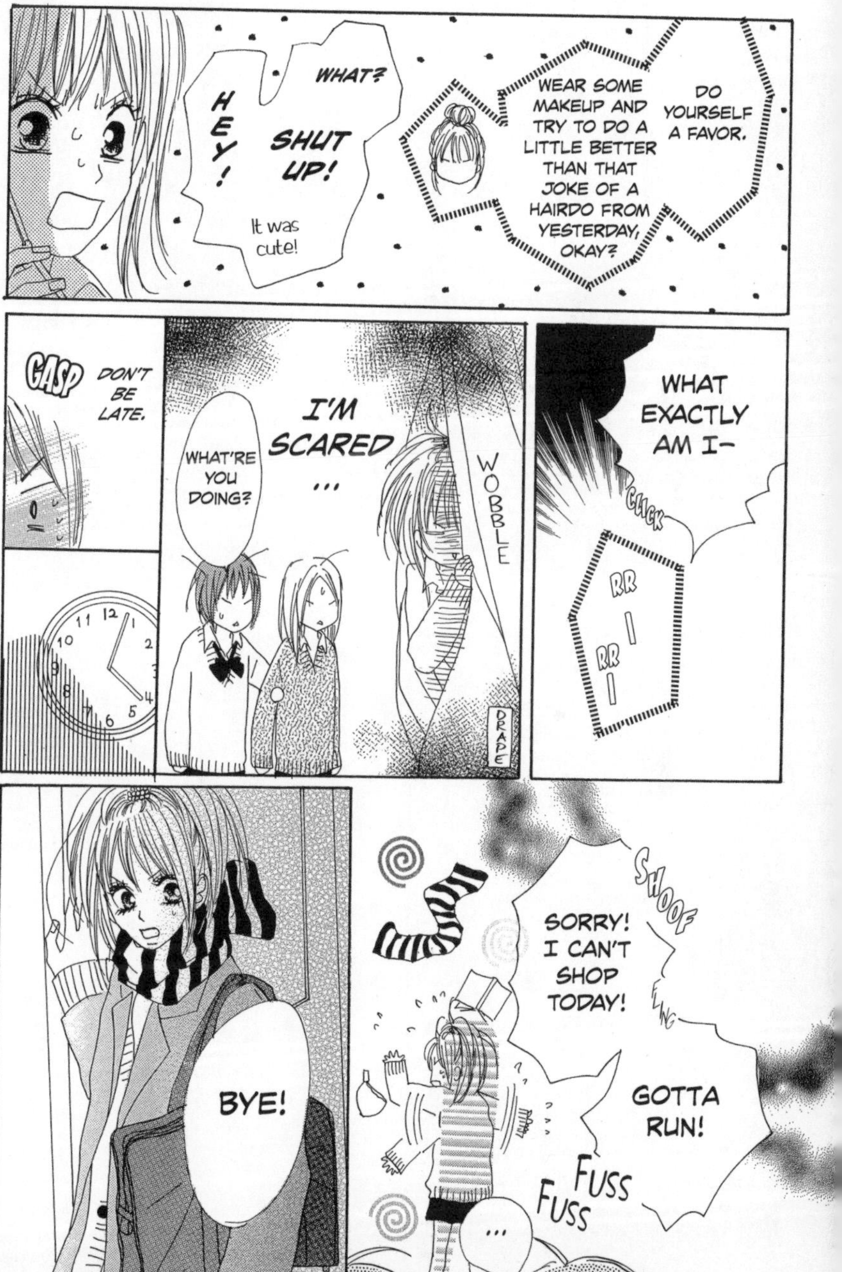
DO YOURSELF A FAVOR.
WEAR SOME MAKEUP AND TRY TO DO A LITTLE BETTER THAN THAT JOKE OF A HAIRDO FROM YESTERDAY, OKAY?
WHAT?
SHUT UP!
HEY!
It was cute!
WHAT EXACTLY AM I—
CLICK
RR I RR I
I'M SCARED ...
WOBBLE
WHAT'RE YOU DOING?
DRAPE
GASP
DON'T BE LATE.
SHOOF
SORRY! I CAN'T SHOP TODAY!
FLING
GOTTA RUN!
FUSS FUSS
...
BYE!

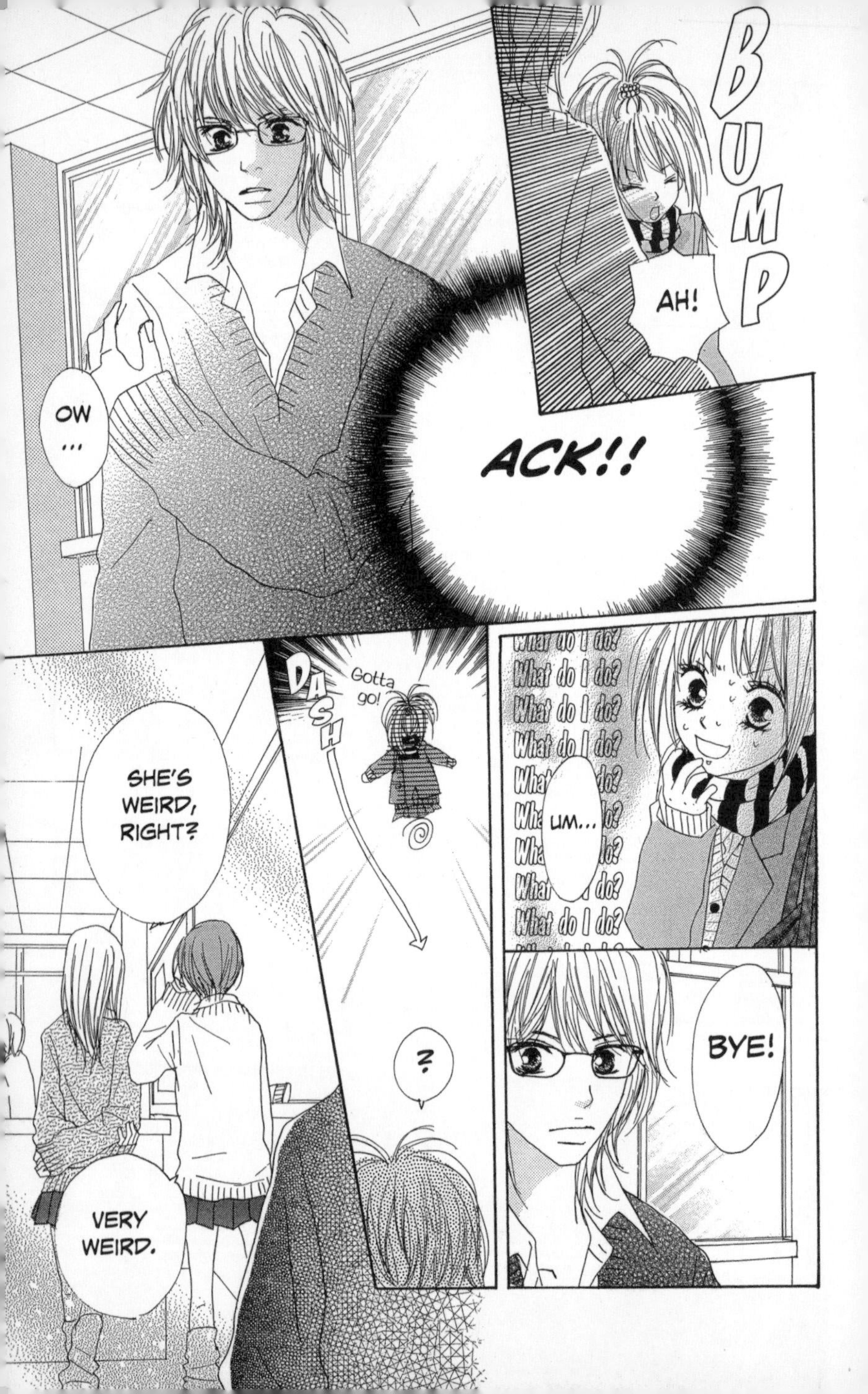
BUMP
AH!
ACK!!
OW ...
What do I do? What do I do? What do I do? What do I do?
UM...
BYE!
DASH
Gotta go!
?
SHE'S WEIRD, RIGHT?
VERY WEIRD.

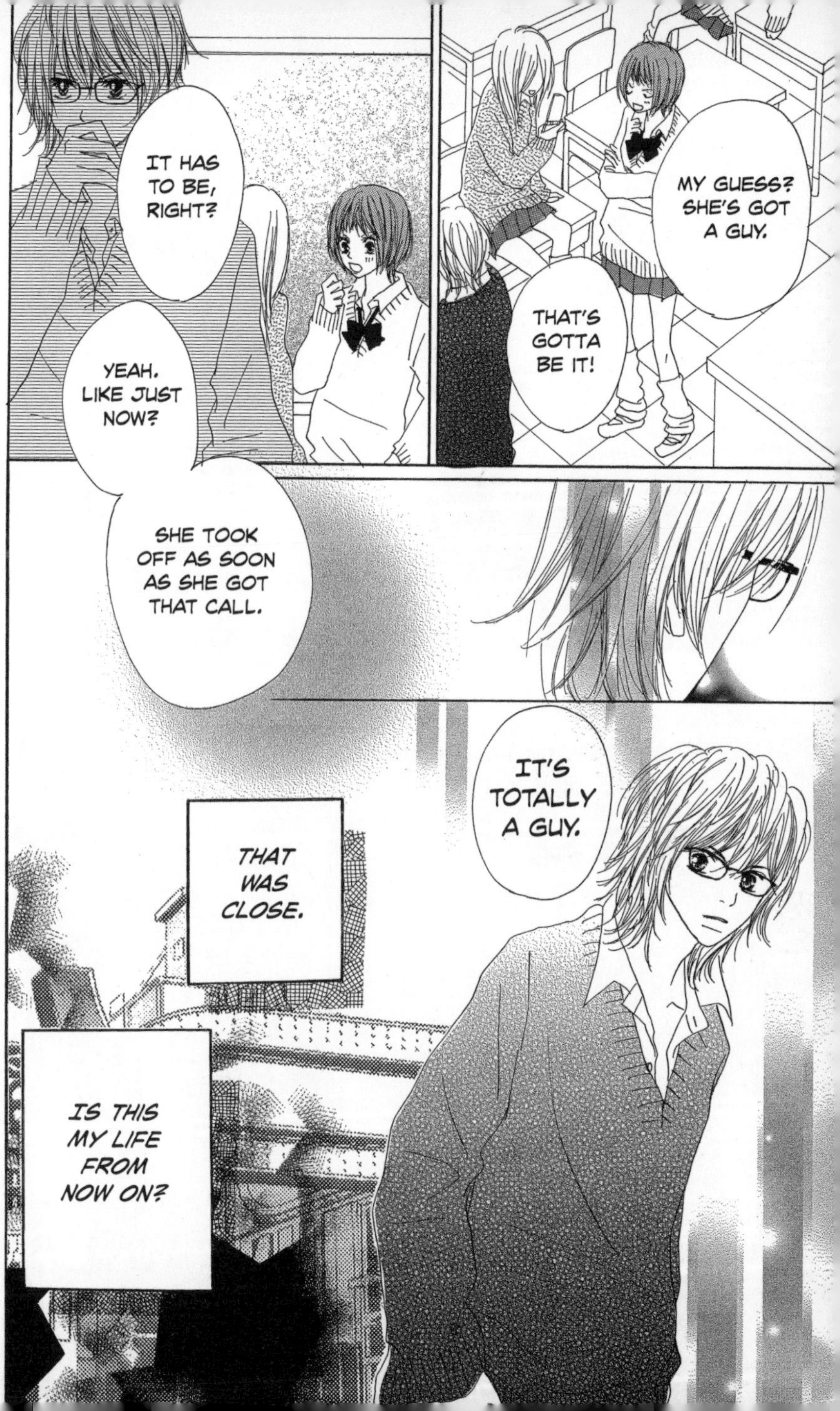
MY GUESS? SHE'S GOT A GUY.
THAT'S GOTTA BE IT!
IT HAS TO BE, RIGHT?
YEAH. LIKE JUST NOW?
SHE TOOK OFF AS SOON AS SHE GOT THAT CALL.
IT'S TOTALLY A GUY.
THAT WAS CLOSE.
IS THIS MY LIFE FROM NOW ON?

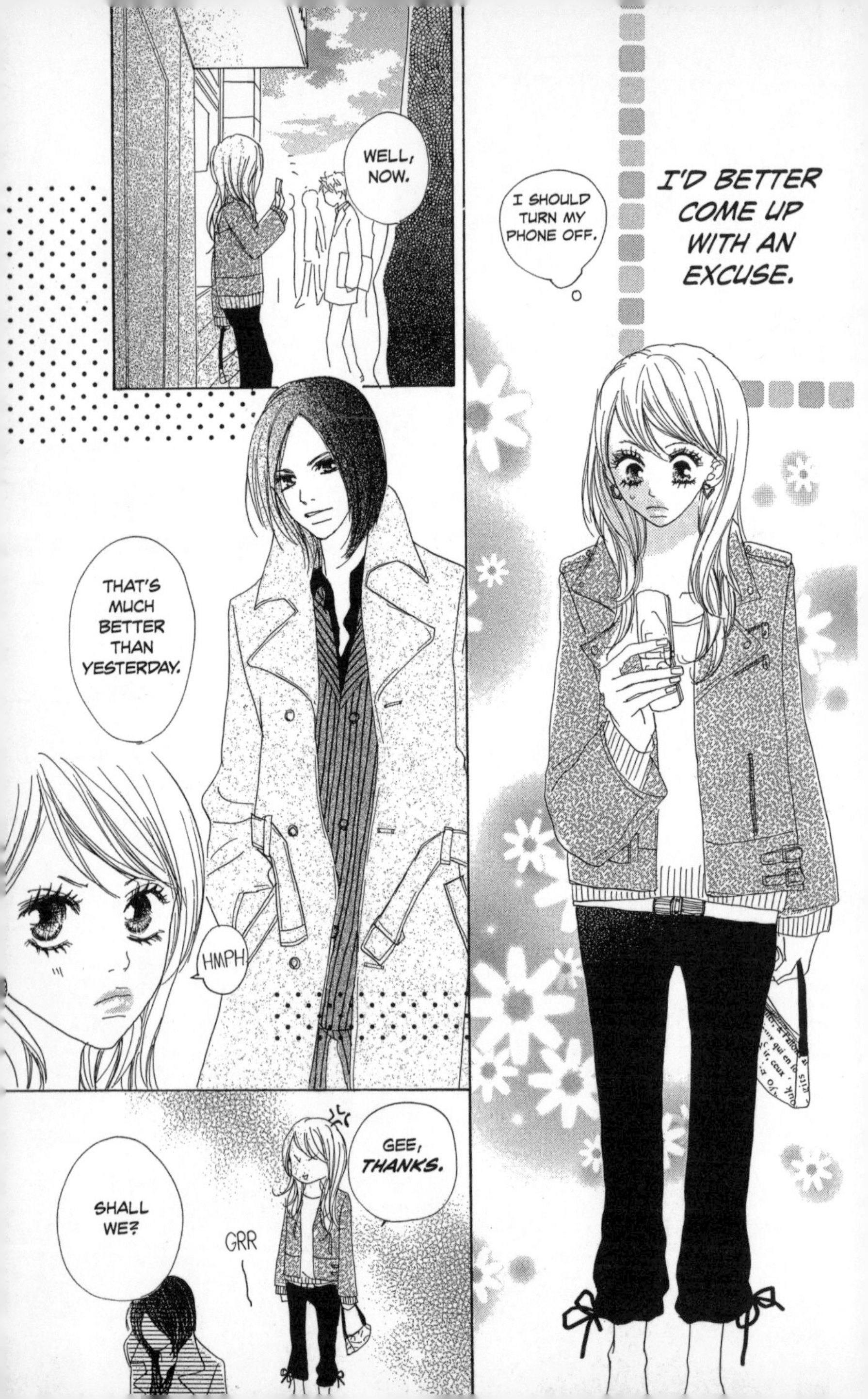
I'D BETTER COME UP WITH AN EXCUSE.
I SHOULD TURN MY PHONE OFF.
WELL, NOW.
THAT'S MUCH BETTER THAN YESTERDAY.
HMPH
GEE, THANKS.
GRR
SHALL WE?

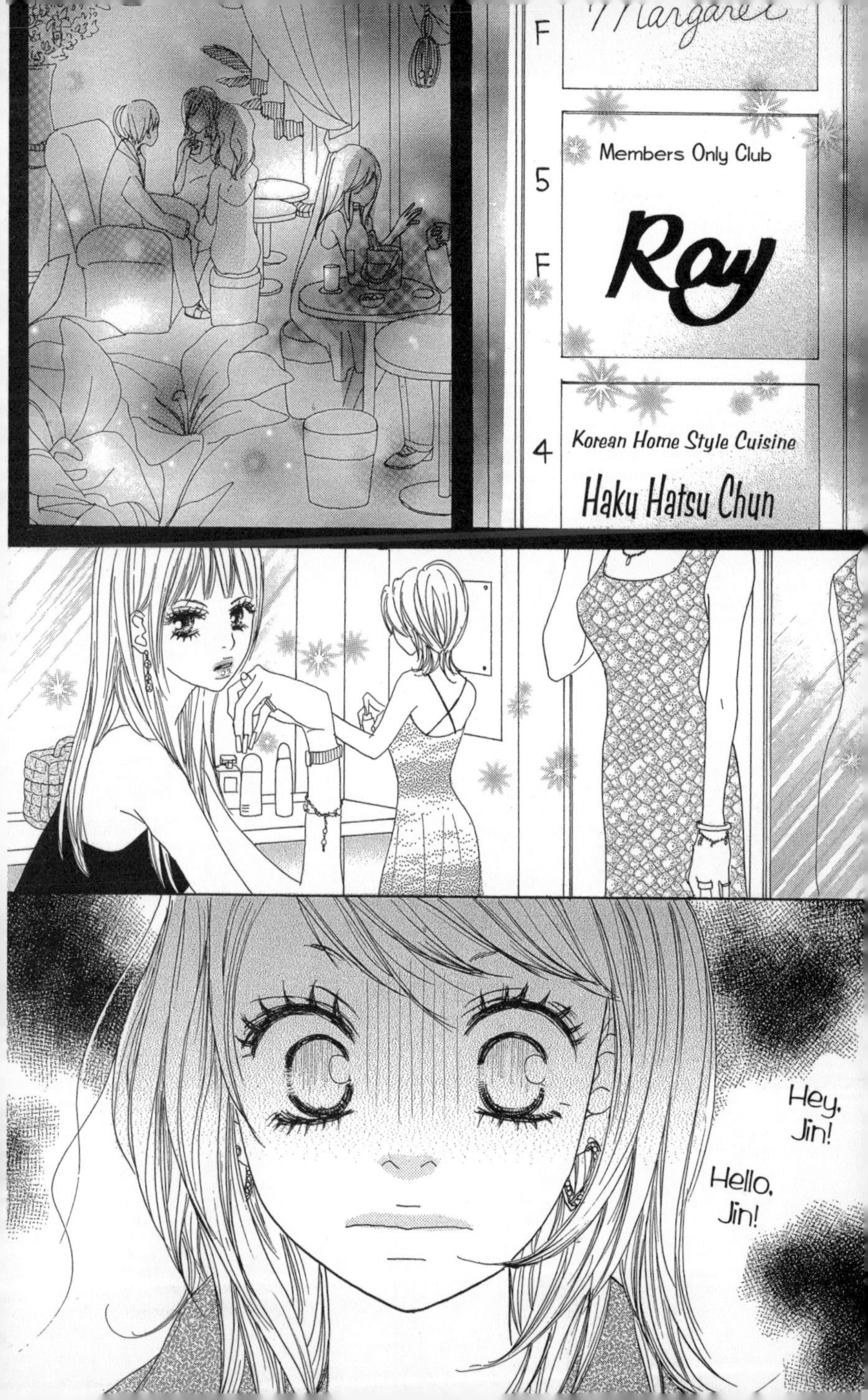
F
Margaret
5
F
Members Only Club
Ray
4
Korean Home Style Cuisine
Haku Hatsu Chun
Hey, Jin!
Hello, Jin!

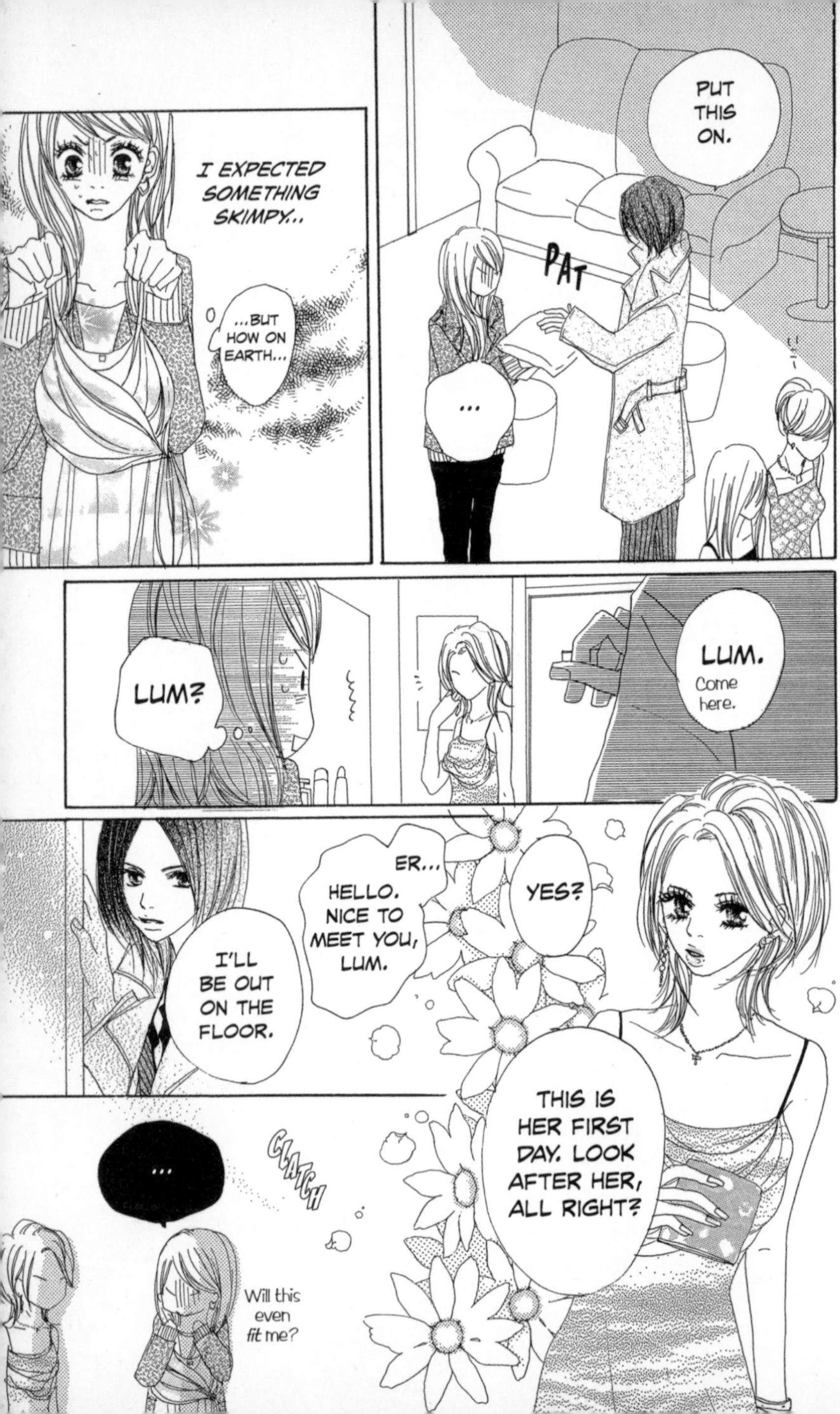
PUT THIS ON.
PAT
...
I EXPECTED SOMETHING SKIMPY...
...BUT HOW ON EARTH...
LUM. Come here.
LUM?
YES?
THIS IS HER FIRST DAY. LOOK AFTER HER, ALL RIGHT?
ER... HELLO. NICE TO MEET YOU, LUM.
I'LL BE OUT ON THE FLOOR.
CLATCH
...
Will this even *fit* me?

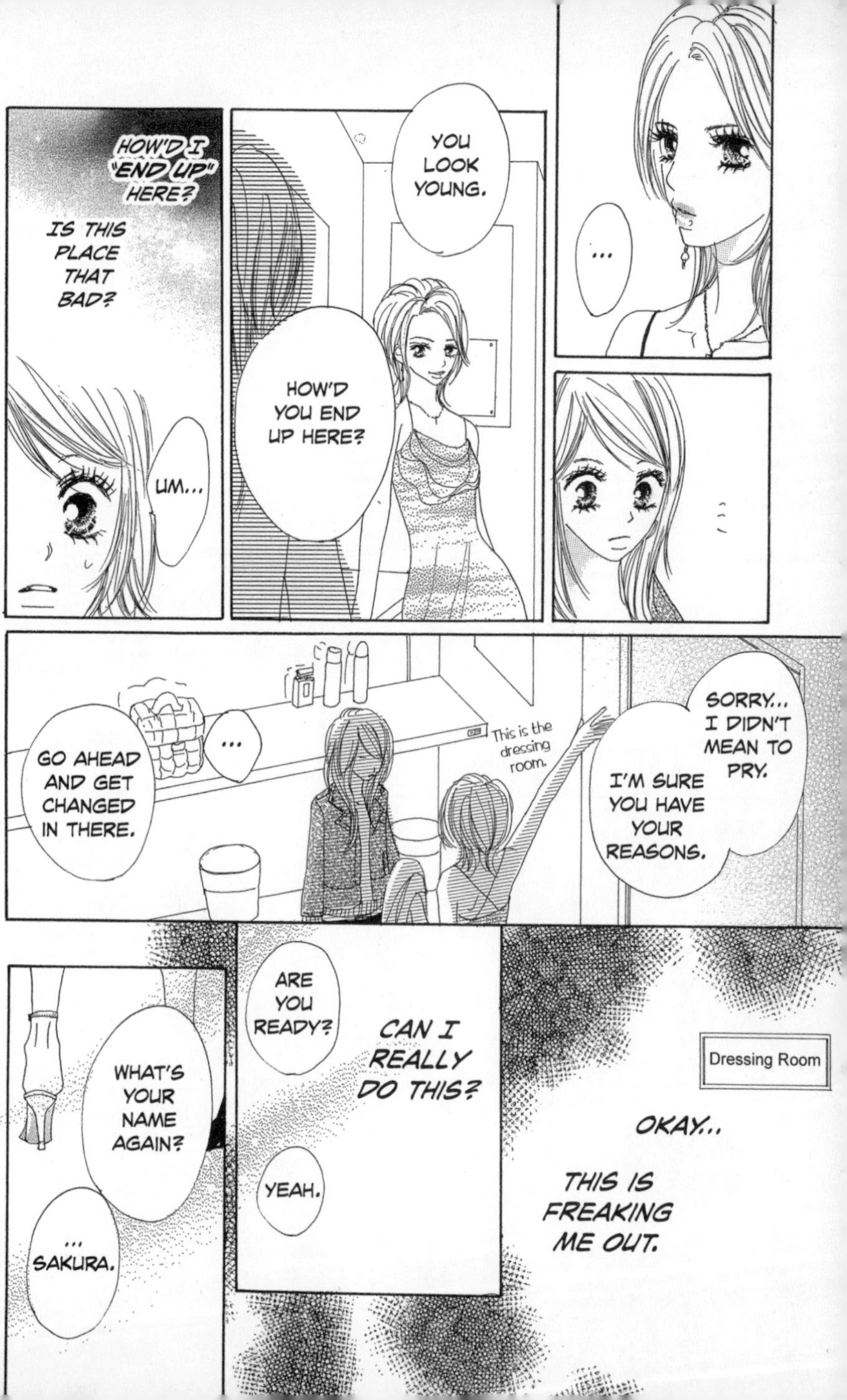
...
YOU LOOK YOUNG.
HOW'D YOU END UP HERE?
HOW'D I "END UP" HERE?
IS THIS PLACE THAT BAD?
UM...
SORRY... I DIDN'T MEAN TO PRY.
I'M SURE YOU HAVE YOUR REASONS.
This is the dressing room.
...
GO AHEAD AND GET CHANGED IN THERE.
Dressing Room
OKAY..
THIS IS FREAKING ME OUT.
ARE YOU READY?
CAN I REALLY DO THIS?
YEAH.
WHAT'S YOUR NAME AGAIN?
...SAKURA.

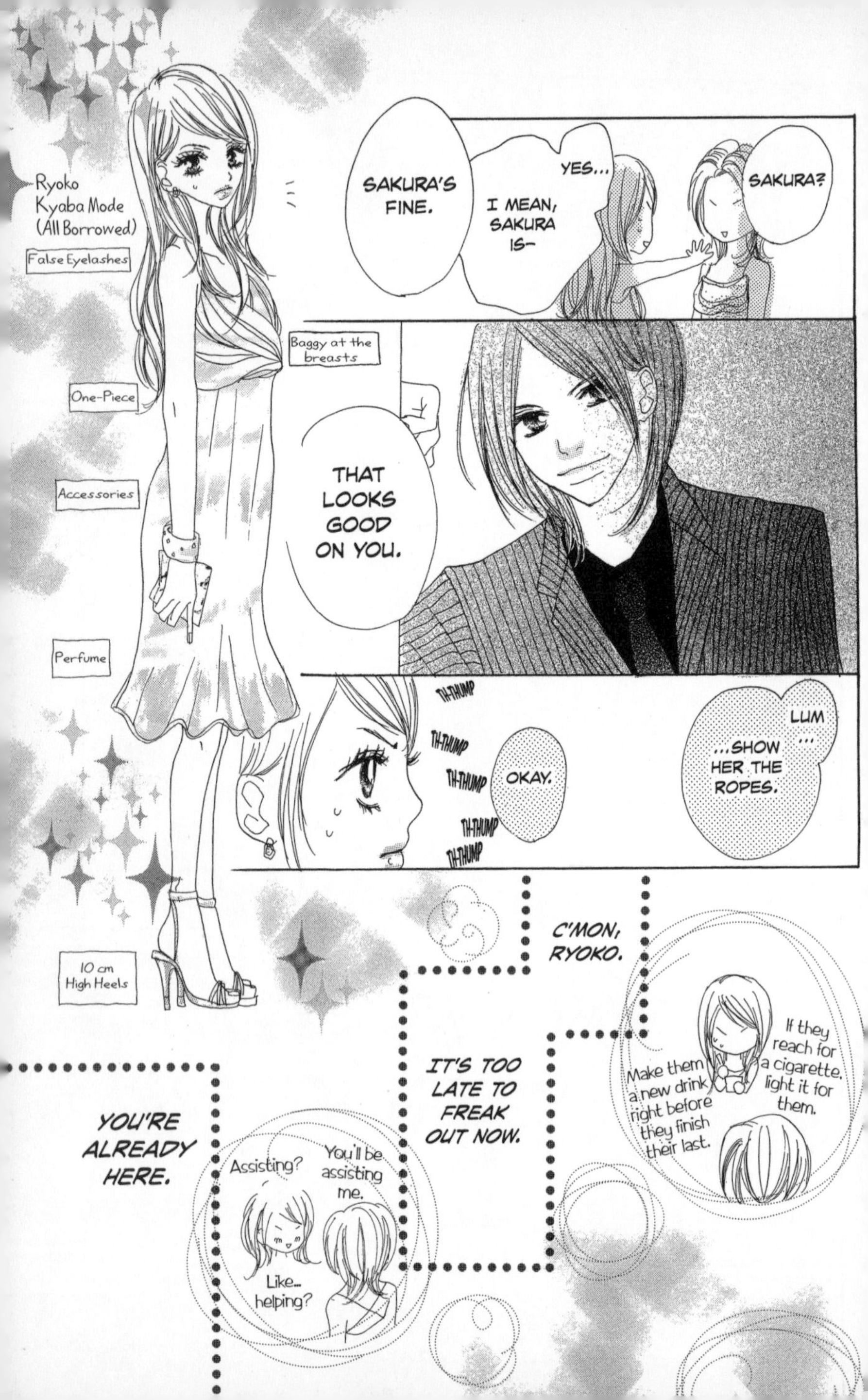
SAKURA?
YES... I MEAN, SAKURA IS-
SAKURA'S FINE.
THAT LOOKS GOOD ON YOU.
LUM ...
...SHOW HER THE ROPES.
TH-THUMP
TH-THUMP
TH-THUMP
TH-THUMP
TH-THUMP
OKAY.
Ryoko Kyaba Mode (All Borrowed)
False Eyelashes
Baggy at the breasts
One-Piece
Accessories
Perfume
10 cm High Heels
C'MON, RYOKO.
If they reach for a cigarette, light it for them.
Make them a new drink right before they finish their last.
IT'S TOO LATE TO FREAK OUT NOW.
You'll be assisting me.
Assisting?
Like... helping?
YOU'RE ALREADY HERE.

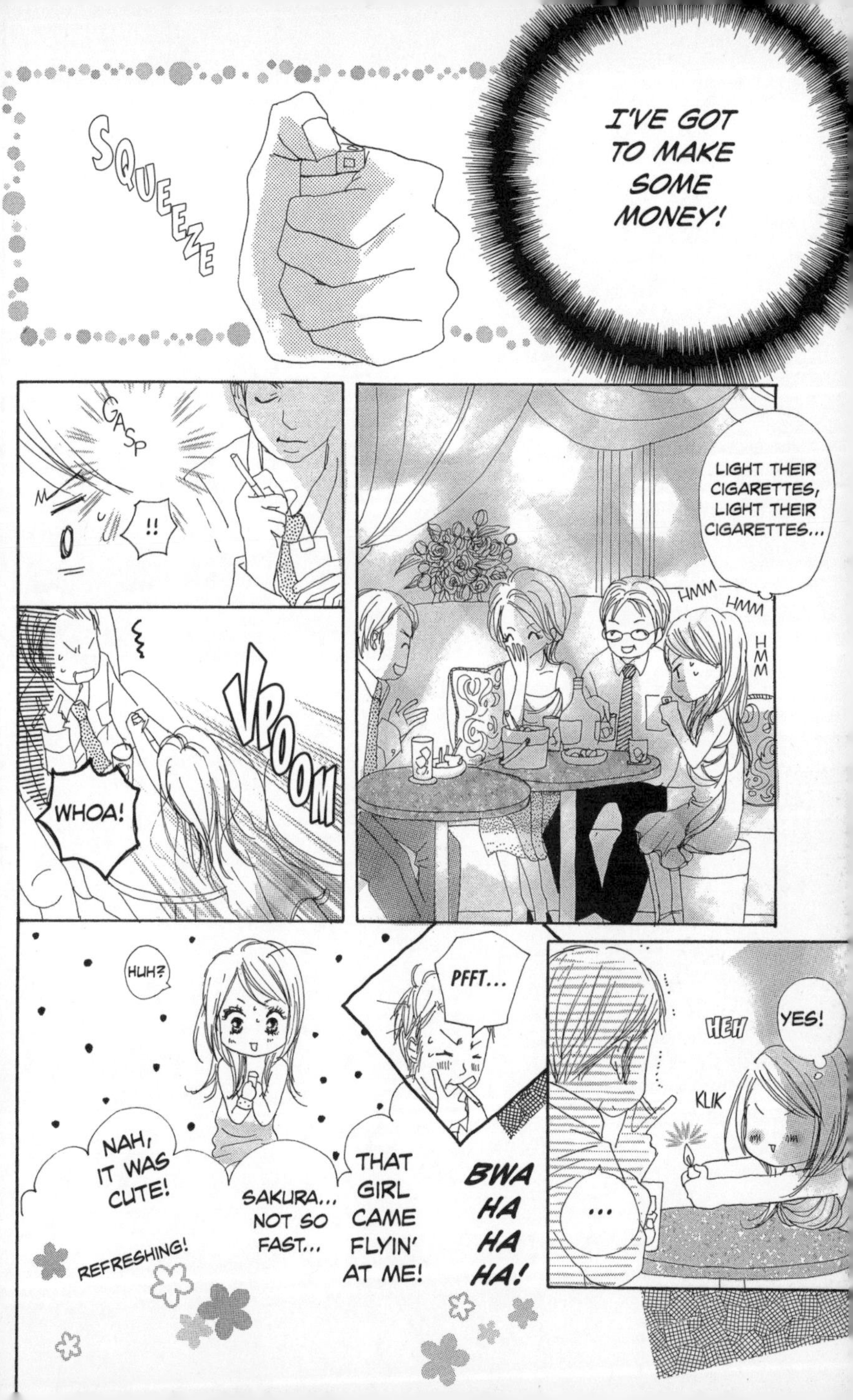
I'VE GOT TO MAKE SOME MONEY!
SQUEEZE
LIGHT THEIR CIGARETTES, LIGHT THEIR CIGARETTES...
HMM
HMM
HMM
GASP
!!
VROOM
WHOA!
YES!
HEH
KLIK
...
PFFT...
BWA HA HA HA HA!
THAT GIRL CAME FLYIN' AT ME!
SAKURA... NOT SO FAST...
HUH?
NAH, IT WAS CUTE!
REFRESHING!

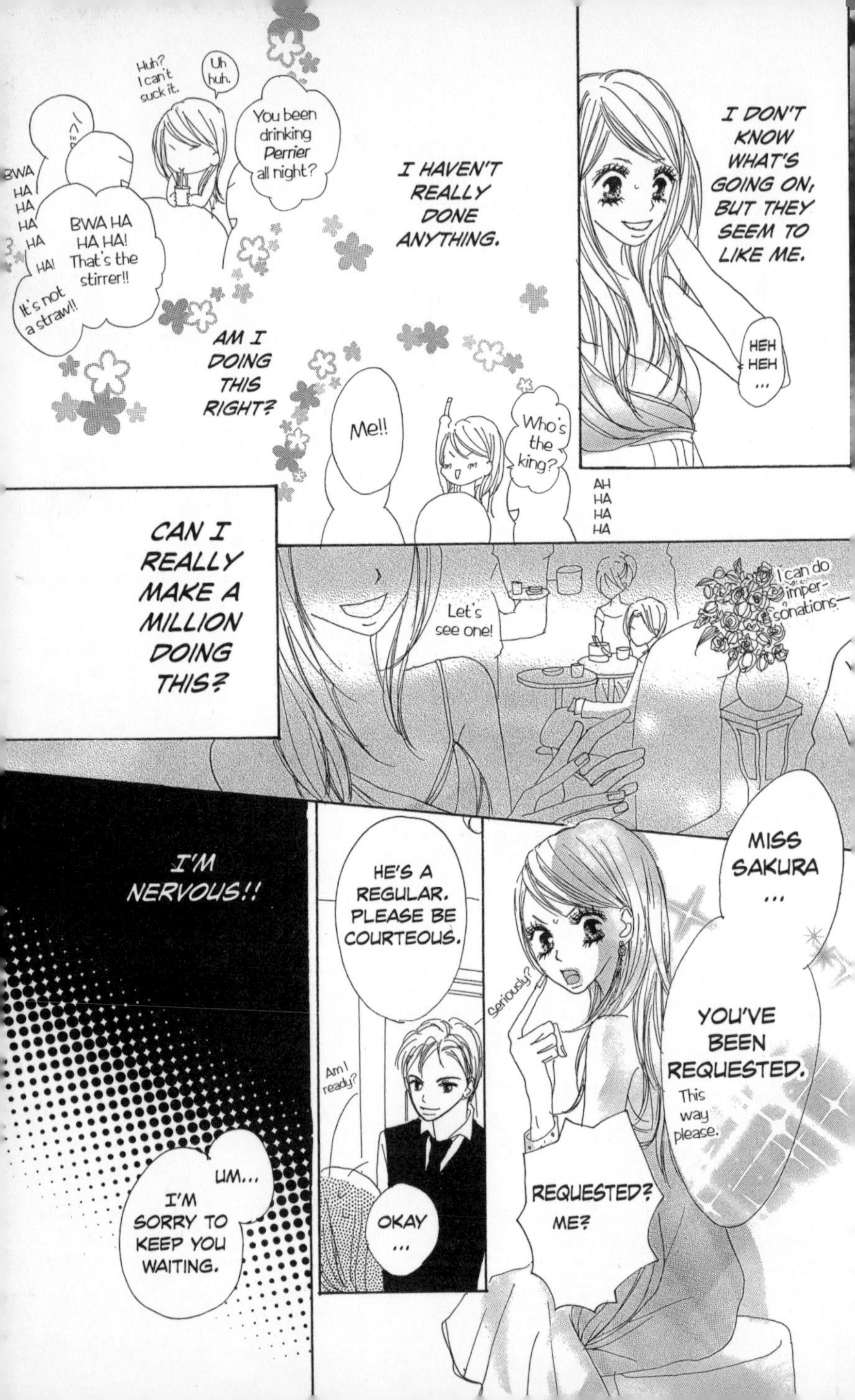
I DON'T KNOW WHAT'S GOING ON, BUT THEY SEEM TO LIKE ME.
HEH HEH ...
I HAVEN'T REALLY DONE ANYTHING.
Uh huh.
Huh? I can't suck it.
You been drinking Perrier all night?
BWA HA HA HA HA HA!
BWA HA HA HA! That's the stirrer!!
It's not a straw!!
AM I DOING THIS RIGHT?
Who's the king?
Me!!
AH HA HA HA
I can do imper-sonations—
Let's see one!
CAN I REALLY MAKE A MILLION DOING THIS?
MISS SAKURA ...
YOU'VE BEEN REQUESTED.
This way please.
Seriously?
REQUESTED? ME?
HE'S A REGULAR. PLEASE BE COURTEOUS.
Am I ready?
OKAY ...
I'M NERVOUS!!
UM... I'M SORRY TO KEEP YOU WAITING.

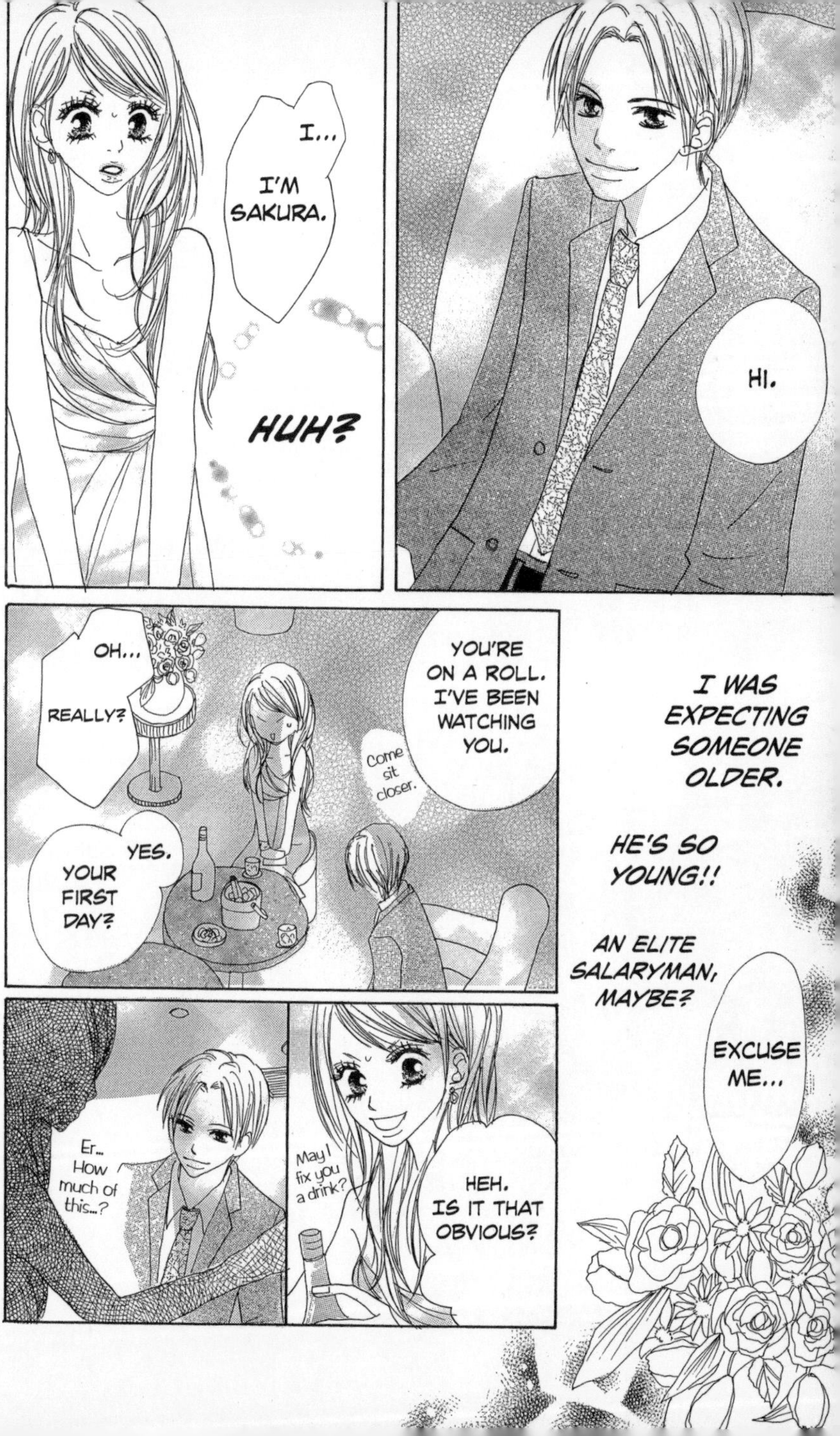
HI.
I...
I'M SAKURA.
HUH?
I WAS EXPECTING SOMEONE OLDER.
HE'S SO YOUNG!!
AN ELITE SALARYMAN, MAYBE?
EXCUSE ME...
YOU'RE ON A ROLL. I'VE BEEN WATCHING YOU.
Come sit closer.
OH...
REALLY?
YES.
YOUR FIRST DAY?
HEH. IS IT THAT OBVIOUS?
May I fix you a drink?
Er... How much of this...?

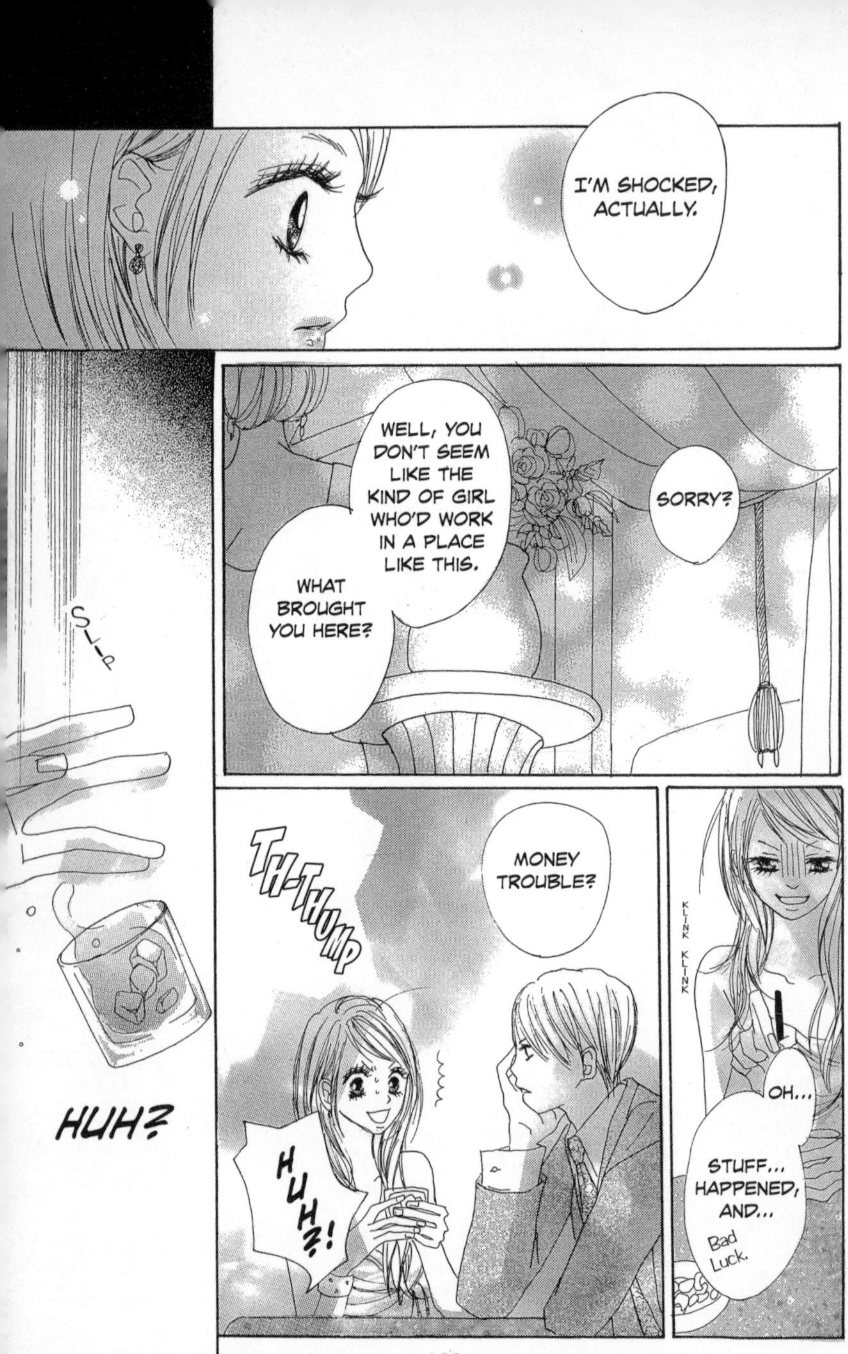

I'M SHOCKED, ACTUALLY.
SORRY?
WELL, YOU DON'T SEEM LIKE THE KIND OF GIRL WHO'D WORK IN A PLACE LIKE THIS.
WHAT BROUGHT YOU HERE?
KLINK KLINK
OH...
STUFF... HAPPENED, AND...
Bad Luck.
MONEY TROUBLE?
TH-THUMP
HUH?!
SLIP
HUH?

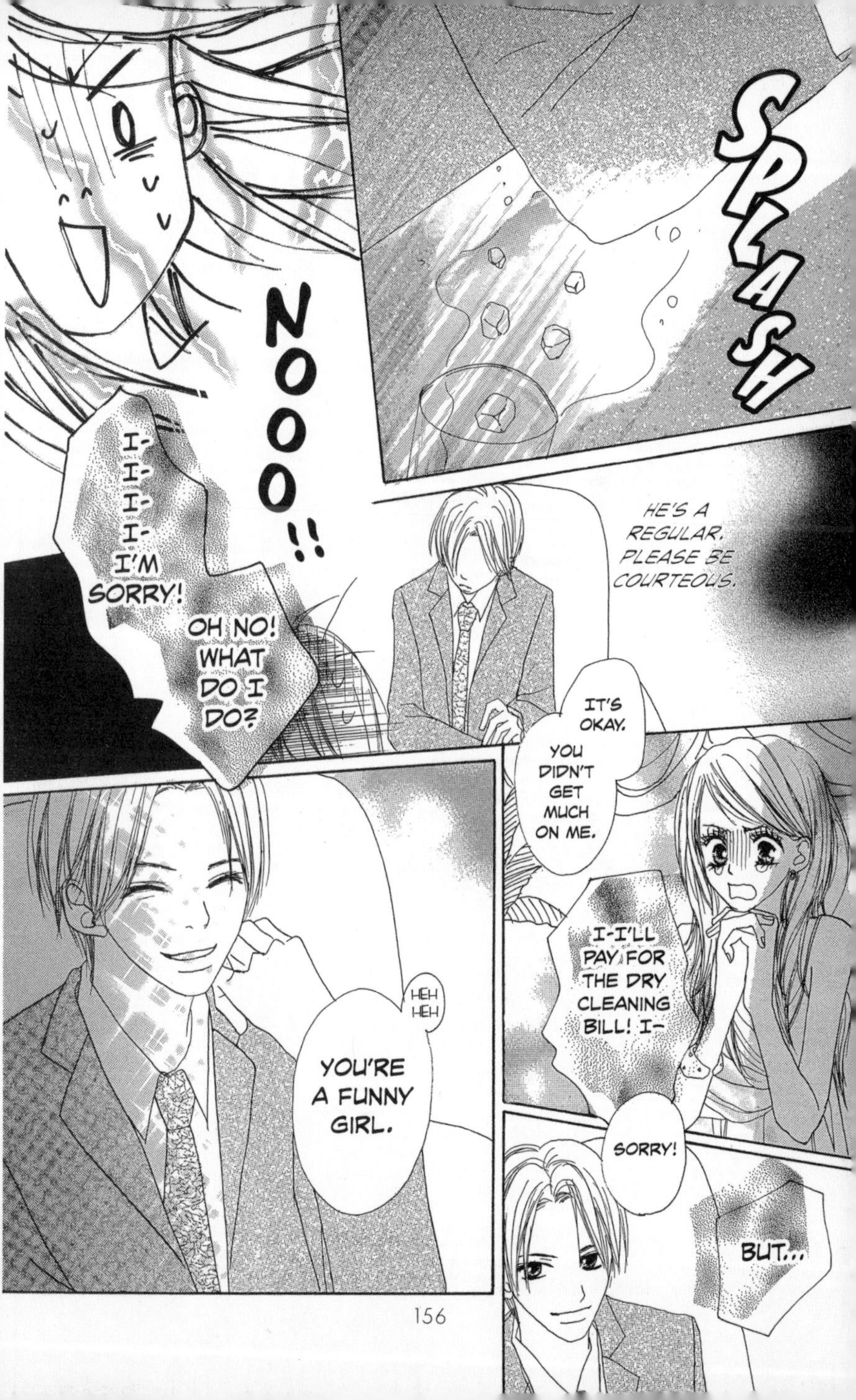
SPLASH
NOOO!!
I-I-I-I'M SORRY!
OH NO! WHAT DO I DO?
HE'S A REGULAR. PLEASE BE COURTEOUS.
IT'S OKAY. YOU DIDN'T GET MUCH ON ME.
I-I'LL PAY FOR THE DRY CLEANING BILL! I-
HEH HEH
YOU'RE A FUNNY GIRL.
SORRY!
BUT...

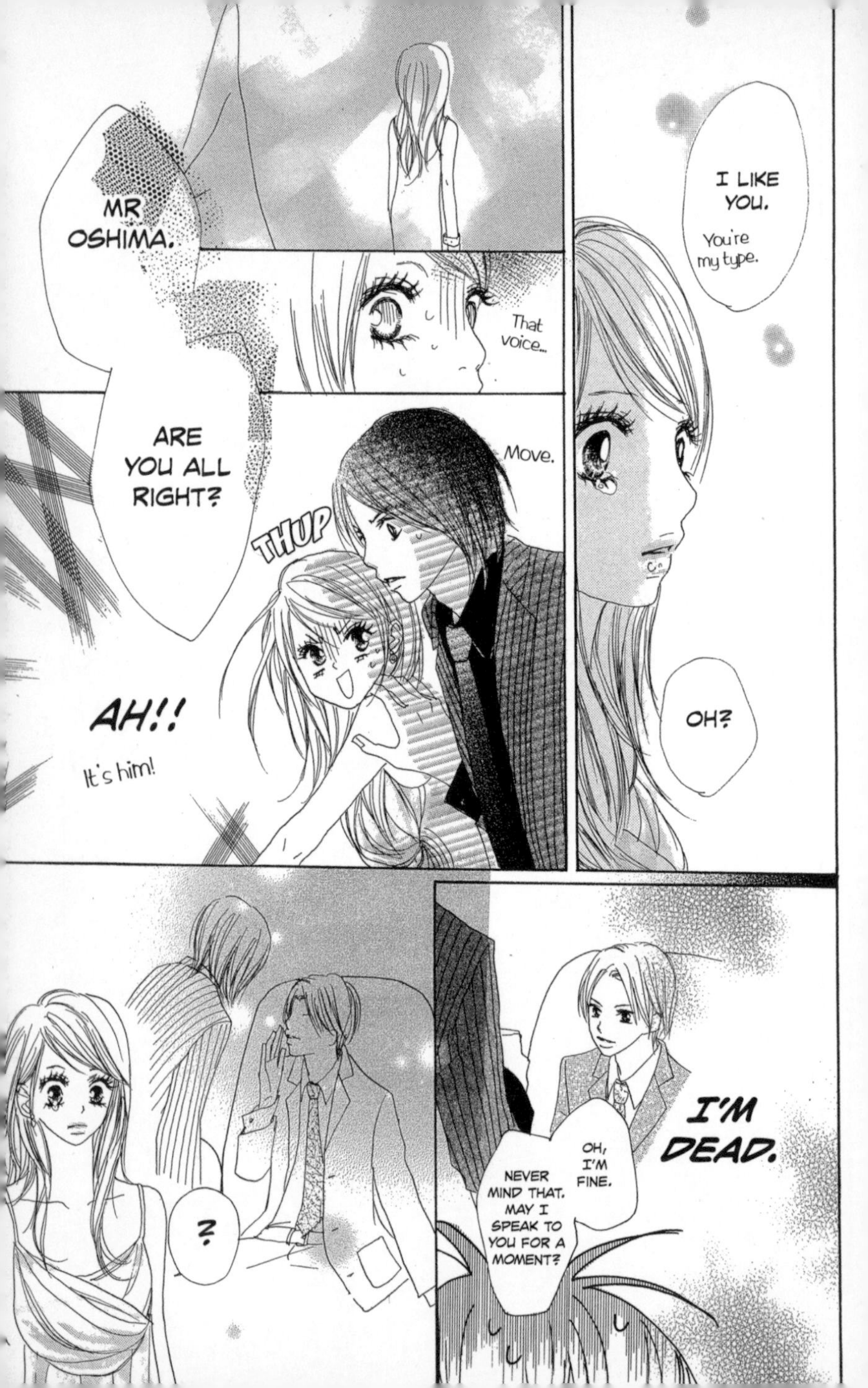
I LIKE YOU.
You're my type.
OH?
MR OSHIMA.
That voice...
Move.
THUP
ARE YOU ALL RIGHT?
AH!!
It's him!
I'M DEAD.
OH, I'M FINE.
NEVER MIND THAT. MAY I SPEAK TO YOU FOR A MOMENT?
?

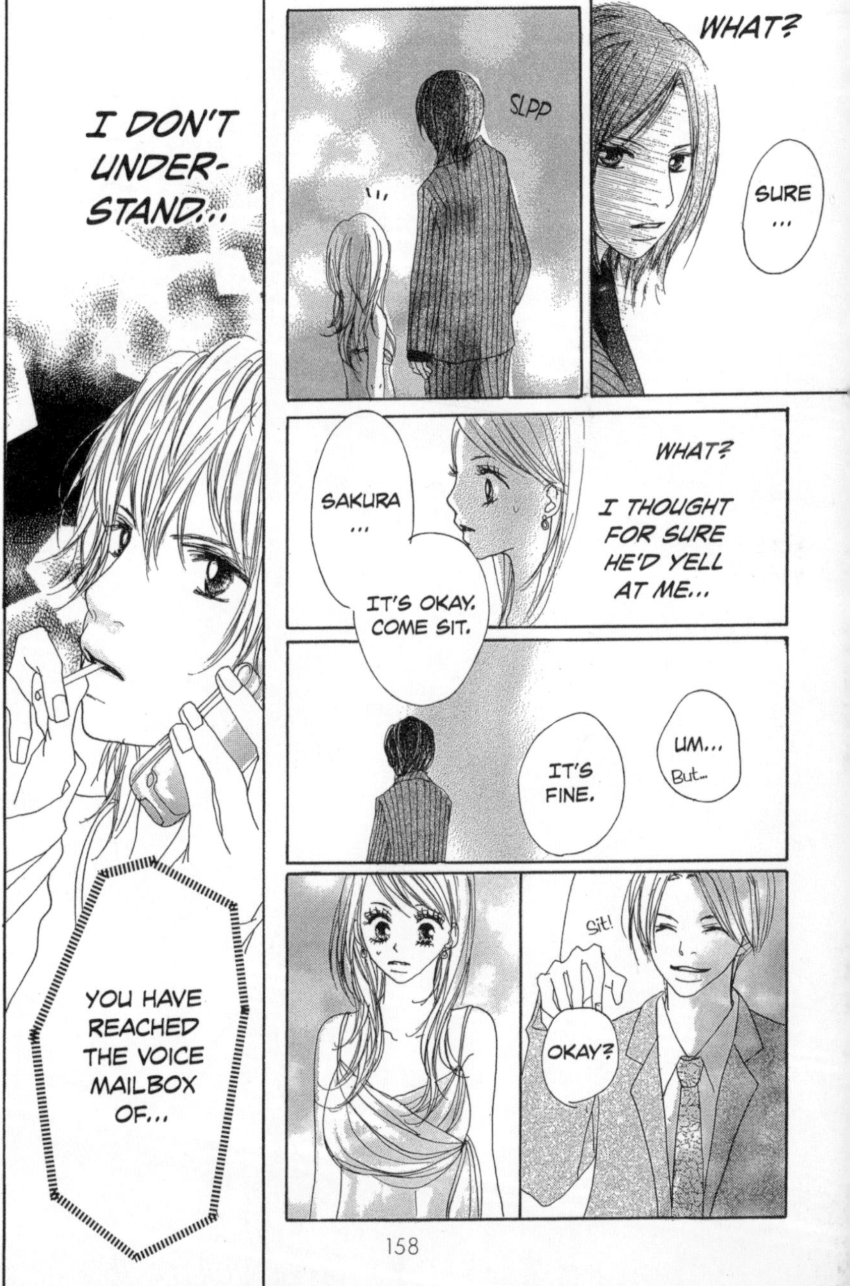
WHAT?
SURE...
SLPP
WHAT?
I THOUGHT FOR SURE HE'D YELL AT ME...
SAKURA...
IT'S OKAY. COME SIT.
UM...
But...
IT'S FINE.
Sit!
OKAY?
I DON'T UNDER-STAND...
YOU HAVE REACHED THE VOICE MAILBOX OF...

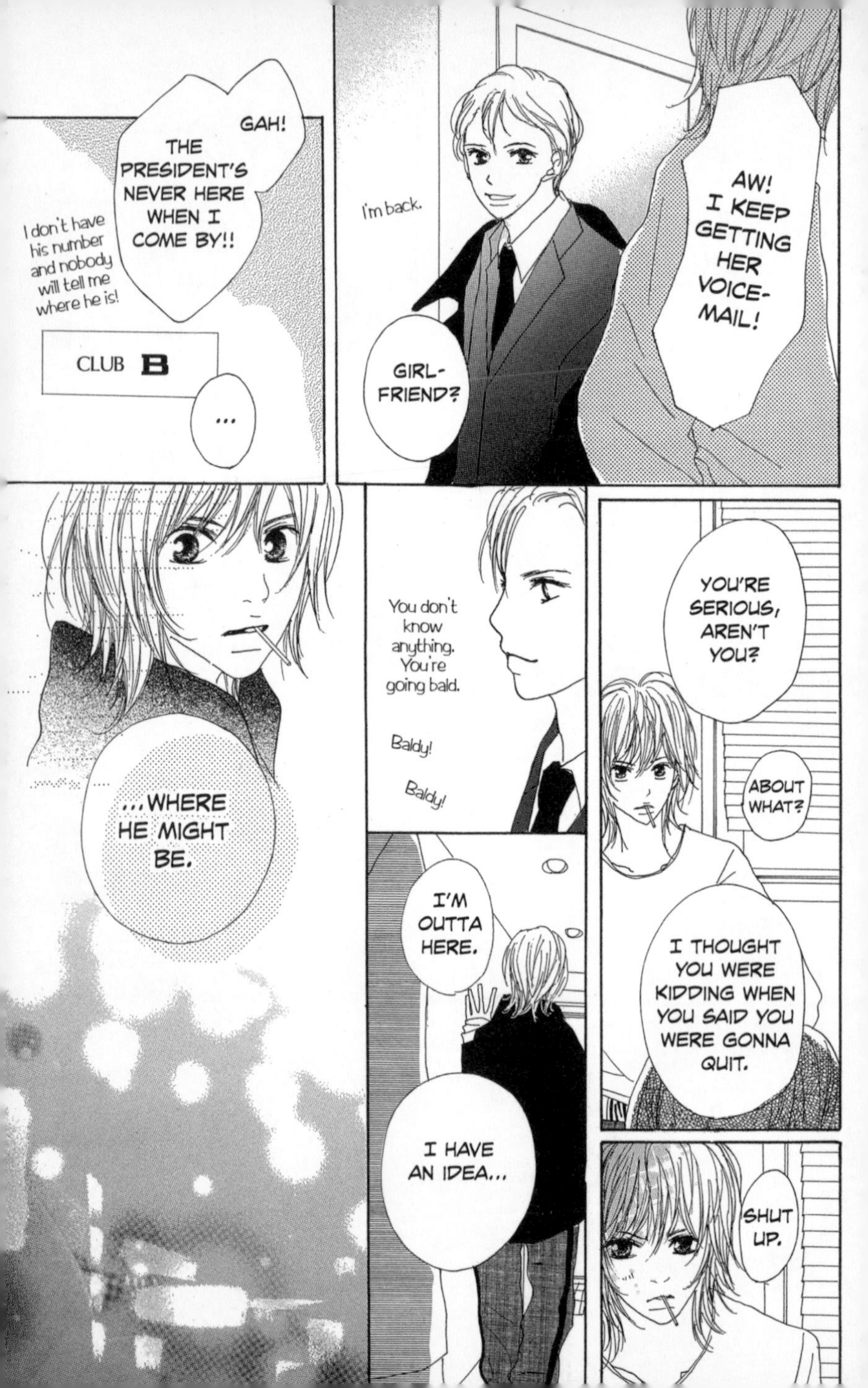
AW! I KEEP GETTING HER VOICE-MAIL!
I'm back.
GIRL-FRIEND?
GAH! THE PRESIDENT'S NEVER HERE WHEN I COME BY!!
I don't have his number and nobody will tell me where he is!
CLUB B
...
YOU'RE SERIOUS, AREN'T YOU?
ABOUT WHAT?
I THOUGHT YOU WERE KIDDING WHEN YOU SAID YOU WERE GONNA QUIT.
SHUT UP.
You don't know anything. You're going bald.
Baldy!
Baldy!
I'M OUTTA HERE.
I HAVE AN IDEA...
...WHERE HE MIGHT BE.

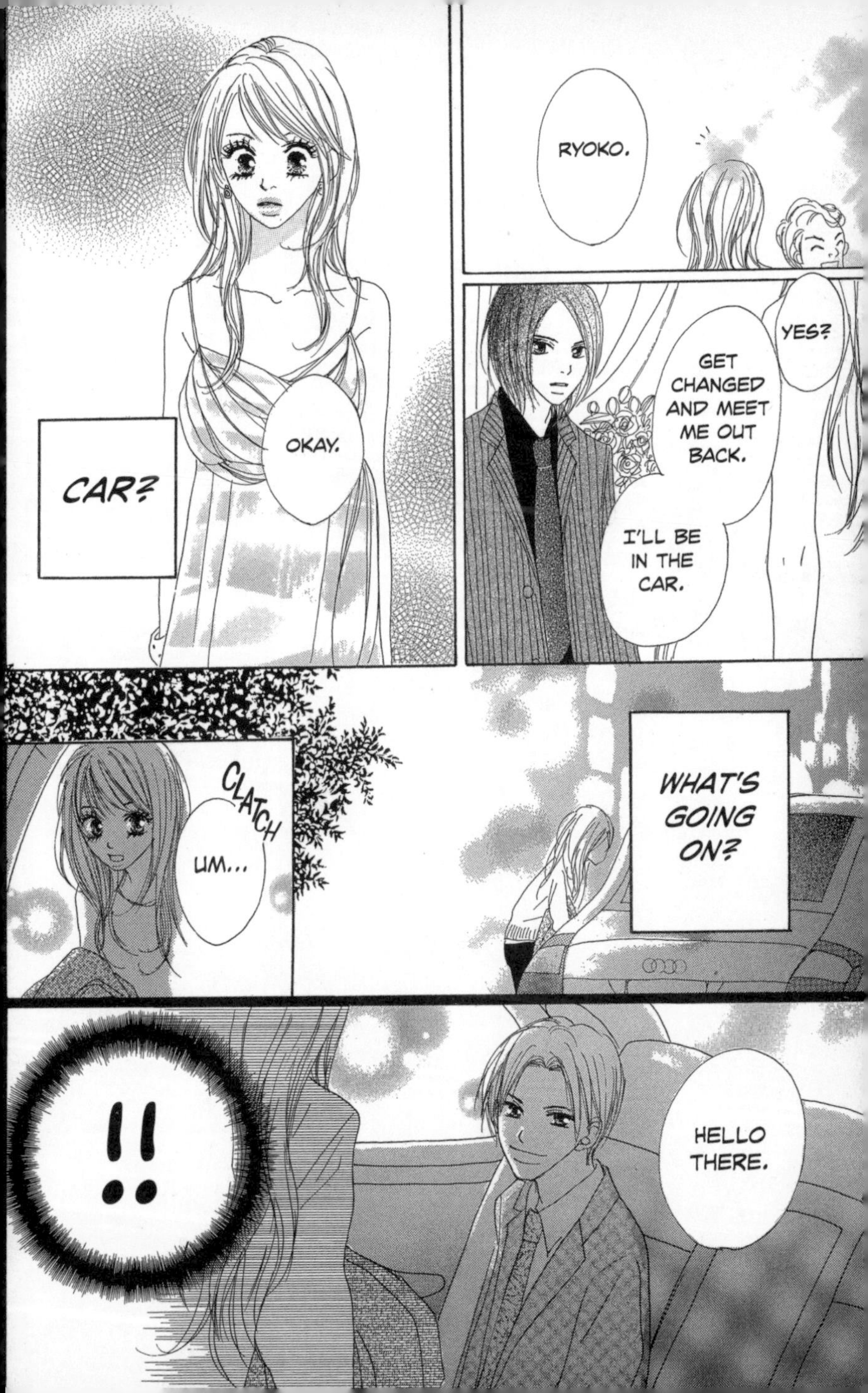
RYOKO.
YES?
GET CHANGED AND MEET ME OUT BACK.
I'LL BE IN THE CAR.
OKAY.
CAR?
WHAT'S GOING ON?
CLATCH
UM...
HELLO THERE.
!!

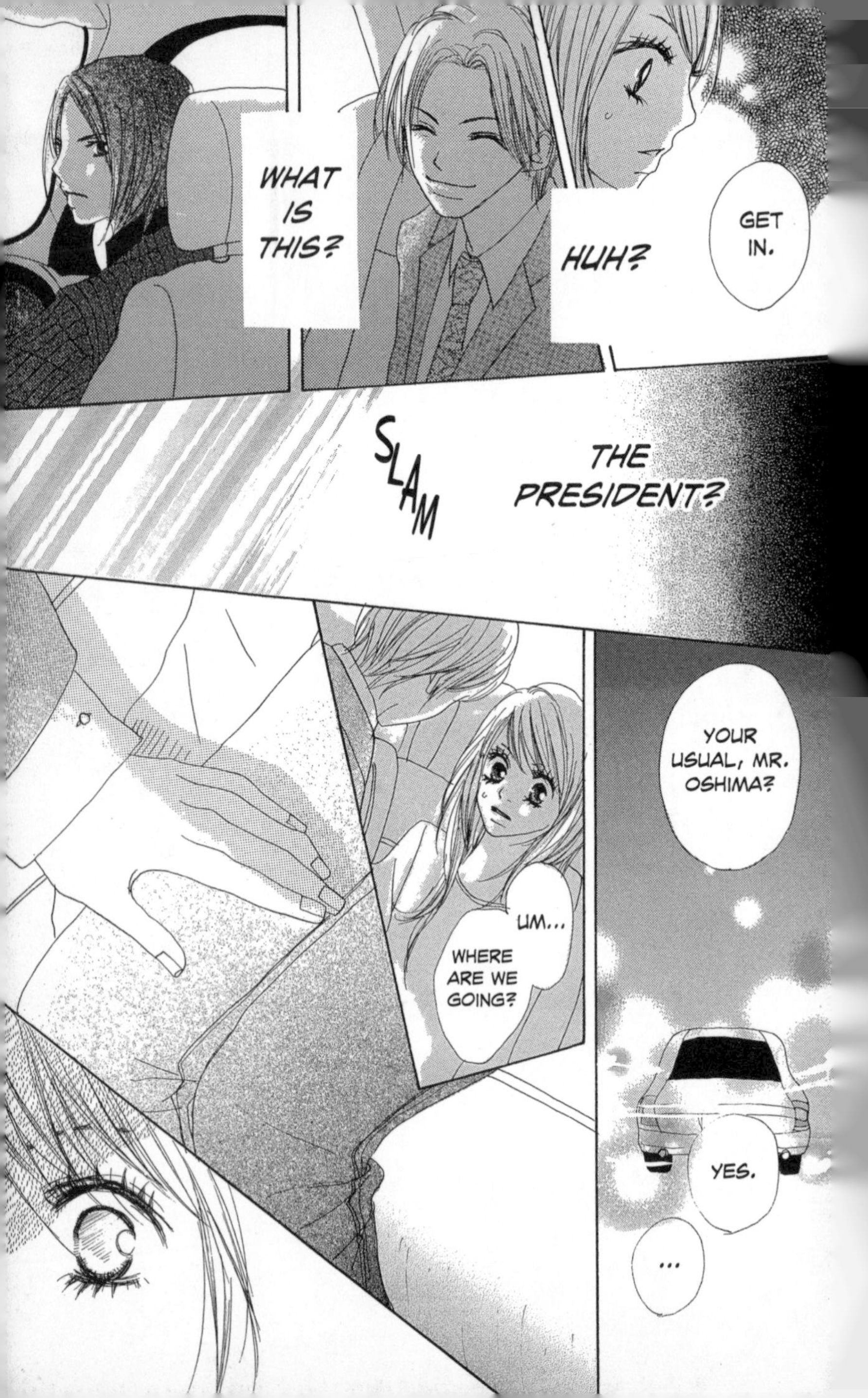
GET IN.
HUH?
WHAT IS THIS?
THE PRESIDENT?
SLAM
YOUR USUAL, MR. OSHIMA?
YES.
...
UM... WHERE ARE WE GOING?

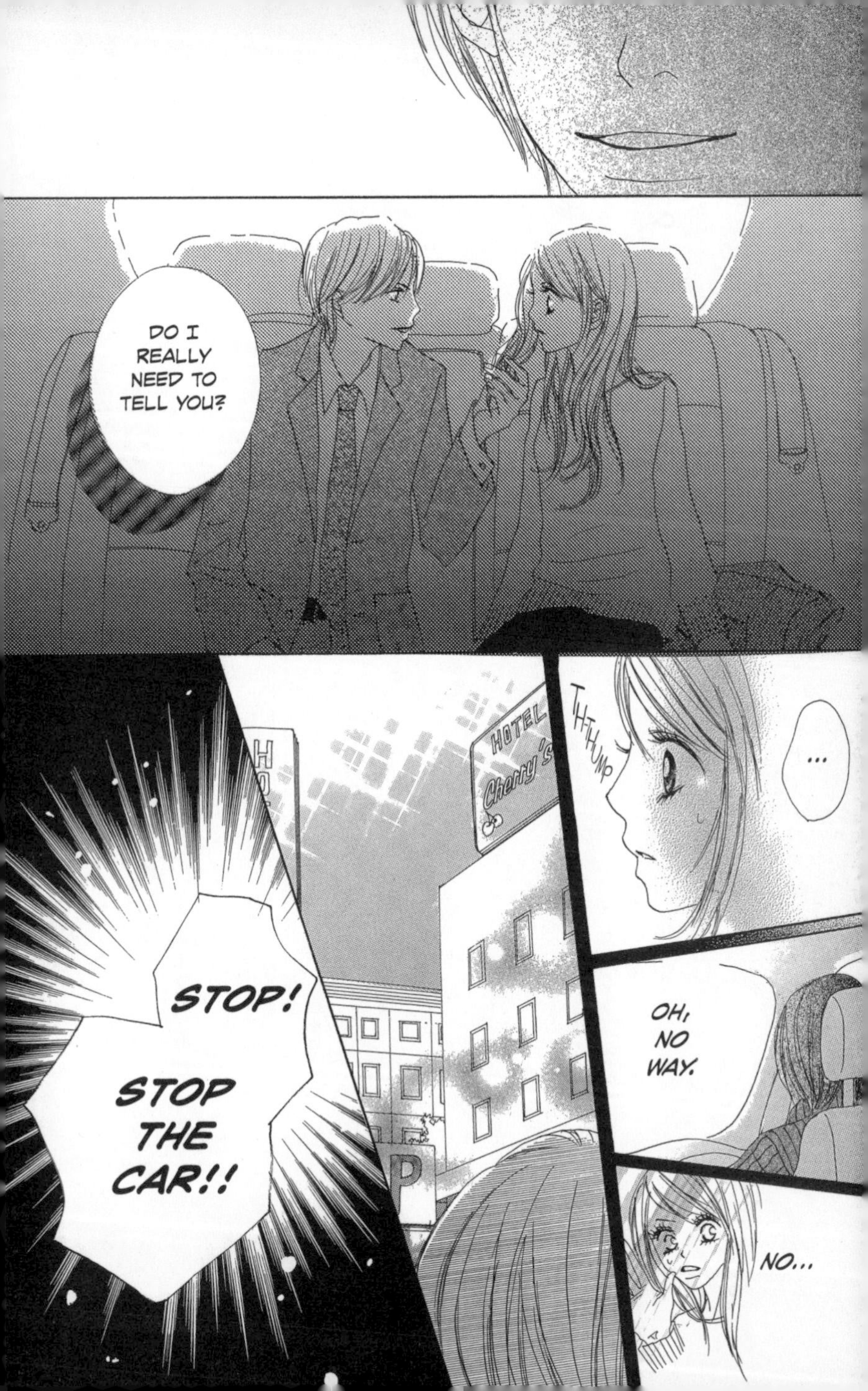
DO I REALLY NEED TO TELL YOU?
TH-THUMP
...
OH, NO WAY.
NO...
HOTEL Cherry's
STOP!
STOP THE CAR!!

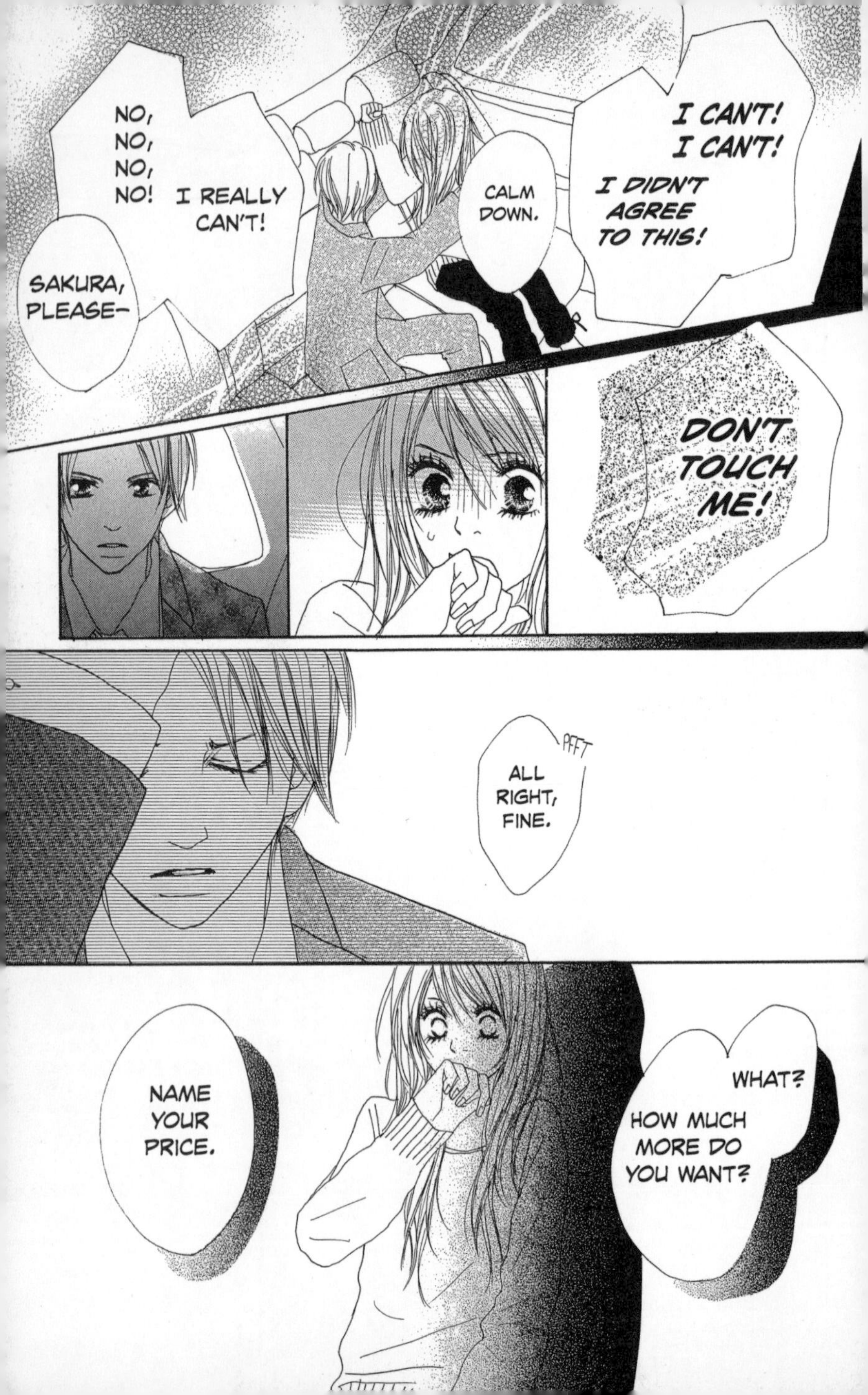
I CAN'T! I CAN'T!
I DIDN'T AGREE TO THIS!
CALM DOWN.
NO, NO, NO, NO!
I REALLY CAN'T!
SAKURA, PLEASE—
DON'T TOUCH ME!
PFFT
ALL RIGHT, FINE.
WHAT?
HOW MUCH MORE DO YOU WANT?
NAME YOUR PRICE.

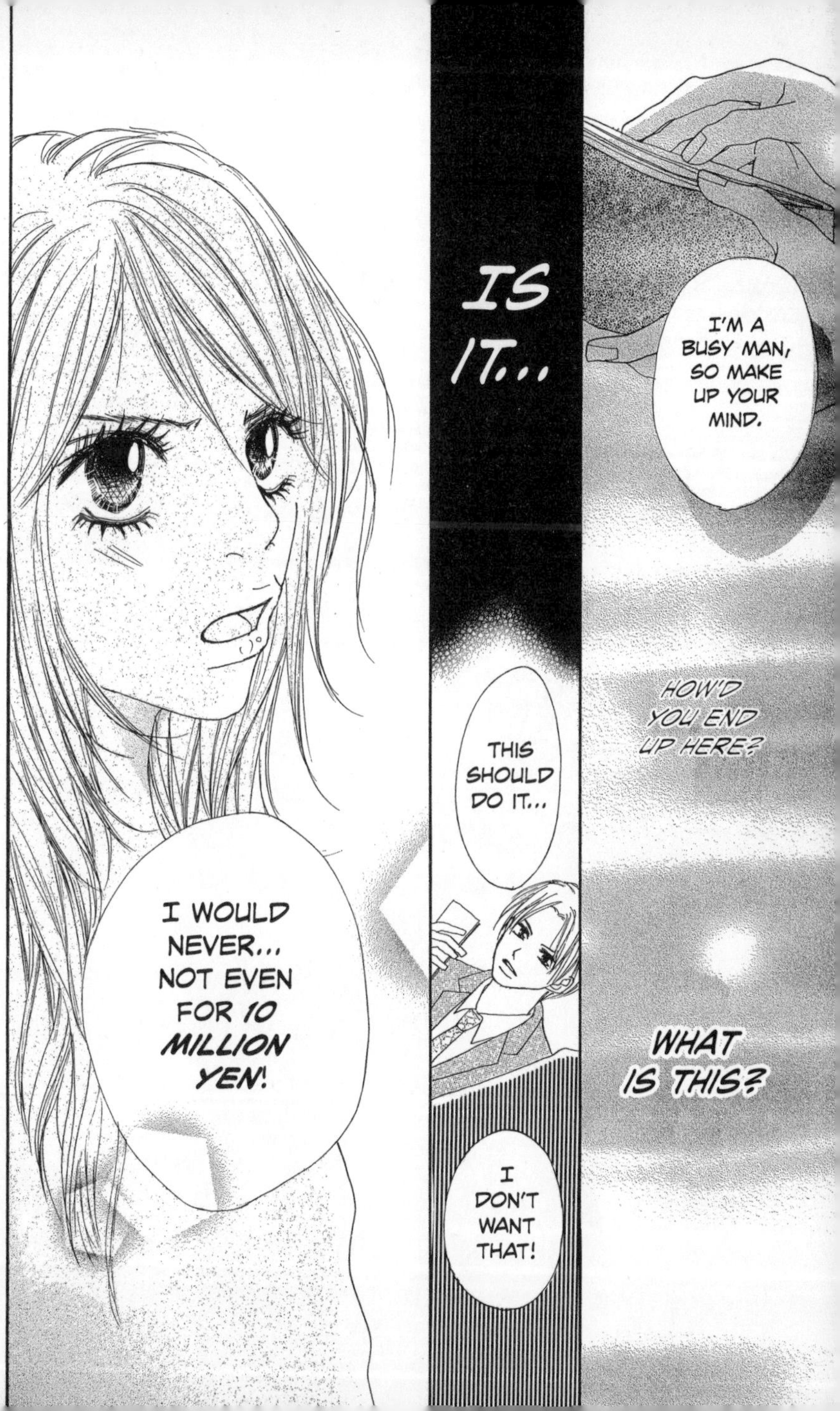

I'M A BUSY MAN, SO MAKE UP YOUR MIND.
HOW'D YOU END UP HERE?
WHAT IS THIS?
IS IT...
THIS SHOULD DO IT...
I DON'T WANT THAT!
I WOULD NEVER... NOT EVEN FOR *10 MILLION YEN*!

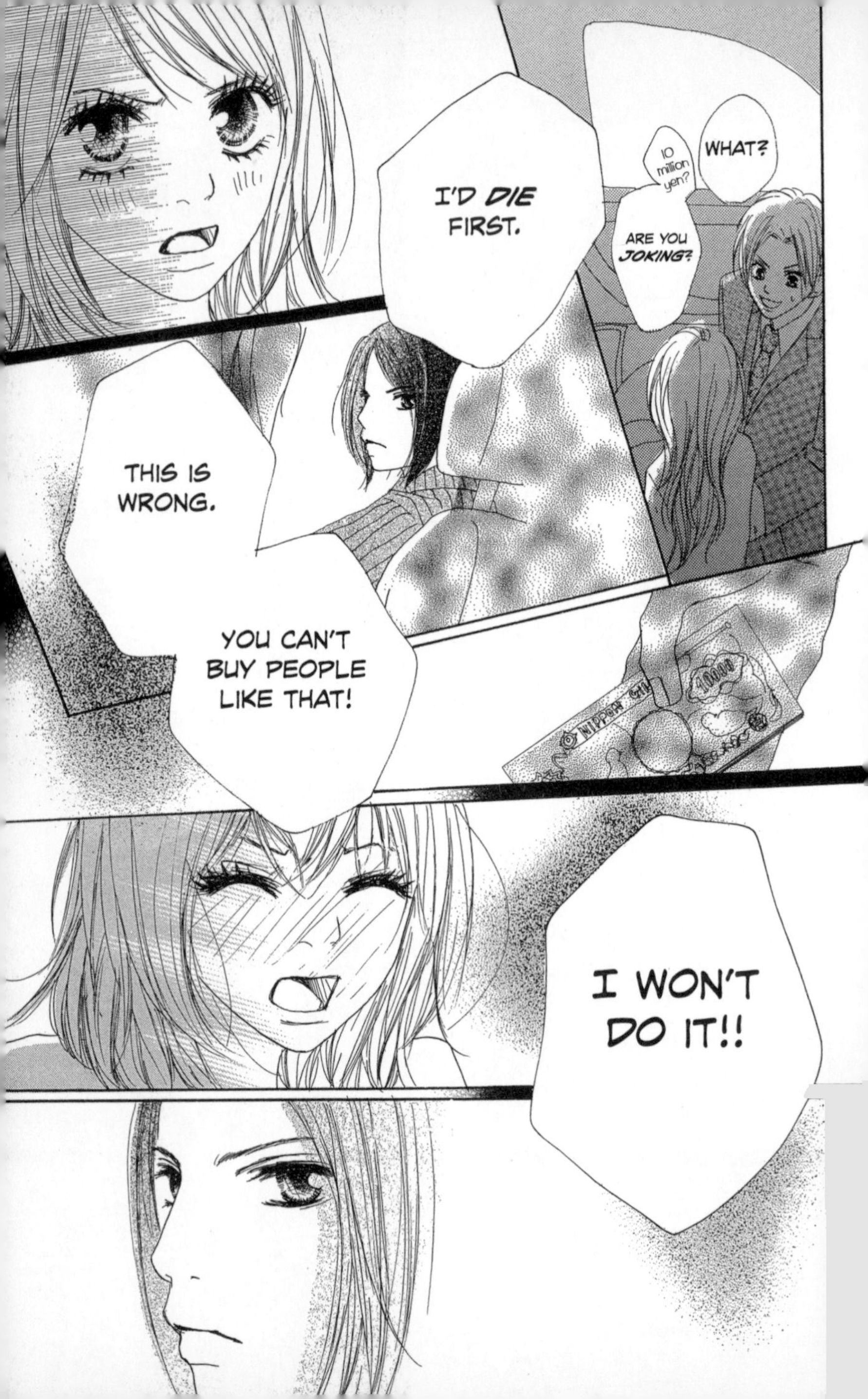
WHAT?
10 million yen?
ARE YOU *JOKING*?
I'D ***DIE*** FIRST.
THIS IS WRONG.
YOU CAN'T BUY PEOPLE LIKE THAT!
I WON'T DO IT!!

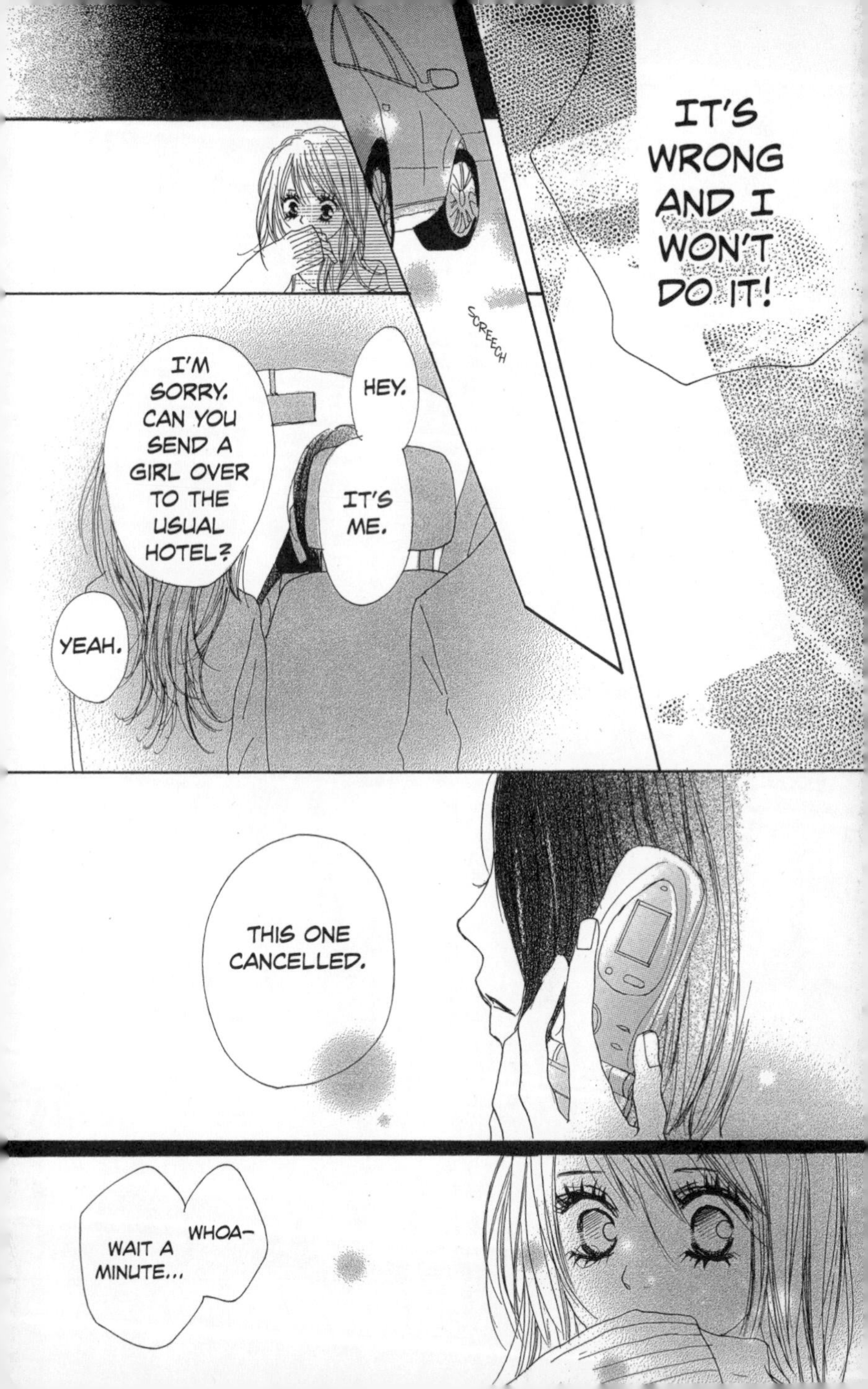
IT'S WRONG AND I WON'T DO IT!
SCREECH
HEY.
IT'S ME.
I'M SORRY. CAN YOU SEND A GIRL OVER TO THE USUAL HOTEL?
YEAH.
THIS ONE CANCELLED.
WHOA-
WAIT A MINUTE...

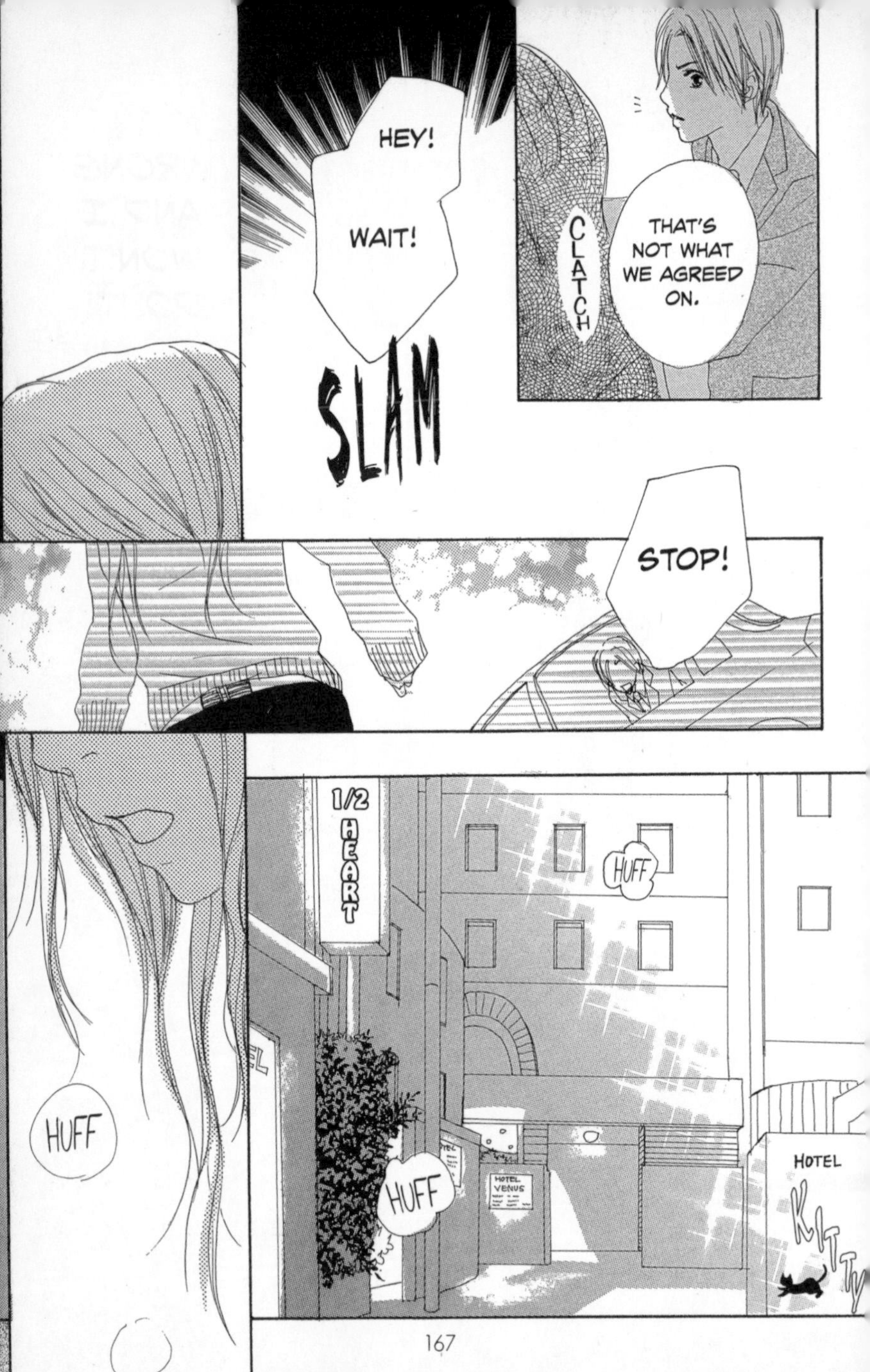
CLATCH
THAT'S NOT WHAT WE AGREED ON.
HEY!
WAIT!
SLAM
STOP!
1/2 HEART
HUFF
HOTEL
HOTEL VENUS
HUFF
KITTY
HUFF

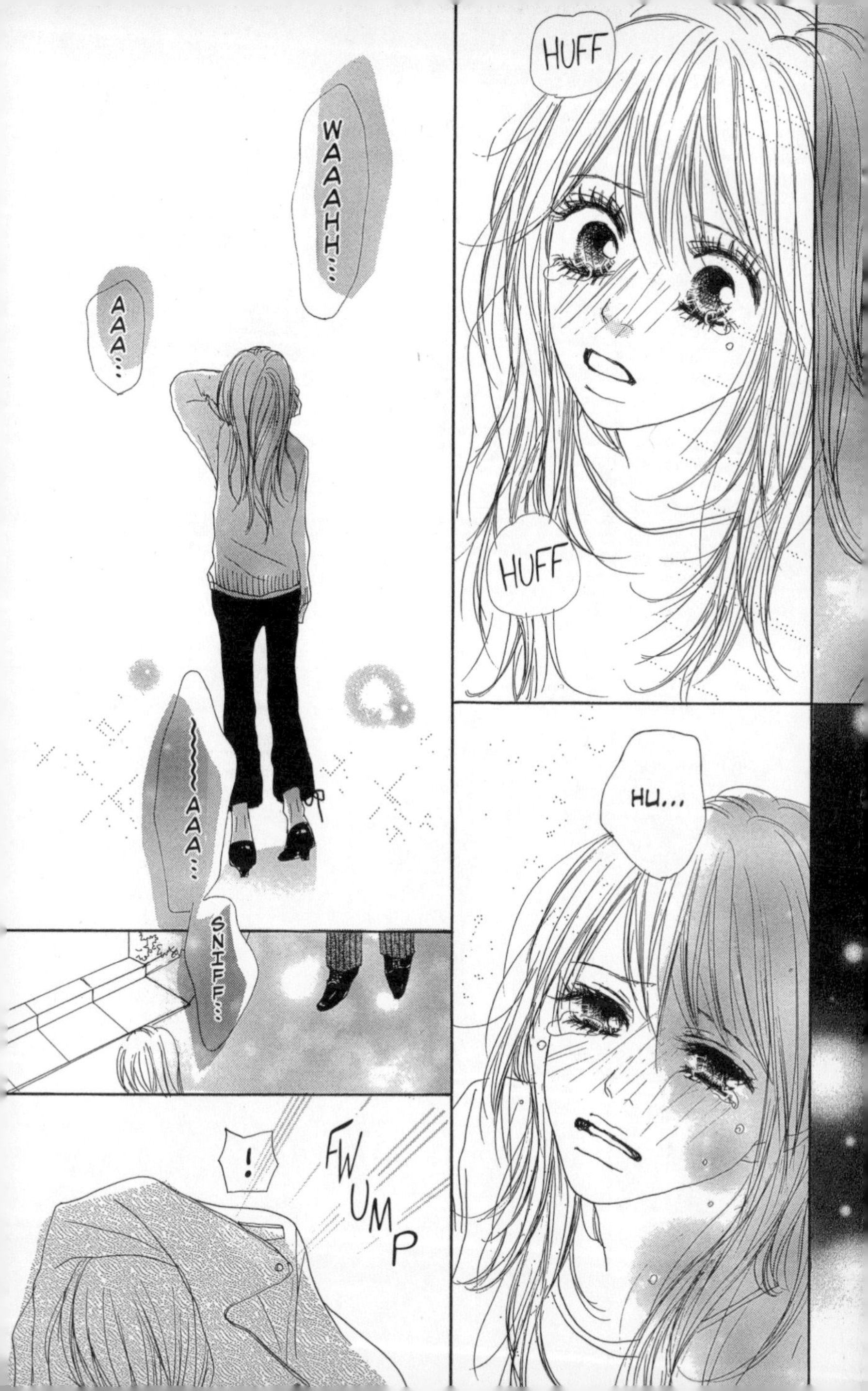
HUFF
HUFF
HU...
WAAAAHH...
AAA...
~~~AAA...
SNIFF...
!
FWUMP
~~~

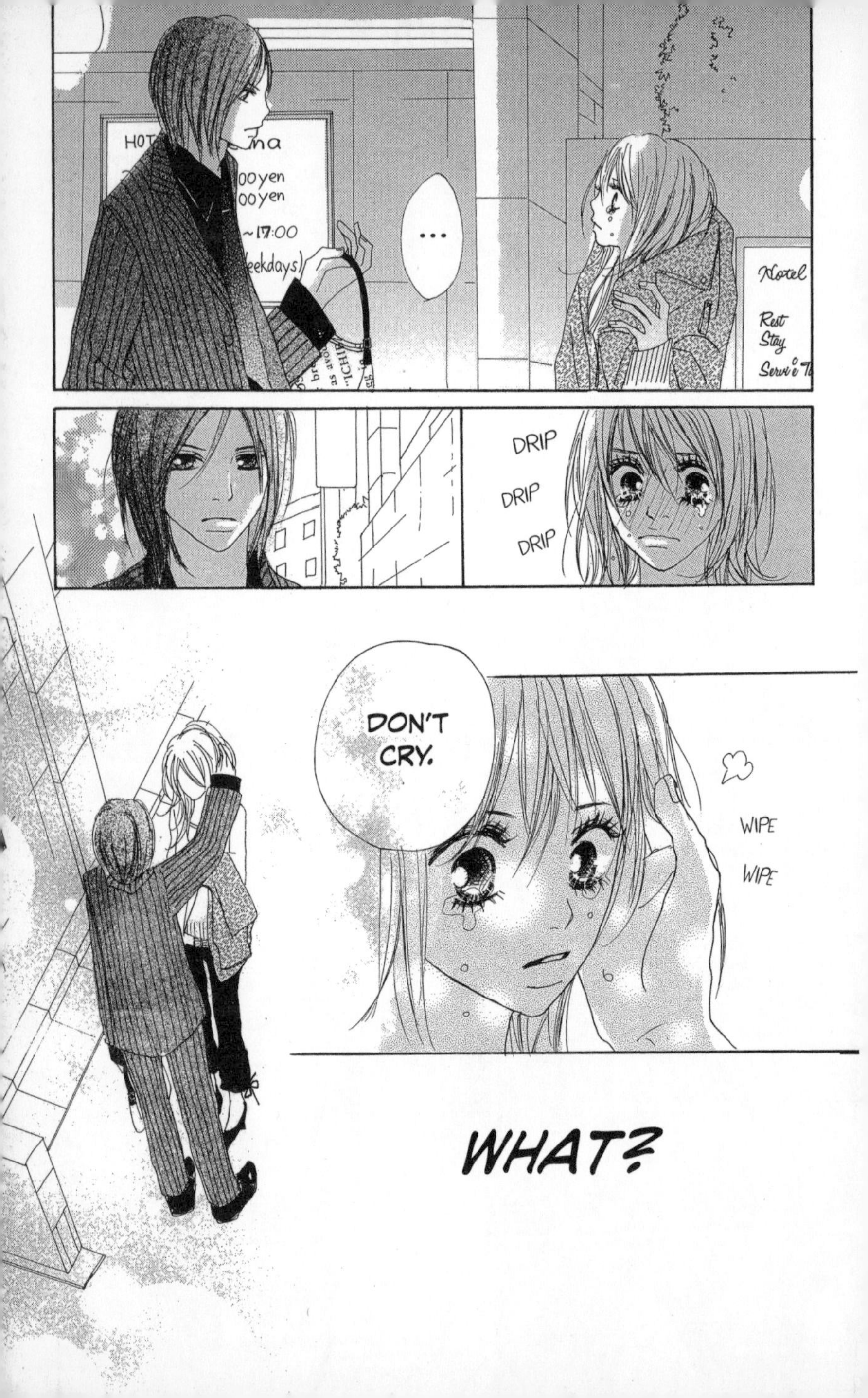
Hotel
Rest
Stay
...
DRIP
DRIP
DRIP
DON'T CRY.
WIPE
WIPE
WHAT?

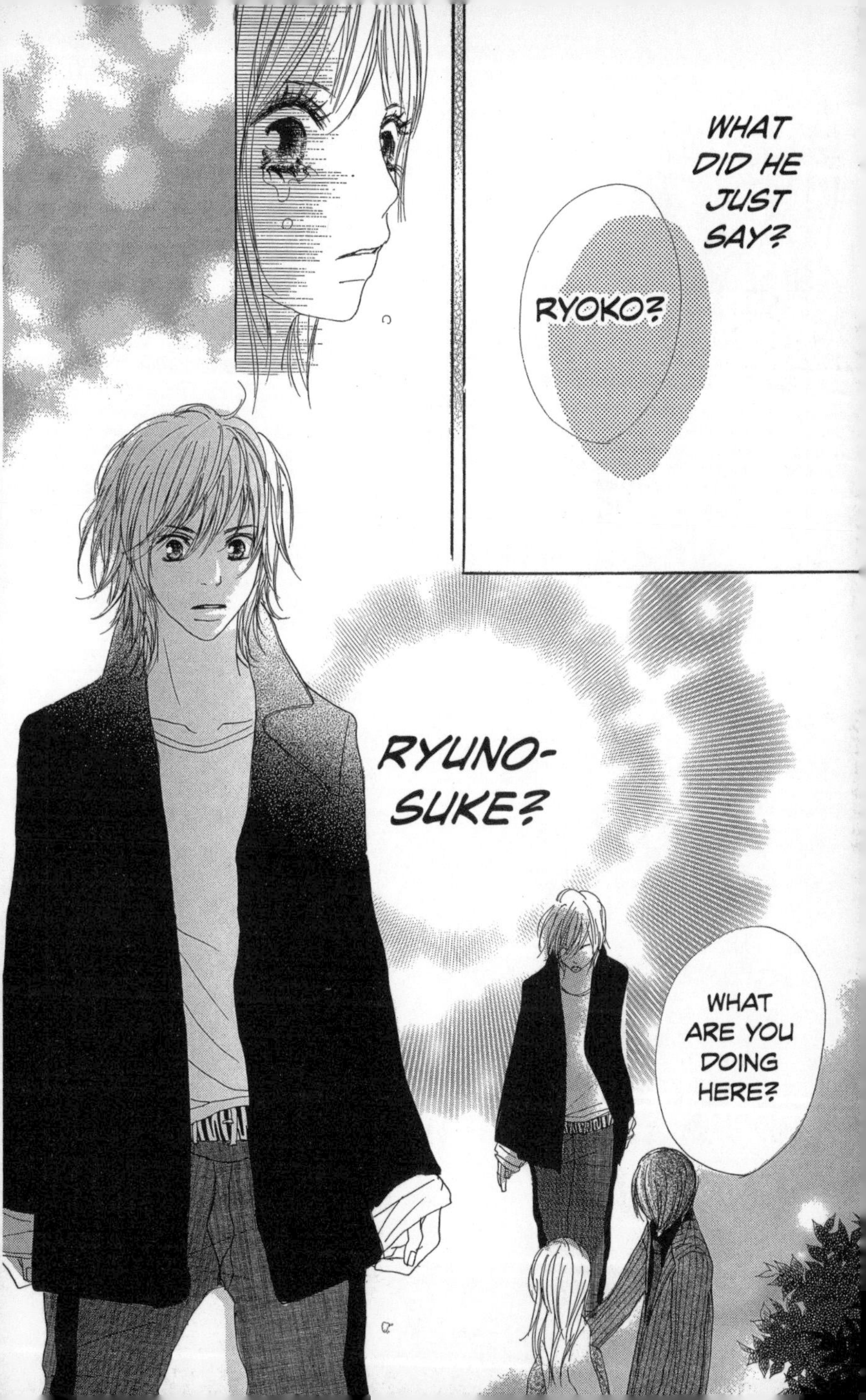
WHAT DID HE JUST SAY?
RYOKO?
WHAT ARE YOU DOING HERE?
RYUNO-SUKE?

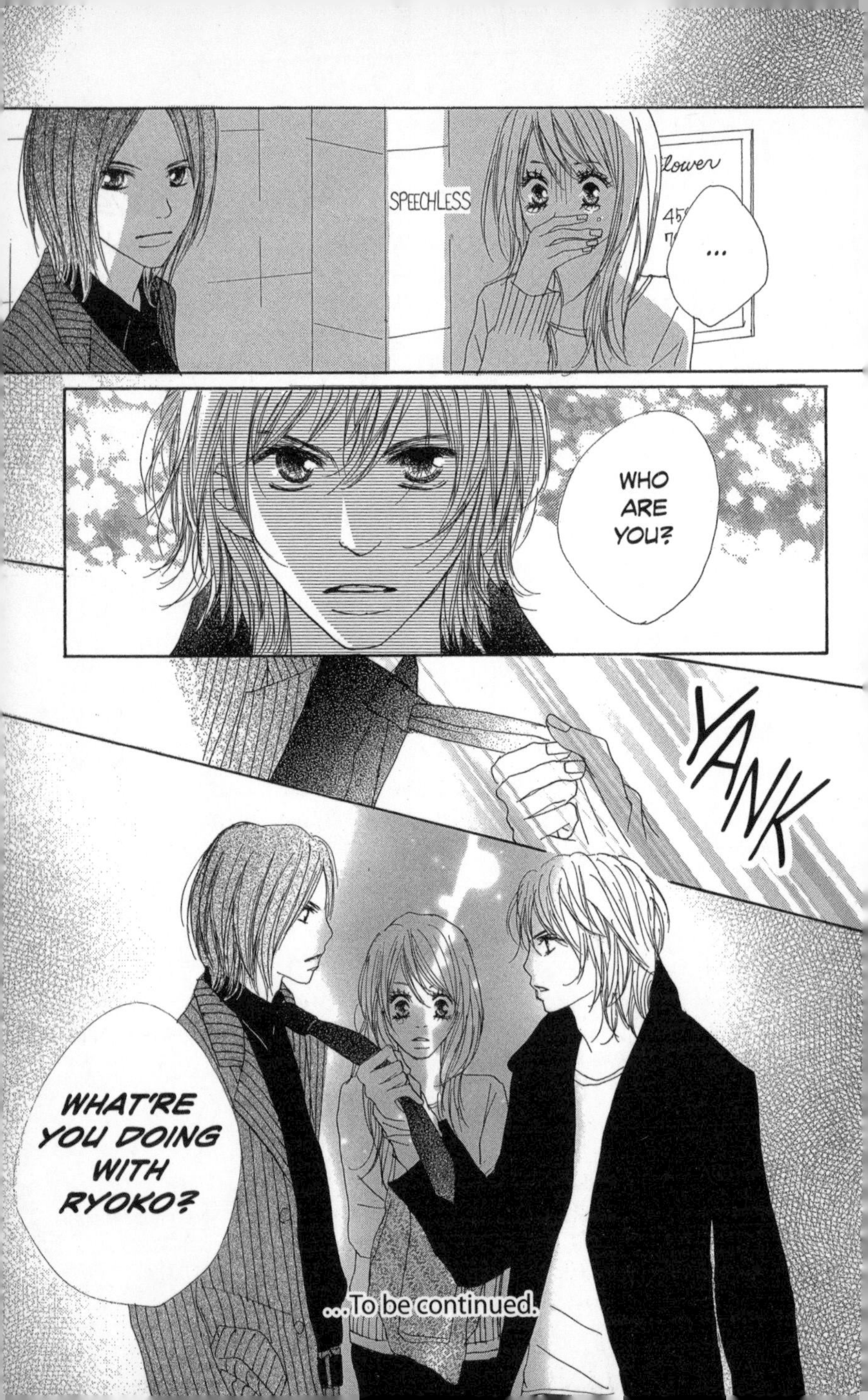
...
SPEECHLESS
WHO ARE YOU?
YANK
WHAT'RE YOU DOING WITH RYOKO?
...To be continued.

Thanks for all your letters and e-mail!

I so look forward to receiving them!! I'm sorry I can't always respond, but I assure you I do read them all!! In fact, I'd like to tell you about a few letters that left an impression on me..

"Hello♡♡! I am a regular person without a job living out in the sticks."

   …"The sticks"? "Regular person"?! I love it. (I'm a regular person too, you know. I totally blend in.)

"I'm an average 9th grade girl who only talks about wanting to be a manga artist."

   …Is this self-deprecation? "Only talks about"? BWA HA HA HA, I got this letter at the same time as the one above and it made me laugh so hard I read it twice.

"When B.O.D.Y. ends I'm gonna cry!!" SNIFF

   …Don't say that, you'll make me cry. From joy.
I'm thrilled that somebody feels that way. I'm so lucky. You make me want to work harder!!

"I especially like Ryunosuke in his glasses♡."

   …I get a lot of these!! Like…a whole lot. Is everybody into glasses these days? Everyone seems to like him, though, regardless of whether or not he's wearing his glasses. That's a good thing. And I've finally started hearing from people who tell me they like Ryoko. Whew!
I know that girl goes a little crazy sometimes. It's out of my control. Just when I thought, "I don't know what I'm going to do with this character!" I got a letter that said, "I can't get enough of Ryoko!" It made me laugh and cry at the same time. Thanks for cheering me up!

TH TWIRL TWIRL AN K TWIRL Y TWIRL TWIRL OU TWIRL

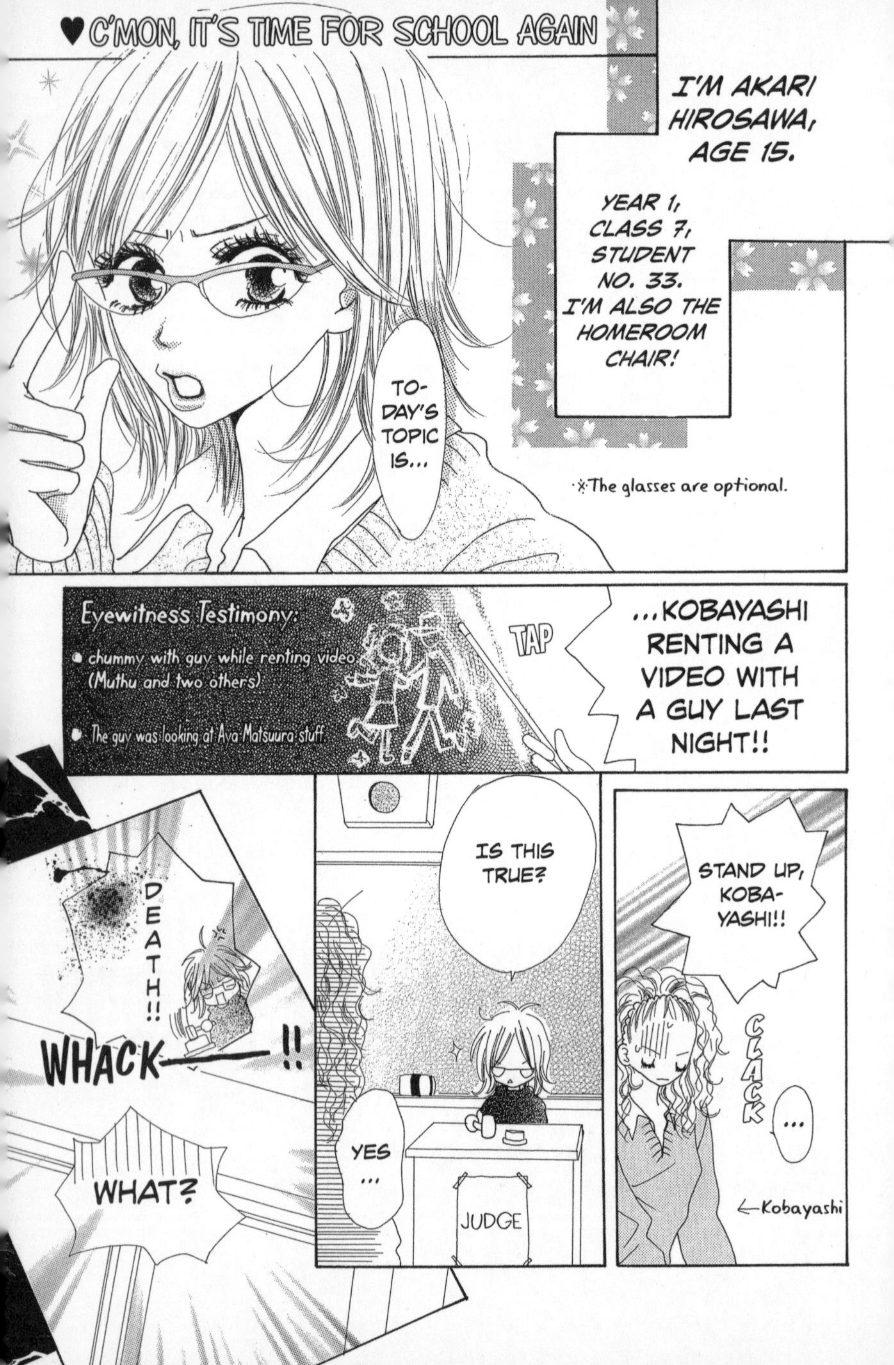
♥C'MON, IT'S TIME FOR SCHOOL AGAIN
I'M AKARI HIROSAWA, AGE 15.
YEAR 1, CLASS 7, STUDENT NO. 33. I'M ALSO THE HOMEROOM CHAIR!
TO-DAY'S TOPIC IS...
※The glasses are optional.
...KOBAYASHI RENTING A VIDEO WITH A GUY LAST NIGHT!!
TAP
Eyewitness Testimony:
• chummy with guy while renting video (Muthu and two others)
• The guy was looking at Aya Matsuura stuff.
STAND UP, KOBA-YASHI!!
CLACK
...
←Kobayashi
IS THIS TRUE?
YES...
JUDGE
DEATH!!
WHACK—!!
WHAT?

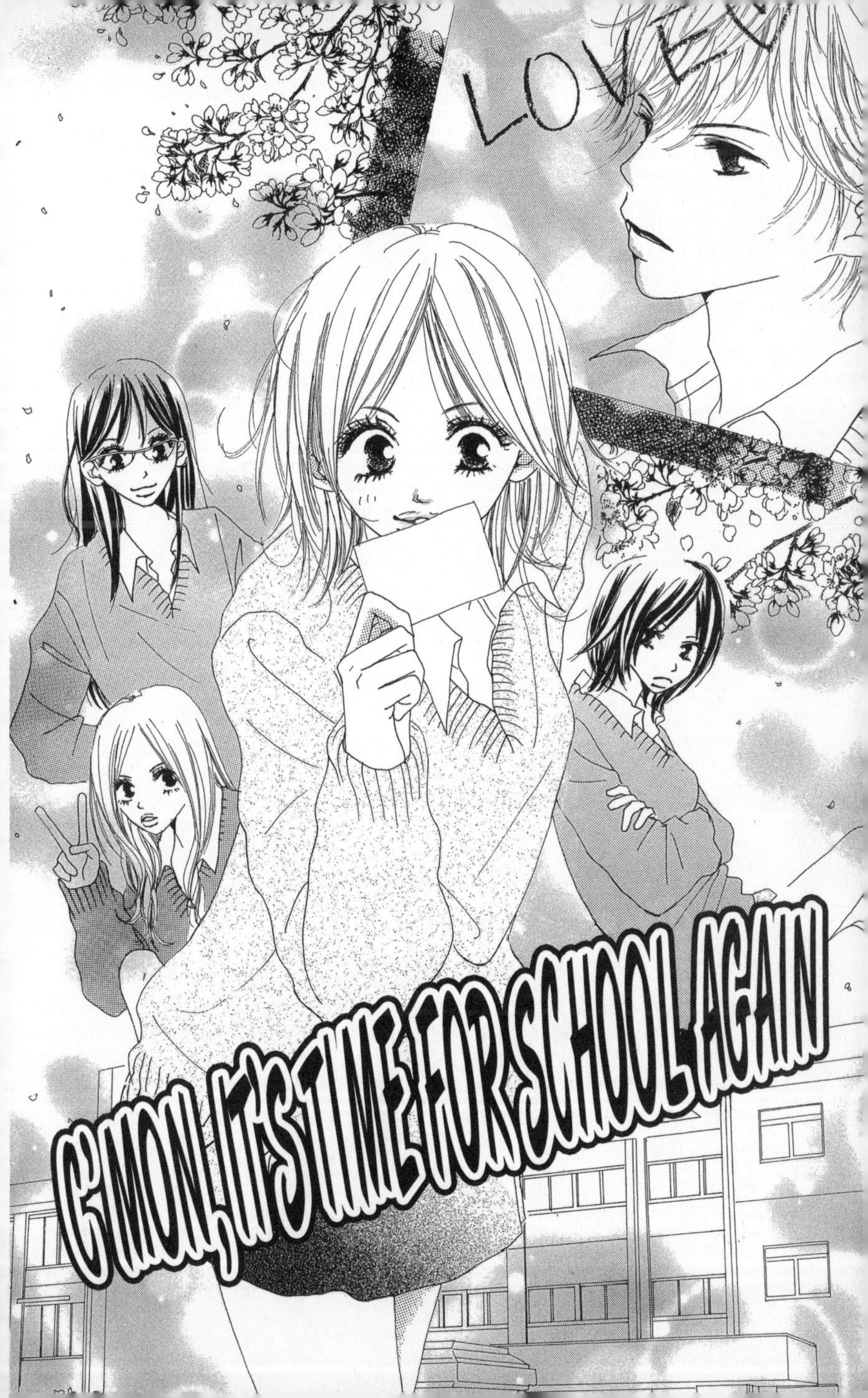
LOVE
C'MON, IT'S TIME FOR SCHOOL AGAIN

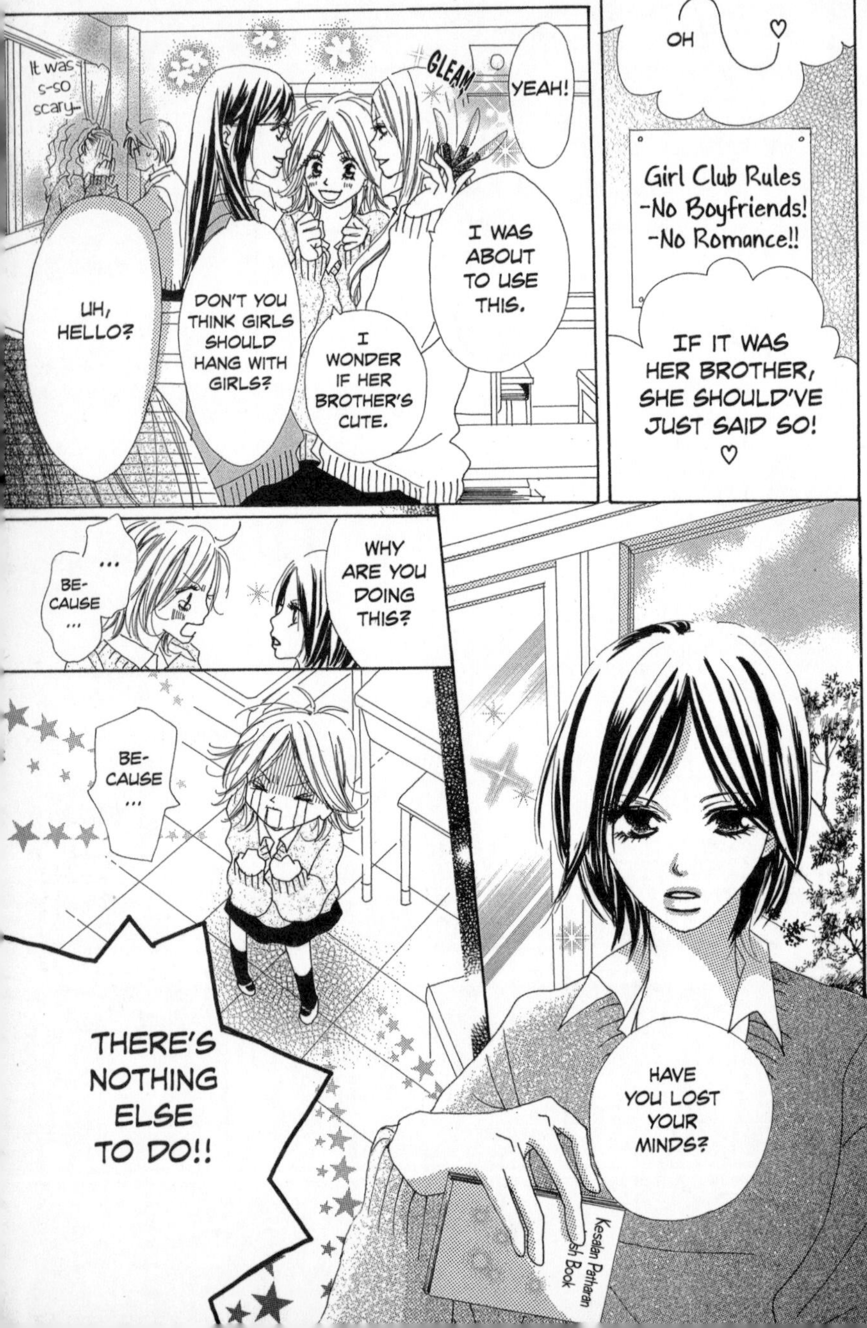
OH ♥
Girl Club Rules
-No Boyfriends!
-No Romance!!
IF IT WAS HER BROTHER, SHE SHOULD'VE JUST SAID SO! ♥
YEAH!
GLEAM
I WAS ABOUT TO USE THIS.
I WONDER IF HER BROTHER'S CUTE.
DON'T YOU THINK GIRLS SHOULD HANG WITH GIRLS?
UH, HELLO?
It was s-so scary...
HAVE YOU LOST YOUR MINDS?
Kesalan Patharan
sh Book
WHY ARE YOU DOING THIS?
... BE-CAUSE ...
BE-CAUSE ...
THERE'S NOTHING ELSE TO DO!!

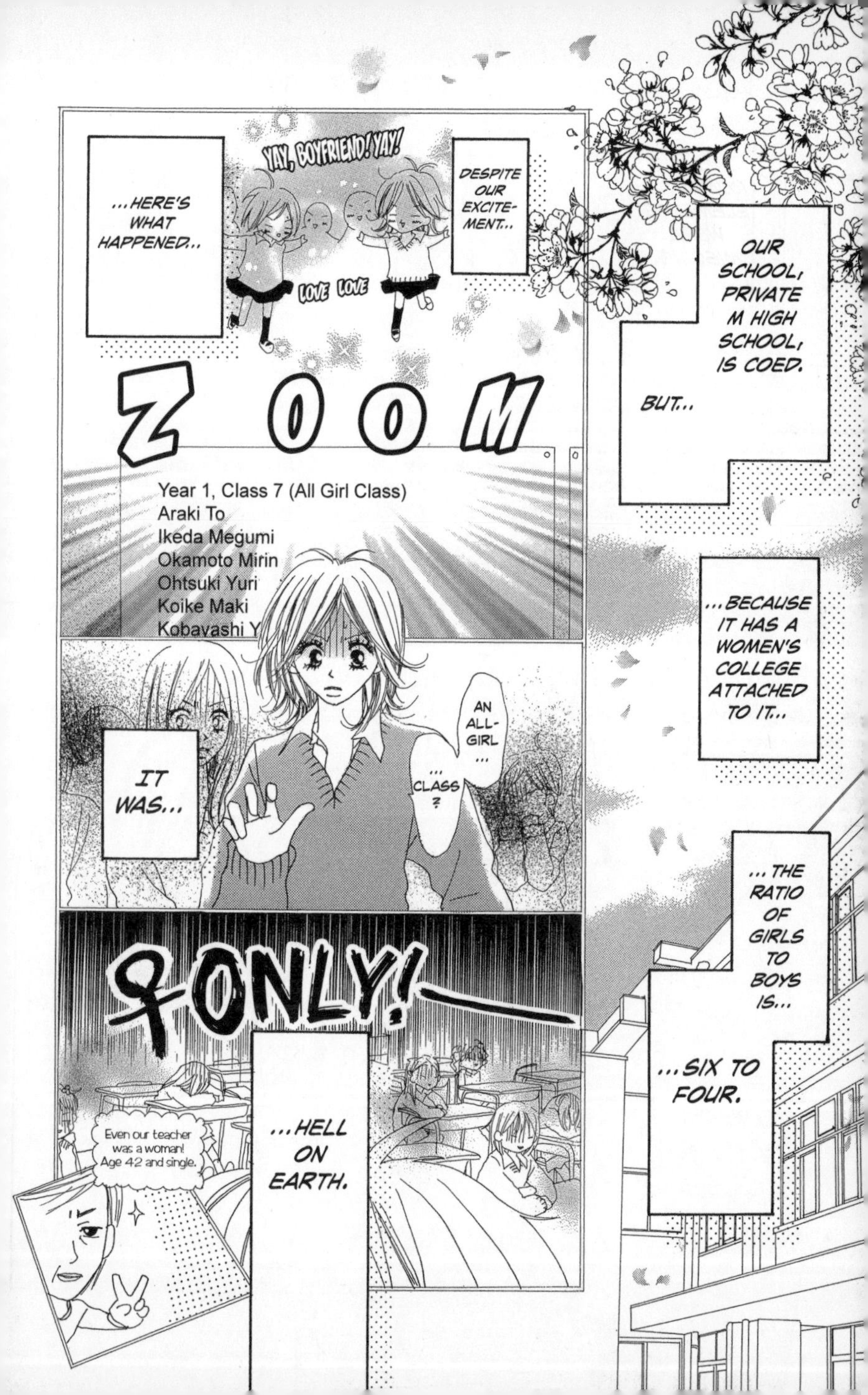
OUR SCHOOL, PRIVATE M HIGH SCHOOL, IS COED.
BUT...
...BECAUSE IT HAS A WOMEN'S COLLEGE ATTACHED TO IT...
...THE RATIO OF GIRLS TO BOYS IS...
...SIX TO FOUR.
DESPITE OUR EXCITEMENT...
YAY, BOYFRIEND! YAY!
LOVE LOVE
...HERE'S WHAT HAPPENED...
ZOOM
Year 1, Class 7 (All Girl Class)
Araki To
Ikeda Megumi
Okamoto Mirin
Ohtsuki Yuri
Koike Maki
Kobayashi Y
AN ALL-GIRL...
...CLASS?
IT WAS...
♀ONLY!
...HELL ON EARTH.
Even our teacher was a woman! Age 42 and single.

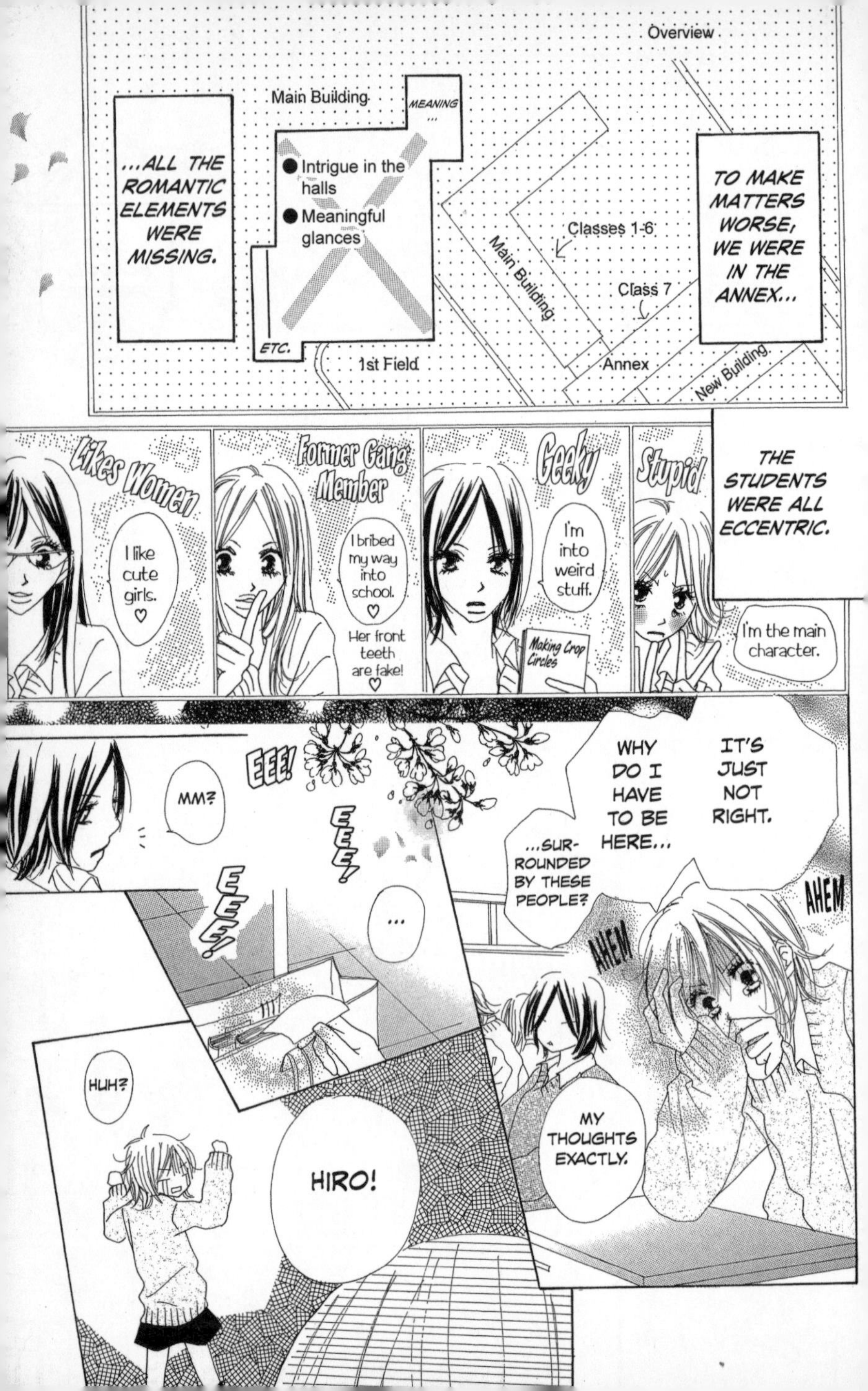
TO MAKE MATTERS WORSE, WE WERE IN THE ANNEX...
Overview
Main Building
Classes 1-6
Class 7
Annex
New Building
Main Building
MEANING ...
Intrigue in the halls
Meaningful glances
ETC.
1st Field
...ALL THE ROMANTIC ELEMENTS WERE MISSING.
THE STUDENTS WERE ALL ECCENTRIC.
Stupid
I'm the main character.
Geeky
I'm into weird stuff.
Making Crop Circles
Former Gang Member
I bribed my way into school. ♡
Her front teeth are fake! ♡
Likes Women
I like cute girls. ♡
IT'S JUST NOT RIGHT.
WHY DO I HAVE TO BE HERE...
...SURROUNDED BY THESE PEOPLE?
AHEM
AHEM
MY THOUGHTS EXACTLY.
EEE!
MM?
EEE!
EEE!
...
HUH?
HIRO!

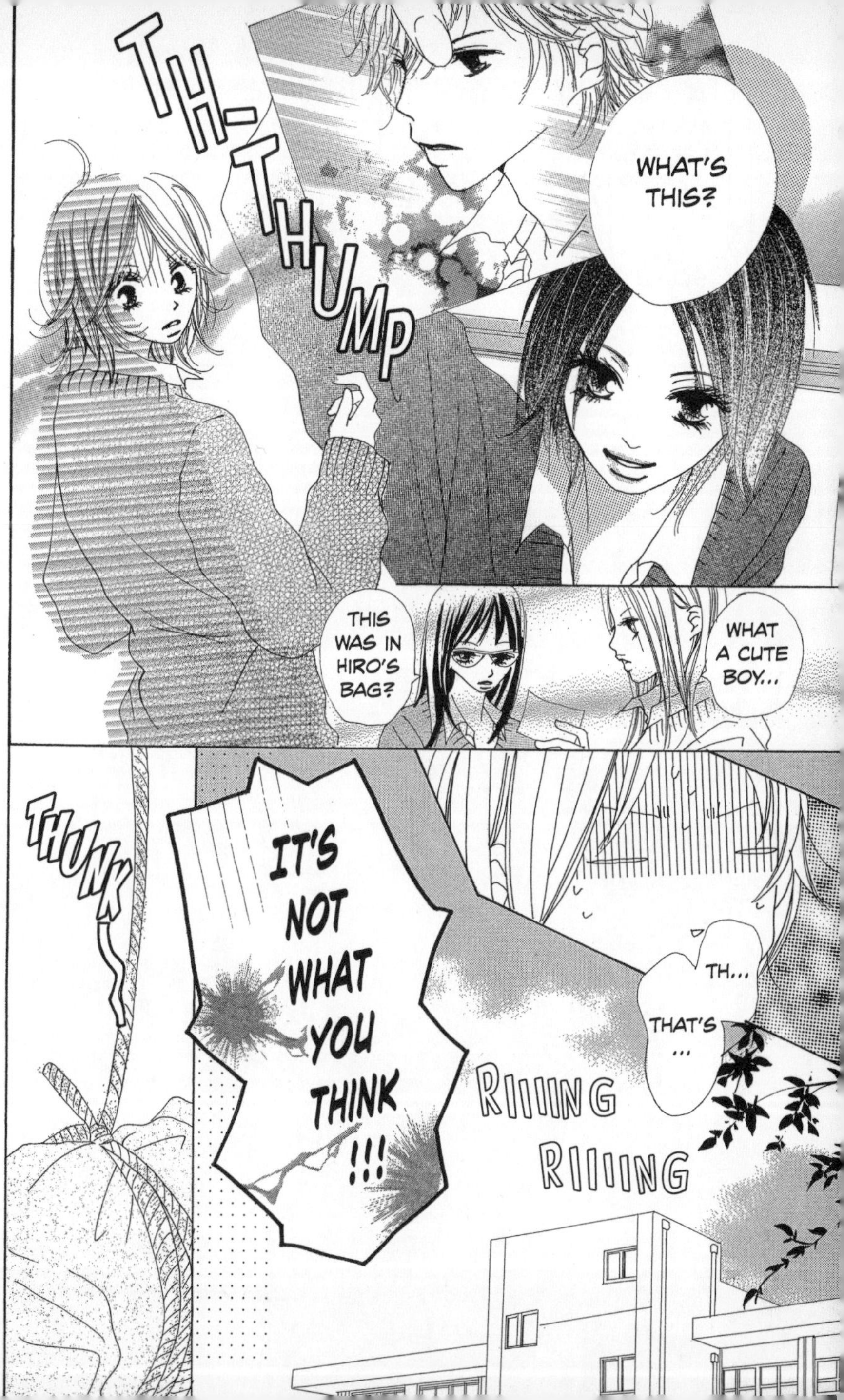
WHAT'S THIS?
TH-THUMP
WHAT A CUTE BOY...
THIS WAS IN HIRO'S BAG?
TH... THAT'S...
RIIIING
RIIIING
IT'S NOT WHAT YOU THINK!!!
THUNK

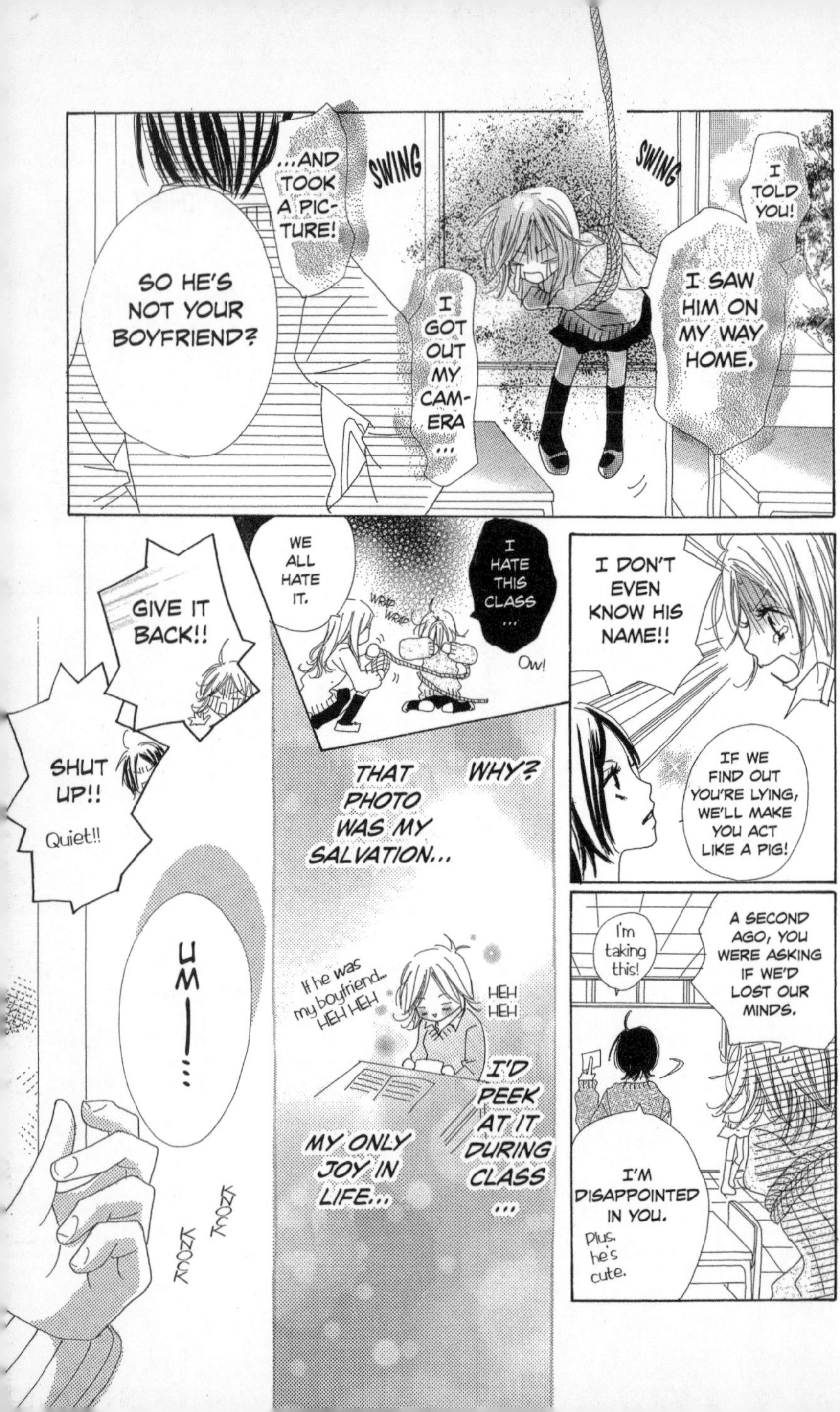
I TOLD YOU!
I SAW HIM ON MY WAY HOME.
SWING
I GOT OUT MY CAM-ERA...
SWING
...AND TOOK A PIC-TURE!
SO HE'S NOT YOUR BOYFRIEND?
I DON'T EVEN KNOW HIS NAME!!
IF WE FIND OUT YOU'RE LYING, WE'LL MAKE YOU ACT LIKE A PIG!
A SECOND AGO, YOU WERE ASKING IF WE'D LOST OUR MINDS.
I'm taking this!
I'M DISAPPOINTED IN YOU.
Plus, he's cute.
I HATE THIS CLASS...
WE ALL HATE IT.
WRAP WRAP
Ow!
WHY?
THAT PHOTO WAS MY SALVATION...
HEH HEH
If he was my boyfriend... HEH HEH
I'D PEEK AT IT DURING CLASS...
MY ONLY JOY IN LIFE...
GIVE IT BACK!!
SHUT UP!!
Quiet!!
UM--!!
KNOCK KNOCK

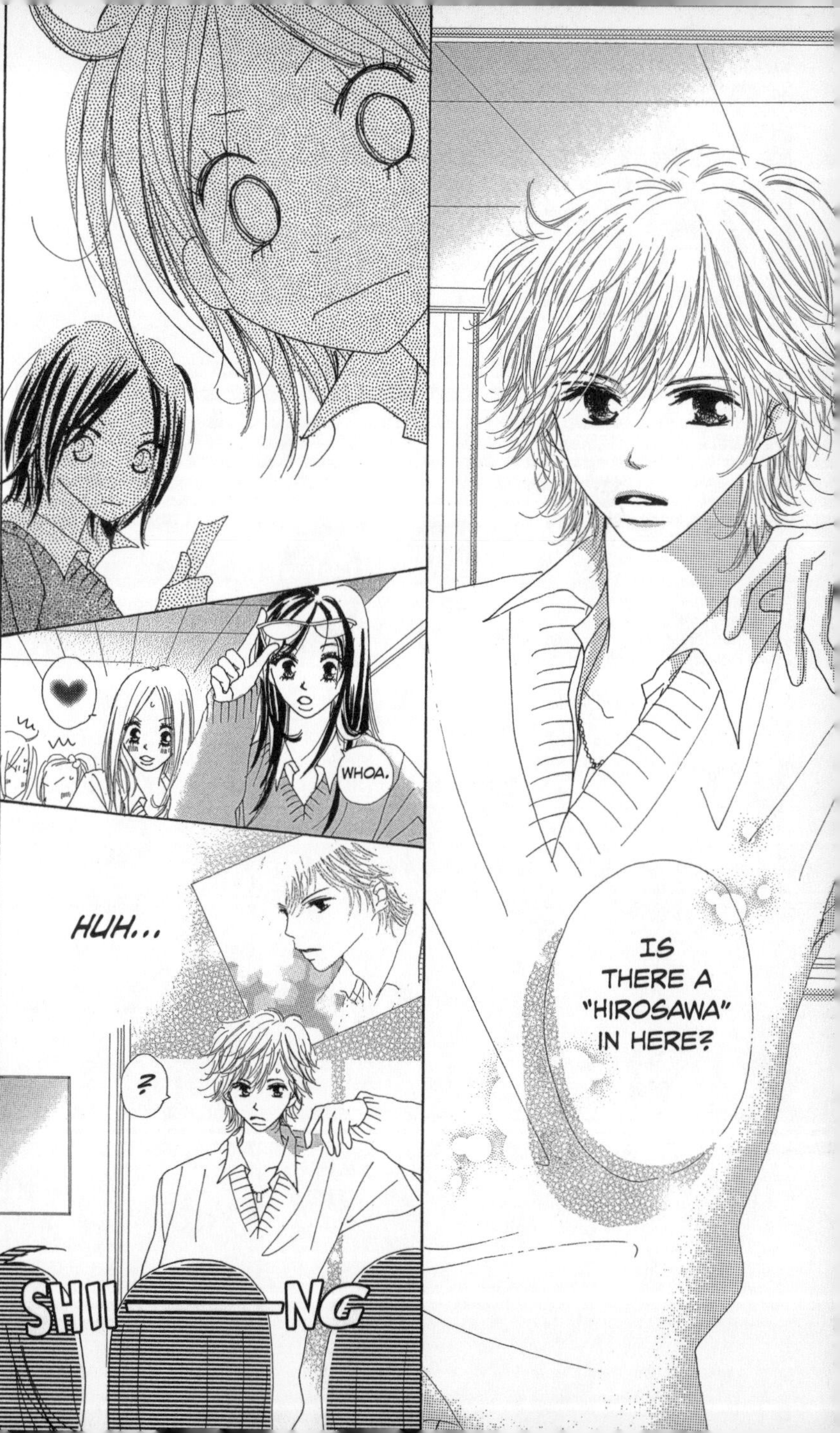
IS THERE A "HIROSAWA" IN HERE?
WHOA.
HUH...
?
SHII———NG

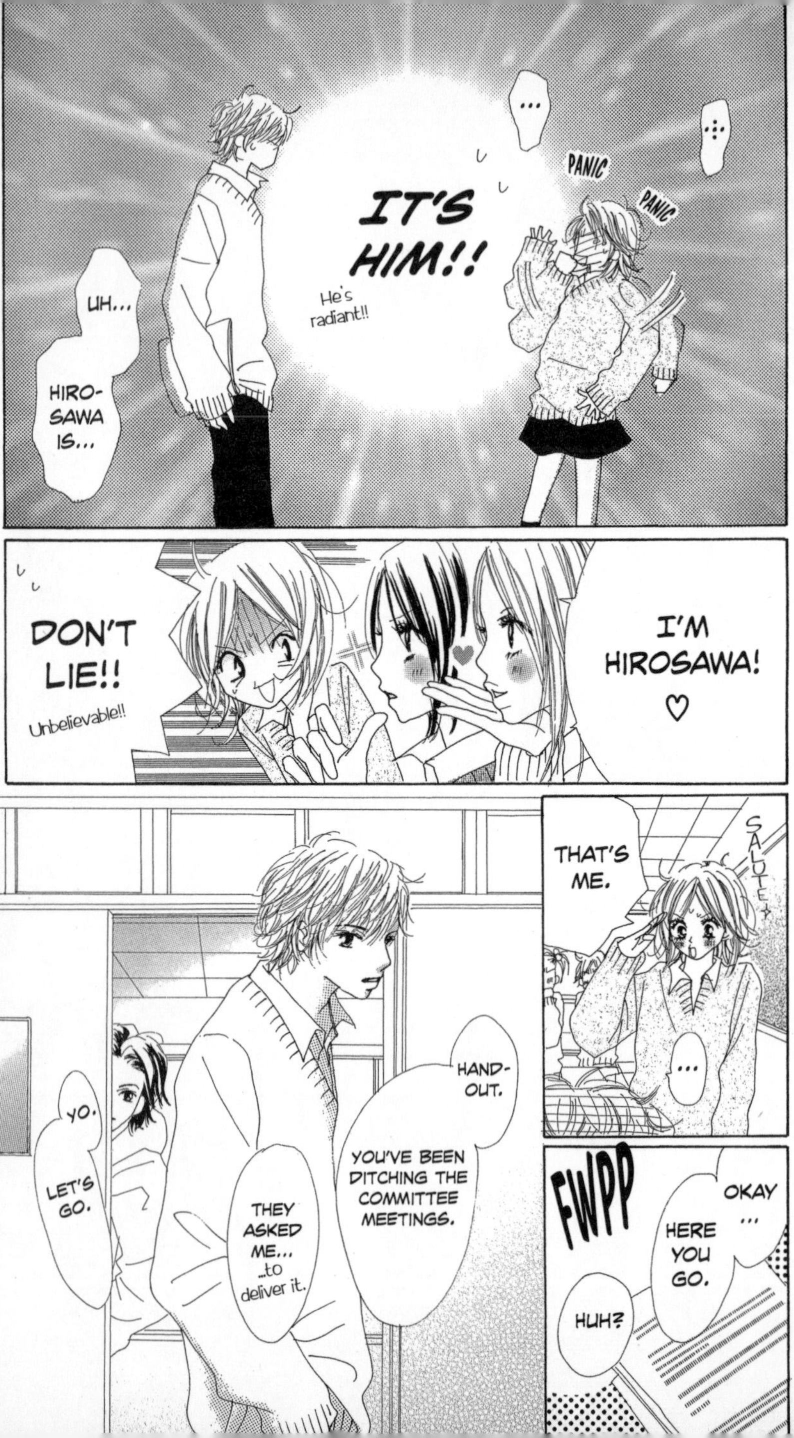
...
PANIC
PANIC
IT'S HIM!!
He's radiant!!
UH...
HIRO-SAWA IS...
I'M HIROSAWA! ♡
DON'T LIE!!
Unbelievable!!
THAT'S ME.
SALUTE
...
OKAY... HERE YOU GO.
FWPP
HUH?
HAND-OUT.
YOU'VE BEEN DITCHING THE COMMITTEE MEETINGS.
THEY ASKED ME... ...to deliver it.
YO.
LET'S GO.

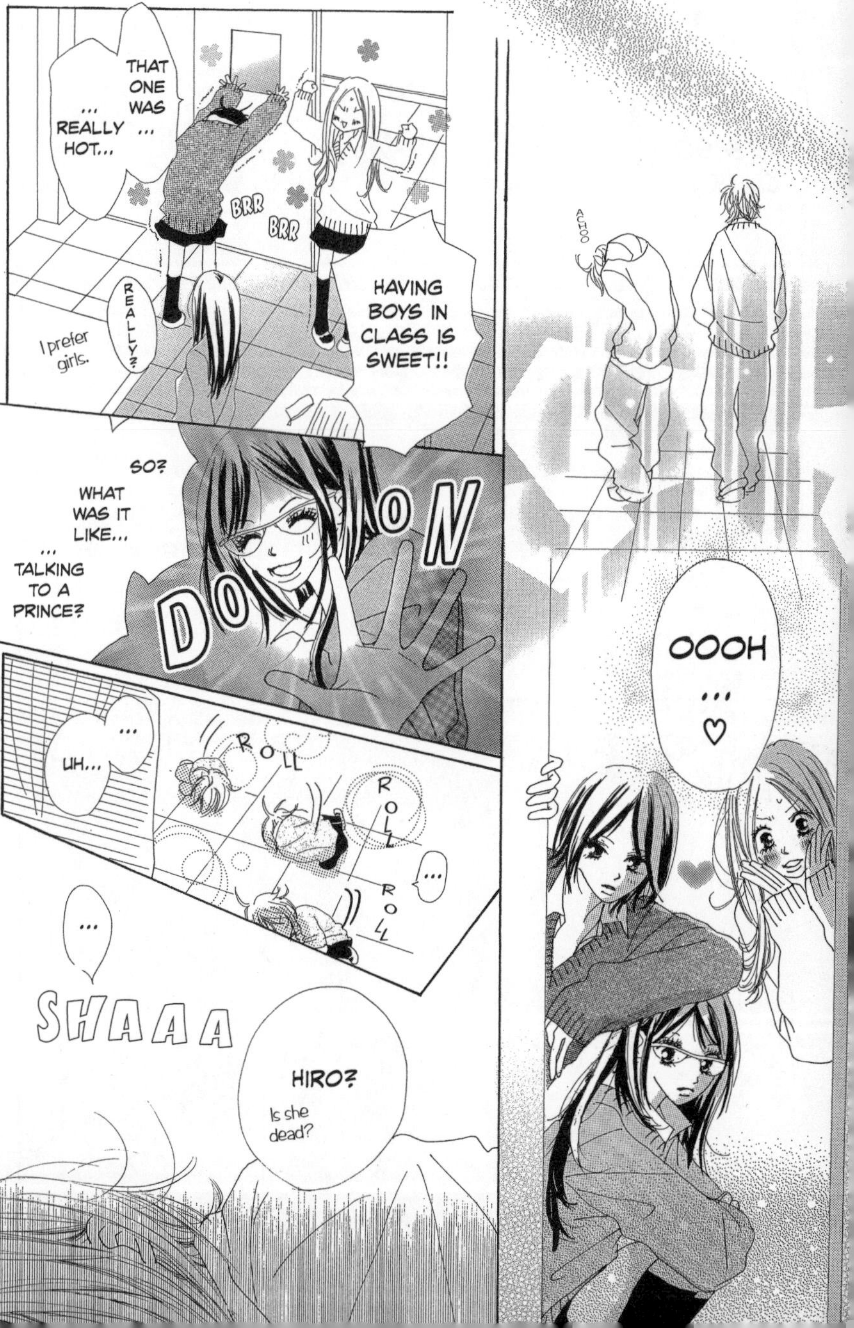
ACHOO
OOOH ... ♡
HAVING BOYS IN CLASS IS SWEET!!
BRR BRR
THAT ONE WAS ... REALLY ... HOT...
REALLY?
I prefer girls.
DOON
SO? WHAT WAS IT LIKE... ...TALKING TO A PRINCE?
...
ROLL ROLL ROLL
... UH...
...
SHAAA
HIRO?
Is she dead?

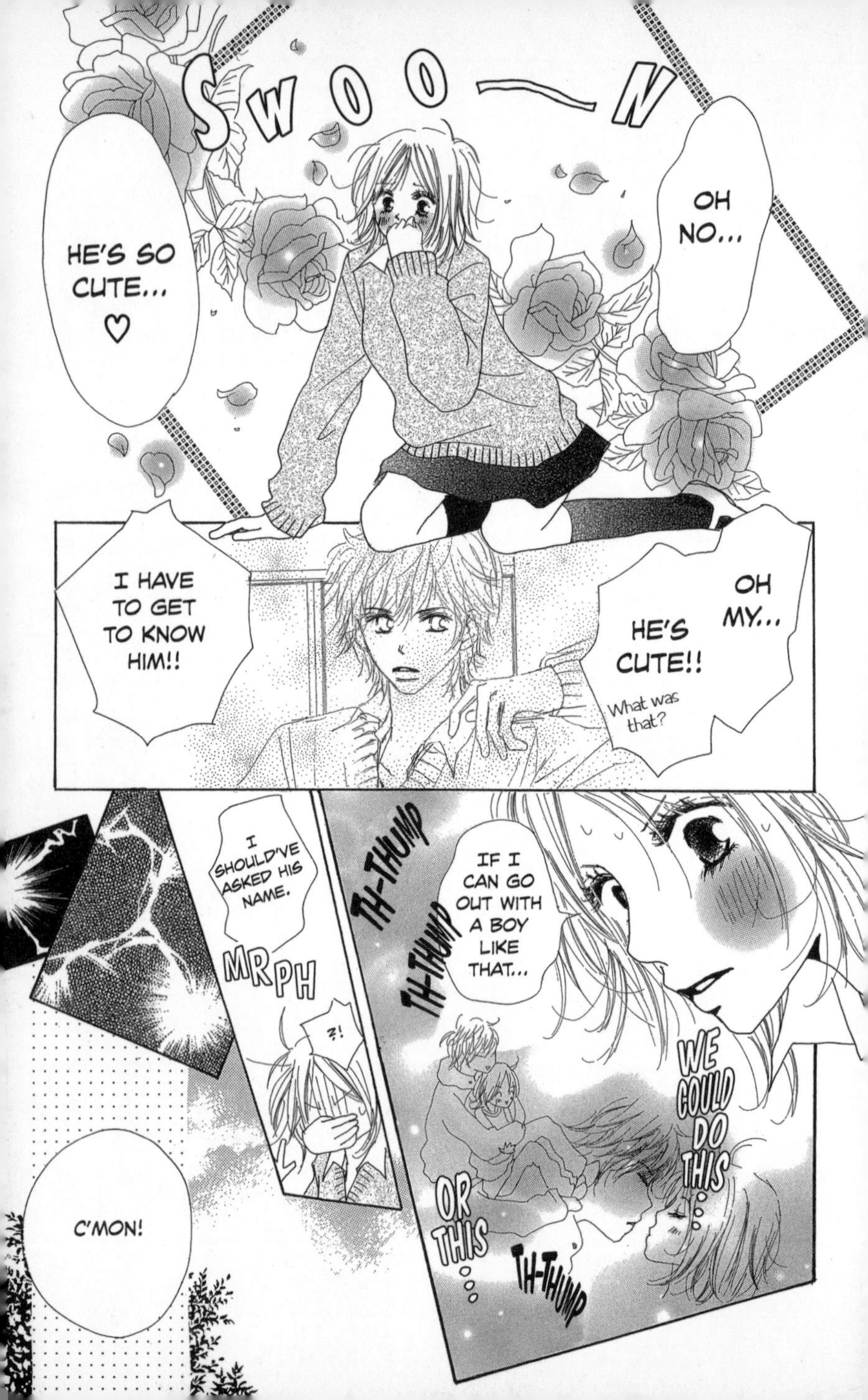
SWOO—N
OH NO...
HE'S SO CUTE... ♡
OH MY...
HE'S CUTE!!
What was that?
I HAVE TO GET TO KNOW HIM!!
TH-THUMP
TH-THUMP
IF I CAN GO OUT WITH A BOY LIKE THAT...
WE COULD DO THIS...
OR THIS...
TH-THUMP
I SHOULD'VE ASKED HIS NAME.
MRPH
?!
C'MON!

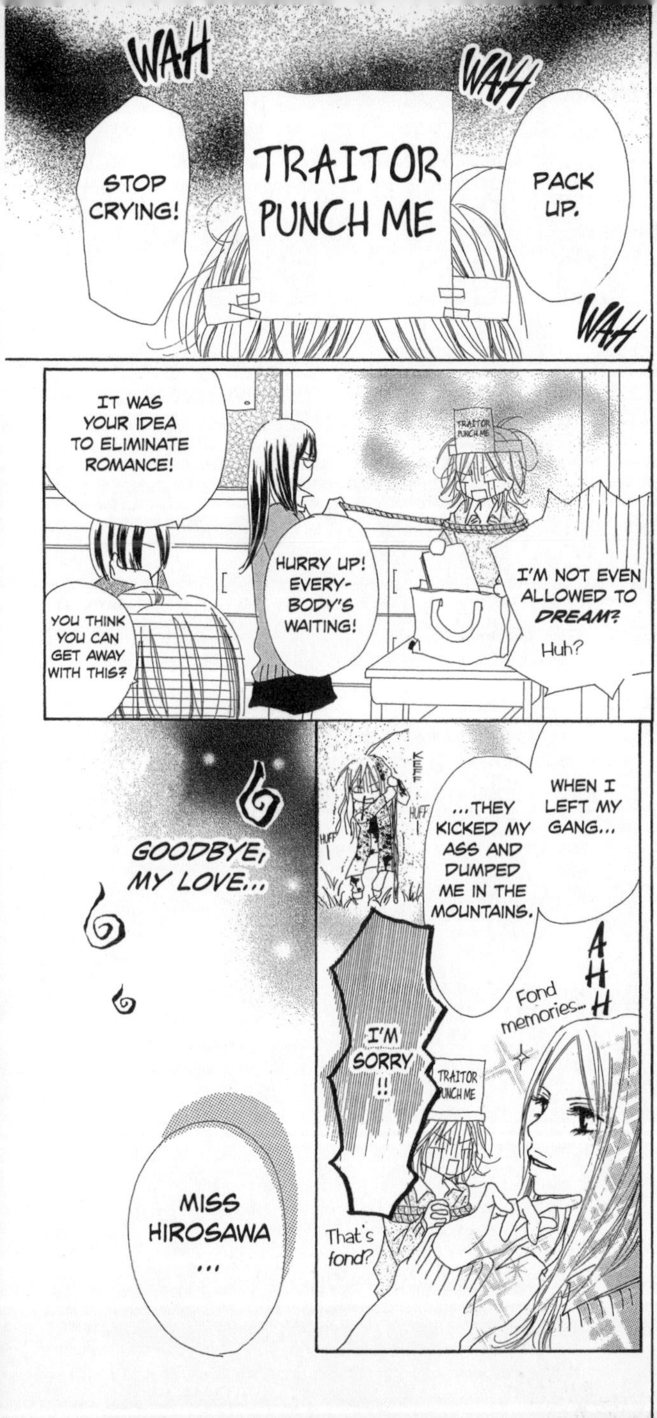
WAH
PACK UP.
TRAITOR PUNCH ME
STOP CRYING!
WAH
WAH
I'M NOT EVEN ALLOWED TO *DREAM?*
Huh?
TRAITOR PUNCH ME
HURRY UP! EVERY-BODY'S WAITING!
IT WAS YOUR IDEA TO ELIMINATE ROMANCE!
YOU THINK YOU CAN GET AWAY WITH THIS?
WHEN I LEFT MY GANG...
...THEY KICKED MY ASS AND DUMPED ME IN THE MOUNTAINS.
KEFF
HUFF
HUFF
AHH
Fond memories...
I'M SORRY!!
TRAITOR PUNCH ME
That's fond?
GOODBYE, MY LOVE...
MISS HIROSAWA...

C'mon, It's Time for School Again

I remember writing this short story. I hadn't done a 30-page story in a long time. I wanted to do something light-hearted... What was I thinking? I probably wasn't thinking about much. I actually like the title quite a bit. Oh, and this was the last piece I did with my first-ever editor!! Ha ha ha...This brings back so many memories. My style's changed a little, huh? It's kinda embarrassing looking at the old stuff...

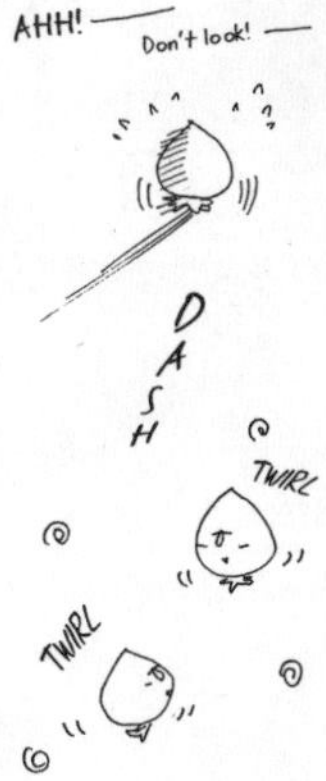
AHH!
Don't look!
DASH
TWIRL
TWIRL

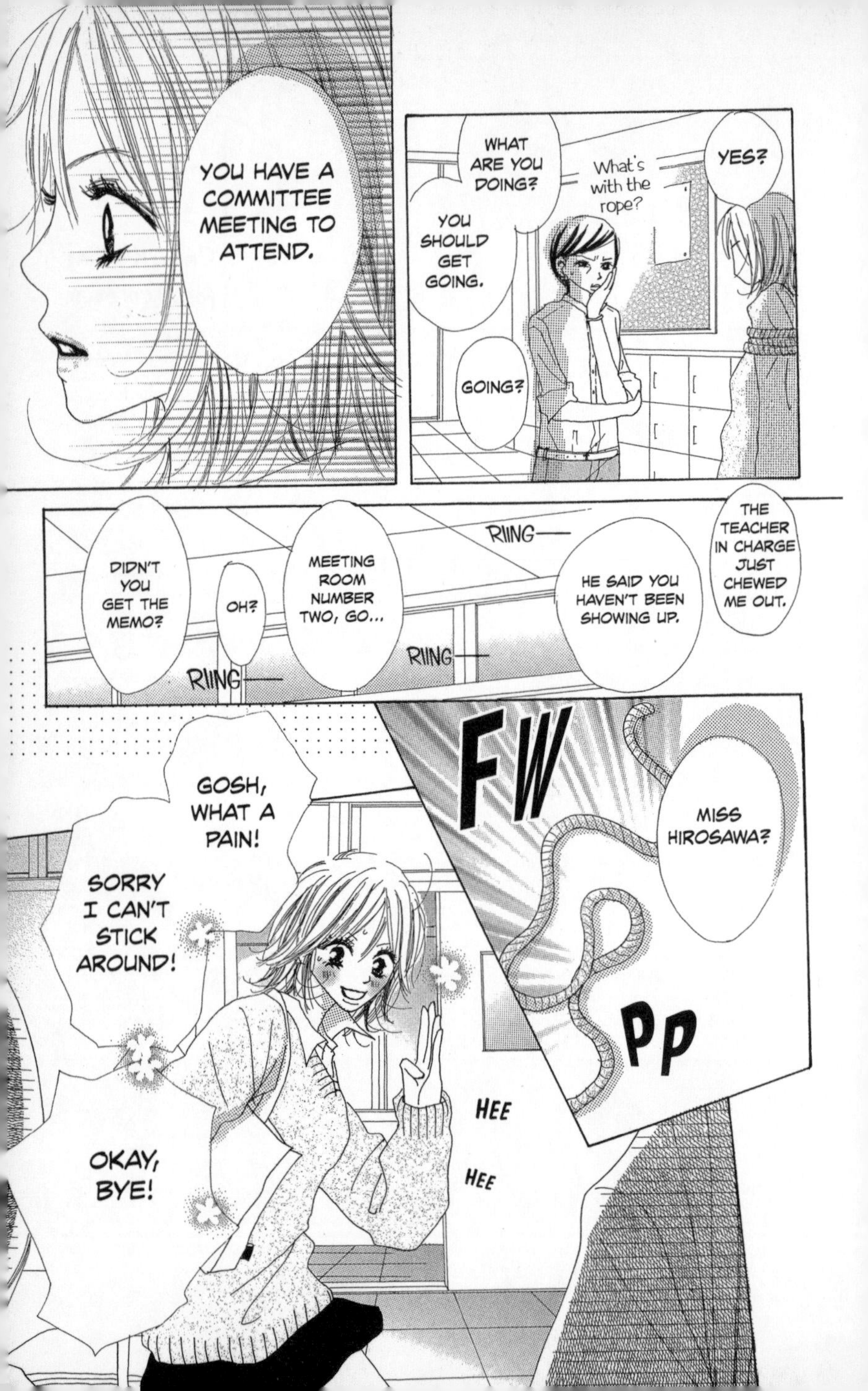

YES?
What's with the rope?
WHAT ARE YOU DOING?
YOU SHOULD GET GOING.
GOING?
YOU HAVE A COMMITTEE MEETING TO ATTEND.
THE TEACHER IN CHARGE JUST CHEWED ME OUT.
HE SAID YOU HAVEN'T BEEN SHOWING UP.
RIING—
RIING—
MEETING ROOM NUMBER TWO, GO...
OH?
DIDN'T YOU GET THE MEMO?
RIING—
FW
MISS HIROSAWA?
PP
HEE
HEE
GOSH, WHAT A PAIN!
SORRY I CAN'T STICK AROUND!
OKAY, BYE!

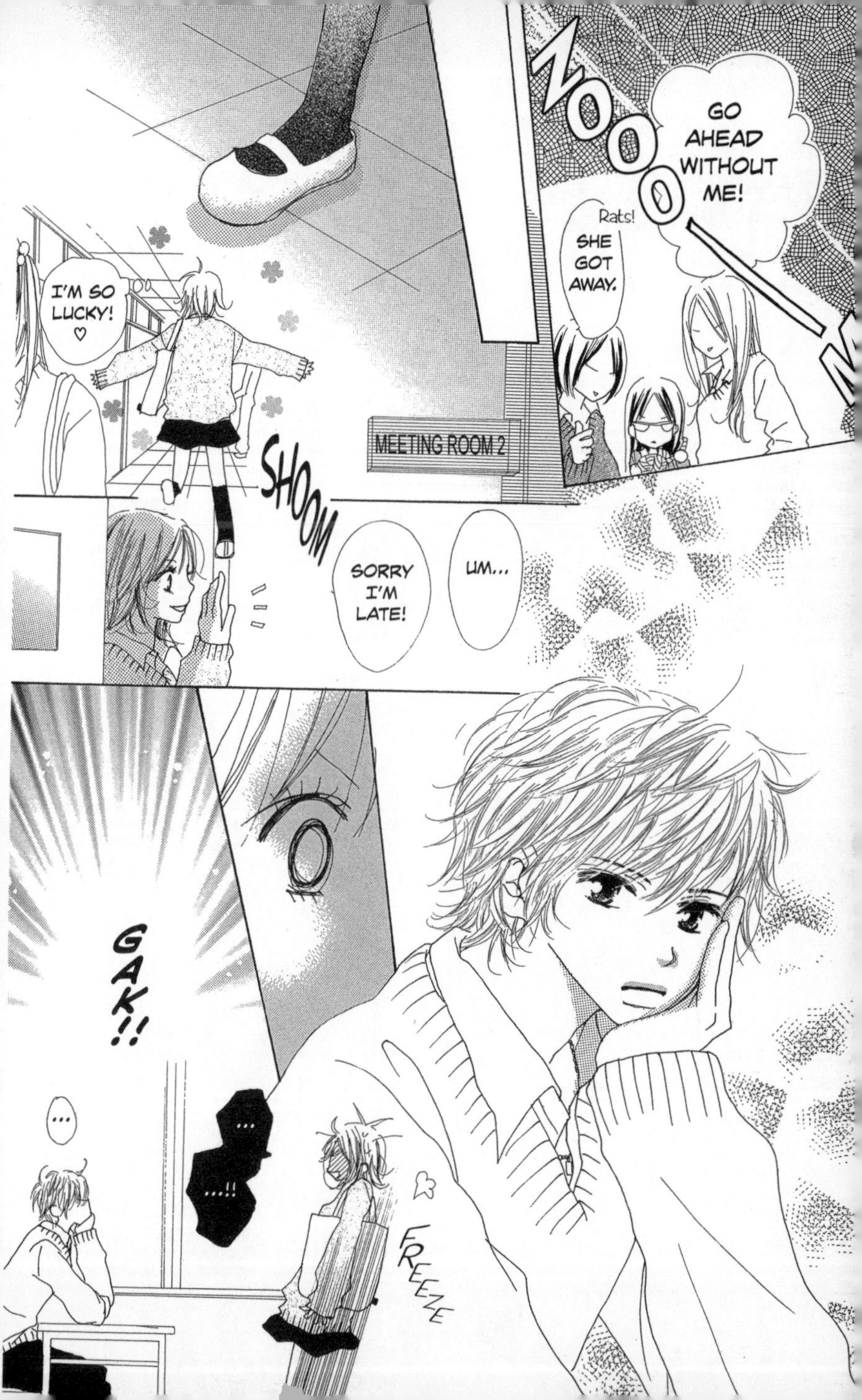
ZOOOO—M
GO AHEAD WITHOUT ME!
Rats! SHE GOT AWAY.
MEETING ROOM 2
I'M SO LUCKY! ♡
SHOOM
UM...
SORRY I'M LATE!
GAK!!
FREEZE
...
...
...!!

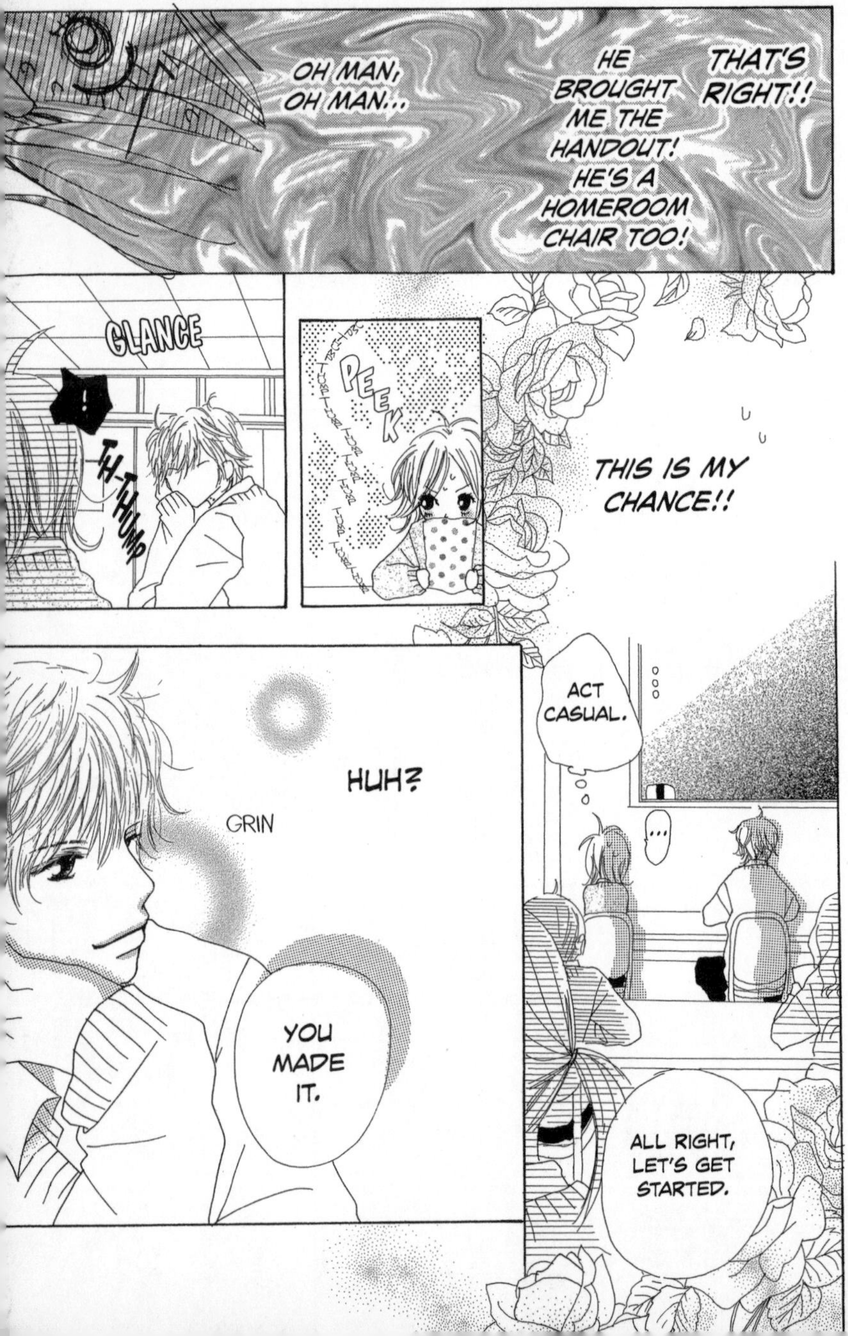
THAT'S RIGHT!!
HE BROUGHT ME THE HANDOUT! HE'S A HOMEROOM CHAIR TOO!
OH MAN, OH MAN...
THIS IS MY CHANCE!!
PEEK
GLANCE
!
TH-THUMP
ACT CASUAL.
...
ALL RIGHT, LET'S GET STARTED.
HUH?
GRIN
YOU MADE IT.

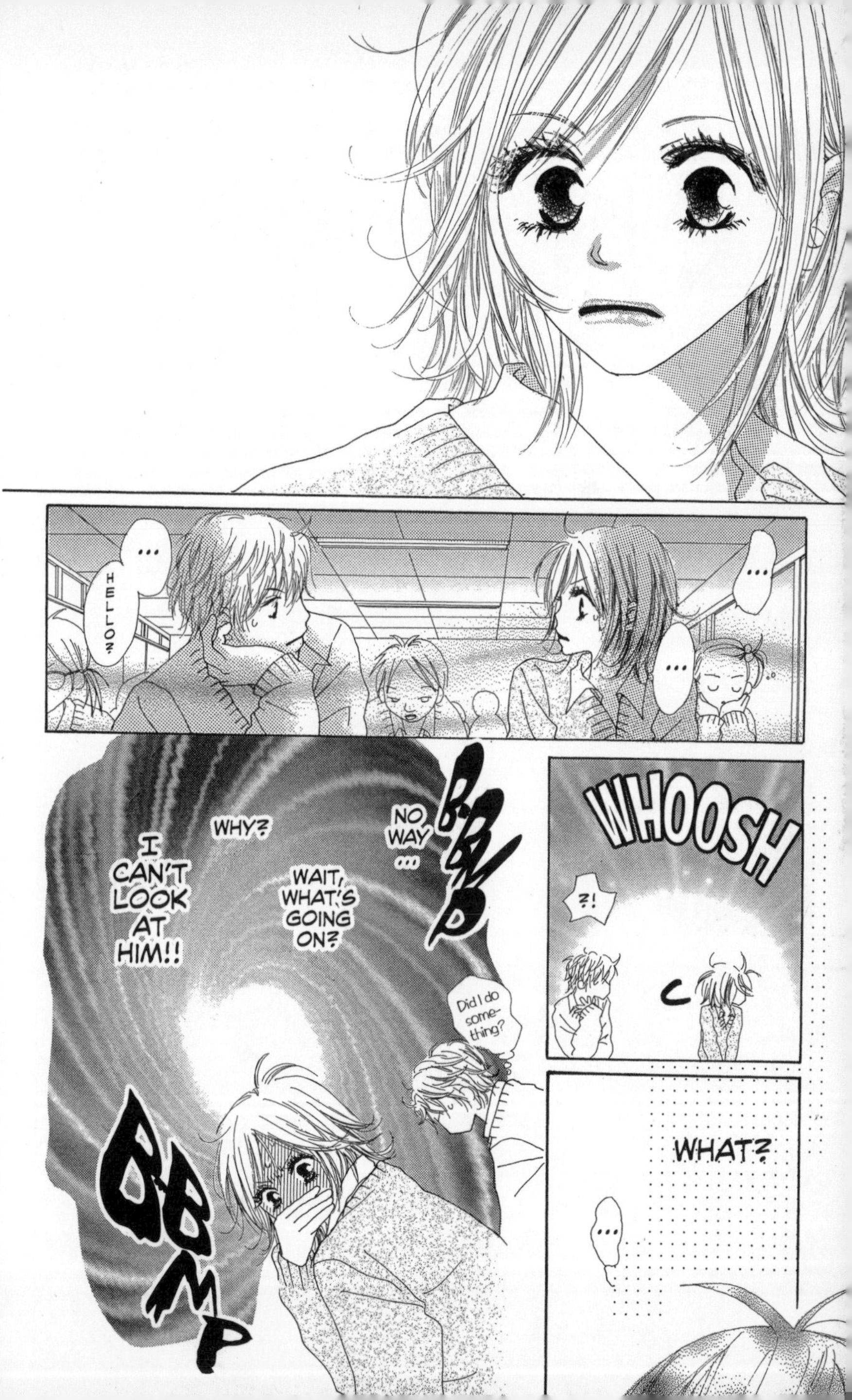
...
...
...HELLO?
...
WHOOSH
?!
WHAT?
...
BBMP
NO WAY...
WHY?
I CAN'T LOOK AT HIM!!
WAIT, WHAT'S GOING ON?
Did I do something?
BBMP

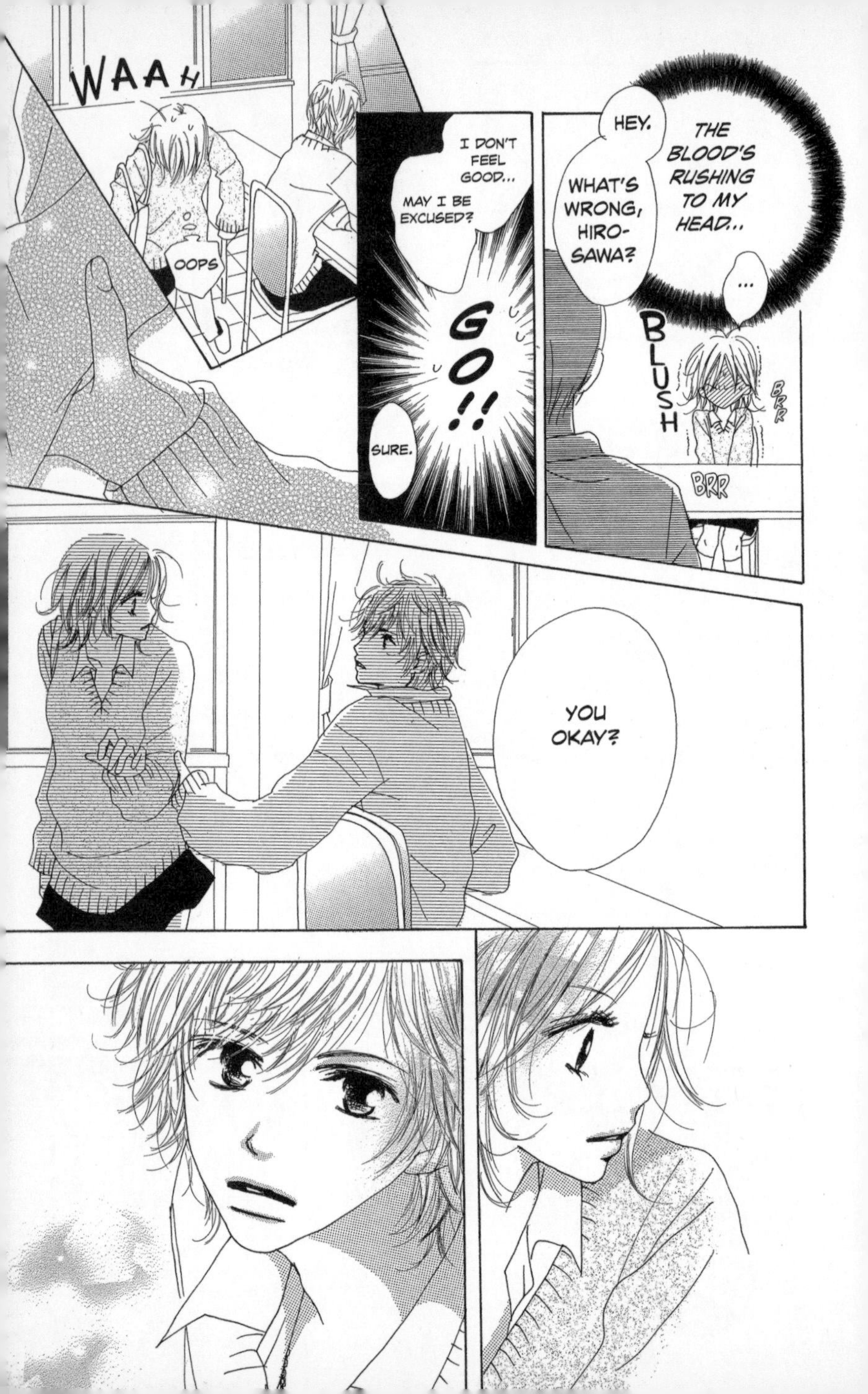
THE BLOOD'S RUSHING TO MY HEAD...
HEY.
WHAT'S WRONG, HIRO-SAWA?
...
BLUSH
BRR
BRR
I DON'T FEEL GOOD...
MAY I BE EXCUSED?
GO!!
SURE.
WAAH
OOPS
YOU OKAY?

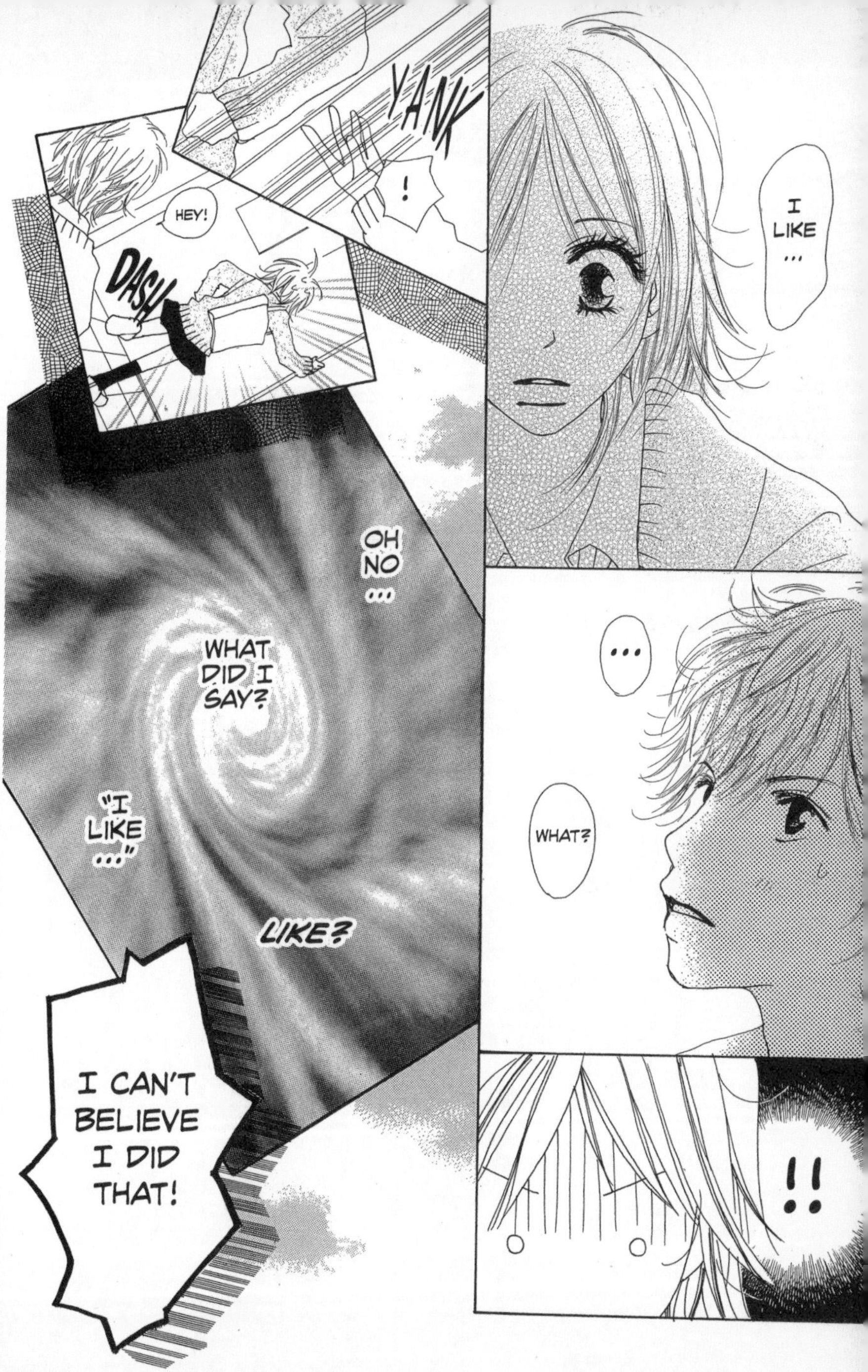
I LIKE ...
YANK
!
HEY!
DASH
...
WHAT?
!!
OH NO ...
WHAT DID I SAY?
"I LIKE ..."
LIKE?
I CAN'T BELIEVE I DID THAT!

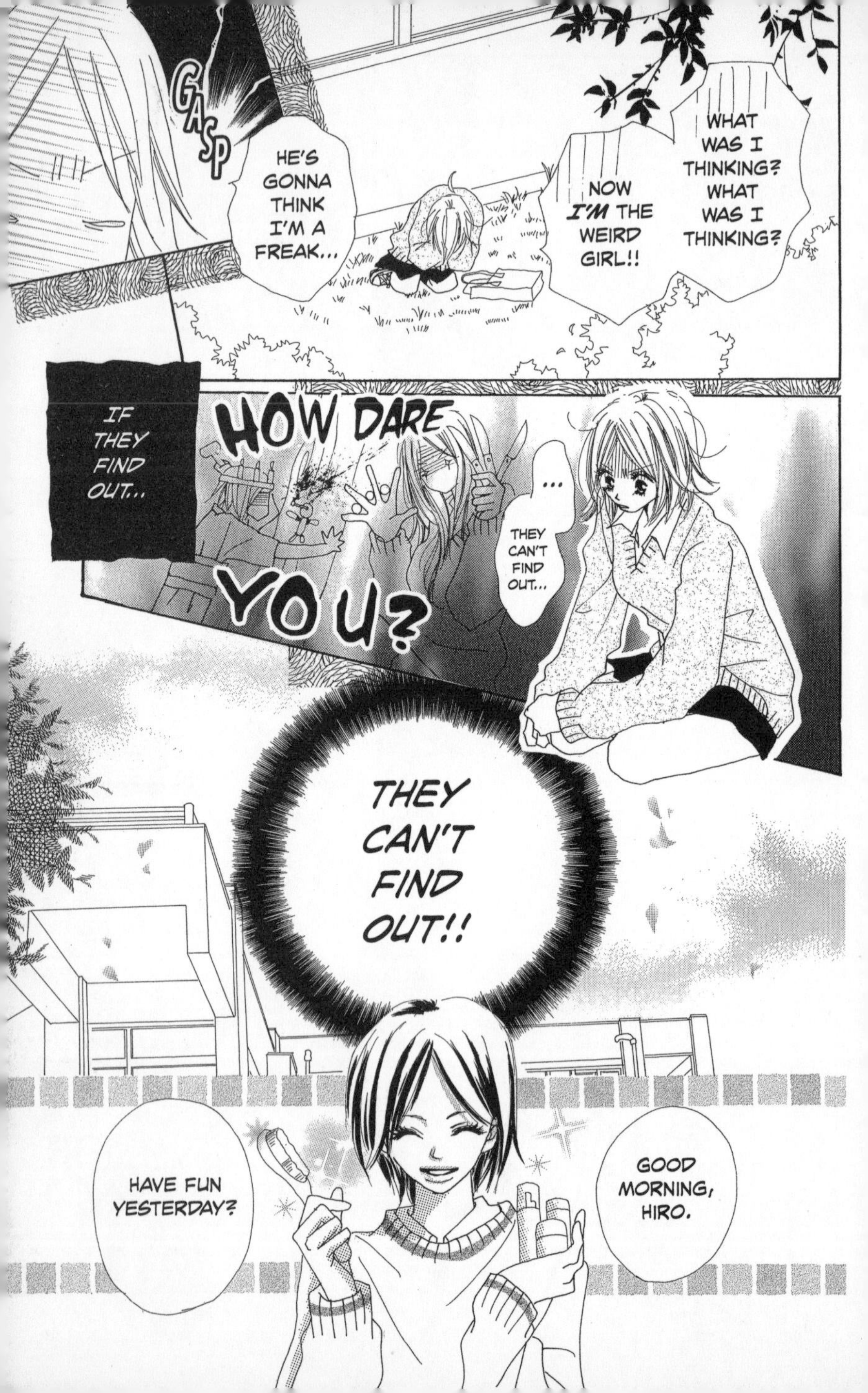
WHAT WAS I THINKING? WHAT WAS I THINKING?
NOW I'M THE WEIRD GIRL!!
HE'S GONNA THINK I'M A FREAK...
GASP
...
THEY CAN'T FIND OUT...
HOW DARE YOU?
IF THEY FIND OUT...
THEY CAN'T FIND OUT!!
GOOD MORNING, HIRO.
HAVE FUN YESTERDAY?

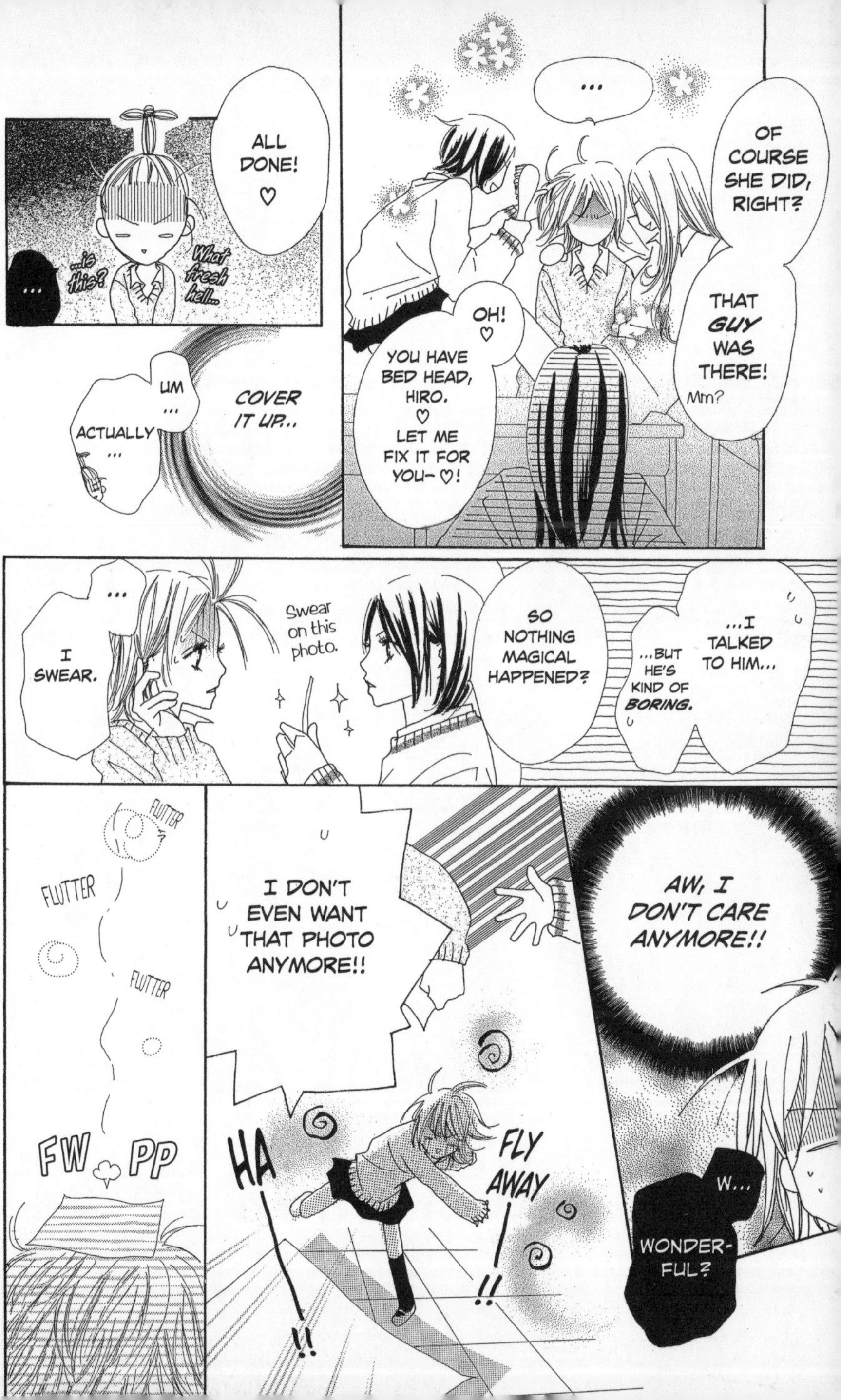
...
OF COURSE SHE DID, RIGHT?
THAT GUY WAS THERE!
Mm?
OH! ♡ YOU HAVE BED HEAD, HIRO. ♡ LET ME FIX IT FOR YOU-♡!
ALL DONE! ♡
What fresh hell...
...is this?
...
COVER IT UP...
UM... ACTUALLY...
...I TALKED TO HIM...
...BUT HE'S KIND OF BORING.
SO NOTHING MAGICAL HAPPENED?
Swear on this photo.
...
I SWEAR.
AW, I DON'T CARE ANYMORE!!
W... WONDERFUL?
I DON'T EVEN WANT THAT PHOTO ANYMORE!!
FLY AWAY-!!
HA-!!
FLUTTER
FLUTTER
FLUTTER
FW PP

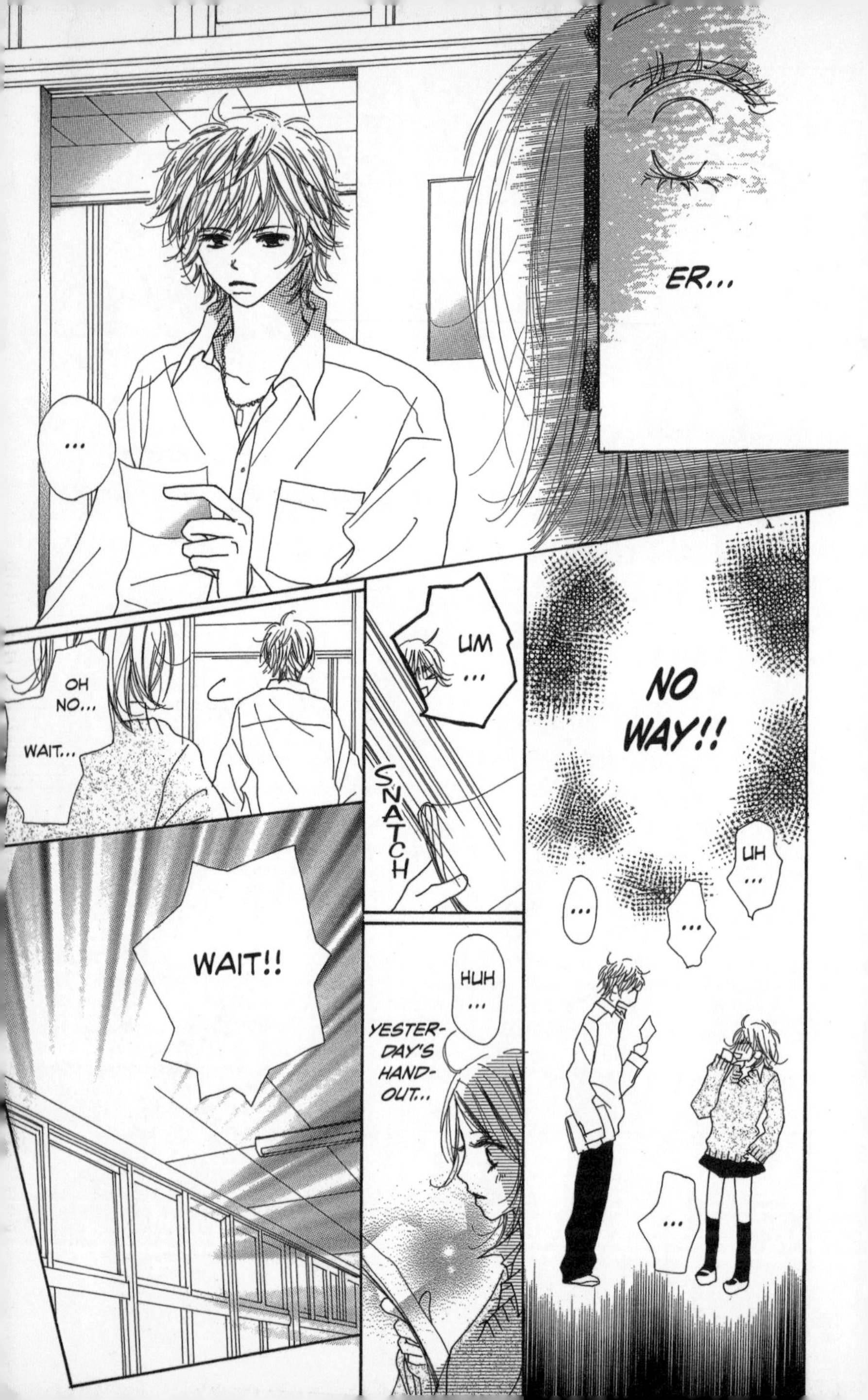
ER...
...
NO WAY!!
UH...
...
...
...
UM...
SNATCH
OH NO...
WAIT...
HUH...
YESTERDAY'S HANDOUT...
WAIT!!

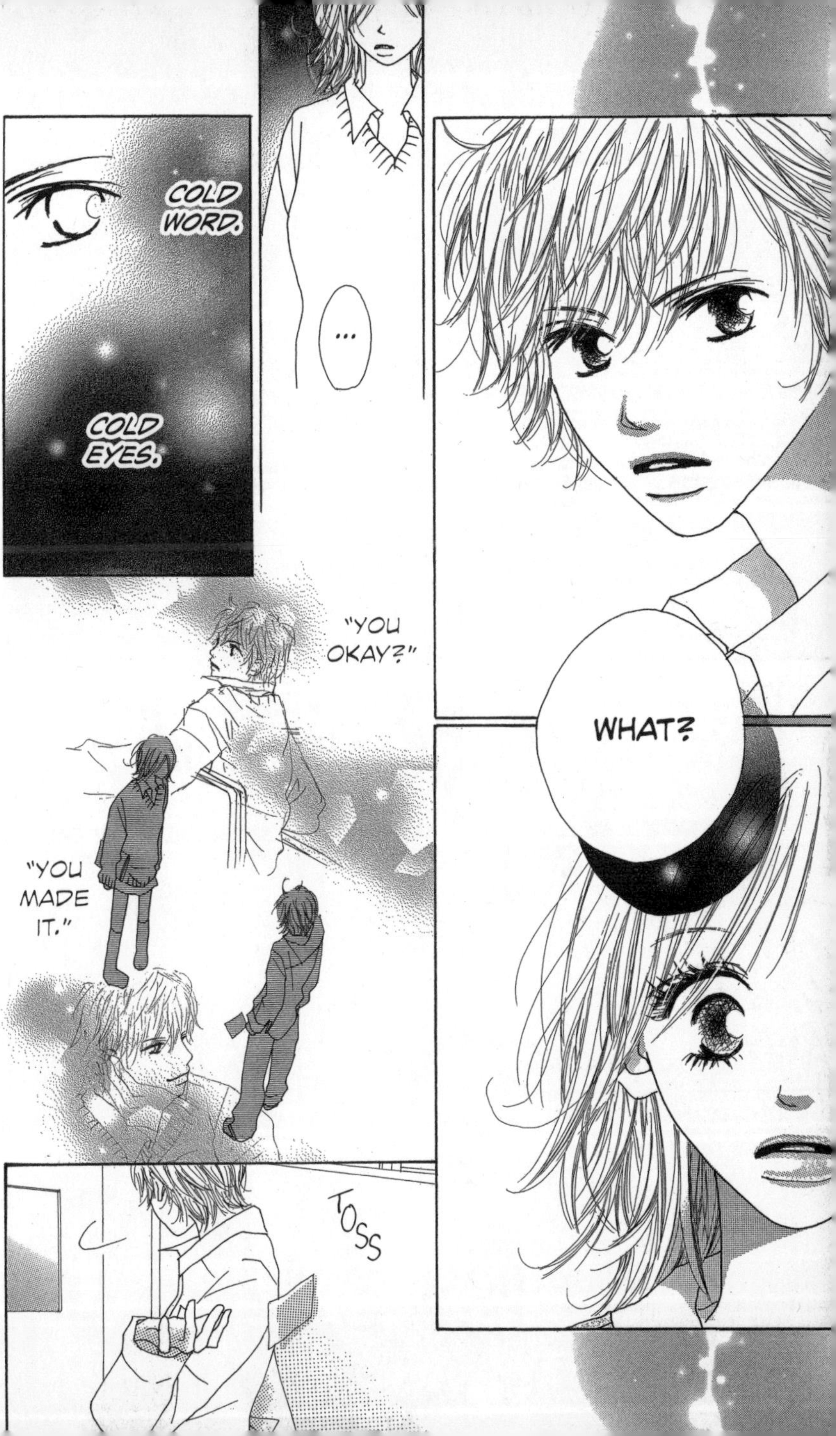

WHAT?
...
COLD WORD.
COLD EYES.
"YOU OKAY?"
"YOU MADE IT."
TOSS

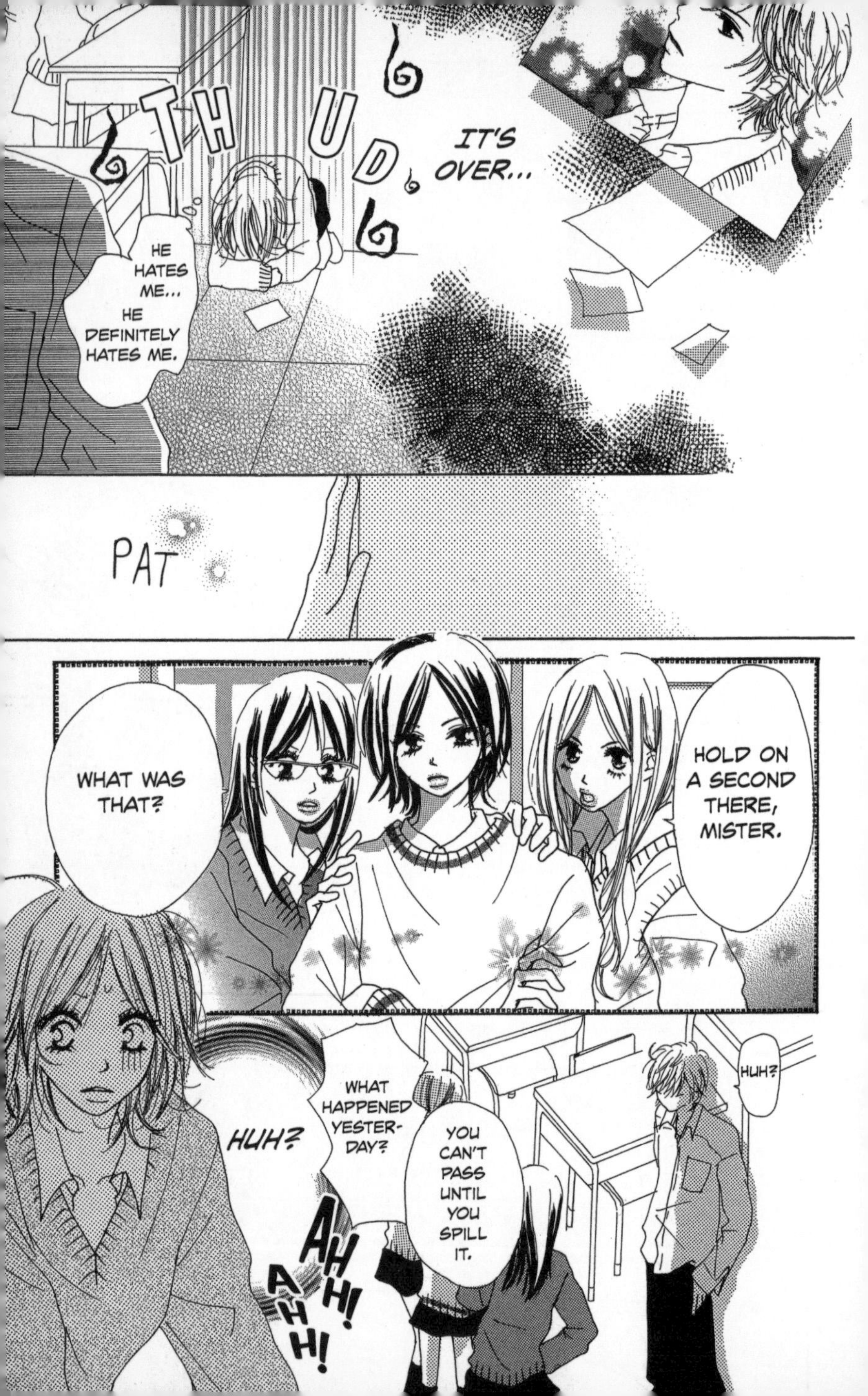
IT'S OVER...
THUD
HE HATES ME... HE DEFINITELY HATES ME.
PAT
HOLD ON A SECOND THERE, MISTER.
WHAT WAS THAT?
HUH?
YOU CAN'T PASS UNTIL YOU SPILL IT.
WHAT HAPPENED YESTER-DAY?
HUH?
AHH!
AHH!

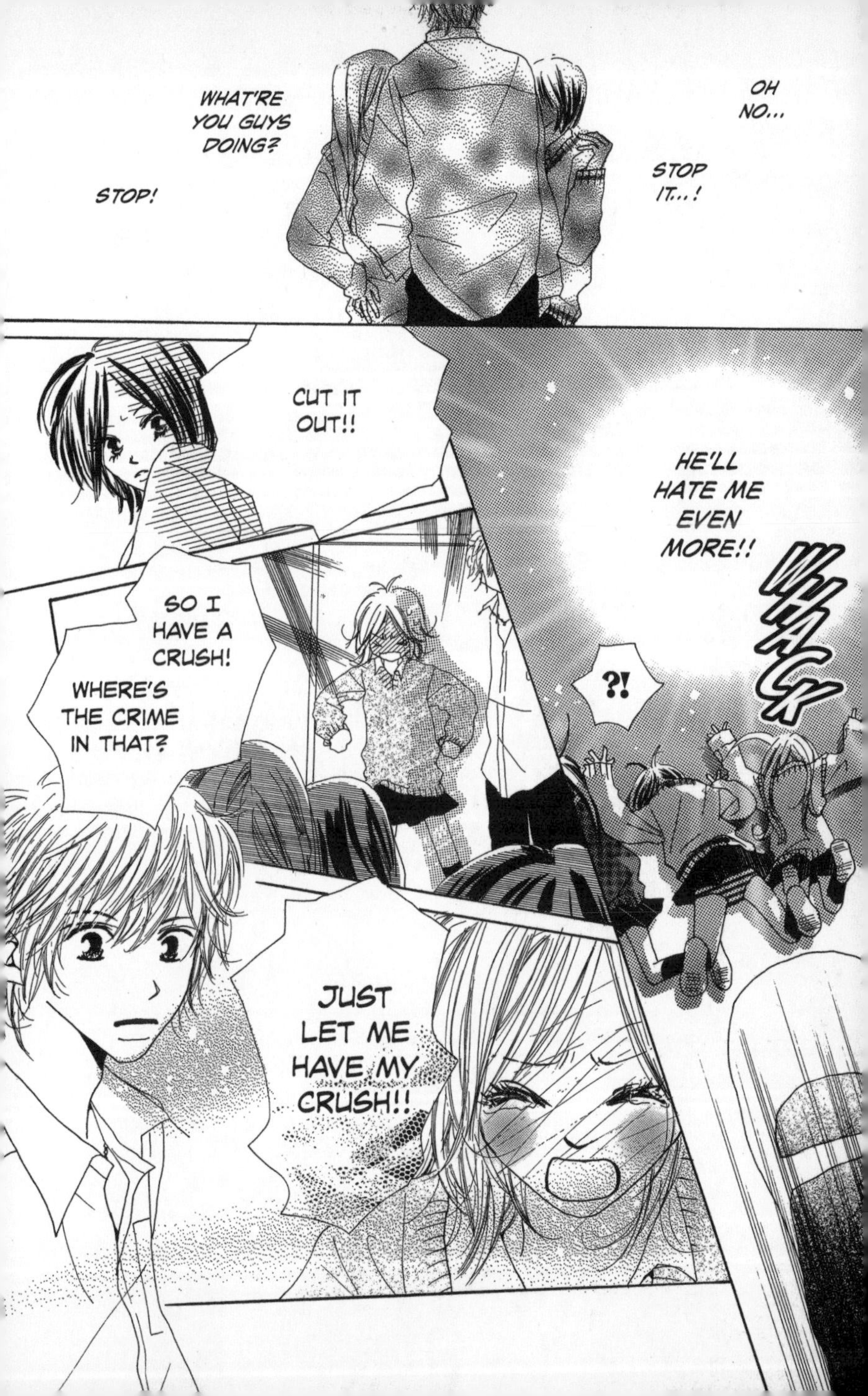
OH NO...
STOP IT...!
WHAT'RE YOU GUYS DOING?
STOP!
HE'LL HATE ME EVEN MORE!!
WHACK
?!
CUT IT OUT!!
SO I HAVE A CRUSH!
WHERE'S THE CRIME IN THAT?
JUST LET ME HAVE MY CRUSH!!

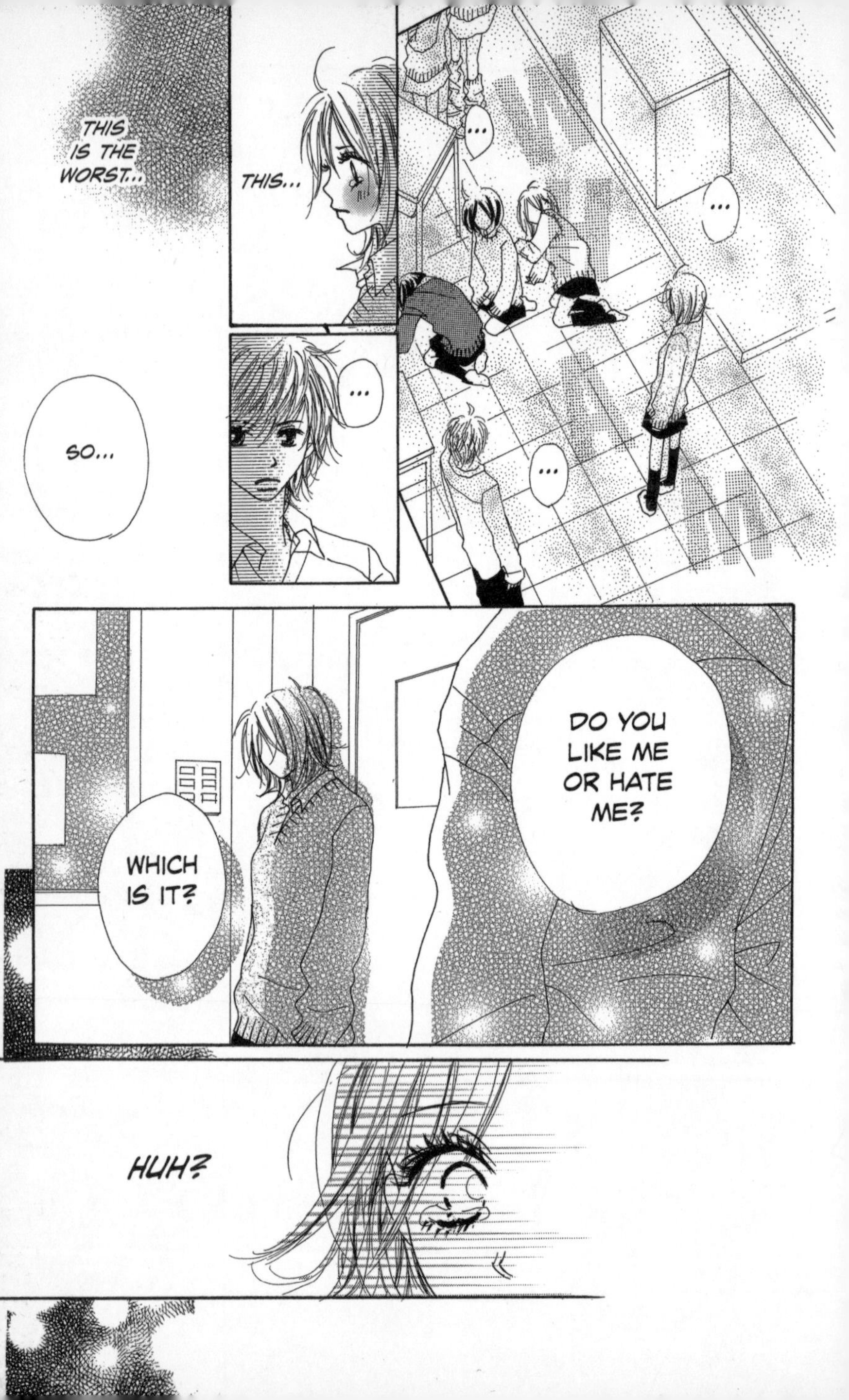
...
...
...
THIS...
...
THIS IS THE WORST...
SO...
DO YOU LIKE ME OR HATE ME?
WHICH IS IT?
HUH?

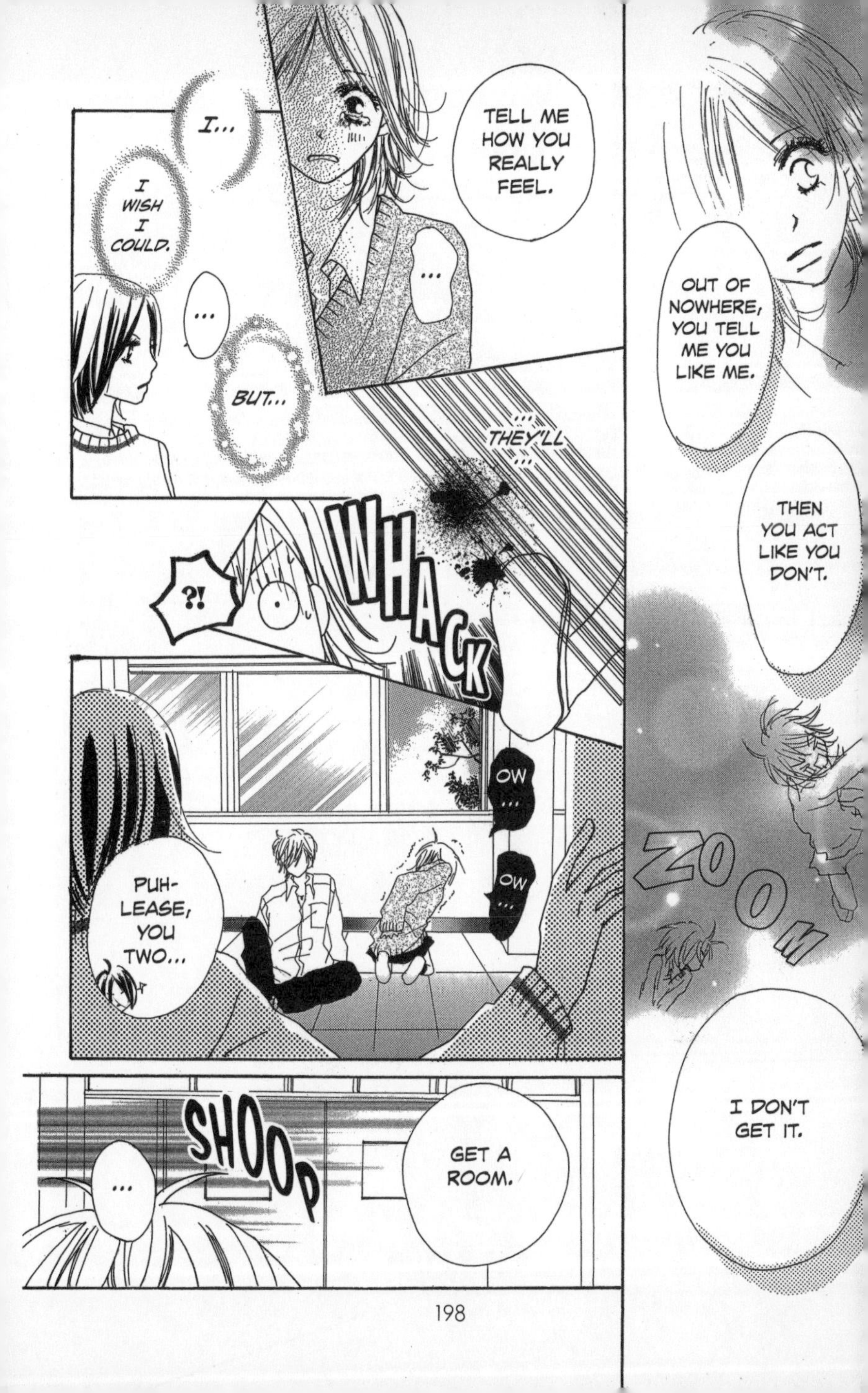
OUT OF NOWHERE, YOU TELL ME YOU LIKE ME.
THEN YOU ACT LIKE YOU DON'T.
ZOOOM
I DON'T GET IT.
TELL ME HOW YOU REALLY FEEL.
...
I...
I WISH I COULD.
...
BUT...
...THEY'LL...
WHACK
?!
OW...
OW...
PUH-LEASE, YOU TWO...
GET A ROOM.
SHOOP
...

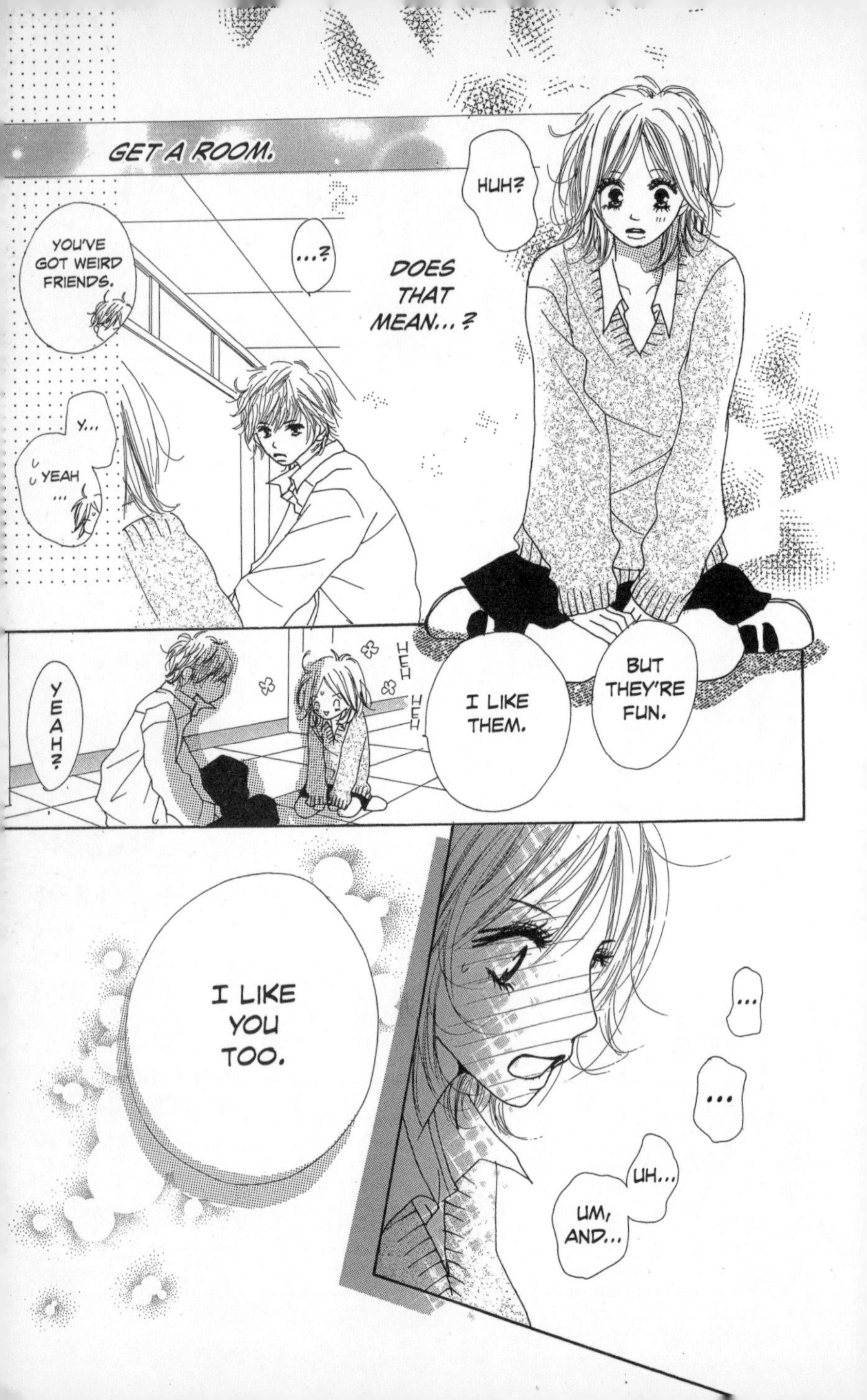
GET A ROOM.
HUH?
DOES THAT MEAN...?
...?
YOU'VE GOT WEIRD FRIENDS.
Y... YEAH...
BUT THEY'RE FUN.
I LIKE THEM.
HEH HEH
YEAH?
...
...
UH...
UM, AND...
I LIKE YOU TOO.

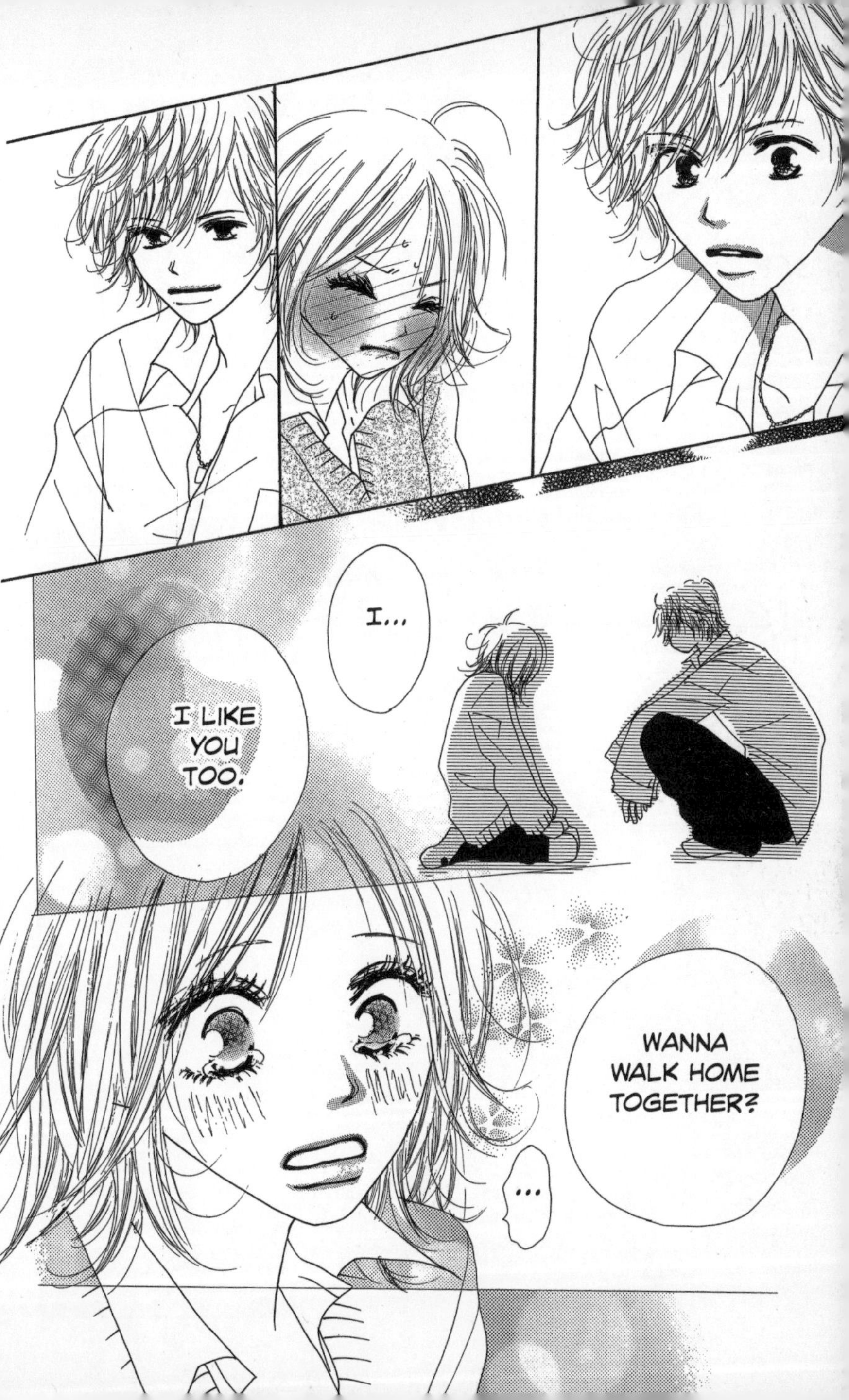
I...
I LIKE YOU TOO.
WANNA WALK HOME TOGETHER?
...

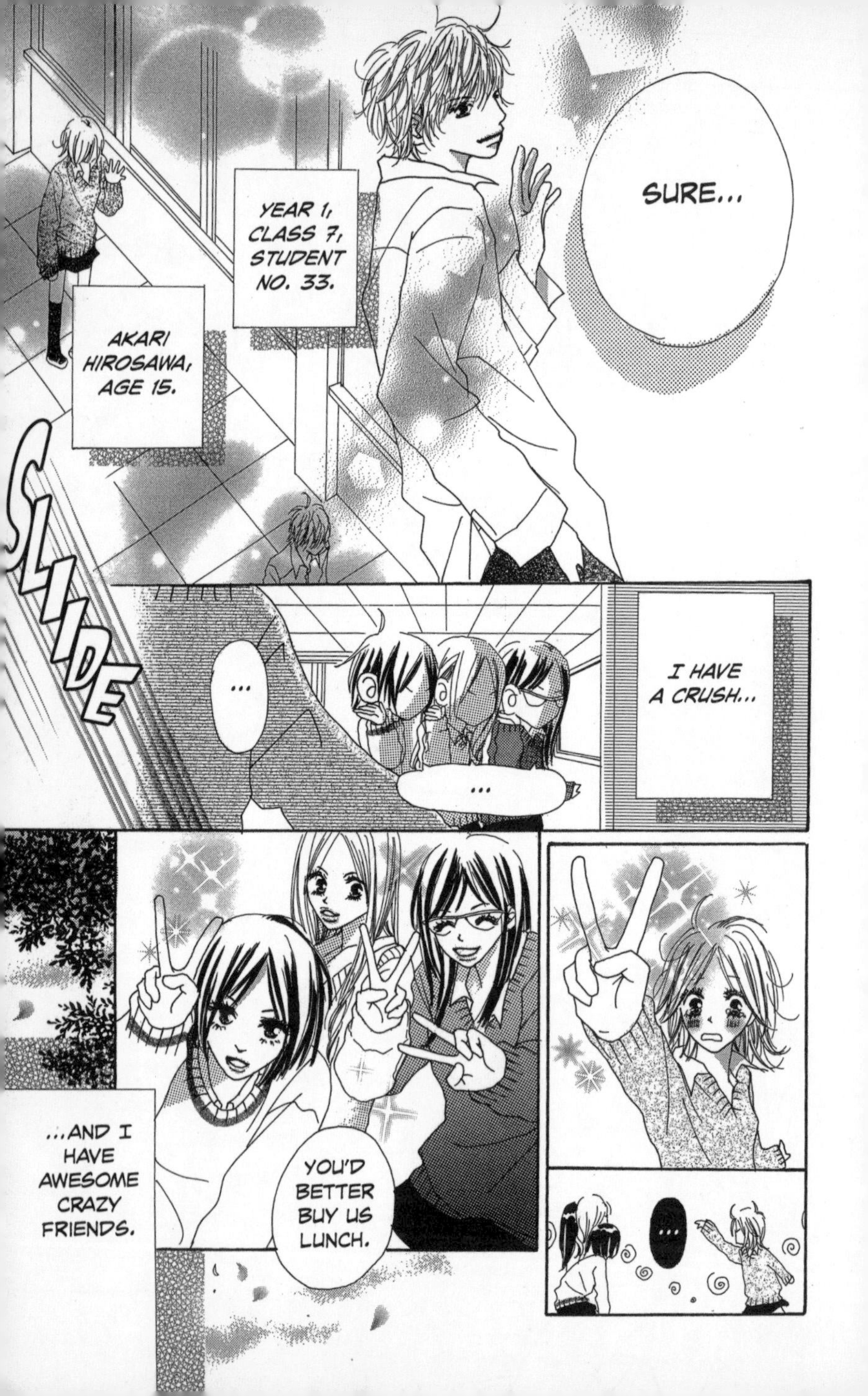
SURE...
YEAR 1, CLASS 7, STUDENT NO. 33.
AKARI HIROSAWA, AGE 15.
SLIDE
I HAVE A CRUSH...
...
...
...
YOU'D BETTER BUY US LUNCH.
...AND I HAVE AWESOME CRAZY FRIENDS.

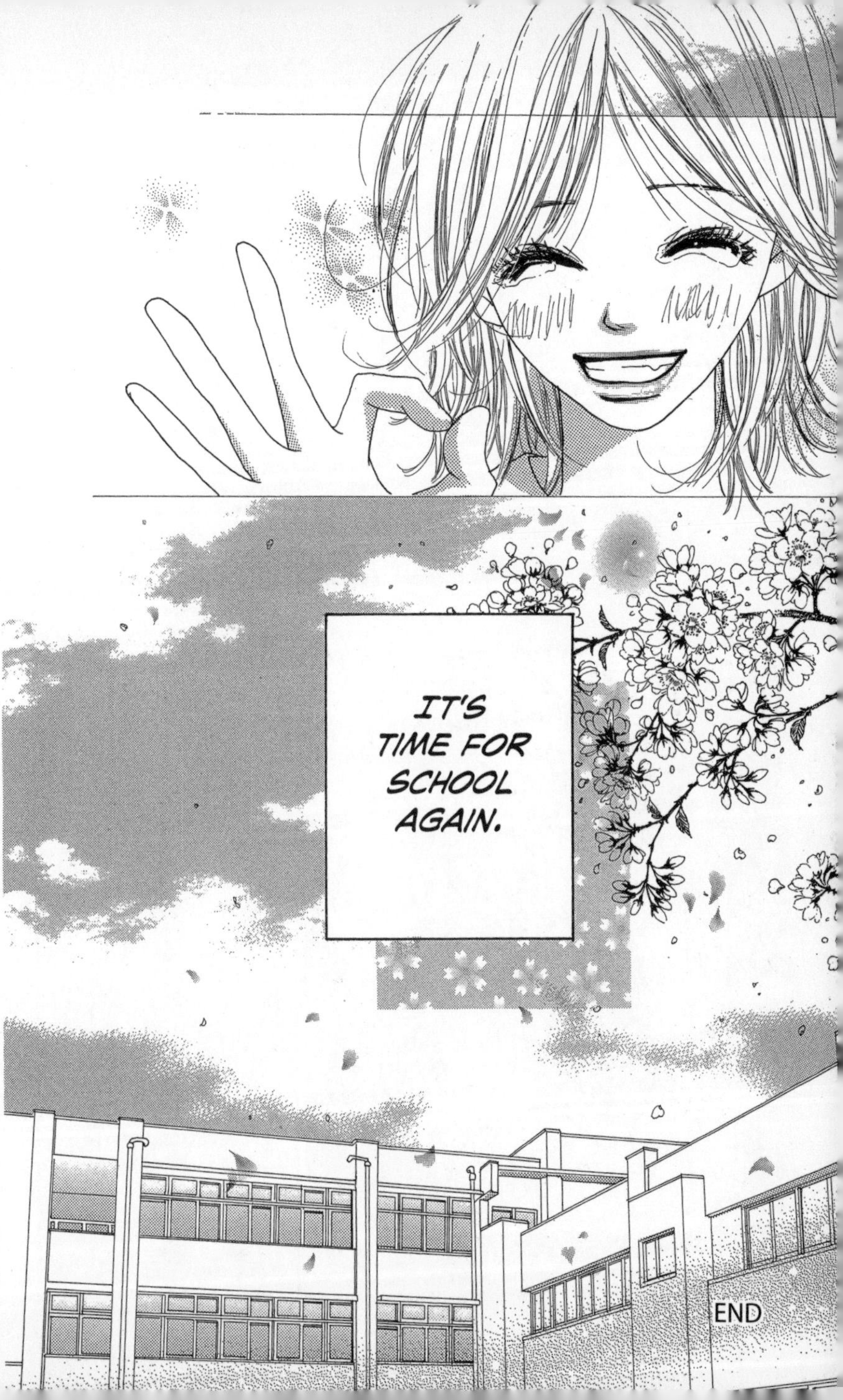
IT'S TIME FOR SCHOOL AGAIN.
END

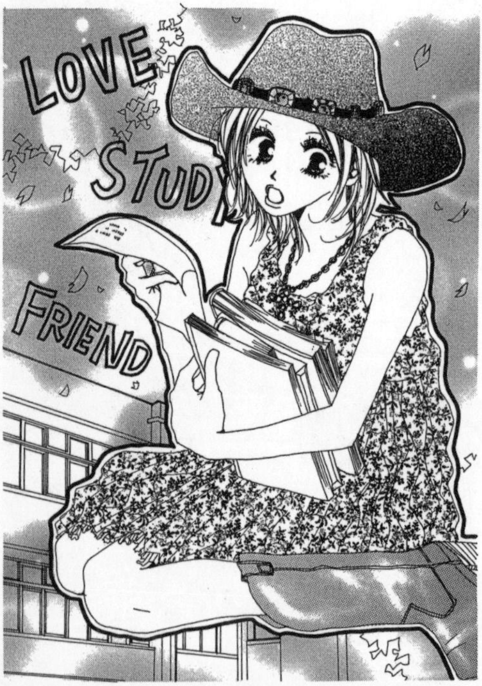
LOVE
STUDY
FRIEND

CHARACTER PROFILE

Ryunosuke Fuji

Born 12/27   16 years old

Height.............................177cm

Weight................................63kg

Blood Type.................................O

Hobby:
.................Changes frequently

Skills:
...............Keen sense of smell

Favorite Labels:
Cabane de Zucca, American Rag Cie

Wants............Driver's license

Ryoko Sakura

Born 11/22   16 years old

Height..............................159cm

Weight................................ 47kg

Blood Type...................................A

Hobby..........Collecting manga

Skills...Running

Favorite Labels:
............Jill Stuart, Hysteric Glamour

Favorite Book:
.... Aopan Monogatari

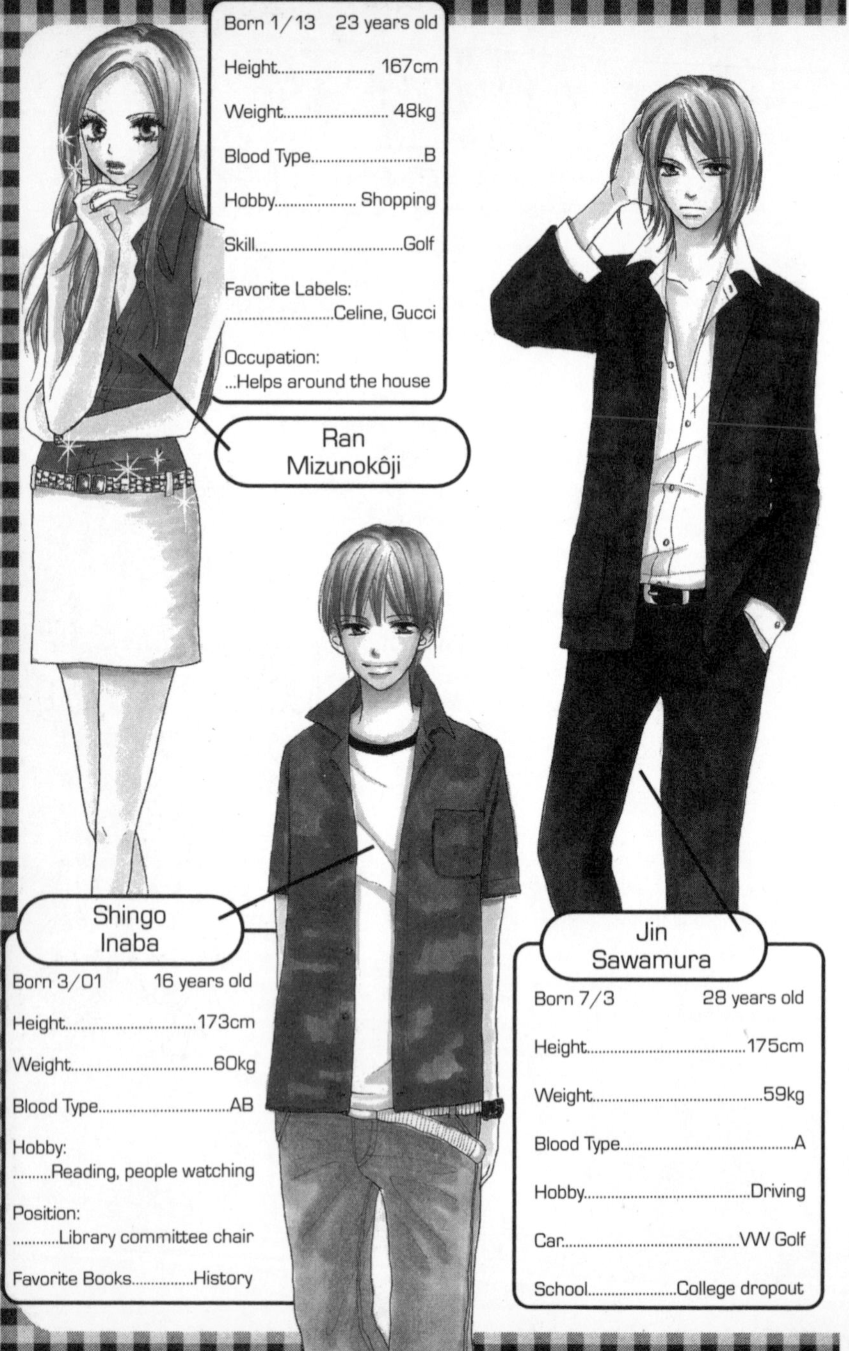

Born 1/13 23 years old
Height.......................... 167cm
Weight.......................... 48kg
Blood Type..............................B
Hobby..................... Shopping
Skill...................................Golf
Favorite Labels:
............................Celine, Gucci
Occupation:
...Helps around the house
Ran
Mizunokôji
Shingo
Inaba
Born 3/01 16 years old
Height.................................173cm
Weight..................................60kg
Blood Type...............................AB
Hobby:
..........Reading, people watching
Position:
...........Library committee chair
Favorite Books...............History
Jin
Sawamura
Born 7/3 28 years old
Height..175cm
Weight..59kg
Blood Type..A
Hobby.......................................Driving
Car..VW Golf
School.....................College dropout

About the Character Profiles

This insert page subtly reveals that the names in B.O.D.Y. were taken from characters in Rumiko Takahashi's *Urusei Yatsura*. Allow me to explain:

* Ryoko Sakura → Sakura + Ryoko ← I mixed them up like this
* Ryunosuke Fuji → Fujinami Ryunosuke

The president's name isn't taken from a regular character in *Urusei Yatsura*...the hardcore fans might catch it, though. (He appears in the episode where Lum goes to a marriage meeting.) Why am I telling you all this? Because I was afraid fans of *Urusei Yatsura* might get upset. I'm kind of a wuss. If anybody is mad, I'm sorry...

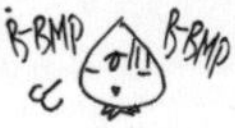
B-BMP
B-BMP

Manga I've Read Recently

I know I'm way behind, but I just collected all the *Dragonball* books. And *Hikaru no Go*. I had to read them, so I bought them all. Akira is so cute! And I like Sai and Isumi.♡ I read them for those three characters. My favorite right now is Umagon in *Zatch Bell*!! Meru Meru Me!!

So cute, so cute...

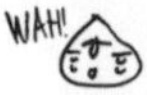
WAH!

I like the anime better because you get to hear their voices. They're so cute they bring tears to my eyes. Umagon is a horse, but his whinny is "Meru Meru Me!" How did they come up with that? Wow...no matter how busy I am, I always read manga. Even when I'm exhausted. It gives me energy!! Plus, there are always more good series coming out.

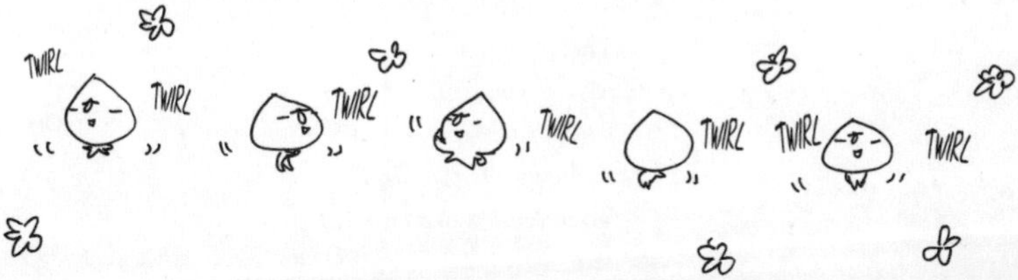
TWIRL
TWIRL
TWIRL
TWIRL
TWIRL
TWIRL
TWIRL

The End

There's going to be a third volume, so I'll see you again soon!! Volume 3... What's gonna happen? It'll be a close encounter of the third kind!! Scary!!

I'll be doing my best, so keep reading!

See ya! ————

HOP

8/14/04
Ao Mimori

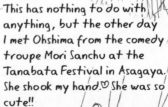

This has nothing to do with anything, but the other day I met Ohshima from the comedy troupe Mori Sanchu at the Tanabata Festival in Asagaya. She shook my hand.♡ She was so cute!!

B.O.D.Y. Language

Page 46, Author's Note: *Bessatsu Margaret*
The manga magazine in which *B.O.D.Y.* runs in Japan.

Page 51, Author's Note: UNIQLO
"Unique Clothing Warehouse," a major Japanese manufacturer of casual wear.

Page 65, panel 6: Shinjuku vibe
One of Tokyo's busiest business districts, Shinjuku is a major center for government, business and international tourism. It also includes Japan's largest red-light neighborhood, Kabukicho, which is filled with bars, pachinko parlors, love hotels and racier establishments.

Page 125, panel 2: a million yen
Roughly $10,000 American.

Page 148, panel 4: "Hello, Jin!"
In the original Japanese, these characters say *ohayo gozaimasu* (good morning). Working people in Japan often use this greeting no matter what the actual time of day.

Page 175, panel 3: Kesalan Patharan
Japanese cosmetics company.

Page 204: American Rag Cie
Clothing chain that specializes in high-end vintage and consignment clothes, especially designer denim.

Page 206: *Urusei Yatsura*
The first hit manga by Rumiko Takahashi, creator of *Maison Ikkoku*, *Ranma 1/2* and *Inuyasha*. A slapstick comedy about a teenage boy who attracts the love of a short-tempered alien girl in a tiger-striped bikini, it attracted a huge fandom in Japan during its run in the late 1970s and 1980s.

Eight volumes...

Author's Commentary

Lately I've been overworked. I get into slumps, I get irritated, I get angry, but in the end, when I see the final product, it puts a smile on my face. I think to myself, "I guess I like drawing comics."

Ao Mimori began creating manga during her junior year of college, and her work debuted when she was only 23. *B.O.D.Y.*, her third series, was first published in *Bessatsu Margaret* in 2003 and is also available in Japanese as an audio CD. Her other work includes *Sonnano Koi Jyanai* (That's Not Love), *Anta Nanka Iranai* (I Don't Need You), *Dakishimetaiyo Motto* (I Want to Hold You More), *I LOVE YOU* and *Kamisama no Iu Toori* (As the God of Death Dictates).

B.O.D.Y. VOL 2
The Shojo Beat Manga Edition

STORY & ART BY
AO MIMORI

English Adaptation/Kelly Sue DeConnick
Translation/Joe Yamazaki
Touch-up Art & Lettering/James Gaubatz
Design/Izumi Hirayama
Editor/Shaenon K. Garrity

Editor in Chief, Books/Alvin Lu
Editor in Chief, Magazines/Marc Weidenbaum
VP of Publishing Licensing/Rika Inouye
VP of Sales/Gonzalo Ferreyra
Sr. VP of Marketing/Liza Coppola
Publisher/Hyoe Narita

B.O.D.Y. © 2003 by Ao Mimori
All rights reserved.
First published in Japan in 2003 by SHUEISHA Inc., Tokyo.
English translation rights arranged by SHUEISHA Inc.
The stories, characters and incidents mentioned in this
publication are entirely fictional.

Printed in Canada

Published by VIZ Media, LLC
P.O. Box 77010
San Francisco, CA 94107

Shojo Beat Manga Edition
10 9 8 7 6 5 4 3 2 1
First printing, August 2008

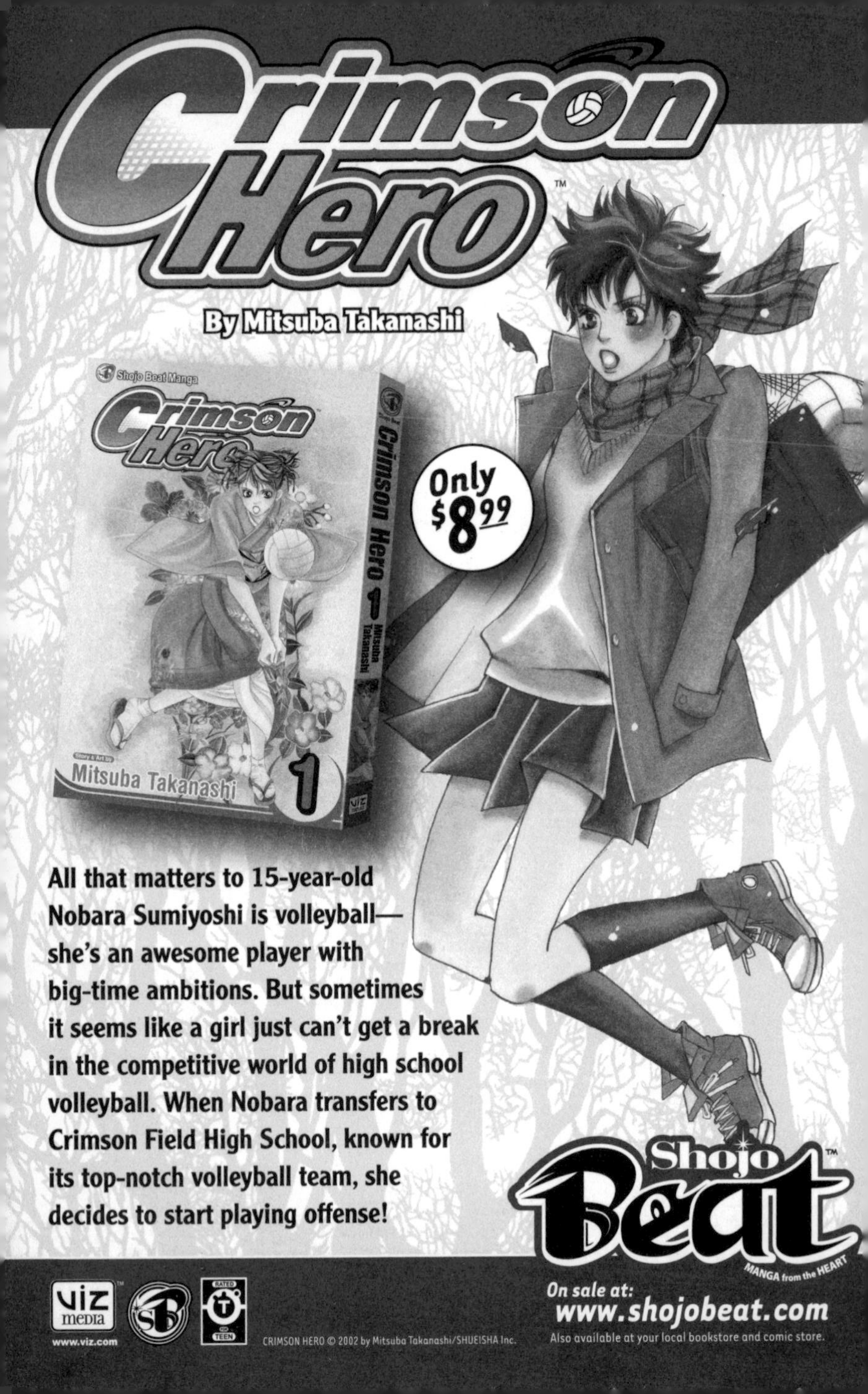

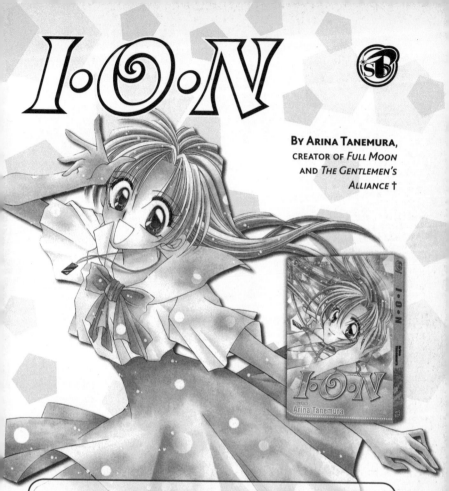

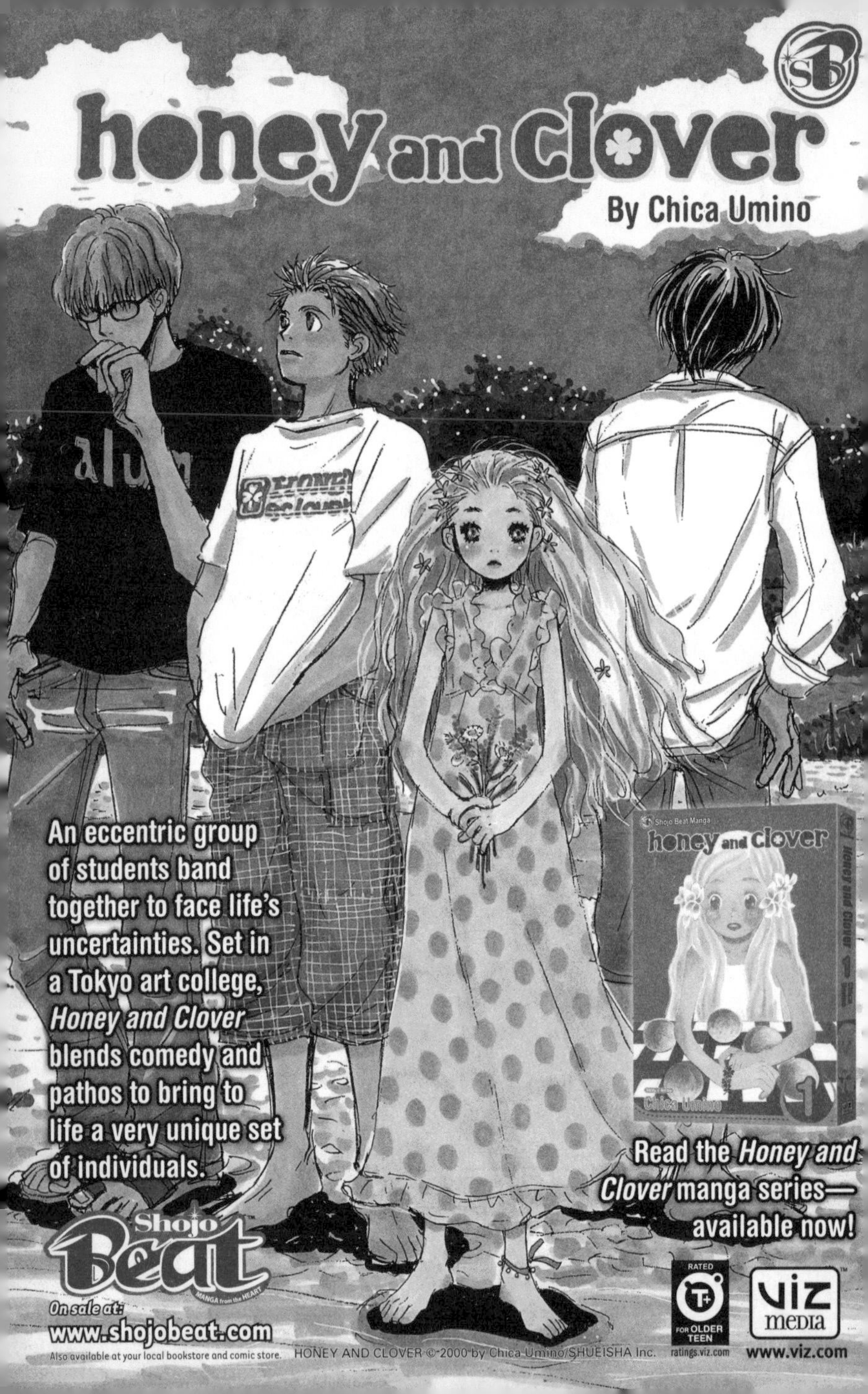

honey and clover
By Chica Umino
An eccentric group of students band together to face life's uncertainties. Set in a Tokyo art college, Honey and Clover blends comedy and pathos to bring to life a very unique set of individuals.
Shojo Beat Manga
honey and clover
Chica Umino
1
Read the Honey and Clover manga series—available now!
Shojo Beat
MANGA from the HEART
On sale at:
www.shojobeat.com
Also available at your local bookstore and comic store.
HONEY AND CLOVER © 2000 by Chica Umino/SHUEISHA Inc.
RATED
T+
FOR OLDER TEEN
ratings.viz.com
VIZ media
www.viz.com

Tell us what you think about Shojo Beat Manga!

Our survey is now available online. Go to:

shojobeat.com/mangasurvey

Help us make our product offerings

THE REAL DRAMA BEGINS IN...